MORE THAN REDEMPTION

A Theology of Christian Counseling

JAY E. ADAMS

BAKER BOOK HOUSE
Grand Rapids, Michigan

All New Testament quotations are from the
Christian Counselor's New Testament.

PHOTOLITHOPRINTED BY CUSHING - MALLOY, INC.
ANN ARBOR, MICHIGAN, UNITED STATES OF AMERICA
1980

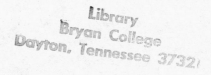
TO BETTY JANE
who knows how to transform
theology into life!

CONTENTS

(*Continued on next page*)

FOREWORD

More Than Redemption is a first attempt to consider a biblical theology of counseling. As such it is woefully imbalanced and incomplete. No one knows this better than I. Yet, it has been my conviction over the years that, though incomplete, materials should be published whenever they can be presented in some sort of systematic form. I know of no better way to test views, provide current help for those who are struggling on the front lines and to further the goal of calling pastors back to the work that their forefathers abandoned. For those reasons—inadequate as it may be—I have released this volume that you now hold in your hands.

In *More Than Redemption* I could take space to restate doctrinal positions that are plainly presented elsewhere by Reformed theologians; I could make observations about numerous aspects of various doctrines that are obvious to all. But this would serve little purpose and would make the book more cumbersome than it is. To note, for instance, that God must be omniscient to know all aspects of a situation in order to answer prayer, that He must be omnipresent to hear all prayers uttered at all times and in all places, that He must be omnipotent in order to respond to every circumstance in any way that He wishes and that it takes a God who is all three to bring about His universal goals through each particular in the universe in relation to every other particular both in the past and future as well as in the present, is (for example) a work of supererogation; the facts are too obvious to take the time to develop. So I haven't. Similarly, many doctrinal implications for counseling, too apparent to mention or for extended comment, have been omitted or merely referred to in passing.[1]

I mention these facts because under each doctrinal section items

---

1. Also, I have made frequent cross-references to my other books whenever there might be extensive overlapping of material. In this way I have avoided unnecessary repetition.

usually found in a volume of systematic theology have not been included. The effect, as a result, might seem somewhat spotty perhaps, but by understanding what I have done, I hope I shall relieve you of some apprehension and (indeed) help you to appreciate the fact that I assume your basic ability to develop the obvious for yourself.

The book may be read for individual benefit or may be used as a textbook in the classroom. A textbook covering such material has been needed for quite some time. Whether, in His providence, God will be pleased to use this one to meet that need, time alone will disclose. It is my hope that He will.

JAY ADAMS

INTRODUCTION

All counselors have one goal in common: change. Moreover, as diverse as the various counseling systems may be—and they are quite distinct fundamentally[1]—they all (1) see a need for change and (2) use verbal means to bring about the change,[2] which (3) is purported to be for the benefit of the counselee.

But, N.B., these are the same three essential elements that I have shown (elsewhere[3]) are inherent in *nouthesia,* the principal and the fullest biblical word for counseling.

The Bible itself provides the principles for understanding and for engaging in nouthetic counseling and directs Christian ministers to do such counseling as a part of their life calling in the ministry of the Word (other Christians also should counsel as God gives opportunity[4]). Therefore, those who develop other systems, based on other sources of information, by which they attempt to achieve these same ends, by the very nature of the case *become competitive.* It is dangerous to compete with the Bible, since all such competition in the end turns out to be competition with God.

It is not that Christians oppose competition as such. That is not the problem. But when they are faithful to God, Christians must deplore any and all concepts, methods, systems, etc., that are set up in competition with God's concepts, methods and systems. When pagan approaches are developed to do what God has given the Bible to do, these approaches must be exposed, rejected, and opposed.

---

1. Cf. Jay Adams, *Lectures on Counseling,* pp. 19ff.
2. Some, of course, add other elements (chemotherapy, E.S.T., etc.). But to the extent that such other means are used, what is done is not (strictly speaking) *counseling.* The very word *counsel,* strictly speaking, implies the verbal element.
3. Cf. Jay Adams, *Competent to Counsel,* pp. 41ff.; *The Christian Counselor's Manual,* p. 14; *What About Nouthetic Counseling?,* p. 63.
4. Cf. Rom. 15:14; Col. 3:16; Gal. 6:1-2, 10; see also pertinent passages in *Competent to Counsel.*

Contrary to what some may think, Christians have not suddenly burst upon the scene challenging psychiatrists and clinical and counseling psychologists; rather (the historical facts show that) the latter are the newcomers who moved in to supplant the church in its work of counseling.[5] Historically speaking therefore, *competition* is quite an accurate word to describe the situation.[6]

At one time counseling was considered to be an integral part of the work of Christ's church. Ministers wrote books on "melancholy" (depression), held counseling sessions with "inquirers" who were concerned not only with conversion but with every phase of their lives.[7] The church ministered to families and persons in every sort of human/human and human/divine relationship (note that this ministry covered a broader scope than modern competitive systems allow for), and the public recognized that it was the task of the church (in general) and of pastors (in particular) to attend to matters of belief, attitude, value, behavior, relationship, etc. Now psychotherapists attempt to usurp that role.[8]

How, then, was it possible for the church to lay aside its God-given task so easily and turn the work over to others who proposed different ways of going about it, ways that not only differed from the biblical

---

5. See my brief history of this subject in *Lectures,* pp. 38ff.

6. N.B. Psychology and medicine are not necessarily in competition with the Bible. It is *clinical* and *counseling* psychology and *psychiatry,* that have (illegitimately) set themselves up within those two disciplines, that are competitive. Legitimate medicine and psychology, while holding no *special* relationship to Christian counseling, can contribute to it in an ancillary way as they would to any other field. But Christian counseling is in no way dependent upon data from either field. Christ the perfect Counselor, Paul and the church have been totally equipped to carry on counseling from early times (cf. II Tim. 3:15-17).

7. They even published case histories (cf. Spencer's *Sketches,* vols. I, 2).

8. Cf. Perry London, *The Modes and Morals of Psychotherapy* (New York: Holt, Rinehart and Winston, 1964). London speaks of the work of psychotherapists as "what religions have long since tried to do," p. 65, and declares, "Psychotherapists are not really doctors, . . . [but] secular priests," pp. 153, 163. In the *National Observer* (May 26, 1973), a popular article entitled " 'Shrinks' Become Pastors to Sick Congregations," affirms virtually the same thing, p. 1. Albert Reissner says, "Eric Fromm shows that psychoanalysis has definitely a religious function," *Essays in Individual Psychology,* Kurt Adler, ed. (New York: Grove Press, 1959), p. 170. In his book, *The Death of Psychiatry* (Radnor: Chilton Book Co., 1974), E. Fuller Torrey says, "The job of explaining unknown behavior formerly fell upon the clergy; psychiatrists have inherited it as they have inherited other aspects of the clerical role" (pp. 91, 92).

pattern but competed and conflicted with it? I have detailed some of the principle factors involved in the psychiatric takeover elsewhere,[9] and I shall not repeat that story here. Rather, I should like to add one more, one that is pertinent to the very essence of this book: *truths that the church does not treat systematically* (i.e., theologically) *it has a tendency to lose.*

Why the Change Occurred

The pressures that had a part in compressing and shrinking the church's counseling role were able to make headway (and indeed, all but succeeded in totally supplanting it) because, even though counseling by its nature was theological through and through,[10] it had been carried on in an unsystematic, atheological manner.

When doctrine becomes creedal (e.g., the Athanasian Creed), it becomes defensible against (Arians and other) heretics. Heresy, as well as truth, becomes identifiable. Before it takes creedal form, however, almost any sort of heresy can claim a place. Controversy over the Bible's teaching on various points led to the formulation of theological statements that have helped us not only to identfy falsehood and defend the truth, but also to teach and to restudy biblical teaching in a deeper and more profitable way. Future generations can stand on the shoulders of past ones and reach even higher on the tree of truth for fruit yet unplucked. Many doctrines have been so defined helpfully. But, to date, no serious theological (let alone creedal) statements have been made about the place or task of counseling in the Christian church.

It is my hope that out of the present controversy over the problem of eclectic counseling within Christ's church (the issue is whether the counseling systems of Freud, Rogers, Skinner, not to speak of scores of others, can be brought legitimately into the church) theological studies will be generated that will lead to clearer definitions of the work of the church and her counseling ministry, so that congregations and their members will better understand the perils involved. In my opinion, advocating, allowing and practicing psychiatric and psychoanalytical dogmas within the church is every bit as pagan and heretical (and therefore perilous) as propagating the teachings of some of the most bizarre cults. The only

---

9. *Lectures,* pp. 38ff.
10. Cf. an article in *What About Nouthetic Counseling,* pp. 37-39.

vital difference is that the cults are less dangerous because their errors are more identifiable, since they are controverted by existing creedal statements.

It is also my hope that this theological study of Christian counseling—primitive and incomplete though it may be—nevertheless will provide an impetus for other such studies, leading (at length) to the sharper redefinitions and theological commitments that are so essential and yet almost entirely lacking.

We often have been told that all truth is God's truth and that if Paul were alive today, he would have borrowed much from modern psychotherapists. Unfortunately, say they, Paul is not now alive; so the point cannot be tested. But, on the contrary, the thesis *can* be tested. We are not left to speculation and guessing about this matter. We can discover whether or not he was an eclectic. Paul does not live on this earth at present, nor did Albert Ellis live in Paul's day. But Epictetus and other Stoics did. And Ellis has gained much from Stoicism (Epictetus is one of his favorites). So we may ask, "Did Paul borrow from Stoicism?" Did he recognize truth in the system and adapt it to his work?

Listen to some quotations from Epictetus (it sounds like Ellis himself writing):

> Men are not disturbed by things, but by the views they take of things. Thus death is nothing terrible. . . . Demand not that events should happen as you wish; but wish them to happen as they do happen. . . . What hurts . . . is not this occurrence itself . . . but the view he chooses to take of it.[11]

Did Paul buy into Stoicism? Not at all. This was not his approach. That he knew all about Stoicism is apparent from Acts 17:18. His neglect was not due to ignorance. And, from that passage it is equally plain that Paul was no Stoic. Indeed, Paul found himself in conflict with Stoic philosophers. He uncompromisingly insisted that they *"must repent"* (vs. 30). Not only was such a *must* out of character with Stoic philosophy, but, by requiring repentance, Paul was calling for a radical change and abandonment of their Stoic thinking that would lead

---

11. Epictetus, *The Enchiridon* [Manual], trans. Thomas Higginson (Bobbs-Merrill Co., 1948), pp. 19, 20, 22. Epictetus was born sometime between A.D. 50 and A.D. 60. For an illuminating description of Stoicism in contrast to Christianity, see F. W. Farrar, *The Early Days of Christianity* (New York: A. L. Burt, n.d.), pp. 9-11.

to a radical change in life style. The thesis of eclecticism, when tested, fails to materialize.

In summing up my position, then, perhaps I can best express it in the crisp form that was necessary for writing a brief exhortation in the September 2, 1977, issue of *Kethiv Quere,* a student publication at Dallas Theological Seminary. Let me quote that short article here in full:

The Basis for Christian Counseling

The Christian's basis for *counseling,* and the basis for a *Christian's* counseling is nothing other than the Scriptures of the Old and New Testaments. The Bible is his counseling textbook.

"Why?" you ask. "After all, the Christian doesn't use the Bible as his basis for scores of other activities in which he engages—such as engineering, architecture, music—so why should he insist that the Scriptures are the basis for counseling?"

The answer to that question is at once both simple and profound (because of its simplicity don't miss the profundity of its implications). The Bible is the basis for a Christian's counseling because it deals with the same issues that all counseling does.[12] The Bible was given to help men come to saving faith in Christ and then to transform believers into His image (II Tim. 3:15-17). The Holy Spirit uses it as an "adequate" instrument that He says has the "power" to do so. That, in substance, is what these verses say.

But note, too, in these verses God assigns this life calling of transforming lives by the Word to the "man of God" (a phrase Paul picks up from the Old Testament designation for a prophet and uses in the pastoral epistles to refer to the Christian minister).[13] And, let me repeat, the Holy Spirit strongly declares that the Bible fully equips him for this work.

So then, it is because counseling—the process of helping others to love God and their neighbors—is a part of the ministry of the Word (just as preaching is) that it is unthinkable to use any other text (just as it would be unthinkable to do so in preaching). A ministry of the *Word* is not such when it is based on substitutes.

The Bible is the basis for a Christian's counseling because of what counseling is all about (changing lives by changing values, beliefs, relationships, attitudes, behavior). What other source can provide

---

12. Engineering, music, etc., do not. I have written about this at length elsewhere. See especially *Lectures.*

13. Of course, informally—not as an official calling—all believers are to counsel, just as all are to proclaim the Word.

a standard for such changes? What other source tells us how to make such changes in a way that pleases God?

That is why other foundations for counseling must be rejected. Not only are they *not needed* (the Bible is adequate—the unique One, Who is *the* Counselor proved that by His own counseling ministry), but since they seek to do the same sorts of things (without the Scriptures and the Spirit), they are *also competitive*.

God doesn't bless His competition! Nor does He bless disobedience to His Word by His servants.

As future ministers of the Word, be just that—only that, and noththing else but that—ministers of the *Word!* Do not forsake the Fountain of living water for the cracked cisterns of modern counseling systems.

CHAPTER ONE

THE NEED FOR THEOLOGY IN COUNSELING

From the beginning, human change depended upon counseling. Man was created as a being whose very existence is derived from and dependent upon a Creator whom he must acknowledge as such and from whom he must obtain wisdom and knowledge through revelation. The purpose and meaning of his life, as well as his very existence, is derived and dependent. He can find none of this in himself. Man is not autonomous.

"In the beginning was the Word" (John 1:1) says it all. Man needed God's Word from the outset—*even before the fall.* His revelatory Word was necessary to understand God, creation, himself, his proper relationships to others, his place and functions in creation and his limitations.

Contrary to Carl Rogers' views,[1] which have been accepted as the preferred counseling stance of so many ministers,[2] man did not come from God's hand with all the resources that he would ever need prepackaged within. Instead of the "autonomous" being that Rogers (and his system) contemplates as the ideal end product of non-directive counseling, the Bible teaches that man was made for God (Rev. 4:11) and dependent upon Him (Acts 17:28). Man was created as a dependent being. Any attempt to transform him into an autonomous being not only constitutes rebellion against the Creator, but is bound to fail. The tragic circumstances with which counselors deal bear unmistakable traces of this sinful rebellion which from the fall onward has been the root of the bitter fruits of human chaos and misery. It is this basic rebellion— thinking we can go it alone—that lies behind, and is the occasion for, so much counseling. To offer more of the same (as do counselors who

---

1. For more on these views, see *Competent,* pp. 78ff.
2. In this reviewer's opinion because of two reasons: (1) simplicity; (2) supposed lack of risk.

stress autonomy), therefore, is to encourage more (not fewer) problems.

Whenever people try to live on their own (whether as the outworking of the sinful propensities of their corrupted natures or as the result of following a system like Rogers'), they must fail miserably. I mean that *literally:* they not only fail inevitably in the course of time (they must, because they were constituted dependent creatures), but their failures bring misery upon themselves and those around them.[3]

Man is dependent upon his Creator and Sustainer for all that he is, has and knows. He was created for a life of joyful, grateful, dependence. It is upon the last one of these three elements, in particular, that I should like to focus attention for a few pages: human knowledge.

From the beginning, God's Word was a necessary factor in human existence; that need did not begin with the fall. Man does not (and did not) live by bread alone; life requires a Word from the mouth of God. Without that Word, a human being has no personal ability to understand, make sense out of, or know how to use the world in which he lives. He doesn't know the ways of living with others, and he can't properly relate to God. As the existentialists have observed, such life is absurd.

Life without God's Word is absurd (it is sheer vanity, as the writer of Ecclesiastes put it) because capacity for knowledge (understanding of facts, properly interpreted and related) is derived, not native to human nature. That means that from the creation on, man was made to be molded by counsel (which is the directive Word of another, given from the outside).[4] Meaning, purpose and function depended upon this interpretive Word. General revelation (in creation) itself does not provide any such interpretation. Without God's Word, therefore, misery was bound to follow. This was inevitable (among other things) because the universe (and man within it) would be improperly interpreted. It would appear chaotic and absurd, and human choices and decisions would be made on the basis of no solid standard. The plague of relativism would descend upon man.

Human beings were created morally and physically good. But the development of neither side of man was *complete.* Perfection, while admitting of no flaws, allowed for advance (e.g., eating of the tree of life with its new effects). Adam, before the fall, had not yet reached

---

3. The Westminster Standards put it well when they speak of sin and misery in close nexus. Counseling has to do with these two elements: sin, and its consequences.
4. God's Word is frequently called counsel; viz., Ps. 119:24; Prov. 25:30, etc.

those states of perfection that are now attained (1) in the intermediate state at death,[5] or (2) in the final state when the body as well as the spirit attains resurrected perfection.[6]

Man's relationship to God, then, was to be a growing one. In the garden he had only begun to enter into the possibilities and potentialities of human existence. These all lay before him. Further development of knowledge, experience, etc., was anticipated in such commands as "be fruitful and multiply" and "subdue the earth." *How* that first command would be followed (with all of the consequent social and political implications of the conduct of human affairs among a *race*), and *what* the subduing (or bringing under human control) of the earth would produce in the course of scientific and political activities, would depend upon the regulatory and interpretive revelation of God's Word. Change, then, even developmental changes in a perfect man, always depended upon God's counsel.

Man was created perfect, but that does not mean that he was ever able to live on his own. Perfection itself implies an acknowledgment of his dependence upon God's revelation. By counsel (he didn't decide to do it on his own) Adam named the animals. By counsel he dressed the garden. By counsel he learned of the trees in the garden and the proper use of them (as well as the possible consequences of misuse). All this came *after* creation, to a man who was *made* to be dependent on God's counsel for all his life, and who was capable of being changed and developed by that counsel.

That is the first crucial factor to grasp at the outset: man was created in such a way that for his own good, and God's glory, it was necessary to depend upon divine counsel and to be changed by it.

If man had obeyed God's counsel faithfully, he would have been changed into a being possessing the eternal life that somehow inhered in (or was symbolized by) the tree of life.[7]

But something happened that led to the misery we have already mentioned: man turned from God's counsel to heed Satan's counsel. In doing so, Adam attempted to achieve independence of God and to assert his own autonomy. He accepted the false counsel to eat and the

5. Heb. 12:23.
6. Phil. 3:21.
7. Cf. John Murray, *Collected Writings* (Carlisle: Banner of Truth, 1977), vol. 2, pp. 48ff.

lie upon which it rested: "You will be like God, knowing good and evil" (knowing good and evil is an expression that means knowing everything[8]). Following false (evil) counsel plunged mankind into sin with all its miseries.

The Adamic rebellion only pointed up the futility of any such attempt at autonomy. Confusion and heartache resulted, humanity was subjected to fear, ignorance and death, and—as it turned out—man had not become autonomous at all. He had only exchanged a holy, beneficent and liberating counsel for a devilish, demonic, enslaving one. In following Satan's counsel, he lost the freedom and capacity to do good and to follow God's good counsel. He became a slave of sin and Satan. In opting for Satanic counsel, he once more demonstrated (in a perverted way) the very facts of his creation:

(1) he was dependent upon outside counsel;
(2) he was capable of being changed by counsel.

Only (tragically) the counsel that he chose to follow brought misery and slavery rather than the promised joy and freedom.

It is clear, then, that from Adam's time on there have been two counsels in this world: divine counsel and devilish counsel; the two are in competition. The Bible's position is that all counsel that is not revelational (biblical), or based upon God's revelation, is Satanic. When counsel is given by those who align themselves with some other counsel than God's the counsel that is given is called "the counsel of the ungodly" (Ps. 1:1). Both the counsel and those who give it are ungodly. It is ungodly (1) because it competes with and tries to overthrow God's counsel, (2) because it is inspired by Satan and (3) because (intentionally or otherwise) it is given by those who rebelliously side with the devil. Over against such counsel (and in direct opposition to it) the psalm places God's Word (vs. 2).

Throughout the course of human history both godly and ungodly counsel always have been present, vying for man's acceptance. The history of individuals, families and even nations, has stemmed directly from whichever one of these two counsels was followed. There is no third counsel, as the psalm clearly indicates. There are just two ways to go: Satan's way or God's way. Man has no counsel that is strictly "his

---

8. Notes from lectures by Meredith Kline; but see also ibid., pp. 50ff.

own."[9] If he rejects God's counsel, whatever counsel he follows instead turns out to be Satan's counsel. Man was made to follow another's counsel; he will do so. He cannot throw off his dependency. Knowingly or unwittingly he always depends upon Satan or God. He was made to be motivated and molded by counsel.

At the beginning, man walked and talked with God in the cool of the day. Doubtless, God counseled him at such times. The pre-fall fellowship was unbroken and entirely open, and the counsel consisted of positive, good, beneficial revelation calculated to develop man's full potential. As he was growing under such counsel, he began to grasp something of the potential of language to bring about order and to express concepts. He saw this in his classification of the animals. He experienced something of the joys of the satisfaction and fulfillment of work as he kept the garden according to God's instructions. He tasted the sweet fruit of understanding and fellowship as he talked with God and communicated with his wife Eve. He discovered that God's counsel was clear, uncomplicated and plain: "eat from all the trees but one." In singularly unmistakable words, God identified and labeled the forbidden tree, "the tree of the knowledge of good and evil." He even located it for Adam: "[It] is in the middle of the garden." And with equal clarity and explicitness He warned, "Don't eat from it or the very day that you do you will die." This counsel was necessary for man's well being. He was dependent upon it and was held responsible for obeying it. Man was a responsible being. It was God's counsel, true and plain; therefore it was good.

In contrast to God's counsel—a counsel that was simple, plain, true and beneficent—Satan introduced a counsel that complicated, confused and contorted God's truth. The third chapter of Genesis tells the sad story.

The first question in history was asked by Satan: "Has God said . . . ?" (vs. 1). By this question, Satan attacked God's Word, i.e., God's good counsel. "Perhaps His counsel is not so simple, so plain or so beneficent as it seems," he intimated. The initial question, however, did not constitute a *direct* attack upon God's revelation; Satan is much too subtle to do that. Instead, to begin with, he merely cast *doubt* upon God's

9. Cf. John 8:34-44. Thinking he is free, man expresses by word and deed his utter slavery to sin: attempted autonomy itself is the clearest possible evidence of the fact of his discipleship to Satan.

counsel. He questioned God's Word and His plain intentions. He has never ceased doing so. Ever since, the method has proved effective.

Having sown seeds of *doubt*[10] about God's Word by questioning it, Satan did not hesitate to continue by *distorting it*. He misstated God's command: "Has God said that you may not eat from every tree of the garden" (vs. 1)? This corruption of truth (typical of the way that Satan throughout history has continued to distort God's truth through his willing servants) was intended both to confuse and to challenge God's gracious gift of all the trees but one. What once had been plain and simple, he now tried to confuse and complicate. Eve's response seems to indicate that she was not totally taken in by this approach, but possibly also reveals that she was sufficiently influenced to the point where she altered the commandment by adding the words, "neither shall you touch it."[11]

Finally, because he had made inroads by *doubt* and *distortion,* Satan was able to attack God's counsel directly. At this point he turns to his last ruse: outright *denial*. That a progression is intended is almost certain.[12] Satan's assertions that eating would not produce death, and that God forbade eating because He did not want man to be like Him (i.e., autonomous, free of dependence upon God for knowledge and counsel) amounted to calling God a liar and a cheat and attributed bad motives to Him. These three attacks—doubt, distortion and denial—were designed to lead to *distrust*. Satan's object was to create distrust in God's Word.

Through the years the situation has not changed appreciatively. Basically, Satan always has concentrated upon this progression as his principal tactic—with great effectiveness. And as you can see, the attack has been upon God's Word.

In counseling, this fact has been more than evident; it has been glaring. Within the church the sufficiency of Scripture (God's written Word) has been challenged. Distrust in God's way, His verity, etc.,

---

10. Interestingly, the Bible indicates that there is a moral rather than an intellectual base for doubt (James. 4:8).

11. It is also possible, of course, that these words reflect a fuller form of the commandment. However, in the context, where the significance of other distortions is the point, it is likely that this addition indicates a growing change of attitude on Eve's part toward God and His Word.

12. And this further argues for finding significance in Eve's form of quotation (cf. previous footnote). Cf. the progression found in Ps. 1:1.

has been propagated by those who have set up rival systems offering different counsel (still) purporting to open men's eyes in one way or another, and still offering autonomy. Satan's approach has not varied; nor has his success in duping the sons of Adam.

The church, throughout the years, like Adam and Eve, either has been deceived by Satan's counsel or has found itself in conflict with it. There is no neutral ground. *Compromise* or *conflict* are the only two alternatives. We are (hopefully) now beginning to emerge from an era of compromise. Hence the present need for conflict with the counsel of the ungodly. For a long time Satan's deceitful counsel has prevailed in the church; only during the 70s has a successful challenge been mounted.

Now, at such turning points it is not unusual to discover Christians who unwittingly continue to side with the enemy, and who fight against their brothers when they try to defend and promote the cause of God's truth in counseling. Frequently this results from good motives, wrongly directed. Yet, their influence is tragic. They not only set back helpful counsel, but confuse many who are in transition. Still, it is not the persons, as persons, whom we must challenge, but their teachings. In bringing such a challenge to the church's sad compromise with the competition, it is time to proclaim the relevance of the first psalm, with its plain contrast between the counsel of the ungodly and the counsel of God's Word. Let us look at verse 1.

The tragedy set forth in that psalm again appears in the progression of compromise with evil (Satan's old tactic, *gradual* defection from God's truth, is plainly marked out). First, the compromiser "walks" in the "counsel" of the ungodly. That is to say, he begins to listen to pagan advice and counsel. He approves of falsehood, mistaking it for truth; he begins to confuse and intermix the two. He defends error, calling it truth. "All truth is God's truth," he declares. Soon he is found "standing" in the "way" of sinners. Intellectually accepting Satanic counsel leads to living according to it. This is sin; he takes the sinful way. He is seen standing in the path of sinners, believing what they believe, doing what they do, saying what they say.[13] At length, he is a leader of those who scoff at biblical truth; he "sits" in the seat of the "scornful."

---

13. Often a desire to be accepted by the world as "scholarly" plays a part in this.

There are Christians today who are so caught up in the views and practices of unbelievers that in their writings they spend more time attacking those who attempt to set forth biblical positions that those who oppose them. They often go to great lengths to defend ungodly counsel.[14]

This might seem incredible if we did not understand how it comes about. The progression of compromise tells us. No Christian sets out to pervert and deny God's truth; the process is gradual. It happens in stages, not all at once. That is the warning of Psalm 1. Such compromise with ungodly counsel, therefore, can happen both to counselors and (sadly) to those who are counseled by them.[15]

It is important to note that neither Genesis 3 nor Psalm 1 leaves any room for a third, neutral counsel. One of Satan's ruses (as an angel of light) is to convince those who claim theological sophistication to accept error under the slogan, "All truth is God's truth." Under that banner nearly every error in the book has been blamed on God!

Of course all truth is God's truth. But there is only one touchstone for determining whether a given statement claiming to be true is, indeed true: Does it square with God's standard for truth—the Bible?

And, when compromisers talk about all truth as God's truth, they call it "common grace." They abuse this concept too. They mean by such use that God revealed truth through Rogers, Freud, Skinner, etc. God does, of course, restrain sin, allow people to discover facts about His creation, etc., in common grace (help given to saved and unsaved alike), but God never sets up rival systems competitive to the Bible. And God doesn't duplicate in general revelation (creation) what He gives us by special revelation (the Bible). That is not common grace.[16]

You can be sure that it is not the result of common grace that two rival ways of counseling exist side by side! God cannot be charged with such contradiction. His common grace is not responsible for false teachings by Freud (man is not responsible for his sin), Rogers (man is essentially good and needs no outside help), or even Skinner (man is only an animal, without value, freedom or dignity). It is nearly blasphemous to claim (as a number do) that such systems, full of errors, falsehoods and anti-Christian teachings, are the product of God's common grace!

---

14. Cf. my monograph, *The Power of Error.*
15. Cf. *Lectures,* pp. 28-37.
16. For more on common grace, see my *Matters of Concern,* pp. 89ff.

Imagine God, in common grace, through these systems, leading people to believe that their problems can be solved apart from Christ! Systems designed to do (apart from the Scriptures) what the Scriptures themselves claim to do are not the product of common grace. This theological language cover is but another of Satan's distortions.

Compromisers—who spend more time studying Freud's views of human misery than the Apostle Peter's—trip and fall over such language and place stumbling blocks in the way of others. Only those who ruminate upon God's Word, day and night, will resist such temptations to compromise. The Christian counselor must be radically into studying the Scriptures, or he too will be deceived.

It is improper to conceive of Freud, Rogers and scores of others like them as great benefactors of the church, near Christians, or persons from whom we can learn much. No; rather, we must see clearly that they have come peddling the wares of the enemy. They are his agents. They offer systems, counsel and a way of life opposed to biblical truth.[17] Their views are not supplemental, but outright alternatives. Surely, they themselves see this clearly enough, and make no bones about it. They plainly say that there is no place for God or His Word. How is it, then, that some Christians are virtually blind to this fact?

In the final analysis, the answer to that question is this—Christians are duped into the acceptance of pagan thought and practice in counseling *when they do not think theologically.*

Because so many who have assumed places of leadership in Christian counseling have little or no training in theological thought, they have become involved in compromising the faith in various ways. Because their backgrounds are marinated with clinical psychology and psychiatry, it is not surprising to find that this is so. The shallow (and often shoddy) theological thinking exhibited in some of their books, the ease with which they slip into syncretizing, the almost total lack of exegesis (or its results) that is so apparent, are all unmistakable watermarks of the problem.

---

17. This is not theory alone. London, for instance, reports that Wolpe cured a man's anxiety over homosexuality by persuading him to disavow his religious beliefs (London, op. cit., p. 120). E. Fuller Torrey (op. cit.) points out that "Jesus was one of the first intended victims of psychiatry." He says, "Between 1905 and 1912 four books were published in an attempt to prove that Jesus was mentally ill," p. 81. Hundreds of similar examples show that the competitive nature of pagan systems is basically anti-Christian.

Theology—a truly large dose of exegetical, biblical, systematic theology—alone can change this situation. Nothing less can keep today's Christian counselors from rushing in to borrow all sorts of things from the latest vendors of such paltry products. Otherwise they will succumb to the successors of Freud and Rogers just as their fathers patronized them. Only when Christians begin to think consistently from the whole of the Scriptures on any given point (i.e., when they think theologically), will they reject eclecticism in counseling. That is why I have written this book. It is an attempt to encourage theological thinking in relationship to counseling. My hope is that it will help to turn the tide.

CHAPTER TWO

THEOLOGY AND COUNSELING

If theology is the answer to eclecticism in counseling, it is important to know what theology is. Some people who think they understand theology may not, and others may have a very feeble acquaintance with it.

What is theology and what is its relationship to counseling? Briefly, let me answer those two questions first, then I shall expand on one or two aspects of those answers.

In its simplest form, theology is nothing more or less than the systematic understanding of what the Scriptures teach about various subjects. Biblical passages concerning any subject—let us say, the teaching of the Bible about God—are located, exegeted in context, placed into the stream of the history of redemption and their teachings classified according to the several aspects of that subject (God's omnipotence, omniscience, omnipresence, for instance). Within each classification, these teachings are compared to one another (one passage supplementing and qualifying another) in order to discover the total scriptural teaching on this aspect of the doctrine. Each aspect, likewise, is compared to other aspects in order to understand the total scriptural teaching about that question (and various subjects also are studied in relation to each other for further amplifications and modifications according to the light that one subject throws upon another). Thus, simply stated, theology is the attempt to bring to bear upon any given doctrine (or teaching) all that the Bible has to say about it. Biblical theology also notes the development of special revelation particularly in relationship to the redemptive work of Christ. And the individual theologies of the various writers of biblical books must be studied and related to one another too.[1] All of these elements are of concern to us in this book.

---

1. Not that their basic theological beliefs differ, but frequently their use of terminology does. These differences must be harmonized.

Let me partially demonstrate how theology can influence practical living by one brief example. In John 14:13, 14, Jesus says, "I will do whatever you ask in My name. . . . If you ask Me anything, I will do it." By itself, that statement seems to constitute a *carte blanche* in prayer. (And too often those who have little concern for theology have taken it that way; they have preached and counseled, saying, "Whatever you want you can get by praying for it.") As a result of a failure to use theology in the exegesis of the passage (asking, for instance, "What does the important qualification, 'in My name,' mean—how is the phrase used elsewhere?"[2] and, "What other qualifications do other Scriptures place upon prayer?"), many Christians have been misled and have been deeply disappointed when they tried to use prayer as an open sesame to unlock their problems and satisfy their desires. They discover—the hard way— that prayer doesn't work that way. Adequate theological study would take into account such passages as John 16:23, 24, 26, 27; Philippians 4:6, 7; James 4:2, 3; 5:15-18 when referring to John 14:13, 14. The qualifications in these references—even if not mentioned to the counselee —must be known (and kept in mind) by the counselor whenever he speaks about John 14:13, 14, so that he will not convey a wrong impression (i.e., an atheological, simplistic one) to the counselee.

In the example just given I have begun to show one of the principal relationships of theology to counseling. Because his counsel is dependent upon biblical principles, a Christian counselor (like a Christian preacher[3]) must understand *all* that the Scriptures say on a given topic in order to give fully biblical direction to their counselees.

One of the principal problems with which counselors must deal (often as a complicating problem) when seeking to help counselees is the problem of counselee frustration and discouragement.[4] Much of the apathy encountered stems from the failure of counselees to understand the Bible theologically. As the result of quite faulty understanding of the Bible, they take all sorts of actions (like using prayer as a rabbit's foot) that fail. Then, on the one hand, either doubts about God and the trustworthiness of the Scriptures or, on the other hand, doubts about themselves ("maybe Paul could do it, but I'm not Paul") arise. Such

---

2. For example, in John 15:21.
3. I have touched on the relationship of preaching to counseling in *Matters of Concern*, pp. 1, 2.
4. See relevant passages in the *Manual* concerning the importance of hope.

apathy, stemming from discouragement and doubt, is avoidable. Exegesis, with a theological dimension, theologically ministered with careful qualifications communicated in preaching and counseling, could have led to entirely different results. So, where the counselee already has received basically untheological instruction, counselors should anticipate (and look for) complications to original problems that stem from faulty solutions. And, it is imperative that the counselor approach such counselees in full consciousness of what theology can do to help.

' In the counseling process, not only is it necessary to have a theological (i.e., a full-orbed, systematically understood) orientation toward the Scriptures to avoid misleading counselees and to correct errors in the thought and practice of counselees, but it is vital also to have this orientation in order to communicate truth authoritatively. The counselor who himself is theologically unsure will communicate his biblical insecurity in the way that he speaks to counselees (and in the way that he writes about counseling). Authoritative proclamation of the Word in preaching and in counseling (not authoritarian[5]) grows only from a sound knowledge of theology. It was because the scribes and Pharisees were speculative rather than theological in their thinking (cf. the Talmudic mentality) that Christ's authoritative teaching stood out in such stark contrast to theirs: "He taught them as an authority and not as their scribes" (Matt. 7:29). The scribes based their teaching not upon an exegetical and theological understanding of the Bible, but upon the contradictory debates, ramblings and speculations found among the body of materials called the "traditions of the elders" which so often made the clear intent of various passages of no effect (viz., Mark 7:13).

It doesn't surprise me, therefore, that Christian counselors today lack authority; there is so much speculation and so little theological depth among them.

Typically, the self-appointed Christian "professional" has spent years studying psychology at the graduate level, but has little more than a Sunday School (or, at best a Bible school) knowledge of the Bible. That is woefully inadequate for a full-time counselor or teacher of counseling! Theological principles and method take not only time to develop and learn, but on top of that it takes years of hard effort in

---

5. Cf. the *Manual*, pp. 15, 16; *Lectures*, pp. 135ff., 187, for a discussion of the distinction between authority and authoritarianism.

applying them to the study of the Scriptures to yield the kind of satisfying results that are needed in counseling.

"Why aren't there more people who approach counseling biblically?,"
people often ask me. The answer is that there are so few persons in
the field who are adequately prepared theologically to do so. I am not
saying that they are ill-intentioned; to the contrary, there are even some
examples of valiant attempts to use what little understanding exists in
proper ways—but these attempts simply fall apart from the outset because of the frightful exegetical and theological inadequacy.[6] How can
a counselor who doesn't even possess the word "exegesis" as a part of
his everyday speaking vocabulary, who has never read Berkhof's text
on theology, who knows nothing of Kittel's *Theological Dictionary,* and
who doesn't even understand the problems of theological reflection
upon the truths of the Scriptures, begin to develop a biblical system?
The very idea is absurd.

In this book, I am assuming at least the basic theoretical theological
adequacy of the reader (acquired either before reading, or as he moves
along). So I am not trying to teach theology (obviously it isn't possible
or desirable to avoid some such teaching; but what I mean is that I
cannot turn this volume into a basic textbook of systematic theology).
What I am trying to do is

(1) to demonstrate the counselor's need for theology, and
(2) to show how theological themes have important (I might say
    vital) implications for counseling theory and practice.

N.B., it is not possible (even for an unbeliever) to do counseling that
is really untheological. All counseling, by its very nature (as it tries to
explain and direct human beings in their living before God and before
other human beings in a fallen world) implies theological commitments
by the counselor. He simply cannot become involved in the attempt to
change beliefs, values, attitudes, relationships and behavior without
wading neck deep in theological waters. I have shown[7] that these theo-

---

6. Actually, such attempts often result in more harm than good; the superficial, untheological use of the Bible confuses and discourages counselees (as well
as misrepresents God by misunderstanding the teaching of the Bible). One of
the saddest failures of all is to appoint such psychologists as professors in theological institutions to teach prospective ministers of the Word. In the end, they
teach them how not to use their Bibles in counseling.

7. Cf. *What About Nouthetic Counseling?,* pp. 37-39. If the reader has any
doubts about this matter, I urge him to read this discussion.

logical commitments may be conscious or unconscious, biblical or heretical, good theology or bad, but—either way—they surely are theological.

If this be true, it is important (1) to become aware of one's own commitments and the grounds for arriving at and for holding them, (2) to make revisions of these and any future commitments consciously on the basis of satisfactory biblical theology, and (3) to study theology continually for further implications of truths that will lead to a more biblical sort of counseling and will lend a proper sort of authority to that counsel.

Thus, in summary, I may say that the relationship between counseling and theology is organic; counseling cannot be done apart from theological commitments. Every act, word (or lack of these) implies theological commitments. On the other hand, theological study leads to counseling implications. The attempt to separate the two must not be made; they cannot be separated without doing violence to both.[8] The separation is as unnatural (and as perilous) as the separation of the spirit from the body. Paraphrasing James, we may say that counseling without theology is dead.

---

8. It is not my place in this book to develop the idea that theology can (I believe, must) learn from the hard questions brought to it by counseling just as it has been impelled to study and define issues raised by the great heresies. Problems demand biblical answers. Theologians and counselors ought to work hand in hand; their interests are common.

CHAPTER THREE

COUNSELING AND SPECIAL REVELATION: THE DOCTRINE OF THE SCRIPTURES

Where were Christians before Freud? Up a tree? Were they bereft of all crucial knowledge about man's relationship to God and his neighbor? Was the church's counseling a hopeless, primitive, stone-age activity that should have disappeared with flint knives? Were Christians shut up to sinful, harmful living before the advent of psychotherapy? Did God withhold truth for living until our present age?

Or did men like Paul, Peter, Augustine, Luther, Calvin, Spurgeon and many others have something worthwhile to say to their converts and parishioners about how to live in a sinful world and about how to solve problems? Isn't the answer apparent?

Drop the question in that form for a moment if it's too hot to handle, and consider this (even hotter) one: How did Jesus Christ become the perfect Counselor that the Scriptures report Him to be apart from the "insights" of clinical psychology and psychiatry that we are now assured by unbelievers (and many Christians who follow them) are *essential* to effective counseling?

A moment's reflection should make one thing abundantly clear—the Old Testament adequately supplied Jesus with all the knowledge and wisdom necessary for Him to counsel others unerringly. He was not inadequately supplied, but (as Paul once put it) "thoroughly equipped for every good work"[1] by those writings. So too, following the Lord, the church (whenever she has been faithful in this matter) has found the Bible to be a rich, inexhaustible source of information for its counseling ministry.

---

1. II Tim. 3:17. Here, the passage speaks of changing Christians by the use of the Scriptures (cf. vss. 15, 16).

Again, we must return to the concept of God's Word *as counsel* (we must never forget that this is one of its prime functions). No wonder, then, that David (in Ps. 119:24) referred to the Bible as his "counselor." Nor should we wonder that, in contrasting what he learned there with human wisdom, he declared that scriptural counsel had made him wiser than all his teachers![2]

So, there should be no question about the fundamental function of the Bible as God's counsel to men, or about the pastor's duty to use it in a ministry of shepherdly counseling.[3] Part of any ministry of the Word is a ministry of counseling.

In this chapter I shall discuss the relationship of certain aspects of the doctrine of Scripture to a ministry of counseling.

First, let us understand plainly that the biblical doctrine of the inerrancy of the Scriptures has important implications for counseling. The Christian counselor has a Book that is the very Word of the living God, written in the styles of the individual writers, who (through the superintendence of the Holy Spirit) were kept free from all errors that otherwise would have crept into their writings, and who, by His providential direction, produced literature that expressed not only what they themselves wanted to say, but what God wanted to say through them, so that (at once) these writings could be said to be Jeremiah's or the Holy Spirit's.[4] This is a God-breathed book. (The word translated "inspired" means, literally, "breathed out by God." "Inspired" means "breathed in.") When God says that He breathed out His Word, He means that what is written is as much His Word as if He had spoken it audibly by means of breath. If the reader could hear God speak, he would find that God said nothing more, nothing less, nothing different from what is written.[5]

2. Ps. 119:99.
3. Elsewhere, I have treated this matter in depth. I shall not repeat here what I have said, for example, in vol. II of *Shepherding God's Flock*.
4. Cf. Heb. 10:16. Cf. especially Heb. 3:7, 8 with Heb. 4:7. The same quotation is attributed to David and to the Holy Spirit. See also Acts 3:21; Neh. 9:30.
5. While ministering in Brazil, I discovered more fully what was behind this assurance. There, in a largely illiterate country, oral speech is supreme. If a secretary were to receive contradictory oral and written orders from her boss, she would always choose the oral over the written word. Here, Paul says, the oral *backs up* the written. Our own heritage reflects vestiges of a time when this was so in English history in such phrases as, "You have my word for it," and "I got it from the horse's mouth."

Counsel drawn from a book like this adds a note of authority to counseling. When faced with plain proposals for sin ("Can I leave my wife for another woman?"), questions about behavior ("Must I pay taxes when they are so unfair?"), etc., the Christian counselor can give an unequivocal answer because it is based not upon his own opinion, upon the probabilities of the consequences, expediency or any other such relative standard, but upon the commandment of the living God, who has spoken.

This makes a tremendous difference. The ministry of the Word in counseling, as a result, is totally unlike counseling in any other system because of its authoritative base. This authoritative character stems, of course, from the doctrine of inerrancy. If the Bible were shot through with human error, and were no more dependable than any other composition—if it were not a God-breathed revelation—this note of authority would give way to opinion.[6] But, because the Bible is inerrant, there *is* authority.

This authority must not be confused with authoritarianism. I have already distinguished between these two at another place,[7] so I shall not repeat what I have written there.

But there is another matter about which I have already said something, but which I wish to amplify somewhat here. It is the matter of scriptural guidance in matters that the Bible addresses in principle, but does not speak about directly. The counselor must distinguish these two matters sharply. In *Lectures on Counseling* I wrote,

> Another factor in the use of the Scriptures is the importance of distinguishing between direct commands of God and valid inferences from and applications of such commands. Some matters are directly enjoined or forbidden; in others, decisions must be made by inference from biblical principles. It is not necessary to spend time developing this theme here since in *The Christian Counselor's Manual* I have already done so.[8] Yet it is essential to stress the importance of making such distinctions. Otherwise, the counselee may fail to distinguish between the authority of God and the biblically informed judgment of others. It is therefore significant when the counselor, in giving advice or in making an assignment himself

---

6. Each counselor would have to determine which biblical passages are true and which are in error. Man would sit in judgment on Scripture, rather than Scripture bringing him into judgment.

7. See also *What About N.C.?*, p. 33; *Lectures*, pp. 133-138, 187.

8. Pp. 16, 17, 447, 448.

makes such distinctions. Compare the following two statements: "Joe, you must stop running around with Bob's wife, and you must stop as of today!" and "Bill, you should study your Bible; I'd suggest that you might begin with the tenth chapter of Proverbs." The second differs radically from the first.

The distinction may be summarized in the following chart.

BIBLICAL COMMAND	COUNSELOR'S SUGGESTION
Command: "Joe, you must stop today."	Specific steps for obeying it: "Phone her and call it off."
General biblical principle: "You must study your Bible."	Specific application: "Read Proverbs 10ff."

The counselor may be very directive about commanding a certain outcome when the biblical commands directly govern it: "Joe, you must stop running around with Bob's wife." When the case is not covered directly, however, one can be directive only about the principles that clearly are commanded: "You must study your Bible." It is not altogether certain biblically *how* Joe must put an end to his infidelity. Indeed, the steps that he takes to achieve this end may vary under different circumstances. If he can make a clean break with a phone call today, under most circumstances he should do so. If, however, Bob's wife keeps on trying to reestablish the relationship, that might call for different steps. On the other hand, studying the Scriptures regularly may be enjoined as a biblical principle, but the passages with which Bill begins can only be suggested. Circumstances, again, might point to entirely different passages (e.g., if Bill is an unbeliever, he should probably not begin with Proverbs, but rather with the book of John).[9]

Thus the counselor's authority at every point is limited by the Bible itself. This is another reason why the Scriptures must be in actual use in counseling sessions. At least a certain amount of biblical exposition ought to accompany any authoritative directive ("Joe, you must stop. . . .") if it is not already absolutely clear to the counselee that the Bible really gives such direction (in the instance cited, very few counselees would question the directive; even many unsaved persons recognize that the

---

9. *Lectures,* pp. 251, 252.

Bible forbids adultery). There are many subjects, however, about which the counselee may be uncertain (e.g., "You must stop worrying because worry is sin"[10]). In all such instances, exposition is necessary

(1) to enable the counselee to "see [for himself] if these things are so" (Acts 17:11);

(2) to bring the full authority of God's Word to bear upon the counselee (so that he may not treat the directive merely as a suggestion, that he may take or leave), and to accord it the full weight that it deserves.

The authority inherent in the New Testament prefacing phrase, "it is written," should be apparent to every serious Bible student. This is the very note that is needed in counseling.[11]

No other system of counseling has authority (even though Ellis and Skinner, *et al.* pretend to it) because no other system has an authoritative base. I cannot help but agree with most criticisms of the use of authority in counseling since they grow out of a recognition of the utter arrogance of any fallible man who attempts to speak authoritatively.[12] No counselee should entrust his life to the hands of another unaided fallible sinner. Unless the counselor has been converted, and is able to demonstrate that there is biblical authority for the directions he gives, a counselee ought to back off.

The Christian's authority for biblical counseling comes not from himself; therefore, he has no necessary problem with arrogance (I say *necessary,* because there are plenty of ways for believers also to become arrogant). The fundamental criticism mentioned above simply does not apply. The authority by which he counsels is divine. The argument from arrogance, when applied to other counseling systems, however, is compelling; but it makes no impact at all on genuine Christian counseling. So, why should those who *alone* have good reason to counsel with authority hesitate to do so?

Albert Ellis can make whatever Stoic pronouncements that he likes from Mt. Olympus, he can denounce codes of morality as the cause of

---

10. It will probably be important to do some (as much as is needed) exposition of Matt. 6 and Phil. 4 in many instances when making such assertions.

11. Cf. *Lectures,* pp. 130, 131, where one (of many) reasons for authoritative direction in counseling is discussed.

12. Indeed, the more authoritatively he speaks (in the name of science, psychology, or from his own opinions), the more dangerous he becomes.

problems in his counselees, declare that "oughts" and "shoulds" *ought* to be abolished—and he is accepted even by some Christian counselors; but just let a believing counselor speak with authority and the ceiling falls in! Yet Ellis speaks only from his own opinion; Christians speak from God's Word. The stance of many Christians, therefore, is utterly absurd[13]—i.e. to say (in this context), untheological.

It is time to sound a crystal note of hope in the wasteland of subjectively based counseling. No one has the right (or should have the gall) to tell another person what changes to make in his life, or how to do so. Who—on his own authority—knows the answers to life's problems for *himself,* let alone for another? By what standard can he do so?[14] In the final analysis, every pronouncement in counseling (even when borrowed from Rogers, Skinner, *et al.*) is made because the counselor thinks (or hopes) it should be.[15] Only an external, divinely delivered revelation provides the way out of subjectivism.

This is so even in the commitment of the believing counselor to the Scriptures as his authoritative source for counseling, because this commitment itself is not subjectively, but divinely, motivated (cf. I Cor 2). Only an infinite, holy God, with comprehensive knowledge, could provide what is needed. All other views of reality, etc., are partial and biased by man's finite and sinful limitations. And this knowledge must be imparted to Christians *by the Spirit's illumination* so that the Christian's limitations do not distort it. That is what we have in the use of the Scriptures in counseling; and that is what makes the difference in Christian authority.

Now these claims to exclusivism, while essential, can lead to the

---

13. This absurdity takes many forms. For instance, Skinner, with no hesitation, omnipotently declares that man is only an animal, that concepts like God, soul and mind are spooky language and should be eliminated, while Christian writers fudge about how far it is valid for a Christian to go beyond Rogerian non-directiveness!

14. See my address, "Change Them—into What?" (Christian Counseling and Educational Foundation, Laverock, Pa., 1978).

15. When Wm. Glasser says that he will bring the counselee into conformity with reality, the reality that he has in mind is the limited, distorted view that a finite sinner has of reality. When Krumboltz accepts the counselee's goals (*Revolution in Counseling* [Boston: Houghton and Mifflin Co., 1966]), he really is accepting what *he thinks* is right—namely, the counselee's goal. Neither the goals of society in general (or what is best for most—Mowrer) nor those of the client provide a way around the subjectivity problem. In the final analysis, the counselor adopts either approach because *he thinks* it is the best.

wrong results (every good and needed emphasis can be—and has been—distorted; Satan tries to get you going and coming). God's call of the Jews to unique living as a special (holy) and chosen (elect) people, who were to represent the true God before the world, *for the world's blessing,* quickly degenerated into a separatism (especially seen in the Pharisees) that despised other peoples. This radical racism led to a state of affairs that was expressed this way: "Jews don't associate with Samaritans" (John 4:9b). Counseling exclusivism can be wrongly distorted in the same way. The Jews were to witness to the world about God's uniqueness, but instead, they closed the door on others. The danger must be noted and avoided.

The biblical separatism in counseling—both in principle and practice —for which I contend is of the opposite sort. We shall not stop unbelievers from setting up their own counseling systems and from doing counseling that competes with the Scriptures; that is a given.[16] But Christian counseling itself must be free from eclectic borrowings and influences *in order to set forth a genuine and viable alternative.* So long as (in substance) there is no real option, so long as so-called Christian counseling looks so much like (and *is* like) non-Christian counseling that for all intents and purposes the two are indistinguishable, the Christian loses his evangelistic opportunity in counseling. This is one of the key factors to remember: separatism in counseling theory and practice (among other things) is intended to provide a cutting edge for evangelism. Only when God's counsel and God's way is set off sharply from Satan's counsel and Satan's way can there be a valid comparison of clear alternatives that allows for the demonstration of the Spirit's power. In other words, exclusivism in counseling theory and technique is not intended to isolate the Christian from the world (or from other Christians), but rather to provide an effective means of breaking in on the world with something *different;* God's something—something *truly* unique.

The "Unique One," the "Counselor" (Isa. 9:6) is just that: "unique" (the actual meaning of the word translated "wonderful"). To dilute the Christian alternative by additions of Freud, Rogers, Maslow, Harris or the speculative views of any other non-biblical thinker in the field,

---

16. In Brazil, for instance, even the "high" spiritist "churches" have a program of telephone counseling!

therefore, is to weaken the witnessing power of Christ's church.[17] Christ's witness always must be kept unique, as it was in the days when He walked among men (no traces of eclecticism can be found in His words or works).

Christians who think they will be accepted by the world (and thereby will enhance their image and opportunity for witness to unsaved persons) only if they pursue the eclectic course are gravely mistaken. They will be accepted all right, of that there is little doubt, but this acceptance means that unsaved persons will accept them *as one of their own*. As a result, there is no alternative. But without an alternative there is no compelling need for the unbeliever to examine the validity of his position. Only by its presence as an alternative can a counseling system set off Christ's uniqueness. We may not put Him on a shelf beside Skinner, Perls or Mowrer. He is truly unique; He stands alone. His counseling too—along with every other aspect of the work to which He called His church—likewise must stand alone.

Now we shall consider an issue of great importance, not only to counselors and counseling, but to the church in general. The issue is thick with problems; no theology of the Word and of revelation ought to avoid it (although many theological textbooks do). Because of its great importance, we shall devote not a little space to the subject.

Personal Guidance

In his work the Christian counselor commonly runs up against the problem of personal guidance. Hardly one in a hundred counselees seems to have anything like a biblical notion of what to do to make decisions that are pleasing to the Lord. And, no wonder. Theologians have ignored the subject; popular books abound with erroneous and confusing teaching. In discussing the implications of special revelation in the Scriptures, therefore, it seems appropriate to say a word or two about this important, practical, day-by-day issue.

Typically, the poor responses of counselees fall into two categories:

(1) those who do not think that the Scriptures have anything to say about everyday decision-making (and so they make their decisions on expedient and pragmatic grounds), and,

---

17. For more on "Evangelism in Counseling," see my article by that title in *The Big Umbrella* and appendix A.

(2) those who disagree with them about the Scriptures but seek further revelation in dreams, feelings,[18] circumstances and "putting out the fleece."

Common to both of these erroneous approaches and widely practiced by counselees (who are Christians) is the opinion that the Scriptures are inconvenient or insufficient, so other sources must be sought.

Now, it is obvious to all that there are two kinds of situations in which guidance is needed:

(1) in those situations about which the Scriptures speak directly;

(2) in those about which the Scriptures speak indirectly.

Usually, it is with the latter sort of situation that the counselee is struggling. If Joe is thinking of holding up a bank, there is usually no confusion on anyone's part about the scriptural guidelines on the matter: "You must not steal." That verse, from Exodus 20, applies *directly* to the matter. If Bill is tempted to become involved in a shady financial transaction,[19] however, he and the counselor *might* not be so sure at first about the proper application of this commandment.

The existence of two facts raises the issue of guidance. The Scriptures are not catalogs of dos and don'ts on all matters of life topically arranged in alphabetical form.[20] Instead, they consist largely of general and specific principles stated in contexts to which they apply and exemplary incidents that are applicable to all of life.

When Phyllis must make a decision, therefore, between two job offers, when Bob must decide which automobile out of many options available that he will buy, and in scores of other such decisions, it is not quite so easy to find scriptural guidance as it is in a case in which they may be contemplating the direct fulfillment or violation of a biblical commandment. That, then, is why confusion exists.

Unfortunately, because the Scriptures do not speak *directly* about all sorts of personal decisions that we must make daily, many Christians abandon hope of ever finding out God's will from them and (as I said)

18. A typical phrase is, "I felt led to. . . ." One Christian leader in Europe told me that when he doesn't have the time to study the Scriptures for help in making a decision, he simply asks God to give him an answer in a dream.
19. By "shady" I mean a transaction that may or may not involve theft—it is questionable.
20. Though there are some such sections (without the topical/alphabetical features); cf. the book of Proverbs.

do what they want to do on grounds *entirely external to scriptural principle* or seek to circumvent Scripture study altogether by the flip-and-point method, putting out the fleece, casting lots, trusting feelings ("I have peace about the matter"), looking for open doors, etc. When people want answers, and demand them *now,* they tend to resort to such tactics.

Yet, as we all know, many terrible and tragic results come from trusting such "guidance" (which, because not sanctioned in the Scriptures, we can be certain isn't guidance at all). We have heard people say, "The Lord led me to. . ." or "The Lord is leading me to do such-and-such." But three months later, in the counselor's room, when the results are in, he hears, "Oh, what a mess I got myself into."[21] More poor decisions have been made under the impression that the Lord was guiding by some means external to the Bible! Perhaps one of the most important tasks that a counselor has to perform, therefore, is to help straighten out Christian counselees on the question of guidance. How does he do so?

The first, and absolutely fundamental, fact to zealously maintain is that there is no way to know God's will and to receive His guidance apart from the Scriptures.[22] This must be made clear to every counselee.

The second fact is a corollary to the first: there are scriptural principles and practices to cover all circumstances of life, available to those who take the time and make the effort to understand and know the Bible adequately.[23] Wise Christians study the Scriptures regularly to learn these, so that when decisions come they will have an understanding of what the Bible says about their situation. This is superior to resorting to dreams!

The third fact grows out of the second, and has been alluded to already: the Scriptures speak both directly and indirectly by implication. They help us to make either/or (yes/no) choices, or they box us up with a limited number of equally legitimate options.

With these three propositions about biblical guidance in mind, we are ready to investigate the matter more fully.

---

21. Or, in its more tragic form, "Why did the Lord do this to me?"
22. The day of direct revelation ceased with the death of the last apostle. And, remember, even the apostles didn't always enjoy direct revelation about all their decisions (cf. II Cor. 12:12; Heb. 2:2-4; II Cor. 4:8b; these passages show that direct revelation was apostolic).
23. II Tim. 3:15-17; II Pet. 1:3.

"Wait a minute," you reply. "What about the two passages that refer to being 'led by the Spirit'; don't those passages clearly speak of some sort of extrabiblical guidance?" That question deserves an answer since so much confusion has resulted from an erroneous interpretation of these passages.

The two passages under consideration (Rom. 8:14; Gal. 5:8) often are used to support views of extrabiblical guidance in decision-making. But the fact is, they advocate no such thing at all. Neither passage has anything to do with decision-making. Rather, in both passages, as their foregoing contexts clearly show, the question in view is sanctification— *walking* in righteous paths by the Spirit's strength. This walk is (according to Paul) evidence of the believer's justification (Romans) and constitutes the behavior of the Christian in contrast to the old sinful way of life of the unbeliever (Galatians).

The Christian is "led" (motivated) to walk in God's ways by the Spirit rather than to walk in the flesh. No notion of guidance in decision-making appears in either passage. To thus construe these texts is to misconstrue them.[24]

How, then, does one make decisions based upon the Scriptures alone when there is no clear word that applies directly to his case?

First, the counselor must help the counselee to search out the relevant principles (or principles incorporated in examples) that have a bearing upon the case. Some of these will be quite general; others, more specific.

If a decision about marriage, let us say, must be made, the general principles about celibacy (in Gen. 2:18; Matt. 19; I Cor. 7) should be considered at the outset. Having applied the biblical tests, and having concluded that the counselee does not have the gift of the single life, principles concerning marriage itself must be applied. For instance, I Corinthians 7:39 (see also II Cor. 6:14-18), makes it plain when it says ". . . marry only in the Lord," that a Christian may not marry an unbeliever. That *broad* principle *narrows* the field of decision-making considerably. However, let us say that in time the counselee has come to the point where he sees three Christian women as potential marriage

---

24. Even if the passages *did* refer (remotely) to guidance in decision-making, the case for extrabiblical revelation would not be made. One could argue (indeed, *should* do so) that the Holy Spirit speaks *through* His Word (Heb. 10:15ff.). It is absurd to suppose that the Spirit would spend years producing the Scriptures only to circumvent them regularly by resorting to other methods of guiding believers.

partners. Given the basic willingness and interest of each, how does he decide among them? By bringing more specific principles into play.

Mary has many good qualities, but there are some serious questions about her concern for Bible study ("It's boring," she says), church attendance and her commitment to living as a Christian in everyday affairs of life. Not all Christians are ready for marriage. Mary, then, may be rejected because at this time (at least) she doesn't seem adequately susceptible to biblical authority and influences, exhibits little growth in her life and (in general) reveals evidence of out and out disobedience to God. To marry Mary would be to set sail on the voyage of marriage with a Jonah in the boat. That narrows the choice to Jane and Betty.[25]

Both Jane and Betty, in contrast to Mary, are vivacious Christians, deeply involved in Christ's work. There is no principle (or group of principles), then, that would exclude one or the other. In fact, after searching the Scriptures carefully, after listing the virtues of each, etc., Herb reaches the conclusion that—on the basis of biblical principle— there are equally good reasons for marrying either one.

In other words, the biblical principles have boxed out all unbelieving women, further boxed out Mary (at this time), but have left Herb with more than one option open *within* the box.

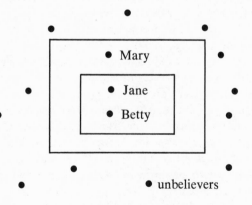

25. Here, the theological "sense" of many pertinent Scriptures brought together without conscious reference to them guides. This can be tricky, because when the "sense" alone is followed, the principles are not apparent as a check on the validity of this sense. But, with many questions, one has already adequately studied to know there is solid ground for this "sense" of the Bible!

"How," asks Herb, "am I now to determine which one is God's wife for me?"

It is precisely the sort of thinking that is behind that language that we must reject. God's will may be thought of from two perspectives. There is the ultimate sense in which we may speak of God *willing* (or determining) a particular event (or a fact). In this sense (articulated clearly in such passages as Ephesians 1:11) we may speak of "God's wife for Herb." There is—and can be—only one person for him *ultimately:* the one whom God in fact has decreed to become his wife (God does not decree that which doesn't take place!). But there is a second sense in which we may speak of God's will, and in that sense Herb's language is inappropriate. This second sense we may call God's directive will—it is His will for man expressed in biblical commands. What God has *decreed* to come to pass (because He will do it) does not necessarily conform to what He has *directed* us to do in a more general way in the Bible. And, it must be observed, biblical directions often are far less specific. It is, therefore, in such cases, wrong to speak as if one knew what God has decreed from eternity *before* it happens. After the fact one may rightly say "God determined that I should marry Betty, not Jane. I know that because I married her, and whatever comes to pass *is* His eternal (or decretive) will." Before the fact, one can only speak about God's directive will.

If, indeed, all other things are equal, and there are no biblical principles that prohibit marriage to Jane or Betty, then Herb may conclude that (in the sense of God's directive will revealed in the Scriptures) marriage to *either* woman is a legitimate option. It is neither right nor wrong, biblically, to marry (or not marry) either one.

God is the God of abundance. There were twelve baskets full of pieces of bread left over. In life's decisions, God doesn't always bring us into places where all choices are between right and wrong. In His greatness, His children often find themselves in the enviable position of choosing among two or more rights! It would have been *right* to take *any one of* the pieces of bread that Christ multiplied. So, speaking from a position before the fact, Herb should recognize that he would not be wrong in marrying either Jane or Betty (provided, of course—for the sake of our somewhat artificial illustration—both women were willing!). Both are options within the area of God's directive will.

Christians often find themselves in such a position. They don't have

to make a definite choice between *right* and *wrong* in choosing to wear
a blue suit or a brown one in most situations. Either (and perhaps the
choice also includes a black and a gray) is acceptable within biblical
principles concerning modesty, etc., that restrict and govern one's
alternatives. And a biblical study doesn't have to be made each time
one selects a shirt. Once having thought through such issues scripturally,
one can operate within the framework thereafter.[26] Frequently, we may
say, many options lie within the box.

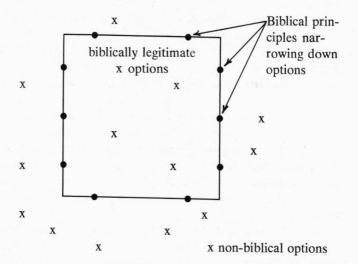

Whenever this is so, it is right for the Christian to choose out of his
own preferences. Thus, Herb has the right, within the options that God
has left him, to decide for Betty (as he does in the end) over Jane
purely on a preferential basis. Decisions between purchasing a Datsun
or a Toyota (or from a larger number of options), between accepting a
call to become the pastor of Church X or Church Y after receiving a
call from each, as well as hundreds of others like them, usually are not
decisions between good and bad, but between two (or more) goods.

It would not be wrong to preach the gospel in India or in Pakistan.

---

26. Though, in counseling, it will be important to raise issues about *assumed*
areas of free choice that the counselee may *never* have taken the time to think
through biblically. He may be making false, unbiblical assumptions; his "box" may
be out of shape.

Both, therefore, in a given case, may be goods (in another, there may have to be a right/wrong decision between the two[27]). At times, not so many options exist, and decisions can be between good and bad in almost any situation.

The important fact to keep in mind is that the case in which one may choose from among many goods (or at least between two) exists *only for those who have eliminated all biblically wrong options* through the proper application of the restrictive scriptural principles that create an option box.

In an absolute or ultimate sense, then, the Christian cannot talk about "God's will" *before* the fact in a multi-option context.[28] He can only say, generally, "I see that it is God's will to marry a girl *like* Jane or Betty."

"But won't circumstances help me to decide what God's will is?"

No.

"No? I've always heard differently." And, doubtless, as the result you've often been confused. Circumstances—often referred to as open and closed doors—only provide occasions (not guidance) for basic decision-making; they do (however) often provide help for making preferential decisions among several goods when you are in God's option box. But circumstances won't help put you there; only biblical principles will do that.

Suppose you plan to become a missionary to India. You complete your studies, get your backing and apply for a visa. But you are turned down—a "closed door"! How will your "read" this circumstance?[29] Are you to conclude:

1. "Well, I guess God doesn't want me to be a missionary"; or

2. "God doesn't want me to be a missionary in India"; or

3. "God doesn't want me to be a missionary in India *now*—I'll wait for His timing"; or

4. "God is testing me to see if I really mean business. What is a

---

27. If, for instance, a missionary wants to leave India for Pakistan *for the wrong reasons,* or when someone says, "I'll go anywhere but India." A decision *against* India *on that basis* may be sin.

28. In I Sam. 24:7, 14, there is a good instance of falsely speaking about what God will do beforehand.

29. On a biblical basis you don't *read* circumstances; they are not revelational.

rejection anyway? It's merely a human decision. I'll go if I have to swim—with or without a visa if necessary!"; or . . .

And so you could go on with other plausible "readings" (or interpretations) of circumstances. It is about as certain as reading tea leaves! Similarly, "open doors" can be variously read; remember, some open doors lead to elevator shafts!

The Bible does not tell us to *look for* open or closed doors as a way of determining God's guidance. True, God often opens and closes doors, but in determining His will beforehand, it is perilous to try to do so on the basis of one's prejudiced (or limited) view of circumstances. Selective interpretation is all too frequently at work.

I shall not take time to discuss the futility of trying to determine God's will by means of "feelings," "urges," "deep convictions," "peace"[30] and "leadings." Behind each are unrecognized *reasons.* Sometimes they are biblical, sometimes they aren't; sometimes they are noble, often they aren't. One must get back to these reasons in counseling to analyze and evaluate them according to biblical principles. Anything less than this results in decision-making that shifts with whims and weather—or worse than that! And what a tragedy when such decisions are stamped with divine approval and authority as "God's leading!"

There is one more fundamental biblical principle of guidance that I call the *holding principle.* It is found most clearly in Romans 14 (especially in vs. 23). The thrust of this holding principle may be stated as follows:

Never act until you are sure that what you are about to do is not sin.

Paul writes, "But whoever doubts is condemned if he eats, because he doesn't eat in faith; and whatever isn't done in faith is sin" (Rom 14:23).

The preceding discussion in Romans has to do with eating meat that had been offered to pagan idols. Many Christians in the early church were converts from idolatry. Soon the question arose, "Is it proper for a Christian to eat meat that has been offered to idols?" Presumably, this secondhand meat was sold in the market place at a cheaper price, and

---

30. The misinterpretation of Col. 3:15 (as *individual* peace—"I have peace about the matter"—as the basis for decision-making must be rejected). The entire passage speaks of *corporate* relations among the members of the church. Peace is the "umpire" for the interpersonal relations of the parts of the body to the whole. This is peace *in the church;* there is nothing about guidance in the passage.

since many Christians also were poor, buying such meat constituted quite a saving for them. But the question arose—how can a Christian eat such meat? Isn't it polluted by idolatry? How did Paul meet the issue? He made it quite clear that eating food offered to idols is not, *per se,* sinful. Such food is not contaminated by the previous use in idol worship (cf. Rom. 14:14, 20b). But there might be other problems involved. What were they?

First, those who agreed with him (not all did) that since an idol is nothing the meat was "clean," had to be careful that by exercising their privilege of eating such meat they did not lead a "weaker" brother or sister (one who didn't see this clearly) back into idolatrous practices. That could not be; it was inconsistent with brotherly love and responsibility (cf. vss. 13-21). It would be better to refrain altogether from eating such meat if their example was leading to such results. That, in itself, is a very important principle for guidance.[31] But the further principle enunciated by Paul has to do with the weaker brother who is not sure whether eating would or wouldn't be sin. "Perhaps," he thinks, "to eat meat offered to idols is idolatry against God" (as Paul puts it, he is *in doubt* about the matter). In such cases, Paul makes clear, the brother sins if he eats, because he doesn't eat in faith.

What Paul is saying is that a Christian may never do anything that he thinks is (or suspects may be) sin. And the point is—it is sin (and he is condemned by doing so) if he does *eat in doubt.* Note, he is not condemned because eating the meat is wrong (cf. vs. 14a), but because he went ahead and ate while *thinking* his act was (or might be) sin (cf. vss. 14b, 23). It wasn't the eating that was sin, but his faithless act. His attitude toward God, expressed by that act, was rebellious. He thought, "This is (or might be) sin, but I'm going to do it anyway." That is where sin enters the picture.

What should he have done? Refrained until he became convinced that to eat was scripturally O.K. That is why I call this the *holding principle.*

The principle, to hold back till certain that you are not sinning, applies to any and all situations in which a Christian discovers that to come to

---

31. Note, the principle is to refrain from any legitimate practices that may cause a brother to sin. (The principle is *not* to refrain from those right acts about which your brother may take offense. In such cases vss. 1-9 must be applied to him.) To "cause to offend" (i.e., to lead by example into sin) is not the same as to take offense.

a particular decision, begin a practice, etc., raises scruples in his mind. Until he is sure that the move forward is proper in God's sight, he may not make it. The holding principle calls a halt to acts, decisions, etc., made when in a condition of doubt. Until he is "fully convinced in his own mind" (15b), he must refrain.

Many good results flow from a faithful application of the holding (or "if it's doubtful, it's dirty") principle. Not all decisions must be made today (nor can all be postponed). Many, if not most, decisions made under pressure (or in haste) are bad because enough time has not been allowed to come to a full biblical persuasion about the rightness of the proposed course of action.

This holding principle can never be used as an excuse for not reaching a decision, however. "Every person" is to "become fully convinced in his own mind" (5b). But until the prayerful, biblical study has been made with its results loud and clear, one must say "no" and mark time. If plain biblical reasons for doing something do not appear, there is a plain biblical reason for *not* doing it. It is better to miss a supposed "opportunity of a lifetime" than to enter on a course of action in doubt. If it seems a shady (or questionable) deal[32] might be sinful, the Christian may not enter into it. If, in the long run, it turns out that there was nothing illegal, immoral or unethical about it, one may have lost an opportunity, money, etc., but not his integrity before God (which is far more important). God will bless him in His way and in His time for this faithfulness. He may be sure that if he sinfully enters into the deal (with doubts about its propriety) God will "condemn" him (23) and that the opportunity or the money will not prove a blessing.

The holding pattern, counseled by this biblical principle, is practical; Christians who regularly put it into practice find that frequently it allows time for new information to be gathered (that brings new clarity to an unclear situation) or new developments to take place (that help clarify the situation). Much of the doubt that arises in counselees grows out of haste. God often wants to slow us down to take a harder look at something before we commit ourselves to it. The holding principle transforms the old saying, "haste makes waste," into a new one, "haste makes sin."

Much more could be said about biblical guidance. Enough, perhaps, has been suggested to give counselors some direction in dealing with

---

32. See above, note 19, for the meaning of the term *shady*.

this all too common problem. The one danger that must be avoided at all costs is following the counsel of the ungodly (even in our own ungodly desires and wishes) by following decision-making processes not sanctioned by the Bible. The Scriptures themselves ever must provide the principles for life.

The Power of the Scriptures

There is power in God's Word. It was by this Word that the world took form (Gen. 1), Jesus Christ Himself is called the Word (John 1; I John 1), and we must not think of the Scriptures which are called God's Word (cf. Ps. 119:9, and throughout) as any less powerful. The Bible is not just another book; it is unique because it is God's Word.

The Word has performative power. God spoke and it was so. No wonder the Hebrew term *dabar* means not only "word," but also "thing." When God speaks, it is so; His Word is as sure as the thing itself. The Bible itself speaks of its own power to change people. Paul wrote, ". . . the sacred Scriptures are able [lit., have the power] to make you wise about salvation through faith in Christ Jesus," and that "all Scripture is breathed out by God and is useful for teaching, for conviction, for correction and for disciplined training in righteousness" (II Tim. 3:15, 16). In those two verses we read of the *power* of the written Word. It has power to bring a person to faith in Christ and power to mold him into the sort of person that God wants him to become. That is the power for which the world (and its counselors) is looking, but has not found. Counselors have sought a system with power to transform human lives, but have failed in the quest; the ever-multiplying new viewpoints, schools, etc., with the ever-increasing confusion that they have engendered, are a sad, but striking, commentary on the fact. But like Simon, who falsely represented himself as "the Great Power of God" (Acts 8:10), who sought to buy the divine gifts that the apostles had when he recognized their true power (vss. 18, 19), the modern counselor knows that he has neither authority nor power. All he can do, therefore, is arrogate to himself titles and respect growing (largely) out of counselees' ignorance and fear. Such power is found in one place only—in God's Word (the Bible)—in the Word that not only brought order and meaning out of chaos on that creative morn, but which alone can give order and meaning to the chaos brought about by modern psychotherapeutic failure.

There are few counselors of any stripe (there might be some, more morally perverse than others) who would not purport to be happy over any counseling program that could assure them that their counselees could become loving, joyful, peaceful, patient, kind, good, dependable, gentle and self-controlled. This is the fruit of the *Spirit*[33] (grown and watered by the Word). Yet, tell them that, identify it as such, and they will turn away. But the fruit will not come any other way than by the Spirit producing it in His people by His Word. The Word has power, because the Spirit wrote and empowers it.

But we have seen that through Satan's influence the world has consistently rejected God's Word from the garden on. To discredit this Word, from the beginning, has been Satan's prime concern. And rightly so, since to do so means, in effect, to remove men from the source of power to become (and to do) good.

Human substitutes, the counsel of the ungodly, do not have power to enable human beings to live harmoniously with God, with his neighbors or with his world. They fail to supply what is necessary to give purpose to living or to provide motivation and strength to pursue that purpose. That is why Satan has encouraged alternative approaches to life from the beginning. No sooner is the utter poverty of one false system revealed than another appears to offer new hope (against all hope). Satan allows his followers little time to investigate the truth. He keeps them too busy buying and selling his futile substitutes.

Harmony with other people, and with the universe, is found only (and even there, imperfectly because of the gradual growth required to replace Satan's ways and Satan's counsel with God's Word) among those who have become "wise about salvation" through the Bible.

For this reason, Christian counselors need never take a back seat to psychiatrists or hover around the tables of the psychological crowd, hoping to pick up crumbs. Indeed, in order to win others to Christ, it is power that is needed—power to transform lives. No one ever need be ashamed of the power of the gospel (Rom. 1:16).

It is just such power that Peter has in mind when he urges Christian wives to win their husbands, not by nagging or by preaching at them, but by demonstrating God's power in their changed behavior (II Pet.

---

33. Gal. 5:22, 23. I shall discuss the fruit of the Spirit in depth at a later point in this book.

3:1ff.). Paul, too, was concerned with that power over against human wisdom (I Cor. 2:4, 5; 1:18).

According to II Timothy 3:15-17, the Word was designed to transform behavior. That transformation has two phases:

(1) *An instantaneous one* in which dead, unregenerate persons are given life to believe by the Holy Spirit. When such persons hear the gospel (from the Word) and depend upon Jesus Christ as Savior, they are *justified* (declared righteous in God's sight). That initial phase is often called conversion (or salvation, in the narrower sense of the word; that sense is probably used in this passage).

The *regeneration* (or life-giving transformation that opens the heart to the gospel) is an instantaneous, unmerited change (what could a dead man—cf. Eph. 2—do to bring about his own resurrection?) of the whole inner life, disposing a sinner toward God for the first time in his life. Regeneration is the first aspect of conversion. The other aspect is justification (a declaration that God has erased the sin from one's record, reckoned Christ's righteousness to his account and declared him righteous because of Christ's active and passive obedience) by faith (faith means *depending* upon Christ's work for salvation). *Justification,* likewise, is an instantaneous *act.* Paul, in II Timothy 3:15, refers to justification when he says that the Scriptures have the power to make one "wise about salvation."

(2) *A gradual one* in which transformation continues throughout the entire course of the Christian's earthly life. This *process* of transformation by which a previously sinfully disposed and habituated life turns into one that pleases God more and more by conformity to His directive will (set forth in the Scriptures) is called *sanctification.* Sanctification consists of a gradual process (not an act[34]) by which the Spirit enables the believer both to put off sinful patterns of life and replace them with holy ones. This second phase I have referred to elsewhere in more depth.[35] It is outlined in the four steps of change listed in II Timothy 3:16.

---

34. But see John Murray, *Collected Writings* (Carlisle: Banner of Truth, 1977), vol. II, pp. 277ff.

35. Cf. the *Manual,* pp. 23, 93, 212; *Competent,* pp. 23, 50ff.; and especially *Lectures,* pp. 26ff., 201.

So then, the Scriptures have the power to transform both our standing with God (justification) and our state (sanctification). No wonder, then, that it is the Scriptures that Satan has spent so much effort to destroy and discredit. He has aimed his attacks at the *source of all godliness*. To the extent that counseling is biblically based, it has *power* to produce godliness; to the extent that the Scriptures are ignored (or diluted through eclectic admixture) it loses this power. That is why Christian counseling may (with ease) be called *biblical* counseling.

CHAPTER FOUR

COUNSELING AND MAN'S BASIC ENVIRONMENT: THE DOCTRINE OF GOD

The unsaved world exists in a completely hostile environment that it neither understands nor likes. I am not referring primarily to the entropy that came in judgment at the fall (Gen. 3:17-19), though that certainly is one significant element of the problem, but I am thinking even more basically. Consider the words of Psalm 139 (Berkeley Version):

> [1]Thou hast searched me, LORD, and Thou knowest me.
> [2]Thou hast me in mind when I sit down and when I rise up;
> Thou discernest my thoughts from afar.
> [3]Thou hast traced my walking and my resting,
> and art familiar with all my ways.
> [4]For there is not a word on my tongue,
> but Thou, LORD, knowest it perfectly.
> [5]Thou hast closed me in behind and in front,
> and hast placed Thy hand upon me.
>
> [6][This is] a knowledge too wonderful for me,
> too inaccessible for me to reach.
> [7]Where can I escape Thy Spirit,
> or where can I flee from Thy presence?
> [8]If I ascend to heaven, Thou art there;
> if I made the underworld my couch, then Thou art there!
> [9]If I were to take the wings of the dawn
> and dwell in the remotest part of the sea,
> [10]even there Thy hand would lead me
> and Thy right hand would take hold of me.
> [11]If I should say, "Surely the darkness will cover me,"
> then the night [would become] light around me;
> [12][for] even darkness does not hide from Thee,
> but night is as bright as day;
> darkness is the same as light [to Thee].
>
> [13]Thou didst possess my inward parts and didst weave me in my
> mother's womb.

[14]I praise Thee because I have been fearfully and wonderfully made;
marvelous is Thy workmanship, as my soul is well aware.
[15]My bones were not hidden from Thee when I was made in secrecy
and intricately fashioned in utter seclusion.
[16]Thine eyes beheld my unformed substance,
and in Thy book all was recorded and prepared day by day,
when as yet none of them had being.

[17]How precious to me are Thy thoughts, O God!
How vast is the sum of them!
[18]If I tried to count them, they would be more numerous than the sand;
when I awake, I am still with Thee.
[19]If Thou, O God, wouldst slay the ungodly,
then would bloodguilty men depart from me!
[20]Those who speak of Thee with crafty malice
exalt themselves as Thy foes to no avail.
[21]Shall I not hate those, O LORD, who hate Thee?
And am I not grieved with those that rise up against Thee?
[22]I hate them with a complete hatred;
they have become my own enemies.

[23]Search me, O God, and know my heart!
Test me and know my thoughts!
[24]See whether there is any baneful motive within me,
and lead me on the everlasting way!

It is true that in this psalm the writer is one of God's children, but
what he says also holds true for the non-Christian (but in a disturbing
rather than comforting way): *God* is man's Environment. And those
who by sin are not in harmony with Him are out of sync with their
environment. He closes in on each one of us from behind, at the side,
in the front; in the dark, in the light. There is no escaping God. The
trees, the sky, the landscape are not neutral; they are His creation.[1]
Even the very thunder and lightning seem unfriendly to those who do not
see His power and glory in them.[2]

Every sinner is aware of the discomfort in his environment. The
existentialists, and those psychologists and psychiatrists who are in-
influenced by them, have described this awareness as *alienation* and an
undifferentiated *angst*.[3] But the unbeliever fails to articulate the true
nature of the problem. He knows something is wrong in himself and in

---

1. Cf. Ps. 8; 19. All creation speaks of Him. To those without ears to hear
its very existence is puzzling, and it has no meaning.
2. Ps. 29:3-9 (especially vs. 9).
3. The Scriptures clarify the nature and source of this angst; Hebrews 2:15
says that people "by fear of death, were subjected to slavery throughout their

this world, but the very thing that creates the problem—his separation from God—also makes it impossible to conceptualize the issues in those terms. The unregenerate man is an uncertain man; he has no absolutes, no standard outside of himself and his ever-changing opinions and values. Down deep inside he is never sure about the life he lives; he can't be because his basic antagonism with his environment constantly unsettles him. He is unhappy and uncomfortable in his environment because he finds himself at odds with it. When sinning, the Christian also shares something of this discomfort, but he knows what to do about it (I John 1:9: "If we confess our sins, He is faithful and righteous so that He may forgive our sins and cleanse us from all unrighteousness"). Confession and cleansing clear the way for a renewed fellowship with God (I John 1:3, 6, 7) that revives a harmonious and comfortable relationship with the environment.[4] Also, in times of danger and concern, the assurance of God's presence brings comfort, courage and cheer.

God is around us, in us and with us. He knows (and cares) about every word on our lips and every thought in our minds. He knows us— indeed has known all about us from all eternity past! The omniscient, omnipresent God is our environment, inescapably so! And though most people rarely recognize it, they are deeply influenced—in all their thoughts and actions—by their environment (I am not speaking about that truncated, superficial and distorted view of the environment that is so much a part of various counseling systems like Skinner's or Glasser's.[5] Rather, I refer to nothing less than God Himself, and a creation that serves and honors Him). In this sense, every unregenerate

---

lifetime. Cf. also I Cor. 15:55-57, where Paul speaks of this fear of death as the *sting (kentron)* of death. What gives death this sting (fear-engendering quality) is the judgment to which it is the door. Men vaguely know that after death they must face the great Judge of all as lawbreakers (Heb. 9:27); they know that they will not be able to stand in the judgment (Ps. 1:5), and that it is "a fearful thing to fall into the hands of the living God unprepared (Heb. 10:31). Christ has removed the sting, with its fear, for those who believe in Him (I Cor. 15:54, 57; Heb. 2:14, 15). The sense of alienation that men have comes from their break with one another in sin, but even more so from their break with God (cf. Eph. 2:12c).

4. This is true even now while the curse (and all its effects) is present because the Scriptures explain these events and remove the confusion, the Holy Spirit gives grace to overcome the effects of the curse (Rom. 5:20), and enables the believer to endure pain and misery with joy because of his hope (Rom. 8:18-23, etc.).

5. See *infra* for more on Skinner and Glasser.

man, and every system he designs, is influenced by his sinful failure to describe the environment properly and, as the necessary consequence, his inability to develop a counseling system (or counseling method) that corresponds to the reality of the environment as it truly exists. A false view of the environment, therefore, can lead to nothing else but a counseling system that is askew, and that rebelliously misrepresents man and the rest of creation because it misrepresents God. Indeed, because it is in such basic error—a system designed to promote life apart from God—it is in competition with God, and at odds with His creation.

When B. F. Skinner, the world's most influential and articulate advocate of Behaviorism, speaks about controlling the environment (an essential plank upon which his entire system rests), when William Glasser talks of bringing counselees into conformity with the reality about them (i.e., their environment), it should be plain to the Christian that neither one knows what he is doing. How can Glasser, a purely humanistic thinker, know what reality is? Can he truly help counselees conform to reality when he himself doesn't know God, and does not think of the creation as His? What he does—if he does anything—is to move counselees from one wrong relationship with their environment to another. The latter—if it seems to work for a time—in the long run may prove a further curse, rather than a favor, if it tends to blind the counselee to the fact that he is still out of harmony with God and a creation that, in reality, is His.

Skinner too talks about the environment. But he is an atheist. How then can he have the faintest notion of what his environment involves? If he cannot even understand the visible environment, because he fails to relate it to the unseen environment which gives it definition and purpose, how can he possibly make good on his grandiose claim to control man by controlling his environment? Can angels, demons and— above all—God be controlled by man? How does one condition an angel? Skinner thinks that he need busy himself only with those things that he can see. But God has revealed that the seen world is inextricably bound to the unseen one.[6] As in this life one cannot separate the body from the soul (another problem of Skinner's) since one is affected by the other, neither can the seen world be separated from the unseen.

---

6. See, e.g., Job 1, 2; Dan. 10:10-31; Eph. 6:12; I John 5:19, etc.

Skinner thinks that he can change and control man by manipulating the environment. But as we have seen, Skinner has an all too shallow and distorted view of his key interest—the environment. To do what he claims, he would have to find a way to manipulate God! God laughs at such efforts even when made by the kings of the earth (Ps. 2:1-4). Skinner thinks he has bottled the ocean when his container holds only a puddle!

In any counseling, then, whether it is systematic or not, a biblical understanding of the environment (or the lack of it) will make a radical difference. To say it another way, whether the originator of the system was a Christian, and whether he brought biblical presuppositions into the structure of the system from start to finish, makes all the difference in the world. That is to say, the world is a different world for the Christian than for the non-Christian. A Christian perspective makes all the difference in how you think about a world of trees, and chairs, and money and persons (I Cor. 2:9, 10).

Is God at work in this world? Then one's counseling system must take this into account. Otherwise, how could it be realistic? Are God's purposes being achieved in the visible environment and in human lives? If so, it is essential to understand what they are and the meaning of this fact. A system that fails to do so fails to take into account the most basic dynamic of all. Has God revealed truth about Himself, about man and about his world? How could a system for living in this world begin to give satisfying direction to counselees apart from serious consideration of any such revelation. Is God concerned? Does He care about people? The answer to this is all-important to persons in trouble. Has He done anything to alleviate human suffering and change the human condition? And if so, what does He say about such change and how it may be brought about? Can counseling even begin—not to speak of proceeding—without such information if it is available? Surely the answers to these questions, and a number of others like them, ought to be of such tremendous significance to all counselors that you would think they would never venture to counsel a single person until they had the answers to them. But, quite to the contrary, system after system has been devised without the slightest consideration of these issues.

Christians should not be surprised by this; the natural man is dead toward God. He has no inner spiritual life (life engendered by the life-giving Spirit who dwells within every believer) from which such concerns might spring. But what are we to think of Christians who enter into counseling as counselors or counselees with much the same attitude? How can they adopt such systems and counsel according to their principles, seemingly as oblivious to their counseling environment as an unbeliever?

It is hard to understand this, but when one becomes aware of the prevalence of such insensitivity to the importance of the issues involved, he must make the attempt and must seek to combat it. Throughout the Western world[7] the concept of neutrality of system and method has been preached almost as a sacred doctrine. The modern man thinks that he can hold his Christianity in one hand and a pagan[8] system in the other. He sees no need to compare and contrast what he holds in his hands. If there is one thing needed, then, it is to awaken Christians everywhere to the facts that I have been discussing above.

Such a viewpoint did not come from biblical theology. It grew largely from the secularizing philosophical theology that Kant and those who followed him have popularized. The "religious" has been conveniently separated from the "secular." A part—the really operative part—of life has been called "secular" (neutral). Churchly, otherworldly things have been called "religious." This bifurcation of the world—intended to "save" the religious realm from the destructive elements of critical attack—instead has had the effect of relegating it to the ash heap of the virtually unimportant. That should be altogether apparent in the way in which system after system simply ignores the question of God, and in the ease with which even evangelical Christians adopt eclectic positions. It brought about a secular week/sacred Sunday mentality.[9] This same mentality fostered the neutrality concept.

The Scriptures present an entirely different view. All of life is sacred; none is secular. All life is God-related; none is neutral. Systems, methods, actions, values, attitudes, concepts are all either God-oriented or sinful. None are *neutral*. Creation was not neutral. The twenty-four elders put

---

7. I have run into this problem on four continents. One might say it is *the* counseling problem for the church today.

8. The word is mine. That is precisely what he would *not* do—label the system pagan. To him, systems are neither pagan nor Christian; they are neutral. But see my *What About Nouthetic Counseling?*, pp. 73-75, for more on this.

9. The biblical view, on the contrary, considers every day holy to God—He is God over all and concerned about the entire week; the entirety of life. Sunday, then, is the holy of holies.

it this way: "Our Lord and our God, You are worthy to receive glory and honor and power because You created all things and by Your will they exist and were created" (Rev. 4:11).

God created all things to bring honor and glory to Himself. Creation is God related; it is committed. It is not neutral; the creation is not secular.

This great verse teaches us that counseling—as indeed all human activity—must presuppose God not only as the Creator, but also as the Sustainer of this world. There is nothing more important to do in counseling than to help the counselee recognize this and find hope in it. The most profound truth, that makes the deepest difference, is the fact that *human problems are not neutral*. God is in the problem! All counseling worthy of the name *Christian* focuses upon that fact. The knowledge that God is in the problem so colors and conditions the problem that it is profoundly changed—from within.[10]

So, if the God of the Scriptures exists, the Christian's approach to counseling will be totally different. Neither that deformed tree growing outside your window nor that arm mangled in an accident by your counselee is merely a tragic happenstance. God was in the events that brought about both. We may never know in this life all the reasons behind those events, but knowing that *there are reasons* itself changes everything. Life is not absurd; it has meaning—God's meaning. Beyond that, knowing that for God's children every happening has a beneficent purpose (Rom. 8:28, 29) is, perhaps, even more significant. There is nothing more important to tell a counselee, therefore, than that God is in the problem.[11]

No other approach honors God, puts Him first and man second. All others are essentially humanistic (man-oriented) and fail to bring hope and satisfaction to human beings precisely for that reason. Happiness comes not to those who seek it, but to those who seek first the kingdom of God and His righteousness (Mark 6:33; see also Mark 8:35 for the same principle

---

10. Cf. my *Lectures on Counseling*, pp. 100-103, for an in-depth study of this fact.

11. Counselors should ring the changes on this fact till it changes the counselee's whole outlook. Christians—because of their secular/sacred neutrality training—approach problems essentially as pagans do. Therefore, it is necessary for counselors to challenge this approach. But how can they do so if their own approach to counseling, for all intents and purposes, is no different? Cf. *Lectures*, pp. 59ff.

stated in a slightly different way). This fact conditions all counseling.

What kind of hope (to take one example) can be communicated by those who do not see life set in just such a frame? At best what one offers can be but an uncertain hope-so. But the Christian's hope differs; it is not a hope-so, but a confident expectation based upon the recorded promises of the living Creator Who sovereignly sustains and guides human affairs to the predetermined ends that He has foreordained. There is a beneficent reason behind all that happens. What a difference from, let us say, Albert Ellis' approach to life: "Well, I guess that's how it is, old buddy; you'll have to live with it, whether there is meaning in it or not!" No one ever stated the alternative viewpoint more plainly than Ellis. It is of the essence of his Rational Emotive Therapy (R.E.T.) to persuade people to abandon value statements like "ought" and "should" (statements that grow out of a God-oriented approach to counseling) in favor of his grin-and-bear-it stoicism. For him, there's no meaning to life, no fairness or unfairness about it all; nothing but what exists. Stress the "is," and accept it, he says. *Que sera, sera.* There are no standards, no values; that's the way life is. Learn to accept it and slide with it. Stop fighting it. It won't do you any good to do so anyway. So, the snow is deep. That's not "tragic"; it's just a fact. Stop making calamities out of life. See it as such and plow through it. It is when you evaluate situations and events as good and bad, tragic and fortunate, etc., that you get into trouble. Your "hope" of living as satisfactorily as circumstances allow lies in taking this colorless view of life.

But Ellis is fighting a battle that he cannot win. God has made human beings incurably ethical. Everybody knows that he lives in a moral world that cannot be divorced from shoulds and oughts (cf. Rom. 2:15). Let him protest all he will, but counselees cannot for long suppress the sense of right and wrong that God put within them. Man was created in God's image as a *moral* creature. He is not a dog. Ellis asks for the impossible when he asks the counselee to erase his moral orientation toward life. Ellis is fighting the environment; he is fighting God.

But even Ellis betrays the futility of his advice in his own writings and tapes. The very counseling concerns that he has belie his position. His strong (at times near violent) insistence upon denial of oughts and shoulds[12] amounts to nothing less than a (distorted) self-contradictory

---

12. He almost makes it a calamity (a no-no for Ellis) to express a value judgment!

ought: COUNSELEES OUGHT TO ABANDON OUGHTS! If he really followed his own dictum, he would abandon counseling altogether, unconcerned about whether people "deceive" themselves with value judgments or not. He *ought* to say, "So what? That's just the way people are—always messing themselves up with oughts and shoulds. I'll live with it. Surely I have no *obligation* to do anything about it. Why *should* I?" A crusading stoicism like this, then, is self-condemning. It demonstrates the fallacy of trying to deny a basic element of man's nature. It is an admission of the untruth of the system at its core.

We have seen, then, that the fact of God's existence has much to do with the success or failure of the counseling system. The system must conform to the reality of the environment in which it will operate. One that leaves God out, however, can only clash with the environment. Why Christian brothers attempt to further godliness by using ungodly systems is hard to understand; yet that has been the rule (not the exception) for a generation. This has been true not only of liberals, who have no inerrant standard (because of their rejection of the Bible), but also of those who claim to believe in the Scriptures as their standard of faith and practice. The use of such systems not only leads to ineffective counseling; more to the point—it is sinful. It is sinful for a number of reasons, but let me mention only one—it shows lack of trust in the revealed Word of God as an adequate standard. To know about God's revelation in Scripture and to abandon it (or dilute it) in favor of the wisdom of men is serious rebellion.[13] It constitutes an attempt to use evil counsel to promote the work of God! It amounts to one form of doing evil that good may come.

Remember, we have seen that from the inception of human history there have been two counsels. Till that antithesis is sharp, not only in counseling, but in every area of theology and Christian activity, the leadership of the church will continue to confuse the members of the church. It is poor theology that fails to distinguish things that differ (cf. Phil. 1:10).

Some Implications of the Fact of God's Existence

God exists; therefore godly counseling must exist. Counseling like this puts God at the center; it doesn't unnaturally tack Him on to the

---

13. Cf. I Cor. 1, 2.

end.[14] God is its goal. The purpose of such counseling is to honor Him and bring counselees into a deeper relationship with Him. It takes as its guiding principle Romans 11:36: "Indeed everything is from Him, and through Him and for Him. To Him be glory forever! Amen." Biblical counseling will recognize God as the Giver of its principles (and even of many of its methods). It will, therefore, be a God-oriented system derived from His revelation about the world, man and Himself.

From start to finish, the fact of God's existence will permeate the counseling context. Counseling will be done *under God*. He will not be ignored, but will be *a very present help* in time of trouble. The very atmosphere that surrounds the counseling session will be dynamically electrified with this great fact. There will be a sense of expectancy to see God work. Care to understand problems in scriptural ways and to frame solutions according to scriptural principles will be noticeable. Dependence upon God, evident in prayer and in the disavowal of human sufficiency, will protrude. Confidence about evaluations and plans that rest upon the unfailing teachings and promises of the living God will be evident in growing hope. Christian counseling will differ at every point because God exists.

If God controls the universe, the counselee's problem may be difficult, but it is not out of control. It is not beyond solution. Indeed, in some way (to be understood now in part, but more fully later on[15]), these problems are a part of God's plan and purpose for the counselee. They didn't just happen; they have meaning. They have a design in God's mind that, at once, will bring glory to His name and blessing to the counselee. How, is not always ours to know in counseling, but acceptance of the fact is essential to a proper Christian response. Counselors, therefore, must themselves believe in the sovereignty of a beneficent God in order to communicate this fact to the counselee.[16] Contrary to Ellis' dogma that things are just that way, so accept them, the Christian believes that things are that way because they are in God's plan and under God's control, and that through them He will work all such things for His good and the good of His people.

Thus God will not allow Himself to become disengaged from Christian counseling. He is transcendent; but He is also immanent. All

14. Cf. *Lectures on Counseling*, pp. 28-37.
15. I Cor. 13:9-12.
16. Cf. *Lectures on Counseling*, pp. 59-72.

deistic notions of a disinterested god out there, who started it all, but went away and left it to run on its own, ideas of a god who has little or no concern (or power to do anything) about the peculiar problems of the counselee, must be abandoned. That concern is demonstrated in the gift of biblical revelation, which is God's concerned counsel to men. That power is revealed in the gift of the Holy Spirit, whose presence in a Christian assures not only his ability to understand the scriptural revelation (I John 2:20, 27), but also his capacity to obey it (Phil. 4:13).

The fact that God is a person is of great significance. God is not a machine; He is not an irrational, blind, unthinking, uncaring force or process that operates according to discoverable (and possibly manipulatable) laws. He is rather the Person who created all things and in His providence sustains and orders them for His own ends. The universe is rational. He is not like high-tension wires to which we can connect our own lines to obtain power. Neither is He a superhuman bellhop who comes at our beck and call; He is not a cosmic dispensing machine that will parcel out whatever we wish if we insert the proper coins and pull the correct prayer levers. God is the Person in charge. He is a sovereign Person. That makes a lot of difference in counseling.

God does what He wants to do. He does it when and how and where it pleases Him to do so. Our prayers do not instruct Him, they do not order Him, they do not manipulate Him. We are *ordered* to ask, but we are *told* that we will receive. All is of grace, and *what* we receive will be the answer that He is pleased to give. It may be yes, partially yes, no, wait or something else. It is our responsibility to conform to His answer, not God's responsibility to conform to the desire behind our request. What we think is right is not always what is best. Counselees often complain of manna and cry for meat. If God gives meat under such circumstances, the way in which He does so is designed to teach us to stop complaining. Counselors will find it necessary, therefore, to instruct counselees in proper biblical attitudes and stances toward prayer that grow out of an appreciation of the personality of the living God; He is the *Person in charge!* Imagine counseling persons apart from any consideration of the One in charge; that is absurd!

Our ways are not His ways. This is true because of our sin and because of our limitations. Counselees must be apprised of this fact. In counseling, their ways will have to be changed to conform to His ways; their thinking to His. God is a Person; He is a Person who is inextricably involved in the counselee's life. A counselee can no more avoid and ignore God than he can live without air. God is his atmosphere. And as an interested Person, God *demands* things of him. It is this change of his ways and of his thinking, and this conformity to His that He is constantly pressing upon the counselee. This is especially true in counseling where the Word is ministered in such a way that these conflicting ways are exposed. God is in charge of the counselor, the counselee and the counseling. He will not strike bargains or compromise with the counselee. He isn't going to abandon His wisdom to accommodate the foolishness of human wisdom (ignorance). He won't stop loving to conform to the counselee's hatred and bitterness. He won't forget His own holiness to overlook the counselee's unholy desires. It is the counselee who must conform to his environment (God), not the other way around.

God does not stand behind a heavenly door with arms full of presents ready to hand out to those Christians who learn the ritual of some religious "open sesame." He is not a force that we may avail ourselves of if only we learn the techniques of positive thinking or (if we live on the West Coast) the routines of possibility thinking. He is the God who tells *us* what to do and what not to do. He is not only the God of shoulds and oughts, but the God of *musts!*

God sustains us. We could have no existence at all without Him; we are in the palm of His hand. Our every heartbeat was decreed by Him from all eternity. "In Him we live and move and exist" (Acts 17: 28). Rogerian autonomy? Nonsense! The very breath by which Carl Rogers speaks the word is dependent upon His everlasting decree! We are all utterly dependent upon Him for all things.

Such a view of man and God makes quite a difference. But everything is changed if you put man in the center of it all (as the humanists do), or if you postulate that the universe is ultimate and is just there—an impersonal brute fact with which we must reckon some way (as the secularists do). In the end, it turns out that every non-Christian counselor reaches this point if he does any serious thinking at all about life and existence. The choice (as Paul put it in Romans 1) is simply between the creature and the Creator as ultimate. If the choice is not for God, at the end point it is for one's self. This is the last choice because if one abandons an objective revelation pointing to the Creator of all things, his viewpoint of life and existence ends with what he himself thinks. Subjectivity is the inevitable result; whatever he believes, rejects, thinks or determines is *his* choice. He then becomes his own interpreter of life and existence, depending upon himself alone for a standard.

But if that is what both counselor and counselee must do, what hope is there? Every man knows also how little he knows and how often he is wrong. What a bad prognosis for counseling!

Who—if not God—can change this tangled tale we call our lives? Who can bring order, meaning and direction into existence? Politicians cannot. Psychologists and psychiatrists have not. Then what is the use of counseling? What is the use of pretending that people can be helped if there are no revealed answers from a personal God who cares, who controls and who counsels? The existence and the acknowledgment of a personal sovereign Creator is absolutely essential to the very idea of counseling. This is no mere academic quarrel; whether God is involved in counseling or not determines whether, in fact, there can be any counseling at all.

Skinner makes no sense out of life and existence. To call men a pack or herd hardly justifies counseling; indeed, it militates against it. To wish to breed and control the human herd, and to counsel individuals for their good, are two entirely different things. Indeed, the two concepts are incompatible. That is why, as a matter of fact, Skinner does not counsel.

In counseling one man sits before another and in effect says, "I'll counsel you." How dare he? It amounts to the exhibition of sheer arrogance if in doing so he depends upon his own ideas. To depend upon Freud's ideas is no better; he too was only a man. And to depend upon Freud's ideas is (in reality) to depend upon one's own ideas about Freud's ideas. The subjectivity of it all is inescapable apart from a revelation from the living God Who also caused us to accept and enabled us to understand it. Subjective counseling logically should lead to the impasse where one ought to be afraid to say (or not to say) anything to a counselee about changes in his life. When a counselor has himself no answer to the basic questions of life, how can he advise another?

Does the reader think for one moment that Skinner or Harris or Mowrer has solved his own problems? Did Freud? Study his biography.

His addiction to cocaine reveals something of his failure to do so. It is amazing that Christians should not see this.

God is the Person Who has all the answers, can communicate all of them that we need and can enable us to understand and live according to them. If He has not done so—as all non-Christian systematizers think—then let's scratch the whole business of counseling and stop deceiving people by arousing false hopes. If there is no God, there can be no counseling (except the counsel of the ungodly)!

The Justice of God

We have said something (all too little) of the sovereignty,[17] existence and nature of God. But we must move on to an equally significant matter. Because of its many applications to counseling, the question of God's justice also must concern us for a time.

One age-old theme, constantly heard in the counseling room in one form or another, is, "It isn't fair." In a pair of psalms, easily remembered by the reversal of their numbers (Psalms 37, 73), both David and Asaph admit to entertaining such thoughts. The theme of each psalm is the justice of God in a seemingly unjust world where the godly suffer and the ungodly prosper. The *final* end of each is contrasted, plus the immediate advantages of the faithful in those things that are of eternal worth. Eternity is contrasted with time, etc. One fact dominates all: God is in control and *the seeming injustice of the situation is only apparent*. The imbalances often experienced are only temporary. The picture is larger than it may seem. This is the theme of the entire Bible. Indeed, it is a principal theme of the cross. The serpent bites the Savior's heel (apparently gaining the upper hand) only as his own head is being crushed beneath it (Gen. 3:15). By His death, Christ conquers death. It is ever so in a world where a good God reigns.

Asaph's personal testimony is informative. The problem of seeming injustice so imbittered him that he almost threw over his faith. But when he went to the Lord's house, heard again about God and thought more deeply about the larger picture, he recognized his error. So too, counselees who are caught up in this problem must hear the message of these psalms: (1) don't envy the wicked; (2) don't fret about the temporary

---

17. For more on this subject, see my essay, "Counseling and the Sovereignty of God," in *Lectures on Counseling*.

imbalances in life; (3) take the long view[18] and (4) recognize that God is just and cares.

The justice of God is one large theme of the book of Revelation. The martyrs, slain for their faith, continually cry out, "How long?" Their cry is for a righting of wrongs, for a turning of the tables. God says all will come in His time; wait a little longer (Rev. 6:11, 12). Finally the time comes. The angel declares that there will be "no further delay" (Rev. 10:6); "the hour of His judgment has come" (Rev. 14:7).[19] The book of Job early dealt with the subject from another perspective, and the theme is dominant in Daniel's prophecy. The great message of God's justice is as clearly proclaimed in II Thessalonians 1:3-10 as anywhere in the Scriptures. The tables *will* be turned: "it is just for God to repay affliction to those who are afflicting you, and to give rest to you who are being afflicted" (vss. 6, 7). But when? Finally and fully, "at the revelation of the Lord Jesus from the sky . . . when He comes . . . on that Day" (vss. 7, 10). Once again the long view is emphasized. The picture does not change throughout the Bible.

As much as counselees would like to hear otherwise, God's justice does not always appear immediately. Injustice all too often does prevail *for a time*. It is true that sinners sow the seeds of their own destruction, but, as the psalmist says, for a time they flourish and spread themselves "like a green bay tree." During that time the imbalance of the scales is not easy for us to take.

But that is what faith is all about; faith looks off to the future (Heb. 11). It takes the long view in dependence upon God's Word. All God's people have had to learn this. Counselees cannot expect to be excepted. The desire to be exempted may be the problem of some. Therefore, counselors must be ready to use the exhortations of the thirty-seventh and seventy-third psalms in counseling. When a counselee says, "That isn't fair!" he must be made aware of the seriousness of his accusation; he is challenging the justice of God and faithfulness of His Word. Moreover, he is exhibiting a clear lack of faith.

God is just. The righteous will be cared for (they don't beg bread),

---

18. And don't miss the many short-range benefits either. Many of the temporary inequities about which counselees complain may be explained by God's generosity and longsuffering toward His enemies and the elect (cf. Matt. 20:15; II Pet. 3:9, 10).

19. For more on this and the book of Revelation, see my book, *The Time is at Hand*.

their ultimate blessing is assured, and God in His time and in His way will right all wrongs.[20] There is no easy way for counselees to arrive at this stance; yet that is precisely the need of so many. Envy, resentment and revenge, mixed with self-pity, constitute the bitter ingredients of very many counseling situations. Therefore, every counselor should arm himself with the basic facts, and a few crucial passages (I have tried to set forth both concisely here) about God's justice. He must warn and encourage. He warns about accusing God of injustice and encourages the long view of faith.

The Trinity

Many fanciful (or at best speculative) ideas have been extrapolated from the doctrine of the Trinity. I do not want to add to these in attempting to draw counseling implications from doctrine. But there are at least some plain facts that seem hard to miss, from which a few important points can be made.

First, when a Jehovah's Witness says, "I can't believe in Christianity [he'll call it 'Christendom,' of course] because of the teaching of the Trinity; who can believe in a god that you can't understand?" the Christian ought to repliy, "I can't believe in your god because I *can* understand him. Any god I can understand is no greater than I." God's infinity and God's trinitarian nature are the very sorts of realities that make worship possible. We can only worship a God Who is beyond us (cf. Isaiah's exposé of the stupidity of idolatry, where he makes this very point—44:9-20[21]).

But this fact, that God is beyond man's full comprehension, raises certain other questions for counselors:

1. Do we have all the answers to all problems?
2. Can we hold out unlimited hope for counselees in counseling?
3. Or are these areas of life, corresponding to the mysteries of the nature of God, that are beyond us and that consequently pose problems that are insurmountable?

---

20. This emphasis is of special importance to those who are bent on "taking vengeance." I have written a practical exposition of Romans 12:14-28 about this issue, entitled *How to Overcome Evil,* to be used as a handout. Cf. also Luke 14:14. At times, to point to the ultimate outcome is the last word that can be given to a counselee concerning God's justice.

21. The same principles hold, even when one's God is like the God of the Russellites.

Again, our response must be yes and no. The mysteries of God—to which certain counselees address themselves in improper ways—of course cannot be solved by finite man. They must be told so. But these cause problems for some counselees only because of another difficulty—entirely of their own making—that *can* be resolved. The attempt to understand that which is beyond finite ability, and the consequent agonies of thought and mental exhaustion into which they cast themselves thereby, is inappropriate, unnecessary and sinful. In essence, it results from disobedience to the Scriptures and (since all matters of disobedience can be resolved) therefore can be set to rest.

Deuteronomy 29:29 reads as follows: "The secret things belong to the Lord our God; but the things revealed belong to us and to our children forever, that we may practice all the words of this law" (Berkeley). Every counselor should familiarize himself with this verse to fortify himself against all counselee attempts to spin counseling sessions off into the realms of speculation that are forbidden by I Timothy 6:4, 5, 20, 21 and Colossians 2:8. There is a class of counselees that invariably want to do just that. Frequently, as we shall see from the thrust of Deuteronomy 29:29, this arises from a desire to divert attention from sins in their lives that they would rather avoid. Others are involved in unrestrained sinful curiosity of the sort that led to the first sin in the garden. Human sinfulness manifests itself in a desire to be like God, knowing all things. It refuses to acknowledge and adopt God's limitations as the standard for human thought and life. Therefore, Deuteronomy 29:29 says several things:

(1) There is an area of knowledge that God has kept secret from us.

(2) There is an area of knowledge that He has revealed to us in the law (Scriptures).

(3) The former area does not belong to us, but to God. To try to pry into it amounts to theft; it is said to "belong" to God. Speculation about it is sin.

(4) What knowledge God *has* given to us must be known and taught to all generations (starting with us and our children). There is more than enough information of this sort to master; there is no need for further revelation.

(5) But this knowledge was not revealed for "academic" or "speculative" purposes either; it was given for practical ends: "that we may practice all the words of this law." The Scriptures

consist of revealed truths all of which are capable of application to life ("practice *all* the words of this law").

The Trinity seems an area of doctrine especially likely to give rise to
speculation among counselees. They often puzzle about various aspects
of the doctrine. Therefore, speculation about unrevealed facts must be
downplayed by explaining that they are forbidden[22] (God has not revealed, for example, how He can be both three and one, how Christ's
human and divine natures interact, etc.). But, on the contrary, revealed
facts about the Trinity, together with their practical applications, must
be emphasized. It is important to replace speculation with practical application.

What are some such facts that carry practical implications for counselees? I shall respond suggestively, not exhaustively.

The fact that we have a trinitarian God has many implications that
bear upon our salvation and the believer's sanctification. The death of
Christ was an infinite sacrifice, adequate in effect to atone for the sins
of all God's chosen ones. The transcendence of God the Father is
balanced nicely by His immanence as Holy Spirit. The majestic other-
ness of His deity (for instance, in presenting God's concern and care)
is conditioned by the humanness of Jesus Christ, who also became man
(cf. Heb. 4:14-16). These facts are readily apparent. But what can a
counselor do with them?

Take the last as an example. In Hebrews 4:14-16 we read:

> Since then we have a great High Priest Who has gone through the
> heavens, Jesus, God's Son, let us hold to our confession. We don't
> have a high priest who isn't able to sympathize with our weaknesses,
> but One Who has been tempted in every way that we are, yet with-
> out sin. So then, let us come close to the throne of grace with bold-
> ness, that we may receive mercy and find help just when we need it.

There are Christian counselees who need help and are afraid to
ask for it. These verses urge them to lay aside all such fear. Christ, by
virtue of His human nature and His life among us in the flesh, knows—
from our perspective—all that we are going through in this world. As a
result He can sympathize with us. He will not reproach us, as James
puts it (James 1:5), but will sympathize with us (see our problems from
the human point of view) when we bring them in prayer. This should

---

22. Cf. also I Tim. 1:3, 4.

be used to greatly encourage counselees to bring their problems to God in the proper spirit (boldly) and with large expectations of mercy and help *precisely when it is needed* (not long after, nor long before, however). Not only this, but because Christ faithfully withstood temptation (without sin), He *knows how* to instruct and help us to do so too.

Curiously, counselees often think, "Well, He didn't sin, so how can He help me—I'm a sinner. I need help from someone who, like me, also has failed." But that is exactly wrong. In every other area of life we understand that fact; we don't go to a music teacher who is an unsuccessful musician, to a coach who can't play the sport, to a two-time divorcee to learn how to have a successful marriage. Here is One Who had all the pressures the counselee experienced (and *more*), yet He *didn't* fail. He best can show another how to succeed. He has "gone through the heavens"; i.e., He is at the Father's right hand of power—and so also is *able* to help others; and He is *willing* to do so (He encourages them to come boldly to Him on His throne, which is the source of all grace (help). He is our High Priest Who intercedes for us with God. So, there is no reason to lose one's grip on his confession; if he does so, he may blame neither God nor the circumstances; only himself. There is great hope and (also) large responsibility that grows out of the doctrine. Counselors should recognize the importance of such truth for many situations where the need for hope and responsibility is paramount.

More about the Trinity will arise as we take up other themes at a later point,[23] especially when we study the atonement and its effects and the application of redemption to man. For now, all I wish to stress is the need for a practical, rather than a speculative, approach to the doctrine.

---

23. See especially chapter 7, which is devoted to one aspect of the doctrine.

CHAPTER FIVE

GOD'S NAME AND COUNSELING
(The Doctrine of God, Continued)

Persons in great misery or distress often need something quite distinct to which they may refer from time to time while going through trial. Throughout the Bible, God has graciously revealed Himself to His people at such times by a name that is appropriate to the situation. When Abraham faced bewilderment and uncertainty over the promise of God in his old age, we read these comforting and reassuring words: "And when Abram was ninety-nine years old, Jehovah appeared to Abram and said to him, 'I am *El-Shaddai*'" (Gen. 17:1). *El-Shaddai!* How those words must have thrilled his soul to know that in all his weakness and inability there was One Who could back up His promises—*El-Shaddai*, translated "God Almighty," means more than that; it means "the Mighty Provider." The Name speaks of God's mighty and infinite power to nourish, satisfy and supply. Abram would not need to depend upon himself or even the usual working of life's circumstances; *El-Shaddai*, the major Name by which God revealed Himself during the patriarchal period, expressed just what Abram (and all the patriarchs) needed to know—their God cared and had both the will and the power to back His care with almighty action. How many counselees as well need to have a counselor write across the head of a homework assignment that seems to the counselee to require of him an almost impossible task, "I am *El-Shaddai*"—Gen. 17:1! In parentheses beneath the name he might write: "The Mighty Provider."

Doubtful, unsure Christians, weak in faith, once more need to reckon with God. Perhaps they are best faced with the unique name: *Jehovah* (or, better, *Yahweh*). It is true that God is the Mighty Provider, the *El-Shaddai;* but that concept does not always meet the center of the problem in the life of the weak, fearful believer. He needs once more to be reminded vividly of God as the covenant-keeping One. Yahweh is the Name peculiarly associated with God in covenant with

His people. By this Name God revealed Himself to Moses, and through him to Israel (cf. Ex. 3:15). It is used about 6,800 times in the O.T. In the new, it is applied to Jesus under the Greek word *Kurios*. This Name is warm and personal in its usage. It is actually a form of the verb *to be* that has been translated variously as " I am that I am," "I am," "I am because I am," and "I will be that I will be." Because of these several possibilities, the N.T. writers refer to its meanings under the phrase, "who was, who is and who is to be." *Yahweh* is the One Who is "the same yesterday, today and forever." It means therefore that He is dependable. The Name, above all else, assures the believer that God will keep His promises. Can the counselee trust God to do what He has said in His Word? Of course! This is the Word of *Yahweh*—the God of promise and steadfast love!

Not only has God Himself revealed something of His nature and character through His Names, but by His Spirit He has led His servants to record Names that *they* used about God to express their gratitude for what He has done for them. These too are very helpful for counselees, especially because they grow out of trying circumstances in which God's people found their God to be faithful to them. It is extremely important to understand that these Names too are a revelation from God—given mediately rather than immediately—but, nonetheless, Names that God intended to be revelatory of Himself. It was He, by the Spirit, who superintended the recording of these Names for our encouragement. Therefore, they should be used by counselors. Here are a few:

1. *Jehovah-Shammah* = "Jehovah (Yahweh) is there"—cf. Ezekiel 48:30-35 for the context (esp. vs. 35) in which this name appears. The returning captives would find Jehovah there in the city they would build. Whenever we move out in accordance with God's revealed will for us, we find that He is there—leading, blessing, waiting for us at the destination we seek to reach.

2. *Jehovah-Jireh* = "Jehovah will provide (see to it)"—cf. Gen. 22:1-19 (esp. vs. 14). This passage, and its circumstances, together with the name, is too familiar for comment. Yet, that makes it none the less precious, especially for counselees afraid to move ahead in directions that seem too questionable, too threatening, too difficult for them to do. The God Who provided the lamb for Abraham, Who provided the Lamb on Calvary for them, will also provide for their needs in this too.

3. *El-Roy* = "God that seeth"—cf. Gen. 16:13. The encouraging

story that accompanies this name is calculated to bring hope to modern day Hagars, wandering alone. This single parent needed to know—as many today do—that in the lonely places, where danger and uncertainty lurk on every side, God's children are not really alone. God overlooks none; He sees them all.

4. *The Rock*—cf. Deut. 32:1-43 (esp. vs. 4). Firm, enduring, protecting as the mountains around Jerusalem—all that, and much more is God, the Rock. Time and turmoil cannot change Him; He towers majestically above it all. Often silent, but always strong, He remains the unfailing refuge of His own. That's what every counselee needs—a Rock. If He knows Christ as His Savior—he has one!

5. *Jehovah-Nissi* = "Jehovah our Banner"—cf. Ex. 17 (esp. vs. 15). Victory is what counselees need; victory over enemies, trials, temptations. How can they win the battle? One way only—by going forth to battle under the banner of God. That means boldly going out to meet the foe when, where and how God says; using only those weapons and strategy that He commands. God marches where His banner flies; His banner flies where His Word of command is obeyed.

There are many other names: The Lord is my *shepherd* (Ps. 23:1); He is *Jehovah our righteousness* (Jer. 23:6); He is the "Lord God of *Sabaoth*"—that is, the Lord of *hosts* (or armies), etc. The biblically aware counselor will search the Scriptures for such help as fully as he can. In the Names of God there is much revealed about God in relationship to His people—all of it of great help both to counselors and counselees.

In closing, one other Name—easily overlooked, but of great significance—is Christ's own favorite designation for God, but one that He taught us also to use (in the Lord's prayer, for instance): *Father*. How rich in content that Name is. All that a father is (or ought to be), with all the familial warmth of care and concern, is contained in it. Develop this fully in counseling; remind God's children constantly of what it means to be a child of the Father in the heavens. Few other emphases can bring about such comfort, encouragement, discipline as this one, rightly understood. There is so much here, and yet such a joy unfolding it, that I refuse to go any further. You are on your own; on the lines that follow—for yourself—work out from the Bible all you can about God as Father of those who have been born again and adopted into His family:

_____

_____

_____

_____

_____

_____

_____

_____

_____

_____

_____

_____

_____

_____

_____

_____

_____

_____

_____

_____

What's in a name? Usually, there is not much in our names today. But God's Names are a revelation of His Person. Through them shine His provisions, His care, His protection, His concern, His faithfulness, etc. What's in a name? Much, when you're talking about the Names of God.

CHAPTER SIX

COUNSELING AND PRAYER
(The Doctrine of God, Continued)

In the Foreword I mentioned the fact that I intended to omit discussions of doctrinal issues that are usually included in systematic theology textbooks when the counseling implications of these are so obvious as to be apparent to any thinking reader. I have tried to follow that practice so far in this book.

But at this point I shall do an about face: I wish to begin to develop a doctrine that has been all but omitted from the study of systematic theology (despite its importance and despite our own ineptness in pursuing it), the doctrine of prayer.

The vast majority of the books on prayer are hortatory, a few are doctrinal, but there is none that I know about that discusses prayer doctrinally with a view to discovering the implications of such doctrinal emphases for counseling. That, therefore, is what I propose to begin to do here in a preliminary way.[1]

The Place of Prayer in Counseling

Prayer has a *central* place in Christian counseling, both for the counselor and for the counselee. Any counseling that is not based upon the idea that it is the power of God that transforms counselees is *essentially* non-Christian. Prayer, then, must have a prominent place, since both counselor and counselee must ask for God's help and depend upon Him to give it. Clearly, this involves prayer. Humanistic counseling of various sorts (whether an avowedly pagan system or humanism in a Christian wrapper) exhibits its fundamental weakness most clearly at

---

1. Hopefully one of the many men in the nouthetic counseling movement who is capable of doing so will write the fuller book (or books) that the subject warrants.

this point—the absence of prayer demonstrates that a counseling system is man centered (humanistic), no matter what its label may be, when in its practice counselors fail to call upon God and rely upon human wisdom and strength to achieve its goals and objectives.

Among other things, prayer is asking God for wisdom, help, correction and blessing upon our undertakings. Without prayer, the Christian counselor should not *expect* God to work by His Spirit through his counseling efforts. (That doesn't mean, of course, that the sovereign God cannot, or even *will* not, work unless prayer has been offered. He is not so tied to us that His work is limited by us. He achieves His purposes as *He* sees fit. But from the counselor's perspective we may surely say that there should be no expectation of blessing upon his counseling unless he truly seeks it.)

So, the first aspect of prayer to be *mentioned* (it is too obvious to be developed very far) is that the counselor must pray for himself and his counselees, asking God to use His Word as it is ministered in the counseling sessions, requesting wisdom for himself in the selection, understanding and use of the Scriptures, in gathering and analyzing data according to biblical norms, and seeking God's help in preparing the soil in the counselee's heart (inner life) for the sowing of the scriptural seed. The counselor will wish to pray specifically for each counselee prior to the next counseling session, mentioning especially those matters that stand out in his notes included in the counselee's file.[2] Among other uses to which the counselor will put them, he will find that his counseling notes can become extremely useful guides for private intercessory prayer.[3]

Prayer in the Sessions

Prayer plays an important role in counseling sessions too. Frequently, at crucial points in a series of sessions, the only appropriate action to take is to pray.

Before coming to an important decision, when a counselee is exerting determined, strong resistance to the Scriptures, after hearing an exceptionally happy, sad or shocking bit of news, where a counselee decides to trust Christ as his Savior, when a great breakthrough has just occurred,

---

2. For further information on note taking and on record keeping, cf. *Competent*, pp. 198ff, 204; *The Manual*, pp. 228ff., 263ff.
3. Reserved for private prayer because such notes should be shared with no one.

and in any number of similar situations, a prayer of commitment, thanksgiving, petition and request, adoration or confession, by the counselor and/or by the counselee, is the natural and spontaneous response in a truly Christian counseling context. Prayer—at any point, during any session—is appropriate when it is natural and spontaneous on the part of either. Probably, because of this fact, such prayer often will be remembered by the counselee as one of the highlights of any series of counseling sessions.

Counselors cannot be told (in a book like this) when to offer spontaneous prayer; by its very nature *spontaneous* prayer flows naturally as the response of one who is accustomed to turn to God spontaneously on such occasions. If his life is characterized by a conscious walk with God, in which talking to Him in response to the happenings of daily life is a regular feature, a counselor will have no need to be taught *when* to offer prayer silently and when to offer it audibly in a counseling session.

Frequently, as the last sentence suggests, prayer will be offered silently. If praying audibly would be "throwing pearls before pigs," if it would interrupt the flow of data being given or if it would confuse a counselee as to its purpose at a given point,[4] the counselor may wish to speak to God silently in his heart without involving the counselee in the prayer at all. But on most other occasions, whether the counselor leads in prayer (using "we" throughout) or whether he prays for him (using "I" and "he" instead), the counselor will want to pray audibly in the counselee's presence.

There are several reasons for this. Often counselors will want to develop greater dependence upon God in their counselees' lives (nothing more effectually does so than involving them in earnest prayer). At other times, it will be vital to help the counselee to confess sin to God, to "call upon the name of the Lord," or to express adoration, thanksgiving and gratitude to God for what He is and has done.

So far I have mentioned two instances in which prayer is appropriate in counseling: prior to each session and (spontaneously) during sessions when it is appropriate. In addition, I might mention also a third: in

---

4. For instance, a counselor may not yet be prepared to discuss with a counselee a matter that he does want to discuss with God; again, a counselor may wish to ask God whether to raise a certain issue with a counselee at this point.

connection with each session (at the beginning, at the end, or at both points). At such times, requesting God's presence and blessing, bringing thanksgiving, confession of sin, commitment to God and such other obvious purposes are paramount. Prayer on such occasions should be made a policy and should be adhered to *in all cases, where it is at all possible to do so* (someone smashing furniture because he is hallucinating may make joint audible prayer impossible).

Prayer by the Counselee

It is desirable for the Christian counselee to be encouraged to pray during the period of counseling for each session, for the counselor, for himself, etc. Consequently, as one regular homework assignment,[5] the counselee may be told to set up regular family (or personal) devotions.[6] Part of the disciplined living necessary for counselees to solve problems demands regularity in Bible study and prayer. It is, therefore, important to give this assignment the very first week (or as soon thereafter as is practicable). From the start, counselees should be taught their dependence upon God for the changes desired. It is the Word and the power of His Spirit that brings these changes, not the counselor (or the counselee). Few emphases impress this fact so vividly as an organized, purposeful, coordinated plan for personal devotions.[7]

At times, too, the counselee will be *invited* (no strong pressures should be exerted; some counselees, however, require, and indeed appreciate, gentle, well-timed pressure) to pray in a particular counseling session. Perhaps at the close of a session that the counselee himself has described as "particularly helpful" is a good time to ask him to lead in a grateful prayer out of the fulness of his heart. In this way, the counselor can move from a position that might otherwise tend to seem "professional" to the proper position of a brother and officer in Christ's church. When the "expert" encourages the counselee to take the lead at such

5. For more on homework, cf. chapters on this subject in the *Manual*.

6. I have prepared a devotional workbook for counselees, entitled *Four Weeks with God and Your Neighbor* (Phillipsburg, N. J.: Presbyterian and Reformed Publishing Co., 1978) as a supplemental aid to counseling. It focuses on prayer, Bible study and the practical application of the Scriptures to life.

7. *Four Weeks* (ibid.) stresses both discipline and change; these two themes are essential in all early counseling. There are also assignments for Sunday sermon note taking and Saturday evaluations of the week's progress. Week four weans the counselee from the devotional guide to personal study and prayer on his own.

times, he goes a long way toward dispelling any *wrong* notions about his authority or expertise.

Another appropriate point at which to invite the counselee to pray is whenever he has made a crucial verbal commitment in the session ("I have decided that God wants me to give up my homosexual way of life"; "I now know that I must go back and straighten things out with my wife"). The commitment made before the counselor is important, but it also should be made to God; it is to Him (not to the counselor) that he must answer (Rom. 4:4). Prayers of commitment following biblical decisions lay stress on this fact.

In general, then, such prayer makes it clear that all that is happening is taking place in the presence of God, for His glory and in dependence on Him. *This understanding is vital for proper biblical counseling.*

Thanksgiving and commitment, we have seen, constitute two of the most significant reasons for extending opportunities to counselees to pray. Some caution should be exercised about inviting them to pray (in sessions) for help. Usually, it is best for the counselor himself to pray such prayers. Most counselees don't know how to pray well— especially prayers of petition (they often violate James 4:3, for instance)—so it is wise for the counselor to guide and model for them in these prayers.[8]

Prayer of confession and for salvation warrants a special word. Here is where the matter of wrong pressure is most likely to enter in unless the counselor is very careful. When praying about something over which the counselee is joyfully thankful, the question of pressure is not likely to arise; there is a wonderful pressure already building *within* that the counselor suggests he release in this manner. Nor do counselees who have *already expressed commitments in a voluntary way* have many problems with prayers of commitment. So, in order to avoid any outward pressures that could lead to hypocritical prayer (forced from *without,* not released from *within*), the counselor should be sure that he has elicited such commitments on the horizontal level before suggesting them on the vertical. If a desire for prayer is not expressed voluntarily ("How do I go about trusting Christ as Savior? I'd like to," or "Shouldn't I ask God's forgiveness for this?"—obviously, these

---

8. There are, of course, many exceptions. And at times the subject of prayer (and teaching about it) may lead to an ideal situation for asking the counselee to pray.

openings are served on a silver platter), the counselor may ask the counselee (as a genuine question, not as pressure in question form[9]), "Would you like to ask God's forgiveness for that now?" or "How about telling God that you want to trust Christ as your Savior; you could do that right now if you are ready to. I'll explain how, if you want me to."

But there are also times to say, "You don't seem ready to make that commitment yet. You ought to do so; delay is sin. But to pressure you into saying words you don't mean would be sin too. I hope you will talk to God about this before I see you next time." This approach stresses the danger of delay and the necessity to forsake sin, but eliminates pressure toward hypocrisy.

Now there also are times (when counseling cannot progress further until a commitment of some sort is made, confession is essential, forgiveness must be sought, a change is made) that the counselor must say, "When you have taken care of this matter, call my secretary for your next appointment; we can't go on till we get past that problem. It is blocking the road." Pressure to do what God says should always be exerted (cf. Heb. 3:7–4:13), even with strong warnings about the consequences of failure to do so; but this should be balanced by an unwillingness to do anything that would suggest that the counselee compromise his integrity.

Because counselees differ—and especially since some actually need strong encouragement ("encourage the timid. . . ."—I Thess. 5:14b)—it isn't easy to know exactly how much pressure to exert on whom and in what ways. Keeping the rest of the verse in mind (". . . be patient with everyone") also helps. If there is any question, extend your patience to the second mile. Yet, never forget, there are some timid persons who need the pressures of encouragement directly exerted.

Feedback from gentle prods (or questions like those above) often will provide the clues that you need to make a decision about whether to exert encouragement-pressure or not. At times, too, it is simply wise to ask, "Bill, are you the kind of person who will need some encouragement to do this?" If the feedback that you receive from offering suggestions (or mild pressure) is an angry response, for instance, usually this is not the sign of timidity *in such a setting*. It is

9. Cf. comments on this in *Matters of Concern*, pp. 87, 88.

time to back off. Questions like, "How do I do it?" or objections like, "But I don't know what to say," on the other hand are usually offhand ways of saying, "I'm embarrassed because I really don't do such things well; will you help me?" and should be pursued. Evasive tactics can be interpreted in any number of ways (so they yield little help in understanding, except the fact that you know there is *something* still in the way of commitment). Postponement (often combined with *mild* embarrassment) perhaps indicates timidity more often than anything else. But remember, read each person in the light of his previous responses—not all respond according to the general type.[10]

At any rate, prayer of all sorts must be encouraged among counselees, not as a magic solution to their problems (too many counselees must be warned against such mystical views of prayer), but because of the importance of establishing regular communication with God, and because of the importance of seeking His help in obeying His Word.

One final note: *As a side benefit only* (*never* as the purpose for inviting a counselee to pray) much can be learned about a counselee from the form and content of his prayers. Counselees should be aware of this.

The Christian Doctrine of Prayer

In this materialistic age, surely one may ask, "What is prayer?" and not in the least be facetious when doing so. The present generation has grown up prayerless. Even where giving of thanks at meals still prevails, all to often it is but the hollow vestigial remains of a worn-out tradition. Few children are taught (or taught how) to bring their problems to God. At home and in school, they are reared according to an uneasy doctrine of self-sufficiency that leads to a radical self-centered pride and arrogance or (conversely) to an unhealthy dependence upon parents and society. Without prayer, God is in a picture on the wall; and for many "religious" people today, that is just where He is. Without prayer, there is no vital connection with God, no confession, adoration, thanksgiving or petition; that is to say, no communication is established with God (of course, there could be none apart from Christ).

But even for Christians—who pray (all Christians do, or they are not Christians)—the universal word is that prayer is the hardest discipline of all. So, on both counts, it is quite proper to ask the question,

---

10. Cf. on this, *Matters of Concern,* pp. 18, 19.

"What is prayer?" An understanding of the biblical teaching will not only give us an answer to that important question, but it also will provide the foundation for drawing counseling implications.

The comment, "Everyone knows what prayer is," is both correct and false. Just about everyone has a vague idea about prayer. The picture of someone with his head bowed talking to God is perhaps the most common connotation of prayer. Yet even that stereotyped image has been shattered recently by the common charismatic stance of face and hands raised toward heaven in prayer. And, members of the Unity cult, for instance, repeat "truth sayings" in an attempt to further indoctrinate one another in the idea that one "prays" to himself, since he is as much God as any other. So it is *not* really true that "everyone knows what prayer is"; clearly, there are quite different concepts of prayer, in content and form, some of which are plainly contradictory to others.

False Ideas about Prayer

Perhaps it is best to begin with some notions of prayer that must be eliminated because they conflict with biblical teaching. Two buildings cannot occupy the same space at the same time. One must be razed before the other can be built.

The auto-suggestion theory must be rejected. The advent of psychological analysis of human behavior combined with unbelief has plowed the ground for such teaching. In one form or another, this theory is widespread today. According to the basic features of this theory, the person calms himself, gets clearer insight, and shifts the burden of his problems from his shoulders when he prays. What happens, of course, is all internal. There is actually no contact with God—if there is a God. The suppliant is fooling himself into thinking that God hears. But since he calms himself in the process, prayer is to be commended to those who care to fall back upon it. Prayer is good, so long as one doesn't become frustrated and discouraged through failure to receive what he asks for.

Of course, this notion of auto-suggestion must be rejected out of hand as bearing no resemblance to the biblical concept of prayer, in which the Bible teaches that "The Lord will hear when I call to Him" (Ps. 4:3). In Christian prayer the praying believer directly calls upon the living God, Who hears and answers according to His will. Communication actually takes place; a transaction occurs. If there is any inner benefit that he receives from the *act* of prayer, it is secondary, wholly a by-product. A Christian does not pray *in order to find solace by the act.* Moreover, even the inner effects of the act itself produce very little by way of secondary effects. True calm comes more from a realization that he is in the presence of the very God of creation and that his need has been placed in God's hands! It is when Christians begin to trust in the *act* of prayer (or its effects) rather than in the God to Whom they pray, that trouble begins. Counselors must be aware of this problem in counselees and warn against it. On the contrary, it is the objective element in prayer that makes all the difference; if prayer is only a subjective experience, there is little comfort or help to be found in that. Such a notion of prayer is sub-Christian.

Closely akin to this is the idea that the only changes that prayer effects are within the person who prays, not within the course of events in history. On this basis, one can believe that there is a God Who answers prayer, but that He does so only by changing the one who prays. This doctrine of inner blessing, taught by some Unitarians and others in the deistic tradition, means that it is quite improper for a Christian to pray for rain. Because this view amounts to a downright denial of the petition that Christ taught us to pray—"give us this day our daily bread"—it too must be rejected.[11] That sort of prayer inextricably involves God providentially in the course of human events.

It is true, of course, that the Bible *does* teach that in answer to prayer God does make inner changes in the one who prays. I have no quarrel with that fact; my concern is about those who limit change exclusively to this inner, subjective sphere.

A third view, found a bit more frequently in orthodox circles than the former two, is the idea that prayer is synonymous with petition. Again, this limits prayer in an unwarranted way. A number of years ago, John R. Rice—who by no means adheres to so limited a view—did us a disservice by entitling a book *Prayer: Asking and Receiving,* as if that title were an adequate description of prayer.

A more recent concept to be rejected is the idea that prayer is meditation. With the advent of Eastern views on meditation, biblical teachings about meditation have been misconstrued at two points: (1) Biblical meditation is not prayer (though it may lead to prayer). (2) Biblical

---

11. To say nothing of the other petitions in the Lord's prayer; e.g., "Lead us not into testing."

meditation (unlike T.M.) is meditation on the truths of the Scriptures about God and our relationship to Him (cf. Ps. 1); it is *never* meditation on "inner space" within the meditator, or some such similar concept. The two ideas of meditation are opposites: the pagan view focuses on self; the Christian view, on God and the truth He has revealed.

The Roman Catholic view of prayer also must be opposed. Prayers to saints and to Mary amount to (1) a rejection of the accessibility of God in Christ (the only Mediator[12]) and (2) an ascription of attributes to glorified human beings that belong to God alone (omniscience, omnipresence, and sometimes omnipotence). Mary is called the "refuge of sinners," the one who is to be asked to "guide" and "teach" us, who is "never implored in vain," to whom "fervent prayers are to be addressed," and the one whose "name alone comforts" (*The Catholic Church the Teacher of Mankind*). She solves the problems of rain and drought, famine and plague according to this book designed to instruct "the Catholic child at the mother's knee" (Title page. The book was published in New York by the Office of Catholic Publications and bears the imprimatur of Archbishop Johannes W. Farley). On page 643 we read:

> Unfortunately, you are still mastered by many faults which prevent your becoming the pious and dutiful child God wishes you to be. To be able to cure yourselves of them you must implore the Blessed Virgin.

Words almost fail in replying to such unrestrained idolatry. This concept of prayer puts Mary in God's place. In fact it seems that according to this doctrine of prayer, God has delegated the answering of prayer to Mary. The response to make must be this:

(1) Nowhere in all of the Scriptures can any such ideas be found. One will search in vain to find anyone at any time praying to Mary; nor is there any injunction to do so. Indeed, the Scriptures tell us to pray exclusively to God in Christ's name (see vss. *supra*). And there is no model of prayer to Mary, any other human being, or to angels. The biblical picture differs considerably from the Roman Catholic one represented in these words: ". . . in his shortcomings, at each instant of his life, and in the hour of his death, the Christian turns to Mary. Her name *alone* comforts him, and gives him confidence" (ibid., p. 642).

---

12. I Tim. 2:5.

(2) When we pray to someone, we thereby ascribe to that one all of God's attributes. For example, we must assume that the one to whom prayer is directed is omnipresent even to be able to hear the millions of prayers that are directed to him from all parts of the earth. But omnipresence is an attribute of God alone. Omnipotence likewise is required of the one to whom we pray; he must be *able* to answer all requests. Omniscience cannot be divorced from prayer either, since the answer must be given with reference to all other matters of all time (past, present and future). Does Mary have such attributes? Some think so ("Mary is all powerful, for she is the mother of God," ibid., p. 642), others have not carefully thought through the issues involved.

The Christian Doctrine

Having taken a hurried survey of some prominent misconceptions of prayer, let us turn now to what the Bible teaches. I cannot do an exhaustive study of prayer here (and, especially, I do not wish to emphasize points commonly stressed by others). I shall, therefore, sketch something of the Bible's teaching and then develop more fully the implications of one or two points.

There are several Greek words in the New Testament that should be understood. These comprise the foundation statement of the Scriptures regarding prayer.

The first word, and the one most closely approximating our English word "prayer" (from the Latin, *precari*) is *proseuchē*. In scope, this word is broadest; it comprises all the rest. It is found more often than the other words and has the general meaning of speaking to God.

The word *euchē*, from which *proseuchē* comes, is used in James 5:15, and is also translated in the same general manner. It is, in a sense, even broader than the former word, but since it occurs only three times, while *proseuchē* is used over 33 times, it can hardly be thought of as the *basic*, comprehensive, broad-scope word of the N.T. Without question, *proseuchē* earns that place by usage and meaning combined.

Trench[13] says that *proseuchē* means "prayer in general," and "always prayer to God." Its use in Acts 16:13, 16 confirms the fact. There it is used as the name of the place where prayer—all kinds of prayer—was made. This use shows clearly that *proseuchē* is the word for prayer in

13. *Synonyms of the N.T.*, p. 189.

general. The more general term is most likely to name the place. Authorities do not differ on the point. Thus, the importance of the term emerges. All other words for prayer refer to either a part or an aspect of *proseuchē*. A verse like Ephesians 1:16 demonstrates the use: I "never cease to give thanks for you, mentioning you in my *prayers*." The thanksgiving and the supplication take place *in* Paul's *proseuchē*.

The second biblical term of note is *deēsis*. This word is more specific than *proseuchē*, although it is frequently found coupled with the latter by the word "and": "prayers and supplications" or "prayers and petitions" or "prayers and requests." At times it does stand alone. Trench points out two ways in which *deēsis* differs from *proseuchē:*

(1) *Proseuchē* is broad and general, while *deēsis* refers to specific requests "for particular benefits." That is to say, *deēsis* is petition; it could never be used as a word to encompass thanksgiving or confession, for instance. It is *asking* for something specific.

(2) *Proseuchē* is always addressed to God; *deēsis,* on the other hand, also is used of making specific requests of men. *Deēsis* describes the petitioner with a clearly understood want that he is asking God to supply; while *proseuchē* is prayer (in general), *deēsis* is prayer in which one goes into particulars. Each particular request is a *deēsis*. Thayer says that the term expresses more explicitly the idea of "need." If that concept of need can be connected to the other, a *deēsis* may be describd as a particular request growing out of a specific need.

Another N.T. word is *enteuxis*. There is a wealth of meaning in this term, but it is used infrequently. The word was in regular use to denote the petition of an inferior to a superior; e.g., a citizen making request of an emperor. In it is something of the idea of boldness, access and confidence. Its translation in the KJV ("intercession"), therefore, can be misleading; *enteuxis* has a broader scope. This is clear from its use in I Timothy 4:4-5, where it cannot have the meaning of intercession. It also carries the idea of conversation or conference. Trench points out its etymological connection with the notion of "falling in with a person." The one who obeys Hebrews 4:16 is engaging in *enteuxis*.

Another word for an aspect of prayer is *eucharista*, everywhere correctly translated "thanksgiving." This is the "grateful acknowledgment" (Trench) of God's goodness in the past; unlike *deēsis*, it looks back and remembers rather than toward the future. There are no special shades of meaning; its connection with gratitude is entirely obvious.

Thanksgiving is vitally connected to happiness. When a Christian suffers financial loss, the death of a loved one, etc., the Scriptures teach that grief (anchored to hope that doesn't drift into despair—cf. I Thess. 4:13ff.) is proper. But because of the promises in Romans 8:28, etc., thanksgiving also is appropriate, even if the specific reasons for it do not appear immediately. The Master Planner is directing the course of events toward the good of His people. The trials and heartaches themselves are an essential part of that plan that ultimately calls for wiping away all tears. The prayer of thanksgiving acknowledges this. The requirement to pray thankfully rather than worry (Phil. 4:6) *demands* of the believer that acknowledgment of God's sovereign goodness. One cannot give thanks meaningfully under adverse circumstances unless he has taken the time to reflect upon the fact of God's providential control. This deeper understanding of the trial in part contributes to the peace that follows (vs. 7). Counselors must point this out.

An ungrateful counselee, even when he finds a solution to his problem, will not appreciate it. Until he has learned to be thankful, even the sweetest fruit will turn to gravel in his mouth. Ingratitude turns all to rust; it leads to unrest and disharmony. Counselors must look for ingratitude and work zealously to overcome it. The word *eucharista* occurs 38 times in the N.T. in a verbal form and 15 times as a noun, its frequency showing its importance.

Two other words must be considered: *aitēma* and *hiketēria*. The first of these is a peculiar word that occurs only twice in the N.T. in the sense of requests or petitions to God.[14] Both times (Phil. 4:6; I John 5:15) it occurs in the plural. "In a *proseuchē* of any length there will probably be many *aitēma*" (Trench). These are the specific requests of which a *proseuchē* is composed. In the Lord's prayer many persons have found seven *aitēma*.[15] Berry equates *deēsis* and *aitēma*.[16] The one element that distinguishes them is the sense of need that always is a part of the *deēsis*. No such notion inheres in *aitēma*.

Finally, we come to *hiketēria*. In this word, the attitude of humility is prominent. (This is seen in the LXX rendering of Job 40:22; II Macc. 9:18.) In the N.T. *hiketēria* occurs but once (Heb. 5:7, where it is linked

---

14. And once in Luke 23:24 it is used of a request of men.
15. See Trench, *Synonyms*, p. 191.
16. *A Greek-English Lexicon of the N.T.*, p. 121.

with *deēsis*). It may be translated "supplication" or "humble request." These words, themselves, indicate much about prayer. The Christian counselor must be familiar with each aspect of prayer since he must deal frequently with the subject. Although God knows all things, He has ordained prayer (Matt. 6:8). Requests, general and specific, given with thanksgiving and offered fervently out of a sense of need and in a spirit of humility are the substance of prayer. God doesn't learn from prayer, we do.

Add to these ideas two other concepts, and the picture will be complete: confession and adoration.

The Greek word for confession is *homologia* (literally meaning, "saying the same thing"). The great passage on the subject is I John 1:9. Confession involves saying the same thing about ourselves that God says in His Word. It means "agreement" or "acknowledgment." It is the fruit of repentance (*metanoia;* a change of mind leading to other changes in life). Confession, therefore, involves a desire to be freed from future sin. Confession with the lips must grow from confession in the heart.

The necessity for confession is found in Proverbs 28:13: "Whoever covers his sins won't prosper; but whoever confesses and forsakes them will have mercy."[17] Good examples of confession are found in Psalm 51, Ezra 9 and Daniel 9.

Adoration is not so much a biblical word as it is a biblical practice. An excellent example is Psalm 103:20-22. In that psalm the author ascribes praise to God for what He is and for what He has done. Adoration is thinking about God and praising Him for Himself. It is the desire to thank Him simply for what He is. It goes beyond gratitude for His works to praise God for His being and nature. In adoration the heart cries "Abba, Father," as the true meaning of those words is experienced. Prayer limited to petition is not Christian. To it must be added not only confession and thanksgiving, but also adoration. Adoration is the *soul* of prayer.

In counseling, it is important to explain and emphasize adoration. Counselees typically are oriented toward the solutions to their problems, and they tend to forget the One Who brings those solutions. Self-centeredness is one common underlying cause of counselee problems.

---

17. I shall have occasion to discuss confession in depth later on in this book.

In those cases where this is prominent, the need for a call to adoration is essential. Often, however, the situation is so bad that even elementary gratitude is lacking. The attitude of a counselee at times may even be, "Well, I'm glad that the Lord finally got around to solving my problem; it's certainly about time." So, thanksgiving frequently is a first priority. But having led the counselee through repentance into thankfulness it is essential to stress adoration too. Especially important is the need to teach counselees to thank God for Who and What He is, *regardless of what He gives*. Not all solutions come as requested, when requested, etc. But the one unfailing source of satisfaction available to every Christian counselee is satisfaction with God Himself. Joy in the Lord is basic to joy in His works (which, in His providence, at times may be contrary to our fondest wishes). Adoration draws the counselee away from self and others to God; it puts the emphasis where it ought to be. Adoration brings ultimate meaning and purpose into life, so that *whatever* God's solution to one's problems may be and *whenever* it may come, he is prepared to accept it because he has learned to love God for what He is. As the spirit of adoration grows, the counselee's ability to handle life in the right attitude grows too. Adoration—though it must be taught and practiced out of obedient love for God, and not for any such personal side effects that might accrue to the counselee—nevertheless does produce such effects. One cannot spend time in loving adoration of God without experiencing the many good effects that accompany adoration. And it is precisely these effects that many counselees need in order to develop a biblical stance toward life and its problems.

A Prime Concern about Prayer

In using the "Personal Data Inventory"[18] over the years, it has been interesting to note the regularity with which certain answers appear. Perhaps the most consistent response of all comes in reply to question 2 on the final page. It is the second in a trilogy of questions that hang together:

(1) What is your problem?

---

18. For a sample of this intake questionnaire see the *C.C. Manual*, pp. 433ff. In *Update on Christian Counseling*, vol. 1, I have discussed the various uses of the P.D.I.

(2) What have you done about it?

(3) What do you want me to do about it?

In response to question 2 (What have you done about it?) there is a one-word answer that appears in isolation on the inventories of most Christians and many non-Christians alike. Do you know what it is? Right! The answer is "prayed."

This usually is both the right and the wrong answer to the question, as further discussion with the counselee makes clear. It is right for reasons too obvious to mention. It is wrong in most instances because it stands alone.

Prayer rarely (if ever) should stand alone as the biblical solution to a problem. To the common complaint, "But I prayed about it and nothing happened," ordinarily the counselor ought to reply, "But what did you pray that the Lord would give you the strength and wisdom to *do?*," or, "Fine. Then what?"

"What do you mean *do* something? I prayed. It is now up to the *Lord* to do something, isn't it?" (so many counselees think).

"He has already done something; in the Scriptures He has told you what to do. Your prayer provides the trusting, dependent background by which you seek God's help in accomplishing His biblically expressed will," you reply, of course.

In many cases, I suggest the following, "You pray the Lord's prayer, perhaps?"

"Yes, I do."

"Well, in that prayer, you ask God to provide your daily bread. This probably refers to all your needs, but let's think about that bread for a moment. Having once prayed for it, you immediately sit down under a shade tree and wait for a loaf to come floating out of the sky on a para-chute, don't you?"

"Of course not."

"Well, *why* not? You prayed for it; now it's up to *God* to do some-thing about it, isn't it?"

"Yes, . . . but. . . ."

"But what?"

"Well, there's something over in Thessalonians or some place that says, 'If you don't work you shouldn't eat'—or something like that."

"Do you mean that you have to *do* something more than pray, then, in order to get that bread?"

"I suppose so."

"Well, then, how about your current problem? Let's turn to the Scriptures to see what God says to do (prayerfully) about it."

"But what about Philippians 4:6, 7? Doesn't Paul say there that peace of heart and mind comes through prayer?"

"Yes and no. I've known a lot of people who have prayed, then complained when peace didn't come."

"I guess I have myself. But what does it say, then, if it doesn't say that?"

"Well, it says pray, all right; *but that isn't all*—you see, that's just the point that I've been trying to make. Prayer is the beginning, but verse 6 appears in a context. And that context requires *other* things *as well*. Let me sketch it for you. First, instead of worrying, Paul says you must pray. And he explains how to pray too:

> but in everything by prayer—namely by petitions growing out of need (*deēsis*), with thanksgiving, let your specific requests be made known.

That means that He wants earnest (fervent) prayer, phrased in terms of concrete items. It means that He wants you to be thankful (even for your problems, knowing that He knows what is best for you) as you pray (not bitter, nasty, revengeful, etc.). Already, you see, Paul has so qualified his explanation of the prayer that you must offer that it is clear that just any old sort of prayer will not do.

But prayer is not enough. He goes on to say that having emptied your heart and mind of your worries by casting them on Him, you must refill your mind with good thoughts that fit the criteria listed in verse 8. If you don't, all the old worries will flood in upon you once again. Your mind and heart cannot simply be emptied; they must be repackaged. Wrong thoughts must be replaced by right ones. There will always be thoughts within; no vacuum can exist. If right thoughts are not carefully introduced, wrong ones insinuate themselves.[19]

But that still is not all that the context requires for peace. First there must be proper prayer; secondly, right thoughts replacing wrong

---

19. Here a Phil. 4:8 "Think List" may help; see *Lectures,* pp. 138f. for more on this.

ones. Thirdly, there must be action. See verse 9:

> Whatever you have learned and received and heard and seen in me practice, and the God of peace will be with you.

The biblical action dealing with each problem must be taken (what Scripture says, the apostles taught and demonstrated, etc.)—*then God will bring peace*. But not *until then*. And notice, the peace doesn't come as you *begin* to do what God says to do—it isn't automatic; it comes somewhere later down the line, *after such action has become your practice*. Now do you see what I had in mind when I said 'yes and no'?"

"I do. But why haven't I been taught such things?"

"There are many reasons. But your concern now is to *do* all the Scriptures require of you—prayer, thought and action to overcome worry. The same is true of a number of other matters. *Always find out all that the Bible requires. Prayer* (important as it is) *is usually but the first step!"*

It is rarely helpful, then, merely to suggest to a counselee that he pray. In the Bible, prayer regularly is coupled with *action*. As action without prayer is presumptuous, so in such cases prayer with action is irresponsible.[20]

Much more could be said about prayer and action in relationship to counseling, but since it is so common a problem I wish to reserve that for another time and place, D.V., perhaps in a separate volume on the subject.

Unanswered Prayer

What about the problem of unanswered prayer? This is a theological/counseling problem that is of interest and significance to both areas of thought.

Sometimes the Bible speaks about God not hearing prayer and of persons imploring Him, "Hear my prayers" or "give ear to my prayer" as though He might not.[21] From this language some counselees have inferred that God (literally) doesn't hear some prayers. If that were

---

20. God, of course, can (and often does) work without human agency; but that doesn't relieve us of the responsibility to follow all scriptural requirements.

21. Cf. Ps. 39:1; 54:1; 55:1, 2; 59:7; 66:18 (note: hearing = giving ear to; see also Ps. 84:8); 102:1; Isa. 1:15; Jer. 11:14; 14:12; Ezek. 8:18, etc.

true, of course, that would be one reason why He didn't always answer every prayer.

But the word "hear" (and similar expressions) in such contexts must not be interpreted literally, as though it referred to the actual process of auditory perception. All things—including all prayers, audible or silent—are known to God. No prayer—not even the prayer of the heathen offered to idols—escapes His purview. That, then cannot be the sense in which passages indicating God does not hear some prayer must be interpreted.

The word "hear" is used not only to refer to the actual physical process of receiving and translating sound waves into sounds and speech, but also in the sense of *heeding* (or, as we often put it, "paying attention to" what one hears). It refers also to listening favorably to a request, and (indeed) to *granting* the request.[22] In Psalm 66:19, the Hebrew *keshev* means to "listen to heedfully," or "pay attention to."

All of those passages in which God is asked to "hear" or to "give ear to" a request, or in which He is said to "hear" one prayer (but not another) must be construed to mean answering or not answering a prayer.[23] When it is said that God did *not* hear a prayer, it means that He did not heed it (or look favorably upon it). Every sense that denies His omniscience or power must be rejected.

In counseling (as elementary as it may seem) you will discover that these theological truths often are not apprehended by counselees. Even the idea that God (literally) hears all prayers may be news for some. Language used in idiomatic ways too often is construed literally by counselees. Bad theological training, or the failure to take good training, accounts (in part) for any number of problems counselors face; this area of prayer is no exception to that rule. The counselor has a responsibility not only to be careful about his own interpretation of the Scrip-

---

22. Cf. Ps. 4:1; 143:1, where *hearing* is in parallel construction with *answering*. Note also Ps. 66:18, 19, 20, where the *contrast* to not hearing is attending to (or answering); cf. Jer. 7:13; Matt. 6:17, etc.

23. It is not always easy to distinguish between heeding a request and answering it. When God "hears" a prayer, it surely means that He looks favorably upon the one praying, and that He pays attention to his words. However, for His own sovereign purposes, He may not grant the request when desired or in the manner desired. Answering in favor of a petitioner, then, may mean saying "no," if granting it may not be best for him (II Cor. 12:8, 9). Saying "not yet" if he is not prepared (or God is not ready) for the request to take place, or saying "Here is something better for you" are also favorable replies that may be styled "hearing."

tures,[24] but also to see to it that he conveys no false understanding by his own use of language. Sometimes a detailed explanation of a passage (or perhaps at other times two or three sentences will do) is necessary to make it clear that God (literally) never fails to *hear* any prayers, but that He doesn't *heed* them all.

The Scriptures plainly teach, as I have noted, that God doesn't "hear" (heed or grant) counselees' requests under certain circumstances. What are these? The counselor will be asked; he must know.

The Bible doesn't specifically outline every concrete situation that might be imagined. Rather, general, guiding principles, applicable to all possible situations, are given. I shall mention some of the principles most frequently encountered in counseling.

1. *God doesn't hear hypocritical prayer.* When inwardly a counselee determines something other than what his lips speak, he prays hypocritically (cf. Ps. 66:18). In this verse, "regarding iniquity" in the "heart" is equivalent to saying one thing with the lips, but thinking another instead. It is praying with the fingers crossed! The heart is the inner person. Delitzsch translates, "If I had aimed at evil in my heart." He says that *raäh* (to see), plus the accusative, means "to aim at," "to have in one's eye," or "to design to do something."[25] The hypocrite is one who says one thing but inwardly is aiming at something different. God will not hear such hypocritical prayer.

Since this is true, it is quite proper (when a counselee complains about God not answering prayer) to ask (as one of several possible probes): "Did you *really* want that to happen?" or "Was that what you wanted in your heart when you prayed?" Counselors, when they ask in love, will find such questions quite productive. Not only will they tend to put down complaints (not the purpose of the question; merely a by-product), but often they will uncover important data that otherwise might not surface. Underline this point and use it often in counseling.

2. *God doesn't hear unbelieving prayer.* I am not saying that in His mercy and goodness God will not determine to do for us what we

24. Matt. 18:19, 20 is an example of the wrong use of a passage. These verses do not refer to prayer (in general) about *any* subject, for anyone. They specifically refer to prayer offered by the church elders during a possible case of excommunication (cf. vss. 15-20).
25. Cf. Gen. 20:10 for a similar use of this verb: "What did you *have in view* to do such a thing?" (Berkeley).

doubt He will do; there are times when He does (cf. Acts 12:1-16). But, as James put it, a doubter "shouldn't suppose that he will receive anything from the Lord."[26] Here, James speaks of the request for wisdom that God promises to give unreservedly to those who ask (without chiding them for asking). It is something every counselee needs, without exception. But He warns in *broader* terms ("shouldn't suppose that he will receive *anything*. . . .") that apply across the board, that doubters will not be heeded. Indeed, the warning is first stated positively ("But let him ask in faith") then negatively ("without doubting").

In giving this warning, James is but echoing Jesus' words when He said, "Everything that you ask for in prayer you will receive if you believe" (Matt. 21:22). Indeed, He went further:

> . . . whoever . . . doesn't doubt in his heart but believes that what he is saying will happen, he will have it. So then, I tell you, in everything that you pray and ask for, believe that you have received it, and you will (Mark 11:23, 24).

Again it is apparent from Christ's words that prayer is not a magical open sesame. Prayer is not a matter of uttering the proper formula or ritual; rather, it involves inner faith and sincerity to validate the words spoken. Once again, the counselee must be led to see that his *heart* condition in prayer is uppermost.

That means that the counselor may with equal concern ask questions of the person complaining about God's failure to answer his prayer: "Did you really believe that God would do it if He wanted to?" or, "Did you really expect what you prayed for?"

3. *God doesn't hear resentful prayer.* In conjunction with his warning about doubt, and the need for faith (Mark 11:23, 24), Jesus went on to say,

> And when you stand praying, if you have something against anyone, forgive him so that your Father in the heavens also may forgive you your trespasses (vs. 25).

Thus, it seems plain, a supplicant may not expect God to give him what he refuses to give to another.[27] Bitterness, resentment, hard feelings

---

26. James 1:5-7.
27. Cf. Matt. 6:14, 15 (see the footnote in *The Christian Counselor's New Testament* at this point for an explanation of these verses). Also, later on, in my discussion of forgiveness in this book, I shall have occasion to say something more about the passage.

(and the like) surely form a serious barrier to the throne of grace. And
as every biblical counselor knows, resentment is one of the most common problems that counselees struggle with. Often resentment is one
strong link in a chain of complicating problems. When an original
problem goes unresolved for a time, resentment often grows as a complicating factor. It, in turn (as the passage indicates), leads to further
difficulties.

While forgiveness must not be *granted* to those who do not seek it
repentantly ("if he repents, forgive him"—Luke 17:3), the one who
"has something against anyone" may not continue to hold it against him
in his heart. Before God, in prayer, he is to forgive him (i.e., he must
tell God that he will hold it against him no longer). He may not *brood*
on it. But this forgiving in prayer (in his own heart before God) does not
preclude his responsibility to pursue the matter with the offender.[28]
He does this

(1) for Christ's sake,
(2) for the sake of the peace of the church,
(3) for the sake of the offender and
(4) for the purpose of reconciliation.

The one who has relieved his own mind and heart of the burden of
the offense in prayer growing out of a truly forgiving attitude, will have
little difficulty *granting* forgiveness to his brother when it is sought.
And, in the meantime, he will avoid the destructive results of resentment.

Again, then, the astute counselor will ask a counselee who wonders
why his prayers remain unheard if he is bearing resentment or grudges
against another in his heart.

4. *God doesn't hear pharisaical prayer.* At least two faults, typical
of the Pharisee, are observed in the New Testament:

(a) The Pharisee often prayed to impress men rather than God
(Matt. 6:5, 6). The one who prays to be heard by others
(Jesus said) gets just what he seeks—praise from men, but no
response from God. The counselor's question, when he suspects such a problem, is obvious: "Who were you concerned
about reaching when you prayed—God or men?"

(b) The second characteristic (in the end) amounts to the same

---

28. He must continue to bring up the issue to him until he repents and reconciliation takes place (Matt. 18:15ff.; Luke 17:3a).

thing (neither type of prayer is prayer at all). In the story of the Pharisee and the tax collector (Luke 18:9-14) we read that the Pharisee "prayed to himself." His prayer wasn't a prayer; it was merely a recital of his own virtues, self-righteous acts by which he sought to impress God through meritorious living. Consequently, Jesus points out, his prayer was not heard. Once more, the counselor's questions are clear, "Did you think your prayer would *merit* what you wanted?"[29]

The counselor must warn against these abuses as well as be on the alert for them. They may take similar form in other contexts: e.g., a husband may utter words he doesn't mean (in sessions or out) to his wife (or in prayer in her presence) *in order to impress her*. But prayer must be to God; it may *never* be directed to others. Ways of avoiding insincere prayer in counseling sessions have been discussed *supra*.

5. *God doesn't hear self-centered prayer.* James is clear about this: "You don't receive when you ask, since you ask wrongly—to waste it on your pleasures."[30] While it isn't wrong to ask for things that one needs, or even those things that he desires, plainly it is wrong for him to ask *basically* (or solely) for things for himself. Things used for one's pleasures only (or fundamentally), James indicates, are wasted. God doesn't answer prayer that is aimed at wasteful results.

In prayer, as in all else that one thinks and does, he is to "seek first His empire and His righteousness." Then "all of these [other] things will be added."[31] James warns against the sin of seeking *"first"* the fulfilment of one's own desires. "Basically, why did you want it—for yourself or for God's sake?" is the counseling question to be asked in one form or another.

The counselee must be shown that his (often hysterically and repetitively self-centered) prayers are wrong. He must *not* come to God (or for counseling) demanding that *his* will be done. Contrary to any of his expectations, he must be taught that *his own desires,* and *his own will,* in any matter take second place to God's. He must learn from Christ's prayers in Gethsemane, in which intense personal desires are subjected to God's will: "Yet don't do what I want but what You want."[32] The words, "If it be Your will," are a very significant addition that every

29. Always make it clear that faith, prayer, worship, etc., are all not meritorious.

30. James 4:3.   31. Matt. 6:33.   32. Matt. 26:39.

counselee must learn to add (in his heart if not in his actual prayer it-self) to every prayer. Either way, the qualification must be the basic presupposition for prayer. When it is, there can be no complaints about the answers to prayer, only thankful acquiescence. The praying Christian farmer who asks for rain and the postman who asks that it not rain, will both be satisfied by the outcome then, since they will be more concerned that the answer further God's work and spread His righteousness than in fulfilling their own desires.

Counselees, in effect, must be taught to pray this way: "Lord, I bring my requests to you, knowing so little. I may not be asking what is best, so please cancel or modify whatever I ask as you see fit, and make me satisfied with the outcome." Close to this is the other basic premise: God's will must be sought for *His* sake. When we rejoice in negative answers to prayer, it is not because of masochistic tendencies, but because of love—the desire to see God glorified. The glorification of believers[33] is secondary, derivative (in conjunction with Christ[34]), largely takes place in the future[35] and even then is intended to enhance His glory.[36] So, then, in prayer, first one is to seek God's will, which is manifested in those things that He does to further His work and His righteousness, and secondarily, his own will as it corresponds with God's.[37] Which leads to another biblical teaching.

6. *God doesn't hear unbiblical prayer.* Jesus warned us about this when He said, "If you remain in Me and My words remain in you, ask whatever you want and it will be done for you" (John 15:7). This apparent blank check has conditions ("If") that must not be missed. The first condition ("If you remain in Me") indicates that it is only the believer's prayers that God is talking about; no such assurance is accorded to the unbelievers.[38] Those who "remain" or "continue" in Him are the saints. This is the doctrine of the *perseverance* (or continuance) of the saints. All true saints will persevere; therefore, all who persevere are true saints.

---

33. I Peter 4:14.
34. Rom. 8:17.
35. Col. 3:4; I Pet. 5:10.
36. II Thess. 1:10, 12; I Pet. 1:7; 4:11.
37. The more scriptural his thinking and living, the more often this accord should take place. But this is in general; behind the scenes heavenly transactions affect earthly ones, as the book of Job clearly teaches.
38. Indeed, the opposite is taught: cf. Prov. 28:9.

But it is the second condition especially to which I wish to call attention: prayer must grow out of and be in harmony with Christ's Word (which today is embodied in the Bible). His Word, stored up in, guiding and motivating the heart,[39] will not only keep one from sin, but also inform his prayers. That is why praying with the mind (with understanding)—not by rote, or in mystical, magical or mechanical ways—is important. It is often wise to use biblical words and phrases (correctly interpreted and clearly understood) as a discipline for learning to pray properly.

It should be obvious (but every experienced counselor knows, from the frequency with which he encounters the problem, that it isn't) that a counselee ought not to request what God forbids (or will not permit). Prayer must be biblical; i.e., requests must be within the range of scriptural norms to be legitimate. To pray successfully is to pray intelligently and out of a knowledge of what God's Word encourages and allows.

Unbiblical prayer also is prayer that is contrary to biblical example. Nonsensical prayer falls into this category. Nowhere in the Bible will you hear a prayer like this (though you will hear it all the time today): "Please, Lord, may last week's meeting have been a blessing." One may pray for that meeting before or during the meeting in that way, or a week later for blessing growing out of the meeting, or for future blessing stemming from it, but he has no biblical warrant for praying for something to happen *after* it has happened!

7. *God doesn't hear self-addressed prayer.* What is the warrant for prayer? What is the address on the envelope sent heavenward? Prayer must be made *in Christ's name.*[40] Prayer, in Christ's name, isn't prayer *on our own* merit, with some special phrase like "for Christ's sake," or "in His holy name" merely tacked on at the end. There is nothing wrong with such phrases if they are filled with meaning for the one who uses them. They must express the true intention and understanding of the praying counselee's heart. The words themselves may (or may not) occur; the understanding beneath the prayer *must.*

What, then, does Christ mean when He speaks of praying in His Name? He means that, in our prayers, we must ask God to answer our requests

(1) because of Who Christ is and what Christ has done;

---

39. Ps. 119:11.   40. Cf. John 14:13, 14; 16:24, 26.

(2) for Christ's honor and benefit.

Believers are assured that God will hear us because of Christ's redemptive work, and under His intercessory lordship. He is the one
Mediator Who can bridge the gap between God and man ripped open
by sin. God will not hear us in our own names because (apart from
Christ) we have no right to be heard—we are but rebellious sinners.
We can demand nothing in our own names. But because of what Christ
has done, and for His honor (Heb. 2:10; Rom. 11:36), we can approach God boldly for all those things that, by His death and resurrection, Jesus Christ obtained for us (Heb. 4:16). He has provided
much, and encourages His followers to lay claim to all of it, but He
makes one thing clear—such claims must be made *in His Name.* Prayer
must honor Christ by acknowledging the fact that all we ask, we ask on
the basis of a saving relationship with Him and that He may be honored by the granting of this request. God will have His Son honored
every time a believer prays; and we will be reminded of this fact in
every prayer.

These seven conditions are not exhaustive, but they are (perhaps) the
outstanding facts to keep in mind when discussing unanswered prayer
with counselees. In many cases, failure in more than one of these areas
will occur; don't rest until you have the whole picture. It would be wise,
therefore, to cover all seven possibilities in your questioning of a counselee. You can write the seven items into your *Christian Counselor's
New Testament,* and even read them off to a counselee when appropriate
("John, there are seven common reasons why God doesn't answer
prayer. Let me read them, and I'd like you to tell me which ones—if
any—fit you").

Keep in mind, too, that unanswered prayer also may be God's
favorable response to proper prayer. (It is not really unanswered in
such cases; "no," "not now; later," etc., are answers just as truly as
"yes.") Because He knows what is best, remember (as I said earlier),
God may temporarily *delay* an answer to prayer, or *deny* it, or *substitute*
another for it—for our good (which is always also the best for His work;
the two are never at odds). Having explored the seven hindrances to
prayer, the counselor may find that this is the final explanation.

Conclusion

In conclusion, let me reemphasize the fact that God is man's basic

Environment. That is why prayer, growing out of Bible study, is so crucial to his life, and why discussion of these areas is so important for counseling. Adam walked and talked with God in the cool of the day. Sin destroyed that fellowship. In Christ it is restored for those who trust Him (I John 1). Prayer now constitutes a significant part of the way in which a Christian comes into intimate contact with his Environment. Apart from the Scriptures (in which God speaks to him) and prayer (by which he speaks to God), a human being is out of touch with reality.

CHAPTER SEVEN

COUNSELING AND THE TRINITY
(The Doctrine of God, Continued)

From time to time in various books I have spoken about discipleship.[1] I have contended that discipleship is the proper method for training counselors, counselees or anyone else because it is the biblical method. I have set it over against the academic method (which we adopted from the Greek academy) as fuller, different, biblical and (therefore) the more effective method.[2]

I have seen Christian education in general—from kindergarten through seminary—suffering from failure to understand the basic elements of and rationale for the discipleship method and a lack of concern to develop this method of instruction at all levels. I have conferred with educators about this and find interest and sympathy. But, in my opinion, there is (yet) no breakthrough from the traditional, institutionalized approach to a more biblical one. If it is going to happen, now is the opportunity. Perhaps in counseling, and among counseling *instructors* in particular (especially, since nouthetic counselors have been and are currently trained through this method), there can be even greater progress that may spill over into other areas of Christian education.

What is the discipleship method? Fundamentally, teaching by discipleship is the "with Him" method. When Jesus chose His disciples,[3] it does *not* say that He chose them to attend His lectures (though at times they did just that) but, rather, "to be with Him" (Mark 3:14). What does this imply? Why were the disciples to spend time *with* Jesus? In Luke 6:40, where Jesus explains His philosophy of education, the

---

1. Cf. the last chapter of *Competent to Counsel,* the last chapter of *The Big Umbrella,* and (especially) an editorial, "Design for a Seminary," *The Journal of Pastoral Practice* 3, 2 (1979).

2. But not *because* of pragmatic reasons.

3. This choosing factor is important, and says something about the discipler's obligation to determine whom he will teach.

answer to those questions comes clear. He says that a student, when properly trained, will *"be* like his teacher." That is a startling statement to many modern-day educators, who would never think of such a goal. But why shouldn't they? Why should they think of themselves merely as verbal deliverers of information, rather than embodiers of it?

Notice, Jesus does not say that good teaching will help the student to *think* like his teacher—of course, that is *part* of what He has in mind. But there is more: he will *"be* like his teacher." In this distinction lies the basic difference (in goals and purposes) between the academic and the discipleship methods of education. The one who *becomes* like his teacher *thinks* like him, it is true, but he will come to resemble him in other ways as well—in attitudes, in skills, in incorporation of values and skills in everyday living, etc. A whole person will affect whole persons on all levels; that is the goal of discipleship training.

Does it work? Acts 4:13 completes the picture. Those that Jesus chose to *be with Him* that they might *become like Him* were so changed by that method that at length they were recognized by others as *having been "with Jesus."* The same can be said to be true of those whose discipleship training at C.C.E.F. in Christian counseling has enabled them to learn counseling. There is a style among such counselors—not so stereotyped that it defaces their own gifts and personalities but—that is recognizable.

Now much can be said about teaching by discipleship (here's another place for study and fruitful writing), but in summary fashion, let me but list some of the salient features:

1. The disciple is apprenticed as a son was by his father (Jesus spoke of discipleship in a Father-Son context in John's Gospel). There is, therefore, something different from the cold, impersonal conditions so common to academic contexts. In discipleship, the focus is not merely on content, but even more so upon the disciple himself—and the disciple in all dimensions.

2. The disciple hears what his teacher has to say about the subject taught, as in the academic method, but also what he says about it in actual practice. Moreover, the disciple hears what he has to say about many other things, and begins to hear how the discipler relates this information to other data and how he uses it in life.

3. The disciple also sees the thing taught *done* by the teacher him-

self. He becomes a model not merely of someone *talking* about his subject, but of someone vitally engaged in pursuing it. Idealism of the classroom (often self-deceiving to the academic teacher who talks about but rarely, if ever, does the thing discussed) is soon washed out by viewing the practical application of theory in action.

4. The disciple may ask questions about what he observes as well as about what he hears. Not only will more questions arise as the result of observation, but the character of questions will change from purely academic (often nit-picking and unrealistic) to more vital and realistic ones.

5. The disciple learns to do the thing taught under the teacher's observation and supervision. Nothing can substitute for this. Too much is left for trial-and-error on the academic model, where years of floundering by the student could have been prevented by a very few hours of such how-to discipling.

These five facts are not exhaustive; but they are all important. Serious reflection on them, drawing out their implications, will show you how much difference there really is.

Now, why have I raised this issue here—under the doctrine of the Trinity—you may ask? A good question, but first let me have one more word with you before responding to that important inquiry.

The issue of how to teach is crucial to all biblical counselors who, by definition, are involved in a ministry of the Word. That ministry, by the nature of the case, requires teaching. Counselors themselves are taught, and being taught. The teaching programs that they frequent ought to employ the discipleship method, and they should *demand* it. You cannot learn counseling well through the purely academic approach.[4] Counselors must teach elders, deacons and other key laymen how to counsel, so they too must understand (and develop) the discipleship method. Moreover, in counseling itself, instruction is vital. All sorts of data must be taught to counselors—and in a practical, concrete, life-changing way. Discipleship is important for this.

I have taken up this issue because teaching methodology is not optional. Biblically, it is wrong to teach in the abstract; all teaching is for life. It all involves commitment to God. Therefore, truth incarnated in

---

4. Cf. my *Matters of Concern,* "On the Teaching of Counseling," p. 50.

life is the goal. For reaching this goal, only one method is possible—the biblical one—discipleship. Whole persons must teach whole persons; the Word must be made flesh. Discipleship isn't one option; it is an imperative—it is the only option. Because we have failed to see this, Christian education (on all levels) is suffering. There is an almost total commitment on the part of Christian educators to the academic approach. Educators pride themselves on "high academic standards" and in accordance with this develop a professional attitude about their work that more often than not turns out to be cold and impersonal. If anything should characterize Christian education, it ought to be a warm, familial approach to learning—but it doesn't. Many Christians, along with their pagan counterparts, soon develop the attitude that "the student is the enemy." Among Christian educators, too often there is almost total ignorance of the discipleship model and its excellencies.

But, why take up discipleship here, under this head? Because discipleship takes its impetus from the Trinity. The method is not to be adopted rather than the academic approach for pragmatic or other arbitrary reasons; rather, it is to be preferred because of its intratrinitarian basis. There is a *theological imperative* for teaching by discipleship.

The Gospel of John most fully expounds the theological relationship between the Father and the Son that forms the basis for the teaching by discipleship that *ought* to undergird all levels of Christian education, including counseling.

In John 8:26-38 Jesus says (among other things) that He does nothing on His own. Rather, He speaks what He has heard the Father speak and does what He has seen the Father do. In the midst of this discussion of His discipling by the Father (note the backbone of the discipling method is revealed), Jesus says, "If you continue in *My* word [as He did in His Father's, He implies] you are really *My* disciples" (vs. 31b). Cf. also these very significant passages: John 3:32, 34; 5:19, 20, 30 for additional confirmation of this emphasis.

In some way—not fully understood because of the mysteries surrounding the Trinity—the Son brought to His ministry such a replication of what the Father is like that He could say, "Whoever has seen Me has seen the Father" (John 14:9). In the context, Jesus makes it clear that His words and works are not only His, but the Father's (vs. 10). This replication, leading to recognition of Whose words and works were involved in Christ's ministry, leads to a powerful impetus for engaging in teaching by discipleship: the way in which the Son says that He learned from the Father.

This basically theological thrust leads to a unique philosophy of education that Christians must exploit to the full. To do so would revolutionize Christian education from within and soon put it far ahead of secular education. Passages in Deuteronomy 6:4-9; 11:18-21, etc., that speak of teaching children only amplify the need for whole persons teaching whole persons in the life-situation, out-of-the-milieu context that is the bread-and-butter staple of discipleship.

Counselors, then, must be aware of the opportunities that teaching by discipleship affords. They must see it as an essential element of counseling (teaching and counseling are constantly spoken of together as two sides of the same sheet of paper—cf. Col. 1:28; 3:16). They must learn to model truth in their own lives (often sharing experiences illustrative of biblical principles). But that is only one way to go. Perhaps the most vital first move they can make in the right direction is to enlist and train (first their own disciples) a network of disciples to whom they can refer counselees for discipling in specific areas. Pastors always ought to have on hand the names of a number of persons equipped (by them) and willing to minister to counselees by allowing them to spend time *with them*. On the basis of Titus 2:4, 5, for example, older mothers could take younger ones who are having various difficulties under their wings. Titus is told to arrange for this; that means you are too, pastor. A single person, perhaps with a bad family background, who is having difficulty understanding Christian living, very profitably could spend a couple of months living in the atmosphere of an exemplary Christian home, where he could observe, ask questions and participate under the authority and discipline of the head of that home. The possibilities for good are all but limitless. Yet—with few exceptions—counselors have failed to develop and use this virtually untapped resource.

It is time for pastors to set the trend in this, bringing (as the inevitable result) great blessings to all involved. The counselee can obtain greater help than if he only talked about his problem in the counseling room, the discipler will be blessed by giving of himself to the one he disciples, and the pastor will be blessed with a ministering (rather than frustrated and complaining) congregation that frees him from much counseling that he ought not to do to give greater attention to those persons to whom he ought to minister.

All in all, then, I cannot recommend teaching by discipleship strongly enough; indeed, I shouldn't *recommend* it at all. To be biblical, I must *insist* on it. Think about this; what part does discipleship training play in your ministry? The right answer to that question could revolutionize your entire ministry in short order.

CHAPTER EIGHT

COUNSELING AND HUMAN LIFE: THE DOCTRINE OF MAN

Perhaps it is the area that I now propose to study that is of most significance to counselors. I say this, not because I think that the study of human beings is of more importance than the study of God, or for any comparable humanistic reasons. Rather, it is the very fact that we live in a thoroughly humanistic climate that raises the concern and that leads me to this conclusion.

During the last century, there has been more focus on the nature of the human race and on solutions to human problems (not only among pagan writers, but also among Christian authors) than on any other one subject. And, unfortunately, because of this emphasis, more errors have been propounded and more misleading terminology exists[1] than in any other aspect of the counseling enterprise.

The problems to which I refer are so dramatic, and the magnitude of the questions that need to be considered is so great, that (I must warn you) I can only touch on the barest minimum of these questions and of the vast number of counseling implications and problems that grow out of this distorted overemphasis and misemphasis. Whole books on nearly every one of the issues that I shall deal with here (sometimes only in passing) need to be written. Moreover, volumes on matters that I would not even dare to raise in a work of this sort must be added to them. I look forward (therefore) to the time when other nouthetic counselors will catch the vision, do the biblical studies required to produce such materials and (as a result) supply adequate instruction at last for those who wish to help men fully in a way that neither misrepresents nor dishonors God by it. The obvious lacks made apparent

---

1. I propose, in time (D.V.) to publish a book on the language of counseling. This is a very vital, yet virtually untouched, area.

by my feeble efforts here (I hope) will stimulate such work and serve (perhaps) as a guide for what needs to be done.

There are two primary reasons why the emphasis in counseling theory has fallen upon anthropology (teaching about man). They are:

(1) The humanistic ascendancy in modern thought that I have already mentioned (and to which Christian counselors and theorists have by no means been immune) has concentrated its interests on man; humanism is a serious problem because (in the end) it puts human beings in the place of God. Man becomes the measure of all things.

(2) The subject matter of counseling tends to focus on human beings; all counseling purports to offer help for human beings by attempting to effect changes in them. That sinful persons (themselves apart from God) should fail to set their discussions of human life and its problems within a framework of creation, fall, redemption and providence (in which the triune God and His glory is of prime importance) is quite predictable. After all, sinners always tend to think self-centeredly. Yet, at the same time, it is inexcusable and deplorable. The extent to which genuine Christians (until recently) have followed their lead in this is far less understandable. That Christians have done so, nevertheless, is the only possible conclusion that any careful student of theology who is even casually aware of the extant literature in the field of Christian counseling could reach.[2] The deplorable situation has met formidable theological resistance only in the most recent years, as biblical critiques of such accommodationism and biblical alternatives to the radical eclecticism, rife among Christians who are counselors (not Christian counselors) at last have begun to appear. There is significant progress—amazingly so—but the total purge of eclectic thought from the evangelical church by no means is complete.

What can be done to successfully expose, encounter and root out the remainder? I can conceive of nothing better calculated to do the job than a torrent of theological studies, practically oriented toward coun-

2. I have documented this claim elsewhere in *Competent to Counsel, Lectures, The Manual,* etc.

seling. These studies must not only hammer out the truths of biblical teaching about human life, but also the full implications of each for counseling.

In considering the human personality, the plight into which it has been plunged by sin and what God has done about it in Christ, it is truly remarkable that *any* Christian thinker or writer can begin at any other point—or turn to any other primary source—than the biblical data that reveal acres of facts about anthropology. The problem is the very bulk. Yet it is not only common, but has been the rule (with few notable exceptions) to find lengthy theoretical discussions of human nature, personality, behavior, etc., by writers who are Christians that rely upon almost any other source than the Scriptures, and use the Bible (if at all) only in a token, superficial or illustrative manner. The Scriptures, when used, rarely provide the true base for the theories that are propounded; rather, they are used (or, I should say, *mis*used) to support humanistic views that not only totally disregard these very same Scriptures, but are hostile to them.

In such writers (whose personal faith cannot be faulted, since it occasionally surfaces in their books) gross inconsistencies abound. By these inconsistencies they do us all—pagan and Christian alike—a disservice by misrepresenting scriptural teaching through attempted integration[3] of materials that (in fact) are altogether incompatible with one another. In the process, the Bible is bent to fit the error.[4] Since I have spoken elsewhere in this book about the ill effects of selling the competitor's wares on God's shelves, falsely labelled as biblical, I shall not elaborate here. However, if the problem exists at all, you can be sure that it is in discussions of the human being that its expression is paramount.

Such distortions of the Bible's view of man constitute an enormous problem, but it is (sadly) compounded by another: the differences and numerous erroneous understandings of scriptural teaching among those who *do* use the Bible as their prime source for understanding human beings.

I am thinking here, not only of the principal differences among evan-

---

3. The dangerous "in" word with persons of this sort.
4. For a concrete example of such accommodationism by a Christian pastoral counselor, see my book, *The Power of Error* (Phillipsburg, N. J.: Presbyterian and Reformed Publishing Co., 1978).

gelical Christians that have persisted for centuries (e.g., dichotomy vs. trichotomy), but also of new serious aberrations stemming from cults, from movements within the church that have shaky exegetical and theological underpinnings (e.g., Arthur Custances' numerous speculative suggestions and assertions) and from freelance "theologians" whose viewpoints tend to unsettle many persons (e.g., Charles Solomon's view of Christians having a *past* eternal existence so that they were actually dying on the cross with Christ[5]).

Truly, the situation is complex (I almost wrote "horrendous"). You can understand, then, why I am begging for *volumes* to be written, and why I make no claims about doing more than making a *beginning* at discussing the many matters of anthropology that confront the Christian counselor who wants to be thoroughly biblical. It is hard enough to know where to begin my sketch, let alone to attempt anything more ambitious.

When one looks at the cocksure confidence with which some Christians who counsel have made firm, but superficial, pronouncements about the nature of man in a couple of pages, seemingly unaware of the large questions that exist for theologians and for counselors alike (and virtually apart from serious exegetical and theological reflection), he sometimes wants to sit down and cry. If it were not so thoroughly frustrating, the situation would be side-bustingly laughable. The laughter wells up when one thinks, "Oh, if it only *were* so simple and clean cut!" The tears come when he considers how many unsuspecting Christians are misled by such writings.

Now, I don't want to imply by such observations that only professional theologians and exegetes are able to learn anything significant about the human personality and human life; surely that isn't true. Many Christian laymen, with a sound, systematic knowledge of the Bible's teachings, are as well off as some theologians and better than many others.[6] What we may know about humanity from the Scriptures is available and perspicuous. All may drink from this well, if they will only draw water with an empty bucket!

5. In personal discussion, 1977. Christians (Solomon said) died with Christ not merely representatively but actually. Solomon comes perilously close to saying (if he doesn't actually say it), that, on the cross, Christians died for their own sins. He would not *deny* it when pressed, but would not flatly assert it either.

6. We must never forget those wonderful words in Ps. 119:99, 100; cf. also Matt. 11:25.

It has been the non-exegetically, non-theologically oriented counselors who have specialized in the systematic study of every other point
of view, but not in the systematic understanding of God's Word, who
especially have confounded the situation. Sometimes, by their abstract
and speculative discussions of Christian doctrine, theologians and exegetes also have added to the confusion. Undoubtedly, then, something
must be done to thread our way through this congested traffic!

Where shall we begin? I propose to start with a consideration of the
origins of human life and the prefall conditions. The effects of the fall
and redemption will follow (the latter under a separate head).

I must say at the outset that I adopt as an unshakable biblical presupposition, stemming from both exegetical and theological considerations, that human life did not evolve from lower forms, but that it was
created *de novo* by God. I believe in the existence of a literal Adam,
from whom (by divine surgery performed under the anesthesia of divinely induced sleep) Eve also was formed by a direct act of God. Exegetical and theological considerations behind these assertions cannot be
detailed here (and need not be, since they have been handled adequately elsewhere; see especially the writings of E. J. Young and John
Murray). Rather than do so, I should like to focus my attention upon
the nature with which Adam was created as a perfect being.

The Nature of Adam

In considering Adam's sinless, created nature, it is also instructive
to learn from the life of Jesus Christ, the second Adam, Who likewise
possessed a fully human nature, that, in His case, remained sinless. The
similarities and the contrasts between the two yield valuable information
for biblical anthropology, and for setting norms for human life as they
illustrate the commandments of God. Christ, not sociological polls, provides the norms for human living.

We are already in trouble if I don't define some of the terms that
I have used thus far. For instance, what is a *nature?* What is *sin?*
I shall consider the first term more fully than the second here (sin will
be considered at a later point).

I used the word *nature* to refer to Christ, Adam and human beings.
The question, "What is the nature of the creature called man?" illustrates the use. By it, among other things, I am asking, "What is a human being like? What distinguishes him from God, the world, and other

creatures? And of what stuff is he composed?" By discussing his *nature,* in this sense, one answers the question, "What is man?" In Romans 1:26, 27 and in Ephesians 2:3, where the English word *nature* is the translation of the Greek *phusis,* the word is used this same way to refer to the basic deposit of "stuff" with which an individual is created or born; it has to do with his inherited and genetic side. Nature refers, then, to what a man is composed of (apart from what he does with it).

N.B., this usage has nothing at all to do with the more popular usage of the term *nature* that appears in the following statement: "He is good natured." This usage is unbiblical and refers to a concept not discussed in the Scriptures, the idea of temperament.[7]

At this point, my principal use of the term *nature* will be confined to the former sense; I am concerned to know what Adam was like, of what sort of stuff he was composed.

Now, for a consideration of the other term, *sin.* By *sin,* I accept the definition in the Westminster Confession of Faith as a quite accurate and succinct statement of the biblical teaching on the subject: "Sin is any want [lack] of conformity unto or transgression of the law of God." Put in more modern terms, that means sin is doing what God forbids, or failing to do what He requires, in the Scriptures. With those understandings of these two terms we may proceed.

Adam Before the Fall

What was Adam (and Eve) like before the fall? We can learn much about him from the early chapters of the book of Genesis. I turn immediately to a study of the biblical data because there is no other source of information available. It seems quite remarkable that no other counseling approach even concerns itself with man's *original* (pre-fall) nature; only Christians raise the question (and then, sadly, many of them inconsistently accept teachings quite at variance with the biblical data).[8]

7. It is interesting that the Bible says virtually nothing about temperament. If it were so important a matter as some make it, the Scriptures would have quite a bit to say. Usually, the various categories listed (in one way or another) go back to the old pagan Greek view of the four humors.

8. For instance, that man's violent social behavior is the result of a yet-incomplete process of evolution. Cf. specifically Skinnerian views of man's evolutionary heredity that simply cannot be squared with the biblical account of man's creation.

But, consider. Where can a system of counseling expect to end up when it shows no concern about what human life originally was like? Indeed, most systems never stop to ask whether there was an original, pre-sinful, human condition. Either the evolutionary theory is assumed, in which human life is said to have been previously sub-human (rather than a higher level, as the Bible teaches), or the theory simply (often naively and uncritically) presupposes that human nature always has been more or less the same as now. In both cases, these erroneous conceptions lead to a string of subsequent errors about man's present problems, the solutions to them and the sort of norms that ought to determine goals for counseling.

So, then, let us try to discover *some* of the biblical facts about human nature as it was originally created.

First, let us ask why it is important to try to discover Adam's nature before the fall. There are several answers to this one question. One (that I have already suggested) is this: when we know what human nature was like before sin, we shall know *something* (not all) about God's norm for human life. Man's concepts and his activities grow out of his nature; God fitted him in this world with a disposition and nature designed to think and act so as to perform certain tasks, and to maintain certain relationships. Every book on psychology or counseling that seriously struggles with the question of normality (or abnormality) ultimately concludes that it is is not really possible to set any absolute norms by which to make a judgment that any given belief or behavior is "normal" or "abnormal." Yet, the authors of these books persist on using these terms anyway, and go so far as to declare various behaviors normal or abnormal. Usually this is done on the basis of sociological theories in which norms are set according to averages obtained in various (often highly biased) ways by surveys and tests. Thus, if enough persons, at a given period, in a particular place, declare their homosexual preferences, homosexuality (presumably) must be declared normal.[9] In Sodom it is possible that the sociologists would have declared heterosexuality abnormal if they could have had a whack at it. Clearly, since a large number of persons masturbate, this is exactly what has happenel:[10] in book after book (Christian or non-

9. Indeed, a couple of years ago, under pressure, the A.P.A. removed homosexuality from the list of treatable mental illnesses.
10. For more on the biblical view of masturbation, see the *Manual*, pp. 399-402.

Christian) we are assured that it is a perfectly normal act. Anyone who speaks against it is identified with those who once taught that masturbation causes insanity. Even Christian writers, who have been caught up in the sweep of sociological pronouncements (Kinsey, not the Bible, becomes the standard), simply go along with the "experts." But if masturbation is normal, then (presumably) Adam, before the fall, and Christ, during His earthly life, masturbated. Does that statement startle you? If so, then recognize that we must not set norms by counting noses on sinful men! If nose-counting were valid, lying would be acceptable.

The consistent Christian refuses to accept sociology as a norm-setting discipline. Sociological studies (based on proper—i.e., biblical—presuppositions) may be of use in describing the mores of a given people at some point in time,[11] but they have no further value. The fact that all are sinners (Rom. 3:23) does not make sin normal. The norm is righteousness—the sort of life that Christ lived. That all people err does not mean that error is normal (Rom. 1 indicates that error is the result of the fall); it means only that error is universal. So then, what is universal is not necessarily what is normal, contrary to sociological dicta. The Scriptures teach that "true righteousness and holiness" is the norm for human living. God sets norms in the Bible; men (not even sociologists) have no such right. Alongside true righteousness and holiness God sets "knowledge" (of the truth; most present-day sociologists and others deny the possibility of absolute truth. They think of truth as relative: true in some respect, for some purpose, etc.) as the last of three qualities that are normal for man, and declares that though they were lost in the fall, He is restoring them to the redeemed (Eph. 4:24; Col. 3:10).

The Christian accepts Adam, as created (prior to the fall), as an example of normal human life. His nature, with its focuses and capabilities, was truly human. But it was not normal for him to sin; that was abnormal behavior for a human being (and so it is today). And, N.B., Adam was not as *fully* normal as he might have been had he eaten of the tree of life and entered into a state in which he could never have sinned again (the eternal state of redeemed sinners[12]). The Ten

---

11. Perhaps for use in sermon analysis or analysis of missionary fields, etc.
12. Cf. Rev. 2:7.

Commandments set the norm for life, and in Christ's own life we see them worked out in detail. So, in the final analysis, we must say that what is normal for a human being is what Christ said and did (we cannot study His thoughts).

If we want to know what normal love is like, then we must look and listen to Christ. The same is true for any other human behavior, attitude or use of emotion. His relationships (from His side) were normal. Everything Adam ought to have done (apart from the redemptive work of Jesus), Christ did. Sociology, by its presuppositions, objectives and methodology, can never arrive at biblical norms. It deals with sinful, abnormal men. But God does not accept sinful norms. He will settle for nothing less than perfection.

Of what importance is it to know about normal human life? A counselor must have proper goals and objectives toward which to move in counseling. Perhaps I stated this most plainly in a talk given to some 500 persons at the psychiatric lecture hall of the University of Vienna in Austria when I spoke there recently. The title of the address, from which I shall quote at length, is *Change Them?—Into What?*

> Christian counseling is entirely fresh; it is totally different from anything that has been offered in our generation in America. Asking the question *why* there has been no consensus, particularly in this field in which people are trying to change the lives of other persons, many of us came to the conclusion that it was because there has been no standard by which this was attempted. You may say that society is the standard, or you may say pragmatically that what works is the standard or that the counselee is the standard; but when you finally boil it all down and strip off the externals, what you have left is this: the individual psychotherapist determines the standard. The problem of subjectivity is enormous. Something from outside of the counselor and counselee is needed; something far more solidly grounded than any limited and biased individual is required. . . .
>
> Why do we need a standard, a yardstick, a rule? Because we are dealing with the problem of changing human lives. What man has the right or the ability to say to another, "I know how you shall live"? What man will take it upon himself to say, "This is wrong in your life, this is right in your life, and this is how I want to change you"? Some think they can divorce themselves from the ethical issues. They think that value can be cast aside. But you can't; you continually get involved in the realm of values when you deal with people and their lives. When you endeavor to change another human being—i.e., to change his values, his beliefs, his behavior, his

attitudes, his relationships—are you willing to say, "What I think his values, his relations, his attitudes and his behavior should be like is best"—are you willing to say that? Unless you are ignorant or arrogant, you must hesitate.

And yet from the very outset that has been the problem, hasn't it? There's been no standard, no one standard, by which to bring about consensus. . . .

There is no common standard for what a human being ought to look like. We sometimes read in popular writings, of course, that "psychologists say . . ." or "psychiatrists say . . ." (but anyone who knows the confusion behind those statements can only take them humorously rather than seriously). The fact of the matter is that there is no agreement on the most basic issue of all—what sort of man is normal? And we won't get that norm by sociological studies either, because they will only tell us what the average attitudes and behaviors that we, in a given period or place, have. And I'm not sure that you or I want to produce more of the kinds of persons that you and I now are: the kind that have brought about the number of wars that our world history records, the kinds of people that do the things we read about on the front pages of our newspapers all the time, etc. Now my point is simply this: there has to be a standard and a model that conforms to it, so that we can both know and see what a human being should be like. There has to be a set of criteria. We have to have a picture of what a human should look like if we're going to try to change people. Where are we going to get such a picture? This is the question that Christian pastors in America have been dealing with for the past fourteen years, and they say that they have an answer.

They say that human beings should look like Jesus Christ! They say that the Bible not only gives a description of what a person should be like in abstract terms, but that in Jesus Christ is a model of such a person in terms of action and speech. Indeed, in contrast to the psychotherapeutic confusion, it has been most powerfully demonstrated in America that a true consensus can be developed, when there is such a standard.

You need to know something about American churches. We have no national churches (*landeskirke*). We have only free churches, and we have many different churches in America. They are in agreement, most of them, on the major issues, but they differ on many minor questions. Now, it is interesting that over many different kinds of denominations this movement in the last fourteen years has swept with a force and power that has led to a movement involving literally thousands of pastors and laypeople (*mitarbeiters*) who are now doing counseling according to this new Bible-based approach. The interesting thing also is that not only have pastors become involved in this work, but many thousands of laypeople also have been successfully counseling all sorts of people along with them. They have been drawn together in a counseling consensus by the Bible.

Now this movement has had quite an impact in American churches and also on the American scene. And it has not kept itself within the boundaries of our country, but has spilled over onto a number of continents—which in my own case (as a representative of this viewpoint) has led to visits just this year in Ireland, Brazil, New Zealand, Australia, Mexico, Guatemala, Germany and Switzerland. . . .

This new view is also concerned with change at a level of depth. It is not concerned about changing people on the surface alone; there is a belief that man and his actions and his attitudes must be changed at the inner core of his being so that his very set of values and the springs of his motivation are affected. The Bible calls this inner power man's heart. It is from the heart that people's problems stem. So a new power from the outside is necessary for him to begin to realize the goal of Christian counseling—to become more like Jesus Christ. In other words, Christian conversion is an essential element in this kind of counseling. If he is not a Christian, the counselee's relationship to God must be changed. He must come to the place where he recognizes that the Christian message about the cross is real and must be taken seriously. This old message from the Bible is that Christ died on the cross in the place of guilty sinners in order to transform their lives, beginning at the very heart of their being and then leading to outward transformations that are needed. Christian counseling has depth, because it goes to the heart of human difficulty.

This old message has been found to be a very new and vital force in the lives of many people. It is altogether possible that you've even heard in the newspapers here, as others have around the world, words like "born again" that have become popular in America these days. That's precisely what we're talking about; in this counseling system God, Himself is asked to give the counselee a new life with new purposes, new goals and new power. This counseling draws upon the wisdom of God in the Scriptures and the power of God in the Holy Spirit. You see, two things happen: the counselee's eyes are opened to God's standard for human living, and, on top of that, God enables him to begin to measure up to that standard for the first time. This is the basic Christian approach. . . .

When you deal with that question of the standard, you're dealing with *the fundamental issue in counseling,* problems that have to do with people ultimately can be resolved only by their Creator and Savior.

If you think seriously at all, after you've talked about everything else you will come back again and again to the issue of the standard. I ask you not to close the door on this matter too quickly. Until it is resolved, you can do nothing. You are planning to help people; fine. But that means changing them. The question is not only how, but (most basically)—into *what?* The Christian replies, "Into the likeness of Jesus Christ." Is there *any other* answer?[13]

That is why the discussion of the norm or standard for counseling is so vital. All counselors believe in change, but can they, indeed *dare* they begin to counsel until they have settled the question of the norm? Biblical anthropology alone can supply this answer. And it does—in detail!

So, let us ask again, "What was Adam like before the fall?" Counselors need to know this because sinful counselees, though converted, will fail to realize their full potential in Christ, often will not know the goals and norms themselves, and frequently will opt to settle for less than the biblical standards. The Christian counselor's task is to help them become aware of and committed to biblical norms, and to instruct them about how to attain such goals, while encouraging them to pursue these. We may say, therefore, that counseling helps Christians to become more normal.[14]

Adam at Creation

1. *Adam Was Created a Material Being.*

When the Bible teaches that Adam was made "out of the dust of the ground" (Gen. 2:7), it is firmly attesting man's material nature. From the beginning, there was an identification, harmony and continuity with this world. Man is earthy, from the earth. The very name, "Adam," means "red (clay)," emphasizing this fact.[15] All Gnostic notions of material creation as sinful, *per se,* therefore, must be rejected; God not only declared the material creation "very good," but made man from it

---

13. Jay Adams, *Change Them?—Into What?* (Laverock, Pa.: Christian Counseling and Educational Foundation, 1978), pp. 10-18.

14. Cf. comments in *Competent,* pp. 73-77, on counseling as sanctification. Sanctification is the process by which the image of God is being restored; i.e., the person is becoming more normal.

15. The name "Adam" early became the generic word in Hebrew for "man," showing how essential an element earthiness is in human existence.

(as the boy said, "God don't make no junk"). Much of the New Testament argues against Gnostic heresies, in which the material universe is said to be sinful. In Colossians and I John, the fact that the sinless Christ came, was baptized, and died *in a body* is affirmed as the ultimate refutation of this heresy (cf. Col. 1:19; 2:9; I John 1:1; 4:2; 5:6-8). That is why, when thinking about death, Paul can speak of his very proper human longing for another body (he wanted to be clothed, not unclothed, with a new body), and of his sense of uncomfortable nakedness without it (cf. II Cor. 5). Death is an *unnatural* state for man; his body is so much a part of him that to be without it (even temporarily), rightly leads to such reactions of discomfort. It is of great significance to us that the state of the risen Christ is a bodily one, and that the eternal state of believers following the resurrection of the body also will be a bodily existence similar to His. That there are new heavens and a new earth, freshly made, in which righteousness will be at home (II Pet. 3:13) indicates that—at least in part—man's eternal redeemed existence will be in that new earth ("righteousness" at home there seems to indicate the presence of righteous beings on the earth).

Now, as counslors, what are we to make of this fact? Man's essential earthiness must be kept in mind at all times when counseling. All attacks upon the material creation (as such), all excuses by counselees resting upon the ground of the materiality of their human nature, must be put to rest. Man does *not* function better apart from the body, as some claim in order to relieve themselves of their present God-given responsibilities; he functions best in it because he was designed to function as a material being.[16]

It is true that the material creation was cursed following man's sin, and that both the natural world and sinfully habituated human flesh now cause problems for the counselee, but that is not because of the materiality of the earth or of the body (doubtless, the sinful, immaterial angels, *without material bodies,* have problems of a similar sort, but it is clear that materiality is not the reason). Remember, too, that the spiritual (non-material) side of human nature (to be discussed *infra*) is equally subject to the blight of sin, and must not be considered more righteous (or any less sinful) because it is non-material. Human materiality is never to be considered (as some, unfortunately, call it) the

16. Of course, not *only* as such; but we shall treat this *infra*.

COUNSELING AND HUMAN LIFE

"lower" aspect of man's nature, and the spiritual (non-material) aspect the "higher," if by that language the intention is to give the former a lesser status than the latter. Both the material and the spiritual creations were equally good and equally as important because both were from God and for God (on the body, at this point, cf. I Cor. 6:14). Both, likewise, have been corrupted by Adam's sin.

Frequently, in sinfully distorted human thought, the spiritual is identified with God and the material with the devil. This too is wrong, for reasons already given. It might be of help to remember (in this regard) that Satan himself is a spiritual (not a material) being, and that his proper realm is not in the material, but in the spiritual creation (cf. Jude 6). Human materiality, then, is no more to be identified with Satan than human spirituality.

Acts of asceticism, in which the body (because it is material) is "punished" or subjected to humiliating and/or injurious practices, cannot be sanctioned biblically and may not be condoned by counselors. Respect for the believer's body, as the temple of the Holy Spirit, and as the form of nature in which Jesus became one of us and died for us, precludes any such denigration of the material body. *Sin* has led to asceticism (Col. 2:23). Therefore, counselors must be alert to ascetic practices that have added complicating difficulties to original problems.[17] In Philippians 2:6-11, where Paul describes the humiliation of Christ in the most carefully worded theological language possible, he makes no point of the fact that Jesus took on a body. Passages that do emphasize the body of Christ are quite positive about it (cf. John 1, etc.). The humiliation, Paul makes clear, consisted of His becoming a lowly human being who suffered an ignominious death (but that includes both the bodily and the non-bodily aspects of human nature).

When, therefore, a counselee complains that "if only" he were not "burdened down with this body" (unless he is referring to the effects of sin in the body), he could do so much for the Lord, etc., the counselor must protest against this outlook. If he identifies sin with the body alone, the counselor must inform him that sin is also in his soul (indeed, *begins* there—cf. Matt. 15:19). If he uses the presence of sin in his body as an excuse, the counselor may point out that sin, itself, is no more in the material aspect of his nature than it is in the spiritual as-

---

17. Cf. long night vigils in prayer that lead to the baneful effects of sleep loss (see the *Manual*, pp. 386, 387, for more on this point).

pect. In fact, it is the sinful inclination of the heart (the inner, unseen life) that causes the aggravating habituation of the material body (Rom. 6) that he struggles with. And, he must be shown that this bodily habituation can be overcome by proper spiritual orientation, and he is responsible for both to God.[18] If he argues that the effects of sin, impairing both body and spirit, limit him, this fact may be conceded. However, they do not limit the Holy Spirit, Who renews and empowers the mind (Eph. 4:23[19]). The point must be made that where sin abounds, grace abounds *far more*. These impairments never directly *cause* sinful behavior in a believer or inhibit a Christian from serving Christ as he should. God's grace causes believers to rise above pain, deformity, etc., turning liabilities into assets for Christ's sake. That, in part, is what the title of this book is all about, as we shall see later on. Where opportunity for change exists, so does responsibility and hope.[20]

So, you can see how utterly vital it is for counselors to have a proper theology of the body and the material creation. But, as I have indicated throughout this discussion, that is but half of the picture; it is also true that—

2. *Adam Was Created a Spiritual Being.*

I could not avoid alluding to this fact in the foregoing discussion; the two are two sides of the same coin. Both elements appear in the creative narrative: Adam was formed out of the dust of the ground, but it was only when the breath (or spirit) of life was breathed into him[21] that he became a living soul (or animate being[22]). That Adam was a "living soul" was not unique. In Genesis 1:21, 24, 30, the same thing is said about other, non-human living creatures. The unique point to

---

18. Cf. *Lectures*, pp. 231ff.

19. "Spirit of your mind" probably refers to the Holy Spirit, Who *renews* the mind. Translate: "being renewed by the Spirit Who influences your mind."

20. Cf. my pamphlet, *Christ and Your Problems*, for more on the interrelatedness of hope and responsibility.

21. I.e., the breath (or spirit) that causes life. The word for breath (or spirit) here, *neshamah*, is used synonymously with the other, more frequent term, *ruach* (cf. Job 27:2; 32:8; Prov. 20:27; Deut. 20:16). The LXX uses *pneuma* for both. Cf. also Kittel, *Theological Dictionary of the N.T.*, vol. VI, p. 377, where the Hebrew word *neshamah* is shown to be "the usual term for the soul as coming from heaven" in Palestinian Judaistic usage.

22. John Murray, *Collected writings*, vol. II (Carlisle, Pa.: Banner of Truth, 1978), p. 8.

note about man's creation is the *manner* in which God brought about this result: He *breathed* into Adam the breath (or spirit) of life. This personal, direct, unique in-breathing constituted a separate act on God's part that distinguished human creation (and human life) from other animate life. There is an earthy side to man,[23] but there is a heavenly or spiritual side as well. Man belongs to both worlds.

The in-breathing demonstrates the fact that man's body is not all; he is *more* than body. God Himself gave life to man's body by breathing breath (or spirit) into him. This special act points up a special case, and a special result. This in-breathing of the spirit is the *source* of human animation (or life), and without it man may properly be said to be dead (James 2:26, ". . . the body is dead without the spirit . . ."). There is an obvious reference to Genesis 2:7 in Ecclesiastes 12:7, where we read, "and the dust returns to the ground it came from, and the spirit returns to the God Who gave it."[24] Clearly, the use made of the Genesis passage by the writer of Ecclesiastes shows that he understood Moses to refer to a duplexity in human nature. Unlike the animals, Adam was formed with an element taken from the earth (*dust,* as he calls it here) and an element that came directly from God which He "gave." At death, these two elements once again become distinct entities and return to their distinct sources. That the writer of Ecclesiastes also understood that human life differed from animal life in its source and composition seems to be borne out by his words in Ecclesiastes 3:21: ". . . the spirit of man rises upward and the spirit of the animal goes down into the ground."[25] Here, where the life-giving or animating force (power, principle) is mentioned, though the word *spirit* is used for both man and beast, a clear distinction between the two is indicated: man's spirit rises upward (to God Who gave it—cf. 12:7b), while the animal's spirit descends down into the ground (from which it came[26]—cf. 12:7b). The human spirit, then, is separable from the human body at death because of the unique features it received at creation (it came directly from God, from above), while the animating

---

23. On the earthy side, human beings share some characteristics with some animals (e.g., they eat food, breathe air, walk on the earth's crust, excrete wastes, etc.). The spiritual side distinguishes man from them.

24. The word here is *ruach,* confirming again its synonymous use with *neshamah.*

25. *Ruach* is used in both instances in this verse.

26. Notice the distinction in sources of the spirit; it is this that leads to distinct ultimate destinations.

force of animals is so bound to their bodies that both are buried (destroyed) at death.

The implications for counseling that grow out of the fact of human nature's duplex form are too vast even to list. Here is one of those places where an entire book (or series of books) is needed to explore these fully. But, before entering into that question in any detail (and, of necessity, that will be scanty), it would be wise to enlarge upon my understanding of this duplex form of human nature. That leads us into a discussion of what (unfortunately) has been called the dichotomy/trichotomy issue.[27]

The question of the number of distinguishable entities of which a human being is composed is important, but the focus has been upon separating these, as the terms *dichotomy* and *trichotomy* plainly indicate (the words mean, respectively, "twice-cuttable" and "thrice-cuttable"). The *emphasis* in the Scriptures, however, is upon the *unity* of these entities. That is why I prefer the term *duplex* (meaning "twofold"). This word stresses the unity of the elements (they are "folded" together), rather than their separability (which, as we saw, is unnatural for man).

The debate about how many elements unite to form a complete human being, however, is important to counselors; to them it is not a hair-splitting issue. Many practical differences result from the two distinct views that are held. The entire stance of Clyde Narramore, for instance, is built upon trichotomy, when he says that the body is to be treated by the physician, the spirit by the pastor, and the soul by the psychologist. That a human being can be so readily segmented and parcelled out is debatable[28] (even were the triplex view correct). But there is no such emphasis in the Scriptures.[29]

---

27. See standard theological textbooks (Charles Hodge, A. A. Hodge, L. Berkhof, John Murray, etc.) for information on this. Cf. also the *Manual*, p. 437, for more on this.

28. See *Manual*, p. 437.

29. There is another dangerous concept abroad that grows out of the triplex view—that the human spirit can gain "spiritual" knowledge and information directly from the Holy Spirit. This is said to be done apart from the mind (or understanding). It leads to an anti-intellectualism, and ultimately results in the teaching that man has special, direct revelation (of a non-propositional sort) from God that acts as a "check" or "prompting." In I Cor. 2 spirit is identified with (not distinguished from) the mind (cf. also Rom. 6–8). I Cor. 14 warns against attempting to enter into non-intellectual relationships with the Spirit (cf. vss. 13-19). The Spirit renews the minds (Rom. 12:2), not merely the spirit of man; Rom. 8:6

The Scriptures do not allow for the triplex (or trifold) view; indeed, the entire emphasis—from Genesis 2:7 on—whenever the Scriptures (reluctantly) speak of separation (remember, the stress is on unity), is that there are two elements that came together, and two (and only two that at death) part company temporarily. In addition to those already cited (and note, Gen. 2:7 allows only for two elements) consider the following:

> Don't be afraid of those who kill the body but can't kill the soul; rather be afraid of the One Who can destroy both soul and body in Gehenna.[30]

In this verse the thought is that the *whole* man suffers in Gehenna; the very emphasis is upon the *entirety* of eternal man suffering over against partial (bodily) suffering now. The statement, "both soul and body" is duplex, not triplex. If triplexity were true, the spirit also should have been mentioned.

Here is another: ". . . that she may be holy both in body and in spirit."[31] It is clear, once again, that *entirety* is in view. It must not be supposed that the father in view desires only two of the three elements to be sanctified (or that only two, not three, needed sanctifying). The same may be said of II Corinthians 7:1: ". . . we must cleanse ourselves from every pollution of flesh and spirit,[32] completing our holiness out of fear for God." The words *"every* pollution" make it clear that the pollution of the whole person is in view (soul pollution surely isn't omitted!).

Such passages are the standard; they weigh heavily against the triplex view. I shall not cite others. "But what of Hebrews 4:12 and I Thessalonians 5:23?" you ask. "Don't they speak of a separation between soul and spirit that indicates a triplex view of man?" The answer is emphatically, "No!"

---

speaks of a spiritual mind. Paul says in Rom. 12:2 that a renewed mind leads to knowing God's will (not merely a renewed spirit). How can one detect non-intellectual (non-propositional) promptings or checks in the spirit when they are supposed to be non-emotional? Spirit is intangible; it cannot be felt, seen or sensed in any other way. One fears that emotional experiences are what really motivate in such circumstances. There is always danger when departing from the Bible as the source of God's revelation. Note that this source requires the intellect for understanding.

30. Matt. 10:28.
31. I Cor. 7:34b.
32. Here it is clear that spirits may be polluted.

Let us first consider Hebrews 4:12. There, we are told, "God's Word, the Bible, is likened to a sharp, flashing two-edged sword that is able to penetrate deeply enough to divide between soul and spirit, just as it can divide between joints and marrow." "See," say those who advoctate triplexity, "if the Scriptures affirm the possibility of dividing soul from spirit, so should we." But the fact is that the Greek doesn't do any such thing. The KJV (and some subsequent translations) mislead the English reader. The point is not that the soul is *divided from* spirit, or joint *from* marrow. Rather, what is said is that God's Word splits the spirit and also the soul, the joints and also the marrow. Many who misunderstand have always wondered why the joints are to be divided from the marrow when they are not in close contiguity. The word *between* has been imported into our thinking about the passage (that is the way that "asunder" is often wrongly understood).

The true idea is that God's Word penetrates deeply enough into man's innermost being to cut open and lay bare his desires and thoughts (vss. 12c, 13).[33] The picture is of cutting open of joints, of marrow, of soul, of spirit. Note: there are two basic categories here—material (joints/marrow) and immaterial (spirit/soul), not three. Just as "thoughts and intents" are not to be separated,[34] but are lumped together comprehensively in order to express the *entire* intellectual side, so spirit and soul are both mentioned *to show that no aspect of the inner man is beyond the penetrating power of God's Word.*[35]

The passage, when not distorted by the insertion of the idea of dividing *between* soul and spirit, becomes a powerful counseling weapon in the hands of pastoral counselors (and preachers). He understands that verse 13 is the application of what verse 12 says. The writer maintains that since the Bible describes and discloses the inner side (heart) of a human being with such penetrating power of judgment,

> before Him no creature can hide [Adam tried it; counselees ever since have done so too], but all are open and naked [two features again stressing totality; not to be distinguished, but lumped] and

---

33. These terms, like the other pair of pairs (joints/marrow; soul/spirit) are not to be set over against one another. Rather, they are cumulative in effect, stressing the whole of the inner life. See following note (34).

34. They are both judged, not judged *between*.

35. Spirit and soul are distinguishable aspects of man's inner nature (as we shall see *infra*), but not distinct entities.

vulnerable to the eyes of Him to Whom we must give an account (vs. 13).

Counselors must not only discover what this verse means, but the power of using it in counseling sessions.

As for I Thessalonians 5:23, again the emphasis in the passage is not upon how many elements man is composed of, nor how we may divide these. Rather, it is upon the *entirety* of man:

May the God of peace sanctify you *completely;* may our *entire* being —spirit and soul and body—be kept blameless.

Paul is not dividing; he is adding. "But doesn't he add two plus one, and doesn't that equal three?" you ask. No, no more than when Jesus adds up heart, soul, mind, strength (and, incidentally, omits body and spirit) should we total these four. Are we now to add strength, mind and heart[36] to the list in I Thessalonians 5:23 and say that man may be divided not two or three but six ways?[37] Of course not!

The Scriptures often pile up terms (sometimes two, sometimes three, sometimes four; sometimes one combination, sometimes a different one) to express entirety, just as we do. In no case is there the slightest notion of dividing man into his essential elemnts. Rhetorical passages, like these, must not be pressed into service for purposes that they were never intended to serve. To do so is to do violence to them, to prove too much[38] and to lead one's self astray by such questionable hermeneutical methods.

To show how superficially those who hold to the triplex view really consider the biblical data, let me ask them, "How do you handle the very frequent scriptural references to the heart?" Why is this extremely important concept ignored? It too represents the non-material side of human nature. Is it separate from soul and spirit, coincidental with both (or perhaps with only one of them)? Tell me, please.

The fact of the matter is that discussion of the scriptural notion of the heart is quite illuminating (and important to counselors), and until it is fully grasped, there can be no real understanding of human nature (and especially the spiritual aspect of it). Therefore, I shall take time to discuss this vital (but neglected) subject.

---

36. Matt. 22:37; Mark 12:30; Luke 10:27.
37. I have actually heard a preacher do exactly that!
38. Six entities, not two or three!

To begin with, it is important to affirm, categorically, that the Western view (modern American, European, etc.) is not biblical. This Western view derives from Roman culture, with its Valentine's Day mentality. In modern thought, the Western view equates heart with feelings or emotion. The word *heart* conjures up visions of cherry-cheeked cherubs, lace doilies and pink paper hearts. Consequently, this concept has carried over into preaching and writing, where, e.g., "head knowledge" is set over against "heart knowledge." The former is said to be merely intellectual understanding and assent, whereas the latter denotes a commitment with feeling. But the distinction is unbiblical.[39] Nowhere in the Bible is the *head* set over against the *heart*. Emotion, in the Bible, is not related to the heart but to the viscera (where, incidentally, many of the strongest, discernible emotional reactions occur).[40]

The reason why head and heart are not set over against one another in the Scriptures is that the term *heart includes the intellectual side* (cf. Job 12:24; 36:13; Jer. 17:9, 10; 23:20; Ezek. 11:5; Hos. 7:11; Matt. 13:15; Mark 7:19-23; 11:23; Luke 5:22; Acts 5:4; II Cor. 9:7; Heb. 4:12; James 1:26; these meager samples show the widespread [universal] consent of a variety of writers, over a wide spread in time, about this fact). In the Bible, human beings are said to talk, reason, plan, understand, think, doubt, perceive, make mistakes, purpose, intend, etc., *in their hearts*. It is clear, then, why the head (which we think of as representing the intellectual side of man) can never be set over against the heart.

In order to help us better understand the biblical meaning of heart, let us ask, "What, then, is set over against heart, if anything?" The answer is *always,* without exception, *the visible, outer man.* Worship that one gives with his *lips* (outer, visible, audible worship) when his *heart* (inner, invisible, inaudible) is far from God is a good example of this contrast (Matt. 15:8).[41] We are instructed that man looks on the

---

39. We should stop using this understanding of heart since it only confuses others, who then read it back into the Bible (and thereby misinterpret the Scriptures). Of course, many preachers who have used this antithesis of *head* and *heart* themselves have not yet understood the biblical usage.

40. The greek term is *splagchnon* (cf. usage in Luke 1:78; II Cor. 6:12; 7:15; Phil. 1:8; Col. 3:12; Philem. 7, 12, 20; I John 3:17).

41. On the other hand, to do something with the heart (or from the heart) is not to do it *emotionally,* but genuinely, sincerely (cf. Acts 2:37; 7:54). To be "pricked in the heart" is to be *genuinely* repentant.

"outward appearance," but (in contrast) "God looks on the *heart"* (I Sam. 16:7). Without multiplying references, it is safe to say that everywhere the Bible uses the word *heart* to speak of the inner man (or, as Peter puts it in a thoroughly definitive way, "the hidden person of the heart"[42]). Plainly, then, heart in the Bible is the inner life that one lives before God and himself, a life that is unknown by others because it is hidden from them.[43]

It is natural, therefore, to identify the heart with the conscience, as some writers sometimes do (cf. Heb. 10:22; I John 3:19-21). And it is in the heart that the fool (Ps. 14:1) or evil slave (Luke 12:45) speaks to himself. From the heart (which is the source or treasure-house from which the outer words and actions spring) come sins (Matt. 15:18ff.; Mark 7:19-23; Luke 6:45). One may sin *in his heart* even though he has not sinned outwardly (Matt. 5:28). Therefore, a person must be *cleansed* in his heart (Heb. 10:22); it is the *pure in heart* who are blessed (Matt. 5:8). To believe *with the heart* and to confess *with the mouth* (Rom. 10:8-10) leads to salvation because both *inner* and *outer* man conform—there is a genuine (not hypocritical or only outward) faith.[44]

Much, much more could be said of the heart, but perhaps this much is enough to indicate the major biblical thrust of the word. It includes the entire inner life. It is the most fully developed, most far-reaching and most dynamic concept of the non-material (or spiritual side of) man in the Bible.

For those who have not yet abandoned the triplex view of human nature, it is important to note that all that is said of the soul *and* the spirit is said of the heart.[45]

It is true also that what is said of the spirit is said of the soul.[46] Both

---

42. I Pet. 3:4; cf. also II Cor. 4:16.
43. Inner life, or place where the inner life is lived; the one is used interchangeably with the other.
44. Jesus is the only truly whole man, since He is the One Whose heart and lips were *always* in harmony. If Freud wanted to discover where conflict lies in man, he might have discovered it here.
45. Cf. Deut. 11:13; Matt. 22:37; Judges 10:16; I Kings 8:48; I Chron. 22:19; Prov. 19:2; Acts 4:32; III John 2; Job 15:13; Ps. 32:2; 106:33; Eccles. 3:21; Mark 14:38; 8:12; I Cor. 2:20; Eph. 4:23; Heb. 4:12, 13; I Pet. 3:4; Ps. 64:6; 13:2; Job 38:36.
46. See parallels cited by Wm. Hendriksen, N.T. Commentary, I Thess., p. 149; John Murray, *Collected Writings,* vol. II, pp. 23ff.

are places of rejoicing, trouble, grief, etc.

What, then, is the distinction between soul and spirit? Why are two words used to describe one entity; and how do they relate to the heart? As we have seen, the heart is the non-material, non-observable inner life of the human being when alive bodily. It corresponds closely to *soul* in this respect. But almost always (if not always), when the word *heart* is used, it has this contrast with the outer and visible in view in some way or other, if only faintly. The word *soul,* however, pictures the whole man in his integrity (rarely is it set over against the body—but see III John 2). Rather, *soul* speaks of man in unity of material and immaterial elements as a living being. So much is this so that *soul* may be used for *human being* (I Pet. 3:20; Gen. 46:22) and one's own self (as it so often means in the Psalms: e.g., 3:2; 6:3, etc., etc.). In interpreting such passages, words like "me" and "I" readily can be substituted for "soul," which seems to be a poetic form for the self). On the other hand, *spirit* always pictures the non-material aspect of human nature *out of relationship* to the body. It speaks of the disembodied state. God, for instance, is never called a Soul, but He is always called a Spirit. The third Person of the Trinity is the Holy Spirit, not the Holy Soul. When Jesus said God is a Spirit (John 4:24), He emphasized the fact that this required more than physical (outward) worship: He must be worshiped in spirit and in truth. When Christ discussed and defined a spirit, He said, "A spirit doesn't have flesh and bones" (Luke 24:39). A spirit is a person without a body. So, as the word *soul* (in one way or another) always depicts the non-material aspect of human nature *in relationship to* (or in unity with) *the material,* so the word *spirit* always refers to the same non-material aspect *out of relationship to* (or disunited from) *the material.*[47] Heart, on the other hand, refers to the non-material side of man *in contrast to* his material side (usually with an emphasis upon the visibility of the latter and the invisibility of the former). That, then, is how the three words differ and may be distinguished. That is why there are three (not one or even two). Yet, all three refer to the same entity: the immaterial person.

Finally, there is the word (or perhaps it would be better to say there are the words) for *mind.* Basically, there are two used in the N.T.:

(1) The *phrēn* group (i.e., words compounding this Greek root with

---

47. The distinction is real, but not substantial. There is one entity described in two ways according to two distinct relationships that it bears to the body.

other Greek words). This *phrēn* word group focuses upon the intellectual side of the inner man—the understanding, thought, reasoning processes, wisdom, etc. *Aphroneo* containing the alpha privative, which negates and reverses a word just as our prefixes *un-* or *ir-* do) means "irrational." *Phroneo* means "to think, to have in mind." *Phronimos* is the "understanding" that leads to prudence, *phronema* is "thought or disposition," and *phrenes* is one's "inner attitude." *Phren* itself appears (in the plural) only in I Corinthians 14:20, and means "mind, thought, inner ways."

(2) The *nous* group (i.e., *nous* itself and those words compounded with it. This word, similarly, focuses on the intellectual side of human nature (sometimes more exclusively than at other times), but is broader, comprising the notions of attitude, perception, understanding, feeling, judging and determining. *Nous* itself is the general term that takes in all these meanings. *Dianoia,* the other principal term in the group, means "thinking through." It involves reflective thought, meditation and reasoning. It also can mean "imagination." *Ennoia,* used in I Peter 4:1, means "thought as intent."

The concept of *mind* also is coupled with the words heart, soul and spirit in the Scriptures. Sometimes, like heart, mind is contrasted with the outer man (see Rom. 6–8). Mind is probably not to be thought of as an entity in itself (like brain[48]), but as the thought life of the non-material side (or inner life) of man. It is a term used to refer to the subjective experiences of thinking, knowing, feeling, willing, etc.

From this all-too-brief survey of the biblical data concerning the non-material aspect of the human being, it is apparent that such notions of man as those presented, for instance, in chapter 5 of Larry Crabb's *Effective Biblical Counseling* are misinformative. The fact is that in that chapter Crabb depends more upon Ellis (p. 89), Adler (pp. 92, 95) and Rogers (p. 96) than upon the Bible for his understanding of human nature. He has spent more time (it seems) devoting himself to the study of these men than in doing the hard scriptural study necessary to develop a truly Christian view of man. The structure of human person-

---

48. The word *brain* does not appear in either the O.T. or the N.T. The brain must be understood as the part of the body that stores and sorts information for later retrieval, and that regulates bodily functions. Like the word *heart* (when not used of the physical organ), the word *mind* describes a functional aspect of man, not a physical entity. Indeed, mind = heart (or some aspect of it) in many passages.

ality described there bears few traces of those things we have been looking at. Consequently, the notions set forth so confidently as "biblical"
by Crabb hardly begin to correspond to the scriptural picture. I would
encourage anyone wishing to understand human nature as the Bible
describes it to avoid such treatments of the subject. Instead, he must
do the sort of tedious work that is necessary to find out for himself
what the Bible says about human personality. My treatment is but suggestive, of course; much more work is needed to supplement and
sharpen it.

3. *Adam Was Created a Moral Being.*

I have thus far avoided the subject of the image of God in man, not
because it does not pertain to what has been discussed already (it does,
vitally), but because until we reached this point, it would have been impossible to handle the question without anticipating too much.

Man was created in God's image and likeness (Gen. 1:26-28). Com-
mentators have differed widely about what this means (narrower and
broader definitions of this image have been given—to say nothing of
Barth's view and others'). All must agree, however, about two facts:
   (a) that it is his likeness to God that makes man different from the
       animals, and
   (b) that (in part at least, though some say this is the whole of it)
       man is an intelligent, morally responsible creature.
Some expositors distinguish between the words *image* and *likeness*
(A. Custance, for instance); most do not (rightly, I think; the Bible
makes nothing of any such distinction and, indeed, seems rather to use
the words interchangeably[49]).

We must discuss this point of universal agreement at some length
since it is of prime significance to the Christian counselor.

From every quarter today unbelieving counseling theory attack's man's
responsible nature. Skinnerians say he is inevitably controlled by his
impersonal environment and may be manipulated in any way that is
consistent with his physical abilities through rearrangement of environmental contingencies backed by a proper reward/aversive control (punishment) schedule. Freud's views were no better. His concept of the
irrational unconscious as the mass of the iceberg beneath the surface

---

49. The words are epexegetical; one explains the other.

by which we are controlled and motivated, and the meager remaining portion protruding above the waters as the rational side (by which we rationalize our actually irrational behavior) again leads to a sort of determinism that removes all responsible choices from us. Obviously, we only rationalize and act self-deceptively when we think otherwise.

Moreover, around us on every hand there is a spirit of irrationalism (in some quarters it may be somewhat on the wane, however). Feeling dominates all. Oriental religions, Rogerian feeling-centered counseling, situation ethics, and a hundred other such movements proclaim with the bumper sticker, "If it feels right, do it." All these forces (again) tend to ignore man's responsible position in the world as a moral creature under God's laws.

So, it is at the very point where man's uniqueness among creatures of earth comes most prominently to the fore that human society has attacked him. Skinner, Freud and Rogers have attempted to dehumanize him. But dogs and cats don't sit in the corner depressed by guilt over some wrong done five years before. Animals are not commanded to pray or love God and their fellow creatures, as man is. God has directed no moral law to the animal world.

That this dual rational-moral element is a fundamental factor in distinguishing human nature is apparent to all who take seriously Ephesians 4:24 and Colossians 3:10. In Ephesians 4:24, Paul speaks of the *renewal* of God's *likeness* (the reference clearly is to Gen. 1:26-28) by putting on true *righteousness* and *holiness*. In Colossians 3:10 (a parallel passage also reflecting Gen. 1:26-28) he adds the concept of *full knowledge* to these two items as a part of that renewal of the image (note, especially, how likeness and image are used synonymously in parallelism in these two passages).

These two verses, of course, also make it clear that God's image in man was so distorted by the fall that man (though still said to retain it in some sense—cf. James 3:9) must renew it by being "renewed in the spirit of [his] mind"[50] (Eph. 4:23). Full knowledge, true holiness and righteousness (or, perhaps, "righteousness and holiness that come from the truth") are said to reflect God's own knowledge, righteousness and

---

50. This unusual phrase, we have seen *supra*, probably refers to the Holy Spirit, Who renews the mind, thereby restoring God's image and likeness in believers (read "by the Spirit, Who influences, [changes] your mind"). Incidentally, "mind" here is *nous*.

holiness; therefore, they unmistakably constitute the image and likeness of God in man.[51] This image, it is clear, is moral and intellectual (or rational).

It is only in the Christian that the image of God once more can begin to be detected in any true sense of the word. Only the Christian can be morally acceptable to God; only the Christian can (from God's point of view) be *thought* acceptable. And these qualities he has, not by personal merit or acquisition in his own strength, but as the result of sovereignly bestowed grace.

It is only the Christian, then, who can be counseled. Anything short of effort to bring about the renewal of the divine image in man is an unacceptable goal because likeness (alone) is God's goal for man. That is why only Christian counseling, stressing salvation and sanctification, is adequate. It is possible to bring about change at a level of depth (in the mind—Eph. 4:23—as the Spirit changes the thinking and informs regenerate men through His Word) only in regenerate people. That is why it is really impossible to counsel (in the biblical sense of the word) an unbeliever.[52] An unbeliever may be helped out of a tight spot, may be helped to see his need for the gospel, etc., but may not be counseled. God's counsel consists in the renewal of the image. Anything less, any approach that doesn't involve the putting off of sin and the putting on of knowledge, righteousness and holiness that comes from God's truth, is unworthy of the label "Christian," misleads unbelievers and dishonors God. God is dishonored because He is misrepresented; He is not in the business of *reforming* lives, but in the business of *renewing* His image in them. God does not want His counselors to aid and abet non-Christians in exchanging one sinful pattern for another (that is reformation); He has called us, rather, to a ministry of reconciliation and renewal.

The image and likeness of God (among other things) is a truth that implies that God holds man responsible for his behavior,[53] as I have already pointed out. He has expressed His will for man in His Word (the good counsel rejected by Adam) and holds him accountable for any and every violation of it. Sin is the failure to do what God com-

---

51. Eph. 4:24; Col. 3:10.
52. See Appendix A for more on this.
53. And, God holds men responsible for their behavior toward one another (cf. Gen. 9:6; James 3:9).

mands or the willingness to do what He forbids. All (Christ alone excepted) have sinned. All, therefore, are held accountable for this sin (for their sin, representatively committed in Adam, and for sin in their own personal thoughts, words and actions as well). Sinners are incapable of fulfilling their moral obligations to God. They neither know nor care to know His will. But God holds them responsible nonetheless. It is, therefore, only redeemed human nature that (like Adam's nature before the fall) is capable of assuming moral obligations to God. That is why Christian counseling is for believers alone, and evangelism (precounseling, if you prefer) is for unbelievers (who come for counseling). Accompanying the ruin of the image of God was the ruin of human capacity for true knowledge, righteousness and holiness.

Regeneration (a new life given by the Spirit) brings with it a new capacity for knowing and for doing God's will. That is the renewal of which we have been speaking. Twice-born persons are morally capable persons—persons who *can* please God. Unbelievers have a sense of morality that they may exercise in their own twisted way, but unbelieving morality turns into legal*ism* and moral*ism* (man thinking he can please God by his own wisdom and efforts) and falls short of glorifying God (Rom. 3:23; 8:8).[54] Unbelieving morality and ethics are based upon the wrong motives and grow out of distortions of God's law. These facts are important to counselors, not only because they are engaged so fully in the discussion of moral issues, but because they must know the capacities of those whom they counsel. Potentially, every truly regenerate person, because he possesses a new life and is indwelt by the Holy Spirit, Who enables him to understand and to obey the Scriptures, has the capacity and resources to do all that God requires of him. Though this is true, in actuality, no one ever lives up to his full capacity in this life. Capacity (or potential) is not the same as actuality. In actuality, the renewal of God's image (with the accompanying realization of the potential of the new life) is a growing thing. Renewal comes gradually; it does not come all at once (cf. II Pet. 3:18). And—another factor—because we are still sinful, that growth takes place irregularly in spurts (and never completely) until we are ultimately freed from all sin and perfected in death or at the Lord's return.

---

54. The book of Proverbs, for instance, consists of morality for God's covenant people; it is not a book that can be followed apart from regeneration. Even believers must take care not to try to fulfill its precepts in their own strength.

Because of these facts, it is always possible for the counselor to find more and more areas in any counselee's life that might need change or improvement. How, then, does a counselor know when to conclude counseling? Theoretically, in one sense, counseling might *never* end. The answer cannot lie in the *number* of problems that he is able to help the counselee solve, because then counseling

(a) would never end in this life (as I said) since there will always be more to discover, or

(b) it would cease at some arbitrarily selected number (but who is to say with what number?).

Instead, the answer lies partially in the quality of the problems solved and partially in other factors. Those difficulties that are presently obvious (or become so during counseling) and that are debilitating him in one way or another, are high priority items for counseling. And, since everything cannot (and should not) be done in counseling, sessions might cease when these items have been handled successfully. But that alone also seems somewhat arbitrary.

Shouldn't the counselor also concern himself with potential difficulties (not perhaps so obvious, but no less real and serious) that counselees might face tomorrow? Is he not committed to preventive measures as well as remedial ones? Surely, he does not want to wait until the counselee experiences these difficulties to help him, does he? Yet, that might include enough material to keep the counselee on the string for years to come. What is the basic answer to this question?

The answer grows out of the fact that the counselor is concerned not merely to help the counselee out of immediate difficulties presented to him (and uncovered) during the course of regular counseling sessions. Beyond that, he wants to teach him how to generalize the principles of biblical problem solving, spiritual growth and Christian living, that are inherent in the solutions they *do* reach together in counseling, to any and all future problems that may arise. In addition to teaching the counselee how to avoid future failure (and what to do to get out of it if he fails to avoid it, the counselor wants to teach him biblical principles and methodology for handling yet unknown difficulties that he will encounter. This stance is basic to all good counseling.

The stance, to which I have referred, grows out of and corresponds to the way that God handles us in His Word. The Bible is not a catalog or encyclopedia of all possible problems with solutions attached to each. Rather, it is a collection of books containing principles that cover all of life, together with a great number of life situations that demonstrate how those principles apply and may be put into practice.[55] Sometimes, as a result of this fact, the very situation that one faces in counseling is dealt with in detail (cf. the discussion of the life style of the wife of an unsaved husband—II Pet. 3). At other times, one must reason from general biblical principles and biblical examples not precisely like the one that the counselee faces. He must learn to use analogy, reasoning (within this framework), etc.

Counselees must be made aware of these facts and taught something of a biblical methodology in using the Bible to meet life situations.[56] The counselor knows that it is the appropriate time to bring counseling sessions to a close when he discovers that the counselee has learned to generalize what he has learned in the solution of the specific problems dealt with in counseling to other situations *on his own.* He knows that when the counselee himself has begun to catch on to how to use the Bible to solve problems, counseling is coming to an end. The answer to the question, "When does counseling end?" is this:

(a) when prominent debilitating problems (or those that turn out to be so during counseling) have been solved biblically;

(b) when the counselee on his own has begun to use the principles learned in solving those problems to solve others;

(c) when he has learned what to do to avoid future failure and how to get out of it when he doesn't successfully avoid it, and

(d) when he has learned to use the Bible to solve problems that arise;

then—and only then— is the counseling ready to be concluded. Now, let us turn to another issue.

Earlier, under this head, I mentioned the problem of determinism in Freudian and Skinnerian thought and its vitiating effect upon human responsibility. The stance of each of these philosophies (and they *are* that) is so seriously opposed to the biblical concept of responsibility that it constitutes an utter denial of man's uniqueness; it leaves no place for the truth of the moral image of God in man. On either basis, man

---

55. Of course, the Bible is *more* than that; but it is that. Often, the principles are imbedded in the life situation discussed.

56. For help on this, see "The Use of the Scriptures in Counseling," in *Lectures,* and *Four Weeks with God and Your Neighbor.*

isn't a moral creature at all—he is no better than an animal, the pawn of circumstances, other people and an impersonal environment. He is driven to his decisions by totally irrational forces. "But," you may have been thinking, "what about the biblical determinism of God's foreordination and predestination—doesn't that leave us with the very same net result?"[57] The answer is a resounding "No!"

"No? How come?"

Fair enough; let me explain. First, predestination is the act of a sovereign, all-knowing God Who is a rational Person, not an irrational force or set of contingencies. That makes all the difference.

"How?"

In at least two particulars:

(1) God is all-wise and all-powerful as well as all-knowing. That means that He is able not only to plan the future (all of the future of all His creatures and all His creation) but that He is able to do so in a way that does not violate their personalities and freedom to make responsible choices within the limits of those personalities. That, of course, is what personal freedom is. One can never be free to be what he is not. God Himself is limited (as we are) by what He is. For instance, He cannot act out of character; He cannot do what is inconsistent with His own nature. That means that when Paul says in Titus 1 that "God . . . cannot lie," He is limited by His altogether truthful personality. But self-limitation—to be limited by what one is—of course, amounts to perfect freedom. It is the freedom to be and do what he wishes (in God's case, infinitely so). Therefore, in predestinating every man's act, God did so *in such a way* that He preserved human moral freedom. He determined to effect His decretive will not by violating, but by using, human personality to bring it to pass. He determined not only the ends, but also the means. One of the means is human choice.

A parallel, somewhat analogous to this fact, is found in the inspiration of the Scriptures. The writers who penned the words of Scripture frequently did not writes as secretaries, taking direct dictation (sometimes they did). Instead, in their own styles and vocabularies they wrote what they thought was appropriate to churches and persons in actual

---

57. Predestination, of course, is a biblical doctrine. The term, *proörizo*, is biblical, meaning to "mark out beforehand" or "set the boundaries beforehand," to "determine beforehand" (cf. Acts 4:28; 8:29, 30; Eph. 1:5, 11; I Cor. 2:7).

life situations. But the Holy Spirit so superintended the entire process (including the development of their styles, vocabularies and thoughts, together with the circumstances to which they addressed themselves) that at one and the same time what they wrote was also what He wanted them to write. He so moved in all that occurred that (a) He preserved their freedom and personalities and used these (b) to produce a perfect, inerrant Book (or set of books) that said precisely what He intended. The result was that the Gospel of John, for instance, was both John's writing and the Word of God. In a similar way, God's predestination of human choices and behavior in no way precludes human freedom of choice and responsibility for it.

(2) God is a Person, and as a Person He has created man in His image. One of the aspects of personality is morality. God is a moral being (He cannot lie; He is concerned about right and wrong, truth and error. He set the standards for these according to His own nature). Therefore, unlike views postulating impersonal, deterministic forces at the base of human motivation and choice (Freud, Skinner, *et al.*), the Scriptures speak of a personal, moral, rational God as the One Who has foreordained whatsoever comes to pass. This personal, beneficent God has determined to achieve His will not apart from, or in violation of human freedom of choice, but by it. His predestination, therefore (unlike chance, blind impersonal, ateleological forces, etc.), is precisely what upholds and preserves moral, responsible behavior in human life.

It is unthinkable (not to mention unbiblical) to suppose that God would frustrate His own plans and purposes by designing a plan for governing all His creatures, and all their actions, that would destroy their moral responsibility and accountability. He did not; rather, He made them in His own image. In ways not altogether understood by us, He both predestined their lives and holds them responsible for the lives that they live. This is the important balance to which every counselor must subscribe.

Now, if that is so, it must have something to do with counseling. It does. Indeed, it has much to do with counseling. But, preeminently, it means that the counselor can assert man's responsibility at every point where the Scripture does, with a firmness born of the conviction that God has declared man responsible to Him for his behavior, and that He has willed him so. God's predestination, then, enhances the doctrine of human responsibility, by providing the only sure foundation for it:

God's will. Neither Skinnerian evolutionary hypotheses nor Freudian socializing determinism could possibly be right, since they are contrary to what the Scriptures everywhere declare to be true—God has made, and holds, man to be responsible.

"But what of the unsaved man's inability to fulfil God's moral requirements?"

That makes no difference. That very lack of capacity, itself, is the result of a morally responsible act. Man's present ability is not the measure of his responsibility. But even the unsaved must not be thought to be bound by God's predestination in such a way that their choices, decisions and nature are violated. They too act according to their natures (sinfully, of course). But, like the rich man, those who do not repent, will not protest unfairness on God's part even though they are suffering in hell. Rather, like him, they will acknowledge their own responsibility (Luke 16). No unsaved man feels any outward compulsion to live and choose as he does. Every sin he committed, he wanted to commit; he will have to acknowledge that this is true. God's predestination *forces* no one, neither the sinner to sin nor the righteous to obey. This is so, remember, because God determined not only the ends but also the means. All that He wills comes to pass, but *through* (not apart from) responsible human agency. That, too, has been determined; therefore, it could not be otherwise.

4. *Adam Was Created a Social Being.*

Adam was not fashioned for solitary, isolated living. From the beginning his capacity for language, his walks and talks with God in the cool of the day, and God's expressed concern that he not remain alone (Gen. 2:18) are all explicit evidences of the social side of human nature. This social side could not be satisfied by fellowship either with God alone (apart from a special gift—cf. Matt. 19; I Cor. 7) or with another human alone. God determined to create a being that would enjoy fellowship on both the vertical and the horizontal planes. Man's capacity for fellowship was wide. He could communicate verbally (as well as through his other perceptual faculties), and he could give and receive love in relationship to others. He was made to love God and his fellowman. While sin has corrupted, perverted and destroyed all of these wonderful social capacities, none has been so effaced as to erase every vestige of it. In distorted form unsaved persons both long for and try to fulfil the longings for social contact. And even those who are "evil" (notice Christ's evaluation of man out of proper relationship to God) know how to "give good gifts to their children" (Luke 11:13). And yet, their best attempts fall short of what God designed when He created man not only to glorify Him, but also "to enjoy Him forever." Their closest approximations to biblical communication, fellowship and love all fail to reach the scriptural standard. But the *fact* of the social nature of human beings nonetheless is evident in these longings and strivings.

It is (again) only the Christian who, in his relationships to God and to his neighbor, in his fellowship with other members of Christ's church and in his love for his/her spouse can begin to experience what man was meant to be socially. Only in "the new heavens and the new earth freshly made, where righteousness will be at home" (II Pet. 3:13), can his relationships be fully experienced. The counselor's task is to help further the process of Christian growth now, to help him to do so as fully as possible in this life.

The social area is so large for the Christian counselor that to explore it here seems frustratingly hopeless. The mighty issues of love for God and neighbor (see relevant material in *Competent*), of church fellowship in all of its ramifications and of marriage and family relationships emerge here, as well as issues of relationship of the Christian to the unbeliever. Many other human movements and institutions could come under review as we consider their social side. But to cover all of these means to write several volumes (not merely one). Clearly, then, that is beyond our scope. One thing that can be done, however, is to point to such specialized books as *Christian Living in the Home* (in which I treat many aspects of marriage and family life) and *How to Overcome Evil* (in which I consider the relationship of the believer to unbelievers as Paul develops this in Rom. 12:14ff.). In my other books I have discussed a number of other questions too (see especially the *Manual*). So here, all I can do is to develop (almost at random) some aspects of this topic that I have not explored (or explored adequately) elsewhere.

To begin with, all asceticism that either excludes or limits fellowship with Christians or proper social relations with unbelievers must be condemned. The second great commandment, "love your neighbor as yourself," prohibits all such exclusivism.[58] In I Corinthians 5:9-11, the

---

58. For further discussion of this commandment pertaining to the matter of love of self, see the *Manual*, pp. 142ff., and *Matters of Concern*, pp. 91ff.

proper formula for sustaining relationships to others is set forth. Moreover, to be the salt of the earth (a preserving influence) and the light
of the world (a guiding influence) are two manifestations of the command
to love a neighbor that illustrate the need to be out and among others.
One's light cannot shine before the world if he is cloistered in a monk's
cell or in a Protestant Christian "ghetto," where his light is under a
bushel. Social relationships are necessary, then, for doing the work of
the kingdom and for becoming the loving person that Christ requires one
to be.

Social relationships (friendships outside the family) also are necessary for our own welfare (as well as theirs). Even Christ "greatly desired" to worship God *in fellowship* with others (cf. Luke 22:15). One
of the trials that He bore was the loneliness of not being understood by
others.

Levels of social relationships must exist (I'm not thinking only of the
distinctions in I Cor. 5:9-11, previously noted). Christ preached to the
crowds (and showed care and concern for them—healing and feeding,
as well as teaching). More narrowly, He developed a much closer relationship with the twelve disciples. These He called His "friends"
(John 15:15; note, Christ defines a friend as someone with whom you
share your concerns). But, in even more intimate relationship to Him
were Peter, James and John. It was these three that He took up the
Mount of Transfiguration with Him; only they accompanied Him to the
Garden of Gethsemane on that last night. And of these three, one—
John—was closest of all. He was known as "the disciple whom Jesus
loved."

So, for pastors (and other Christians) to develop levels of friendship
is not wrong (when handled properly). Jesus, Himself, set the example
of this in His own social relationships. Persons with no friends (or
only superficial acquaintances) need help. Counselors must look for
and detect this problem when it exists, to guide those with difficulties
in making or sustaining close social relationships.

Christ's words in John 15:15 about friendship consisting (at least in
part, but a significant part) of relationships in which one is willing and
able to share his concerns at a level of depth are of great importance to
counselors. In biblically constructed questionnaires, tests, or simply in
data gathering in counseling sessions, it is of significance to ask questions like, "Do you have two or three persons who are close enough to

you that you can level with them?" It almost can be written down as a rule that any counselee who doesn't is having trouble in this area.

Helping one person solve his social problems, however, may be somewhat different from helping another. The causes behind his problem may differ significantly from those of the last counselee; there are any number of possible difficulties (or combinations of them). One counselee, out of pride (this is the difficulty behind much so-called *shyness*, incidentally), may refuse to allow others to get close to him and share his concerns. Embarrassment at such knowledge is the key element to look for (of course, he may have a guilty secret he doesn't want found out). Another counselee may be wary of close associations and friendships because in the past he has been betrayed by a friend who spread to others (or used to his own advantage) the intimacies that he shared with him alone. He was "burned once" and doesn't "want to be burned again," he may say. A third simply may be awkward and inexperienced at making or keeping friends. He may not know (1) what friendship involves, (2) where to find friends, (3) how to go about establishing or (4) maintaining friendships, etc. So, while a common social problem exists—with its common baneful effects—there is no one cause for it. Each case must be examined separately by doing careful data gathering, closely reading the results of homework assignments, etc., to discover its own particular roots. The cause will lead to the cure.

Perhaps the greatest areas of interest in social problems today (among Christian counselors) have to do with Christian fellowship and Christian marriage. We live in an era in which the world speaks increasingly of *alienation*. Persons are said to be social beings (as, indeed, we have seen them to be) who are out of intimate relationship with one another. Many of the ills of our "society" are attributed to this alienation of person to person. Attempts of every sort (self-help groups, marriage encounter, etc.) have been made in programs designed to bridge the gaps at various levels. But Christians know that those efforts are not the answer. Christian counselors know that the answers, instead, lie in good old-fashioned Christian fellowship and in properly functioning Christian marriages. It is here that the sharing of intimacies should occur. Converted sinners characteristically develop and pursue both of these relational areas very inadequately.[59] Even so, the joys experienced in both

---

59. More help must be given in an organized, systematic way to enable them to discover how to overcome this problem.

relationships (sometimes fleeting and frequently marred) give promise of what sinless social relationships will be like in eternity, and of what (increasingly) we can begin to experience here.

Let us take an example. Today we live in what has been described as a rootless society. Mobility has brought about this condition. Many people stay in a community for only a brief span of time; then relocate. Truly this must be traumatic for unbelievers. How will they develop new friends and associations? How long will it take to do so if it is possible? Such questions plague families today. But Christians are a family, stretching across the country and throughout the world. Wherever they go, they can plug in immediately with other Christians by visiting a church and developing new relationships with its members. What a difference this makes!

Christian fellowship was an important matter in the New Testament. Apostles sent greetings in their letters from and to individuals and churches in order to promote it, traveled back and forth from place to place strengthening ties among brothers in various places, wrote whole letters about hospitality (II and III John), etc.

Adam was a social being, and all his posterity has been too. In His people, the family of God, our Creator and Redeemer has provided for their need. Alienated *Christians,* then, must be encouraged to strengthen their ties with other members of the body. Counselors have not always seen the great importance of this emphasis; yet it is a constant one in the Bible (simply trace the various beneficial aspects of Christian fellowship in the "one-another" passages). Alienation is a consequence of sin. One can understand this alienation of man from man when he realizes the basic alienation of man to God that exists among unbelievers. But among Christians, who have been reconciled to God, there is no reason for this; if they find themselves alienated, they can blame no one but themselves. God has provided almost limitless opportunities for fellowship.

There are times when counselors must tell Christians so. The "lone-wolf Christian" is sinning. He sins against God, the body, the world and himself. The life of a hermit or recluse may never be tolerated (he fails to obey the second great commandment). At length, too, it leads to further problems that may require counseling. How important it is, therefore, for parents, Christian school teachers, youth leaders, etc., preventively to do all they can to counter such attitudes at an early age, as soon as they detect them.

Christian marriage offers the most intimate of all purely human social relationships. Nowhere does the opportunity and potential for intimacy stand out more clearly than here. And nowhere is the contrast with the world's alienation more evident. Marriage in the Western world is in serious trouble (I almost said chaos). True intimacy is virtually unknown. And yet, the very purpose of marriage is companionship (cf. Gen. 2:18 with Prov. 2:17 and Mal. 2:14). Careful exegesis of these biblical portions shows that marriage is *a covenant of companionship*.[60]

Companionship, then, constitutes the fundamental relationship between a husband and wife. This companionship must be cultivated. It does not develop automatically by putting two persons under the same roof. They must have something basic in common about which they can grow together more and more. The only thing durable enough to provide this is their faith in Jesus Christ.

Marriage *fundamentally* was not designed to provide for the propagation of the race. Animals procreate quite successfully without the institution of marriage; it is plain that human life could be propagated that way too. Animals mate; humans marry. There is a vital distinction between the two. In mating, there is no further commitment than to the fulfillment of the sexual drive (though instinctively animals may carry other rituals of family life). But, by instituting the covenant[61] of companionship, God demands more of the human relationship. In marriage there is to be a unity of persons in an intimacy (that surely *includes* sexual union and the propagation of offspring) that (above all else) requires the commitment of both husband and wife (note again Prov. 2:17; Mal. 2:14, where both are bound, in similar terms, by this covenant; cf. also the equality of responsibility in I Cor. 7:4) to the idea of meeting the other's need for companionship. This intimacy was to be so complete that not even clothing was to separate them (Gen. 2:25), and they were to become "one flesh" (Gen. 2:24).

The expression "one flesh" has been widely misinterpreted as refer-

---

60. N.B., the covenantal aspect accompanies the companionship theme. Note also that in Gen. 2:18 Eve's creation is said to serve the purpose of meeting the need for companionship: "it is not good for the man to be *alone*."

61. A covenant is a binding, solemn agreement that involves sanctions upon those who violate, and blessings upon those who keep, its terms.

ring directly to the sexual union. Certainly, one factor included in the one-flesh concept is sexual union, but that is not its larger, over-all, inclusive significance. The Bible uses the phrase "one flesh" quite differently (e.g., in Eph. 5:28-30, where Paul argues that the two have become so much of a unit that whatever a husband does for his wife he, in fact, does for himself). In the light of the New Testament interpretation of Ephesians 5:28-30, the Genesis 2:24 passage must be interpreted to mean "one person." And when we investigate Hebrew terminology (from which this usage of flesh came), we discover that it has precisely that meaning (cf. Gen. 6:17; 7:22; 8:21, where "all *flesh*" is exactly equivalent to our English expression "every*body*." In neither the Hebrew nor the English should the words *flesh* and *body* be taken *materially*. Also, in Joel 2:28 (quoted in Acts 2) the word *flesh* means "person." Thus, for the two to become *one flesh* means that the two enter into a relationship so close, so intimate, that this new unity can be referred to as becoming "one person."[62]

The answer to human social alienation (or, as the Bible calls it, "loneliness"), then, is intimacy (each at a different level) in Christian fellowship and marriage. Openness on a level of depth that issues in a communication,[63] and concern that transcends that which exists in any other human relationship is available—for Christians. Counselors must hold forth this hope and set these goals for counselees.

The tragedy of our times is that forces *on all sides* demean and attempt to undermine marriage. Christian counselors, therefore, should make every effort to help believers to make the most of their marriages. In this way they can become salt to others whose marriages have lost zeal and flavor. A solid Christian marriage proclaims the intimate relationship that exists between Christ and His church (the model for a Christian marriage relationship—cf. Eph. 5—which, in turn, should exhibit it too). For biblical studies on marriage, see my book, *Christian Living in the Home* and (for matters pertaining to sexual relations in

---

62. The reference to Gen. 2:24 in I Cor. 6:15, 16 (the only sexually related passage) at first may seem to argue against my interpretation. But it does not. Paul again speaks of intimacy of relationship with Christ (one *spirit*, vs. 17) that is destroyed by prostitution, in which one becomes "one *body*" (vs. 17) with a harlot (note this is as different from one *flesh* as is one *spirit*), and quotes Gen. 2 (the broader concept: intimacy of oneness, encompasses the narrower: intimacy of sexual relations).

63. See sections on communication in *Christian Living* and in *Competent*.

marriage) *The Christian Counselor's Manual.*

Now, at one point the title of this book, *More Than Redemption,* comes prominently into view (though I shall discuss this more fully later on under the doctrine of salvation). When Christian counselors listen to the tragic tales of broken and miserable marriages, they have real hope to offer. To Christians[64] they may say: "I realize that your situation is grave; I don't want to minimize it in the least. However, the solution that I have to offer you in Christ is far greater than your problem. Not only is there no problem too difficult for Him to overcome, but (1) He wants to solve it for you, and (2) He wants to do so in a way that will give you a far better marriage than you ever have had before. I am not interested in patching up a marriage; repairing a mess. Our goal in counseling can be nothing less than a marriage that sings! And you can have just that if you mean business with Christ! The Bible teaches that 'where sin abounds' (and in your marriage it certainly does) 'grace far more abounds'[65] (and that is what we are aiming at)."

Thus, the Bible (in Christ) holds forth hope not merely for a return to a previous marriage state that was lost (good or bad as that may have been), but for something that is far superior to anything that they had before. God delights in turning crosses into crowns, emptying tombs through glorifying resurrected bodies, etc. He transforms tragedies into triumphs. Let us take this stance always in counseling. But more of this at a later point.

In concluding this section it is significant to note that Adam—and Christians today are called to manifest this fact as well—was acknowledged to be a social creature. One of the largest tasks of the Christian counselor is to help Christians to restore and more fully develop proper relationships with others.

5. *Adam Was Created As a Working Being.*

So far we have seen that Adam was a material, spiritual, moral and social being. Since, *now,* all human beings are totally depraved (i.e.,

---

64. To non-Christians, of course, they can hold out hope *on the other side of the Door.* Until the counselee has come to God through Christ, the Door, however, there is no hope.

65. Rom. 5:20b. Note how the counselor must not minimize the problem, but must maximize the Savior.

corrupted in all areas of life, though not totally corrupt in each), we must recognize that they develop problems in all life situations. We have been contrasting God's norms for man in Adam with some of these problems. Counselors must discover and help Christians find God's solutions to these human problems caused by sin. Work is no exception.

Work is not the result of sin. God works. Prior to the fall, Adam was called to provide companionship for Eve, dress the garden, name and rule over the animals, subdue the earth and propagate the human race. This was work—and it was intended to be a delight. If he had not sinned, it would have been.

There was *variety* in the work to which God called him. The various sorts of work were to occupy both the *mind* and the *body*. The work involved *relationships* to persons (including God, *the* Person with Whom we have to do) and to the non-human creation. His work related to *all* of animate and inanimate creation. If he had pursued it fully, he would have become a *very* well-rounded individual.

This work was to be carried on in an ideal setting and in a very friendly environment.[66] While money was not yet of any significance to human life (and, incidentally, this makes it clear that money itself is not the factor that brings about satisfaction in work), it is clear that a number of the tasks that God assigned him were of a type that would have been non-remunerative in an economic culture. This is important to note (and to stress with counselees, many of whom identify as *work* only those activities that bring in income)—that work is not necessarily attached to earning a living. In any number of counseling situations, this important biblical principle will come into play.

The necessity for work—to be a creative,[67] productive being—is built into man: Adam was created to be a working being. There is a built-in desire to produce. Even today, the scientific urge with its sense of curiosity and desire to learn,[68] the home-building, house-furnishing and decorating interests that so often crop up in women, etc., all manifest

---

66. Clearly, Adam's sin demonstrated that rebellion against God cannot be blamed on genetic causes (like temperament) or on environmental ones. Both his heredity and environment were perfect.

67. Not, of course, in the primary sense of God's creativity, but reflecting His creativity by bringing forth new and distinct accomplishments (to His honor) *from* the material creation. God creates *ex nihilo* (from nothing).

68. So long as it respects Deut. 29:29.

something of the remnants of Adam's original working nature.

It is never right not to work. There are, of course, *times* for work and *times* for leisure and rest. But no man, woman or child (play is work for very young children; chores and schoolwork follow) should be without work six days a week. God has ordained that this is so. When he doesn't work (and this is a problem with *many* counselees—particularly with depressed counselees) a human being becomes dissatisfied, unhappy and meddlesome (cf. II Thess. 3:8, 10, 12). This sense of dissatisfaction grows from two prime, but not mutually exclusive, sources:

(a) *Physical.* The writer of Ecclesiastes observes: "The sleep of the workingman is sweet" (Eccles. 5:12). We become sluggish in body and brain when we do not work. Laziness is denounced continually in Proverbs; Paul, in II Thessalonians 3:10, rules that those who won't (he didn't say couldn't) work shouldn't eat. He denounces their idleness and *disorderly* (a key word associated with persons who avoid work) lives.[69] Counselors must understand the dynamics here and work hard (also as an example) at this problem.

"Why," someone may ask, "am I so tired on a day when I haven't done anything?" or "Why am I so tired when I wake up after a full night's sleep?" Often the answer must be something like this:

"Because, in spite of what you think, you *have* been working so hard. When you go to bed after a day when you've done little productively, you have probably worked harder than if you had dug a five-foot ditch. You were nervous, worried, concerned, angry or dissatisfied with yourself and/or others. This brought about muscular action in which your muscles became tense. But, because you did nothing physical to *productively* release that muscular energy, your muscles didn't relax. They went on, hour after hour, taut as ever, using up energy *unproductively* and tiring you out. You may have gone to bed with those muscles still tied in knots and worked (*unproductively*) all night long too! No wonder you were tired in the morning.

---

69. Cf. II Thess. 3:6-15. The adverb used in vs. 11, *ataktos,* "disorderly," is a military term referring to soldiers out of step, etc. It has the idea of chaotic, unstructured living. Such persons need to develop patterns of regularity and order. A regular, scheduled job helps. Counselors will find undisciplined, *ataktos*-living a prime counseling problem, frequently associated with other difficulties it occasions (Paul notes how it leads to becoming a "busybody").

"When you work hard during the day physically,[70] you expend energy and muscles relax. Then, the sleep of such a workingman is sweet. He goes to bed relaxed, with a sense of accomplishment. That is the difference between the tired-but-satisfied (Eccles. 5) and the tired-but-dissatisfied feelings we have been discussing."

Even a shut-in confined to a wheelchair (or bed) can expend energy productively in profitable enterprises like letter writing and prayer (but resentment, worry and anger complicate a physically ill patient's situation for the reasons just stated).

(b) *Negative Self-Evaluation.* When we are told to carry our own load (Gal. 6:5, as well as the II Thess. 3 passage quoted above), and we don't, we sin. Conscience[71] then triggers bad physical feelings (and muscular responses) to awaken us to the need for change. The economic responsibility attached to some work, and God's command to work six days each week, lay plain obligations upon us that we cannot escape without bringing misery into our lives. Counselors will be aware of the fact that the "idle rich" (cf. the Gal. 5 passage), or the "idle sick" (a more modern category that fits a wider constituency) are miserable, discontented persons.

Retirement (when interpreted as a cessation from work, and a time to indulge in loafing, the sole pursuit of hobbies, sports and other self-interests) is a non-Christian concept.[72] If, (however) one interprets it as an exchange of one sort of work for another, and enters a new phase of productive activity (possibly doing many non-remunerative things for Christ's church that he never had the time to do before), that is good. When God speaks of doing "all your work" in six days, He refers to more than one kind of work (not merely remunerative work). Work that is biblically proper and satisfyingly productive, whether it pays or not, is work. Doing such work fulfils God's requirement.

When a counselee says, "I have no job,"[73] we always respond, "Oh, but you do." When he asks for an explanation, we say, "God gave you

---

70. Productive brain work is physical; it burns up calories.
71. On the conscience, see the *Manual,* pp. 74, 75, 86, 94, 95, 123; *Competent,* pp. 67-70.
72. Cf. material on this in *Shepherding God's Flock,* vol. II, pp. 110ff.
73. He means, of course, a remunerative job. The response is calculated to teach the facts about work and provide the dynamic for obtaining a remunerative job.

a job—to work six days a week! You have a job. So, spend eight hours a day, planning for and working at obtaining the right remunerative job; you will soon find one. Those who do *never* have difficulty obtaining work—*very* soon."

The work ethic in Colossians 3:22–4:1 (also Eph. 6:5-9) is vital to proper Christian labor. It, fundamentally consists of this: (1) Christians work for Christ, as His slaves, (2) no matter what their tasks may be (so long as these are biblically legitimate), (3) regardless of who their earthly employers may be, (4) or what they are like, (5) or whether they recognize their hard work and efforts, etc. (6) Therefore, Christians work well (heartily), (7) knowing that Christ sees and will reward their efforts, (8) and that He never treats them unfairly; (9) and they neither pilfer, nor cut corners, nor complain, (10) working not to please men, but Christ (Who sees all). (11) Employers must treat employees fairly, trying to put themselves in their shoes, (12) by recognizing they too have Someone (in the heavens) Who is over them, (13) to Whom they shall have to give an answer for how they have served Him in this, (14) and remembering that "the laborer is worthy of his hire" (Luke 10:7; I Cor. 9:14, etc.).

The man who is out to get as much as he can for as little work as he can do will never enjoy the satisfactions of work. By his sinful attitude, he has turned a God-given blessing into an onerous chore. He works *fundamentally* to get money, rather than *basically* to please Christ (and, as a by-product, to enjoy the satisfactions of labor). Such a person makes work a misery for himself by his whole approach to it. Counselors encounter this more often than not in dealing with miserable Christians. A man's work at his job (or a woman's work at home, or a child's work at school) will be pleasant or unpleasant according to how he views it and how he works at it (review the first ten principles listed above).

What of work within the church, and (in particular) the use of gifts designed to be used (some remuneratively, some non-remuneratively) in the service of Christ in that realm? I only *mention* this here because of its great importance, to *remind* counselors of this crucial issue. But I shall not repeat what I have taken an entire chapter to discuss in "Gifts That Differ," in the *Manual* (q.v.).

Obviously, my all-too-superficial treatment of work here is unsatisfactory. At least five solid books need to be written (right now) on the subject to cover various aspects of this thorny, important, and (yet) virtually untouched subject.[74] Most of the books written so far are anecdotal and do not get at the heart of vital issues that (for far too long) have been neglected by Christian counselors.

So, then, we see what Adam was like. He was created to live in an exciting, productive, God-honoring manner that would bring joy and satisfaction to him. But something happened—and that is the subject of the next chapter.

---

74. Here's hoping several will be published as a result of this plea.

CHAPTER NINE

COUNSELING AND HUMAN SIN
(The Doctrine of Man, Continued)

The subject that we now begin to consider is a sad one. Indeed, it is the very reason why *remedial* counseling exists (remember, man was made as a creature whose welfare was dependent—even *before* Adam's sin—on God's directive, guiding and preventive counsel. He received such counsel in the garden and benefited from it by the fellowship and communication that it established with God. Human life depends upon God's Word). Counsel *per se* was always needed.

But, like work (which became toil), counsel has changed since the fall, adding dimensions not previously necessary. Now the need for rebuke, for correction, etc., must be added to the counselor's repertoire.[1]

Consideration of sin and its effects upon the human being, and the implications of this for counseling, is an enormous undertaking that requires several books of various sorts (you are probably tired of hearing me say things like this, but I believe that it is important not only to warn about the sketchy nature of this chapter, but also to issue a call for help from readers who can contribute something to our knowledge and practice).

Now, let me say one thing at the outset and be done with it. The notion that is so widely spread abroad (sometimes by those who ought to know better), that nouthetic counseling considers all human problems the direct result of actual sins of particular counselees, is a gross mis-

---

1. Whether or not there would have been human *counselors* had man not sinned, is a moot point. Adam *may* have counseled his wife as head of his home; it seems that they would have counseled their children. But the *office* of counseling (like the *office* of preaching) may not have existed (cf. Jer. 31:34, where more ideal condition would seem to preclude such a necessity). The idea that all counsel is rebuke (as some wrongly have represented me as teaching) should be countered right off by this emphasis.

representation of the facts. From the beginning (cf. *Competent to Counsel,* 1970, pp. 108, 109) I have stated *clearly* that not all problems of counselees are due to their own sins. In *Competent,* I cited the cases of Job and the man born blind (John 9:1ff.).[2] Those who persist in attributing to me views that I do not hold are culpable. Either they ought to know better before they speak and write (by reading the material available—nouthetic counseling has not been done in a corner!), or they should have investigated on their own what they accepted as fact (but was actually only gossip).

While *all* human misery—disability, sickness, etc.—does go back to Adam's sin (and I would be quick to assert *that* biblical truth), that is not the same as saying that a *quid pro quo* relationship between each counselee's misery and his own personal sins exists. *That* I as quickly deny. It *may* be true in one given instance, but not in another. Neither is it true that all the suffering that some deserve they get in this life. Nor is it true that all the suffering that others receive in this life they bring upon themselves. Suffering, in a world of sin, comes to all in one way or another in the providence of God,[3] but before investigating each case, that is all that may be said about it. Apparent inequities (not really so from the perspective of eternity) can be resolved only in the purposes of God, who hasn't yet been pleased to reveal to us everything we'd *like* to know. We have all that we *need* to know—which is quite sufficient. The counselor's task, therefore, is to summon counselees to

(1) trust in God's providence (I Pet. 2:23; 4:19) and

(2) develop a proper perspective on suffering (which, according to II Cor. 4:17 and Rom. 8:18ff., flows from a comparison and contrast of present suffering with eternal glory).

Corruption

The Bible teaches that by Adam's sin the human race became both guilty and corrupt. This corruption (or depravity,[4] as theologians have

---

2. See also *What About Nouthetic Counseling?*, p. 29.

3. For more on this, see my address to the third assembly of the National Association of Nouthetic Counselors, Chicago, 1978, entitled "The Suffering of Pain." Tapes of this address are also available from Christian Study Services, 250 Edge Hill Rd., Huntingdon Valley, PA 19006.

4. The English word *depraved* was derived from words that meant "crooked" or "warped out of shape." The word corresponds with a biblical term for sin, *Avah,* that will be studied *infra.*

called it) is total. But when we speak of total depravity, we must make it clear that this does not mean that every person is as bad as he might be. Rather, the idea behind the word *total* is that *in all parts and aspects of his life he is depraved*—no area has escaped sin's blighting effects. When we speak of the inner person (or heart) as corrupt or deceitful and wicked (cf. Gen. 6:11; Eph. 4:22; see also Jer. 13:10; 16:12; 17:9; 18:12; 23:17; 49:16 for a study of iniquity in the human heart), with Jesus we affirm that the heart (the inner life) is like a storehouse (Matt. 12:34, 35) from which sinful acts and habits (behavior patterns) stem (cf. Matt. 15:18, 19). This corruption of the entire inner life is to the non-bodily aspect of man what sickness, malfunction, injuries and malformations are to his body. To speak of the effects of sin upon the soul of man as amoral, or to call it sickness (unless, like the Bible, one speaks figuratively about inner sin as sickness) is to miss the crucial point that the corruption of the inner life is what constitutes one a child of (i.e., one headed for) wrath *"by nature"* (Eph. 2:3). Thus, God calls this heart *evil* and *wicked* (see vss. *supra*) and depicts it as devising only wickedness with which it then began to fill the earth in outer behavioral manifestations (Gen. 6:5). The flood wiped out the early effects of this heart-corruption in the human race and on the earth, and the confusion of tongues at the tower of Babel (which also contributes to cultural distinctives that clash) was a gracious act (as well as judgmental) because it restricted all of mankind from ever combining its wickedness again.[5] Wicked men against wicked men, misunderstanding one another, and pitting wicked intentions against one another, has restrained the growth of wickedness from expanding to such proportions ever again.

But the point to be made here is simply this—those who see the corruption of the non-bodily side of man as amoral[6]

(1) have no biblical evidence for this position and

---

5. The Pentecostal reversal of the confusion of tongues (Acts 2) at the institution of the worldwide empire of God that consists of some from every nation, implies that the possibility of the true union of all who are in Christ without such effects is possible.

6. Nor is there the slightest *hint* in the Bible that there is *another* inorganic, amoral aspect of man in addition to the heart (the so-called psychological) which (according to the advocates of the view) is so important for living. If it were as influential as Narramore believes ("Psychology for *Living*"), the Bible would have something to say about it. Biblically, the emphasis is the *Bible* for living.

   (2) do violence to all the biblical data that declare that the situation is so bad that the old heart must be replaced by a new "heart of flesh" (Ezek. 36:25-27).

The picture in the Scriptures is that the heart (the *whole* inner life, no other inner life is identified in the Bible) is *totally* corrupt—i.e., no aspect of it *isn't* corrupt. It is extremely dangerous, biblically (and therefore theologically) to speak as if there were a part of human nature that was not only not sin-affected, but also not sin generating (in the next chapter we shall see how even the sin-habituated *body,* because corrupt, generates sinful acts—for now, cf. Rom. 6:16, 19). All of man, then, is both affected by sin and is a source of further sin. Those who see in man some non-bodily psychological area *affected* by sin, but not *effecting* sin, fail to speak biblically. The heart, the inner, non-bodily side of man—all of it without exception—is "deceitful and desperately wicked." Man needs a new heart.

Prior to the reception of the "new heart" (Ezek. 36:25, 26) that replaces the old stony heart at regeneration (when the Spirit comes into the inner life and transforms it—cf. Ezek. 36:27; Rom. 5:5; 8:10), it is impossible either to understand or to obey God's Word (Ezek. 36:27; I Cor. 2). But the new heart makes this a genuine possibility (cf. Ezek. 36:27). "As a result, it is now possible to live the remainder of your time in the flesh no longer following human desires, but following the will of God" (I Pet. 4:2, NTEE).

From this inner corruption flow all sinful attitudes, words and actions. Man is not a sinner because he sins; he sins because he is a sinner. By *nature*[7] (Eph. 2:3) he is a sinner. He was *born* that way (cf. Ps. 51:5). The Berkeley Version says, ". . . in sinful state I was born." This sin is David's, not his mother's (see also Ps. 58:3, a parallel passage that even more clearly makes the teaching of original sin explicit). In Psalm 51:5 David says, "I was shaped in iniquity" (not by God, but by the process of conception leading to birth). David is saying, "I was *formed* as a sinner." In Genesis 8:21, human beings are declared "wicked" from their "youth" (*naar* = "infancy" or "youth"; in this context it can make sense only to take it in the former sense). Proverbs 22:15 declares that foolishness is *bound up*[8] in the *heart* of a

---

7. The deposit that he inherited at birth, the non-learned side of personality.
8. The picture is of a child coming into the world with foolishness (i.e., sinful behavior in contrast to wisdom = wise behavior) tied to his heart. It is an in-

child (no one ever had to teach a child to sin).

Corruption of the whole person, but especially of his inner life, is a dominant and essential theme for every counselor to know, to teach and upon which to base all his work. Clearly, he cannot bring about biblical change by means of the old heart, since from it flows only sin. He will counsel, then, only believers (as we have said before); he will evangelize unbelievers. But, conversely, he also will recognize the tremendous potential of the new heart. He will not give up on truly regenerate persons (or those who through profession of faith he must presume to be so); in them is the capacity to understand and obey God's counsel (Ezek. 36:27). The indwelling Spirit makes this a genuine reality. He sees matters in a clear-cut way: either counseling is possible, or it is not. There is no middle ground, there is nothing in unsaved man, untouched by sin, to which he can appeal. His only point of contact with unregenerate persons is at this very point of corruption. He can speak of sin and one's need of a Savior and pray that God will open his heart (another expression, used in Acts 16:14, for giving a new heart) to understand and believe. Short of a new, open or cleansed heart, he will attempt no counseling.

Guilt

But it is true too that one is born guilty. Adam's sin was representative (Rom. 5). By it all "sinned" (Rom. 5:12—the aorist indicates in one final act of Adam) and were constituted (Rom. 5:19) sinners. And even children (though they haven't sinned as Adam) are held guilty (vs. 14). One person (Adam) by one sin (note vss. 12, 15, 16, 17, 18, 19 all speak of one person and one sin) plunged the entire human race of all time not only into corruption but into guilt.

The wages of sin is death (Rom. 6:23—that includes *all* death, spiritual as well as physical), but even newborn babies (and unborn children) die. That means they were held guilty of Adam's sin. Jesus Christ could not have died (being sinless) unless He died (as indeed He did) as a substitutionary sacrifice, bearing the sin of others (I Pet. 2:24; Isa. 53, etc.). Adam, before the fall, could not have died. Death came *as the result* of Adam's sin (Gen. 2:17; Rev. 20:14). Without question,

---

separable part of the heart with which a child is born. The link is always there. Only discipline, creating conditions for learning of and submitting to God in salvation, can drive it out of the heart.

then, the Bible teaches that all are held guilty of Adam's sin because He
was their representative.

It is important, at this juncture, to distinguish between *guilt* and *a
sense of guilt*. In psychological and psychiatric language and literature,
usually the two are not distinguished. Pastors must be aware of this
when reading such material. In the past the word *guilt* always meant
culpability; but with the advent of psychology the word came to mean
a sense (or feeling) of guilt.[9] Because of this change in the meaning
of the term, many who have read deeply into modern psychology and
only superficially into the Bible read the idea of "sense of guilt" into
the word *guilt* in Christian literature. Christian counselors should make
their position clear—what they believe, and how they use the terms—
whenever discussing guilt. Because the idea of guilt as *sense of guilt*
has so permeated modern language, it is also important to clarify the
term for counselees, many of whom otherwise will misunderstand. It
is too easy, also, for eclectic Christians to read culpability ideas into
the word guilt when it appears in some psychological treatises. Care
must be taken, always to understand how each writer uses a term (in
books or chapters, or even paragraphs—writers themselves are not
always consistent in this matter).

As *guilt* is the basis for a sense of guilt (or bad feelings triggered
by a guilty conscience—that is the actual dynamic involved), Christians
should recognize

(1) that it is not adequate to treat feelings alone[10] (by medication,
     shock, transcendental meditation, biofeedback, home-brew,
     etc.), and

(2) that it can be dangerous to do so (since this may lead to sear-
     ing the conscience described in I Tim. 4:2—searing the con-
     science is the result of not heeding it). Christian counselors,
     instead, will treat the cause.

The guilt of original sin (guilt stemming representatively from Adam's
act of transgression) can be removed only by judicial, representative
forgiveness in Christ (see "Forgiveness," *infra*). Guilt from the Christian's actual sin also must be dealt with by the parental forgiveness that

---

9. Still to be distinguished from Freud's misuse of the words *guilt feelings*
as a technical phrase meaning false guilt. On this matter, see *Competent*, pp. 14ff.
10. See *Competent*, pp. 94ff., for a discussion of desensitizing the conscience.

God extends to His children in Christ.[11] Of course, guilt (and guilt feelings) comes from both.

Now, in the psychiatric literature (as I have said) much is made of guilt (meaning the *sense* or feeling of guilt), guilt feelings (Freudian *false* guilt), and the supposed damage that such guilt does. While it is altogether possible (indeed, highly probable) that unconfessed and unforgiven sin, carried with a deep sense of guilt over a long period of time, does do harm[12] (organically), a sense of guilt, *per se,* is not harmful. As a matter of fact, the painful bodily state that is aroused by the conscience (once it has made the self-evaluation that there has been a violation of one's standards) is intended as a friendly warning. Pain in the fingers, when touching a hot stove, is intended as an early warning device designed to preserve those fingers. The pain itself doesn't do damage; rather, it warns against trouble that might damage one's body. So too, when painful, unpleasant or anxious bodily states develop from negative self-evaluation, these are intended to alert and warn one that his attitudes and actions must be changed. Similarly, conscience doesn't damage, but only warns against that which might lead to further damage.

While any pressure on the body may become stressful (and therefore harmful) if the stressful response is prolonged for an extended period of time (just as the fingers will be seriously harmed if not quickly removed from the hot stove), there may be harm from not heeding the sense of guilt. But that is quite a distinct thing from declaring that the sense of guilt is an enemy to be eliminated (by tranquilizers, etc.). To do so is to commit an error as foolish as claiming that the nerve endings in one's fingertips should be desensitized. The problem is not in the warning device. Pain is a friend; guilty feelings (which are essentially painful, or unpleasant bodily states) likewise serve a beneficent purpose. The pain in the warning device is to be deactivated by heeding its warning, not by destroying it.

Instead of attacking the pain (or focusing on it) the wise counselor will recognize that a sense of guilt flows from true guilt (a violation of

---

11. See footnote in *The Christian Counselor's New Testament,* p. 14 (Matt. 6:12, 14, 15). Murray says, ". . . it [justification] must mean that God constitutes a new judicial relation to himself in virtue of which the person may be declared to be righteous in his sight." John Murray, *The Imputation of Adam's Sin* (Grand Rapids: Eerdmans, 1959), p. 87.

12. See "Stress" in my book, *Update on Christian Counseling,* vol. 1 (Phillipsburg, N. J.: Presbyterian and Reformed Publishing Co., 1979).

one's standards) and can be removed properly only by dealing with the guilt (violation) itself. Masking the symptom will do no good. Yet much in current medicine and counseling is aimed squarely at deactivating by damaging, debilitating or destroying the warning system.

Here, I should like to make an important distinction. First, as I have often taught, violating one's standards makes him guilty of actual sin before God. This is true *even when the standard is unbiblical* (e.g., believing that playing Old Maids is, or might be, sin). Thus, the guilt feelings arise *properly* (not improperly—there is nothing "false" about such a sense of guilt) because the one who plays Old Maids sins when he does. He is guilty before God (take note) *not* because playing Old Maids is a sin in and of itself, but because he played *even though he thought it was* (or *might* be) *a sin.* He has violated the precept in Romans 14:23. Note too, if the standard is wrong, there is an obligation on the counselor's part not only to deal with the sin (a rebellious attitude toward God), but with the faulty understanding of God's Word. In such cases, the counselor,

   (1) must call the counselee to repentance (he treats the guilt as real and the sense of sin as appropriate) and,
   (2) must show the counselee what the Scriptures actually teach regarding the matter, in order to strengthen his conscience.[13]

So, when Christian counselors speak of guilt, they refer to culpability (i.e., action or attitudes making one liable to punishment) before God. This culpability may be for original sin or for actual transgressions by the counselee. When they speak of a sense of guilt, they mean painful bodily discomfort aroused by the conscience. They may speak also of false standards (or a "weak conscience"—because it is activated by unbiblical criteria), but one thing they do *not* accept is the notion of false guilt, which (I have shown) is an incorrect designation on two counts:

   (1) "Guilt" is used for "guilt feelings" (or sense of guilt).
   (2) "False" is used to describe situations in which there is, indeed, true guilt.

Sin

Earlier in this book, I have referred to sin as any failure to do what

---

13. Even on the basis of faulty scriptural interpretation, there is real guilt—the counselee *should* have developed better standards of conduct.

God requires or any transgression of what He forbids. It is doing what God says don't do or not doing what He says to do. Sin, therefore, is "lawlessness" (I John 3:4). Sin is disobedience to God. Quite to the contrary of what O. Hobart Mowrer and Karl Menninger have to say about sin, sin *always*—first and foremost—is related to God. Menninger and Mowrer (the two psychotherapists who write of sin) redefine the term in ways that destroy its meaning. For both, sin is purely horizontal; it has only to do with improper relationships and offenses toward other human beings. Indeed, even many Christians have been tempted to speak of sin primarily in terms of its effects upon human relations—calling it, for instance, *alienation,* etc. But before all other dimensions of sin (alienation or separation surely is one), sin is a personal affront to the Creator. Sin is saying to God (not always knowingly so), "I want to do as I please, regardless of what You command."

Now, as I have just noted, sin does have many dimensions; it is many-faceted. We know this because the Scriptures treat sin from a multidimensional standpoint (in the Bible, for instance, there are more than 17 distinct terms for sin). God has gone out of His way to give us a *very* clear picture of sin and its effects (sometimes people wonder why we stress sin; answer: because God does). Let us consider these 17 words; each says something about the *act* or the *effect* of sin that a Christian counselor ought to understand.

1. *Old Testament Words*

    A. *Avah* (lit., "bent"—cf. C. S. Lewis' "bent" people in *Out of the Silent Planet*). This word is similar to our English word *wrong* (i.e., *wrung* out of shape). Picture a bent key that will no longer fit into the lock. Because it has been twisted out of shape, it cannot be used to accomplish the purpose for which it was intended. So man, designed to image and honor God, *has* (by sin) been twisted and warped so that he *cannot* please Him (Rom. 8:8). Moreover, bodies are disfigured, misshapen and malfunction. Minds are perverted, etc. No human being functions as designed originally. Counseling involves straightening bent lives to enable believers to function once again as God intended. It is (from this perspective) *restoration* (cf. Gal. 6:1; the word *katartizo,* "restore," is used of mending broken bones and torn nets *so as to make them functional once again*).

B. *Ra* (lit., "breaking up, ruin"). Here is a picture of destruction. The idea is that what God has made has been ruined by iniquity. Often, the word comes to mean the *trouble* that such ruin occasions. Sin causes trouble by breaking marriages, ruining homes, careers, etc. Both the *act* and the tragedy it *effects* are contemplated in the word. Sin deteriorates. Everything in a sinful world—houses, cars, even bodies—goes to pieces. Ever since Adam's sin, human beings have been busy ruining both their world and themselves. Counseling seeks to reverse these destructive patterns of life. Constructive solutions to problems are encouraged (e.g., Eph. 4:29: "Don't let a single rotten word [i.e., a destructive one] come from your mouths, but rather, whatever is good for constructively meeting problems that arise, so that your words may help those who hear").

C. *Pasha* (lit., "rebellion against a rightful authority"; "revolt"). Sin is treason; it is rebellion against God, His law and His government. Clearly, what happened in the garden was an attempt to overthrow God's rule. The Father of lights was rejected for the father of lies. Here, in this term, is the *core* element. The thought is, "Not Thy will be done but *mine!*" Modern aspirations for autonomy in scientism, existentialism, Rogerianism, humanism, etc., express the essential concept in the term. This *wish for autonomy,* so prevalent today, must be identified and countered by counselors, or they shall fail. At bottom, this emphasis is rebellion against God.

D. *Rasha* (lit., "hubbub, confusion, tossing"). The picture in this word sees someone running here and there, agitating others, stirring things up, causing confusion. There is no rest; agitation is the kernel thought. People, agitated, running to and fro, *not knowing which way to turn* (the idea emerges plainly in Isa. 57:20, 21). Biblical counseling guides and directs. It is concerned with scriptural structure—order and discipline—from which come the freedom and peace of God. Having no standard, man cannot find his way; counseling (when biblical) points to that way.

E. *Maal* (lit., "a breach of trust, unfaithfulness, treachery"). Judas, an adulterous marriage partner, Aachan's sin (Josh. 7:1; 22:20), all set forth the essential ideas inherent in the term. The word points to the serious nature of breaking faith, violating a covenantal agreement, with God or neighbor. Sin is spiritual adultery; it is covenant-breaking. When counselors fail to recognize and stress this aspect of sin, they neglect the need for confession and repentance. Reconciliation and peace with God are essential prerequisites for successful counseling.

F. *Aven* (lit., "nothing, vanity, unprofitable behavior"). The notion here is *effort with no result;* the word refers to worthless, pointless, unprofitable, unproductive living. The ultimate result of all sinful living is *aven* (cf. Prov. 22:8). The existentialists (rightly) have declared life (that is lived apart from God) "absurd." Counselees are concerned with helping people to abandon "their meaningless ways of thinking" (Eph. 4:17). Instead, they encourage *renewed* thinking (Eph. 4:23) that leads to purposeful living.

G. *Asham* (lit., "guilt" through negligence or ignorance). When someone was *asham,* he was required to offer an *asham* (guilt-offering). Sometimes the word is connected with the idea of restitution. No sin can be *overlooked;* all must be dealt with— even sins of ignorance. Not only is restitution often necessary for counselees, the recognition of guilt for both known sins and sins of ignorance is important.

H. *Chatha* (lit., "to wander from, fall short of, miss the mark"). Probably, like its N.T. counterpart, *hamartia, chatha* came to mean sin (in general). It is the biblical equivalent to our English word *sin.* In both the N.T. and O.T. terms, the notion of not measuring up to God's standards, failing to meet His requirements, is prominent. It implies blameworthiness (one *should* have hit the bulls-eye on the target), is used frequently in confession and has to do with *acts* of sin rather than the *condition* of sinfulness. All counselees have fallen short of God's standards of knowledge and holiness; otherwise they would need no counsel. Yet, in the process, some forget and must be reminded of this.

I. *Amal* (lit., "labor, sorrow"). Hearkening back to the curse on Adam and Eve, this word stresses the fact that sin has made life a burden. Pain, heartache, the whole "problem of evil" is bound up in this idea. Trouble, travail, weariness are elements of *amal*. That is why counselors echo Christ's words, "take My yoke . . . My burden is light." Sin brings misery and trouble; righteousness simplifies and lightens living.

J. *Aval* (lit., "unjust, unfair"). This word for iniquity (the English term is connected with inequity, inequality) depicts a departure from what is equal and right just as our English words do. The concept is clear in Malachi 2:6, where the word is contrasted with its opposites. The self-centeredness of sin emerges here. It is the counselor's task to help the counselee focus upon God and his neighbor. Where his concern is others, such problems will disappear.

2. *New Testament Words*

A. *Hamartia* (lit., "missing the mark") corresponds closely with its Hebrew equivalent *chatha* (q.v.). The arrow was aimed poorly and falls short of its target. The one who sins misses life's purpose. Again, this is the common (general) word for sin in the N.T. Once more, it is important to recognize the place of the Scriptures as a standard (and Christ's life as a fulfillment of them) against which human conduct must be measured (Rom 3:23). Counselors not only must help others to identify God's targets (the *what*-to of the Scriptures), but also must show them how to shoot accurately (the *how*-to of biblical application). They are archery instructors, as was Paul (cf. I Tim. 6:20, 21 in *The New Testament in Everyday English*).

B. *Parabasis* (lit., "crossing the boundary line"). The word pictures someone disregarding a "No Trespassing" sign, violating a property line. The word means "trespassing." God has drawn the line; in his insolence, man steps across. In the garden God posted a No Trespassing sign on the tree in the center of the garden. Man disregarded it. Romans 4:15 illustrates the use of the term. Man's sinful nature makes him want to touch to see if the paint really is wet, again, disregarding the sign. This perverted desire to do what is forbidden will be encountered regularly in counseling.

C. *Anomia* (lit., "lawlessness"). The lawless are those who live as though God had issued no laws. Every counselee is an outlaw. The description in Judges, "every person did that which was right in his own eyes," puts it well (Tit. 2:14 is a typical usage). Man's great self-deception is to think he is his own law-giver; no counselor may avoid confronting him about this. The clash in counseling occurs when God's requirements do not please the counselee who wants to go on living as a criminal in God's sight. Counselors are lawmen!

D. *Parakoe* (lit., "disobedience to a call"). "Johnnie," his mother calls; but there is no response. So too the (outward) calls of God go unheeded. Cf. II Corinthians 10:6 for the use of *parakoe*. Counselors echo God's calls for counselees; they remind God's children of their duty to heed God, their great Father. Counselors help their counselees to want to respond, and show them how to respond to God.

E. *Paraptoma* (lit., "falling" when one should stand upright). Our expression, "falling down on the job," catches most of the nuances in this word. It is failing God by our lack of dependability. Faithfulness, perseverance, trustworthiness are qualities that God expects. Counseling endeavors to develop these qualities in counselees.

F. *Agnoema* (lit., "ignorance" of what one ought to know). "Ignorance of the law is no excuse," puts it exactly. There will be people in hell because of ignorance. Lives, homes, relationships, churches are ruined through ignorance. Cf. Hebrews 9:7; Christ died for what we didn't know to do (or not to do), but should have. Again and again in counseling it is necessary to *instruct* counselees in God's will as it is revealed in the Scriptures. Biblical ignorance accounts for many counseling problems.

G. *Hettema* (lit., "defect or shortcoming"). When we try to give God a *part* of our lives, attempt to departmentalize our faith or separate it from other activities, we fail this way. God must be at the *center* of all we do. The Sunday-only, one-day-a-week way of life won't do; God is sovereign over all. Eclecticism in counseling makes it defective. It will fail at those points where something else has been substituted for God's truth. Sin endeavors to defeat by defect. Counselors must stress the need for committing *all* the soul, mind, strength and heart to God in *all* things. Too few counselors have a grasp of this problem and God's solution to it. One defect may ruin all.

From this study it seems evident that sin takes many forms. Many of these terms speak of aspects of the *act* (or state) of sin, others speak of the *effects* of sin. Some seem to move back and forth over both territories. Either way, it is obvious that sin has many dimensions, all of which bear upon counseling.

Counselors, aware of something of the depth of biblical description, insight and exposure of sin, can look for problems *from various angles.* For instance, when someone protests, "Well, I didn't do anything," he usually thinks of sin only as some plain affront to another (*pasha*) or as some grossly perverted deed (*avah*). The counselor, on the other hand, may need to say, "That's just the point—you didn't do anything when it was expected of you" (*asham, paraptoma, hettema* or even *agnoema* may fit here, according to the details of the given situation). In another situation, the idea in *hamartia* (or *chatha*) may best fit the circumstances: "It isn't enough to 'do the best that you can'; God requires perfection, and you have fallen short." Clearly, then, the counselor (who must continually be dealing with sin in all its forms) needs to be aware of the scriptural picture as it is presented to us.

Misery

Some of the words in the preceding list describe various aspects of the misery that sin brings into human life. I do not wish to speak about this at length, since I have done so already in my discussion of the subject in *Competent to Counsel* (see especially pp. 105-127). It is enough here to consider the matter from an additional angle or two.

Human misery is the result of God's judgment upon man's sin. There was no misery in the garden *before* the fall, and all pain, crying, etc., will be eliminated in the eternal state as well (Rev. 21:4). Pain, sorrow and the other forms of human misery came as the result of the curse.

Prior to sin, man worked—but it was pure joy—work meant fulfillment and satisfaction. It was never a "chore." When the curse was pronounced, God turned the world *against* humanity. Man could henceforth earn a living only through "painful toil" and "sweat" (Gen. 3: 17, 19). Thorns and thistles (the former, incidentally, were used to bring suffering and pain to Christ as the sin-bearer Who, thereby, bore the full effects of the curse for His people) grew to impede man's efforts. Work became burdensome, and clouded the joy and satisfaction associated with it. But God did not remove entirely the satisfaction of

productivity (cf. Eccles. 5:12). To the joy of bringing life into the
world was added the pains and travail experienced in childbirth (Gen.
3:16), not to speak of the risks it now involves to both mother and
child.

Plainly those elements do not constitute the whole of the misery experienced as the result of God's judgment upon human life for Adam's
sin. The pronouncement of death as the penalty for eating of the forbidden fruit entailed not only death, but all the numerous miseries that
are associated with it, and for the unbeliever (and uninstructed Christian) a sting (something to be feared and avoided) and fear that en-
slaves (cf. I Cor. 15:56; Heb. 2:15). Alienation from God and one
another took place (Gen 3:8, 10). Love for God and neighbor fled, etc.
Misery was the third consequence of Adam's sin.

Consider pain briefly. Pain in a good God's world is inexplicable
apart from man's sin. Culpability by Adam's representative act alone
provides a satisfying basis for understanding and enduring pain. Approach the problem of evil from this viewpoint, and you will discover
that there are three possible responses to the presence of pain in God's
world. The first two must be rejected; only the third will meet the requirements of the Bible.

(1) *Deny the reality of pain and suffering.* The Christian Science
Church (as well as certain Eastern religions), denies the existence of pain from a pantheistic viewpoint. If all is God, and
God is all, then we are a part of God. God does not suffer pain.
Therefore we do not suffer pain. Christians reject this view as
unbiblical on several counts, not the least of which is the explicit denial that Christ suffered for our sins.

(2) *Admit the reality of pain and suffering, but say that God wants
to but can't do anything about it.* This viewpoint appears in the
works of various writers who refuse to accept the sovereignty
of God as both the Creator and Sustainer of the universe. They
postulate (sometimes wittingly, sometimes unwittingly) the
existence of a second, negative, evil, force (or person) as ultimate as God Himself. Again, Christians reject the dualism of
this essentially Zoroastrian approach as unscriptural; God created and controls all things (including Satan and his activities).
God must not be confused with what He makes. He makes
lakes, He is not a lake. He can make Satan; He is not like him.

It is not necessary to resort to a doctrine of equal ultimacy in order to believe in a good God.

(3) *Admit the reality of pain and suffering and say that God brings it about.* This is the Christian viewpoint. Although we do not understand all the reasons for God's decretive (or ultimate) will, we can assent to it and leave the full explanations for eternity. We do know that, at the fall, *God* cursed man with pain and misery. It was His act. He is sovereign over suffering. Human misery was a just penalty for sin (the Latin, *poena,* from which our word *pain* comes, means, literally, "penalty, punishment." This very word, therefore, is an acknowledgment and reminder of the origin of pain in human life).

Now, the first two viewpoints are often found, in one form or another, in the minds of counselees. Questions like, "Does God care?" or "Is God really in control?" or "Do you really think a good God would permit this if He could do anything about it?" reveal such thinking.

Outright denial of pain is rarely seen, but counselees trying "to keep a stiff upper lip," or who minimize the depth of human tragedy ("Oh, well, it could have been worse") come close to it. The Bible lends no support to any denial of the reality of pain and suffering (either as a whole or in part). Pain is to be recognized for all the bitter misery it can inflict. Counselors must make this plain to all. Grief sufferers, who unlike the Lord at Lazarus' grave) attempt to bridle their emotions, are wrong, and must be told so. Jesus wept. Others, looking on, saw this not as weakness of faith, but as an expression of genuine love. And so it is, when real and unrestricted.

In the midst of serious loss and all the sorrow that accompanies that, the Christian has a solid response. Because of his hope (hope in the Bible is not hope-so, but confident expectation) of the redemption of the body, he does not grieve *hopelessly,* "as others who have no hope."

When Toccoa Falls dam broke in 1977, flooding the Toccoa Falls Bible Institute and drowning 39 persons, many of whom were children, the government sent psychologists to help the survivors. Their help was rejected as unwanted and unnecessary. Robert Nuttal, a psychologist himself, reported that the experience had changed the way government researchers view the aftermath of natural disasters." He continued, saying that the Christians at Toccoa, who had suffered the loss of loved ones,

. . . were in better mental health than the other communities we studied, who, for the most part, were not hit as hard.

He explained,

Their very strong religious commitment gave them an understanding and an explanation for what had happened to them, which the people in the other communities did not have. . . . Because of Toccoa, we had to change our theory about psychological reaction to disaster to include cultural values.[14]

He continued,

But as the college buried its dead, survivors expressed faith that the tragedy somehow was a part of a divine plan.[15]

This belief, Nuttal opined,

. . . allowed the Toccoa survivors to avoid the hostility felt by most victims of natural disasters [i.e., to say the Lindemann view is not the norm for believers].

He noted also,

The people of Toccoa were far easier to deal with than those in other communities. They were helpful and friendly and less hostile.

Nuttal quoted one student (Thurman Kemp) as saying,

People [outside the college] couldn't understand why there wasn't more sorrow, more suffering and more crying out[16] [Kemp lost a seven-year-old son in the flood].

Kemp explained,

Things happen for a purpose, and if God had wanted that dam to hold, He could have done it with a Band-Aid.

The place of the church also was significant in supplying funds and

---

14. It is about time for such a change, which is long overdue. The idea that the salvation of the grief-sufferer makes a difference is not new to Christians. In *The Big Umbrella,* 1972, I pointed out that in grief the Christian faith ". . . makes the great difference between hope and despair" (p. 73), and that "Paul . . . distinguishes between two kinds of grief: grief in despair and grief in hope" (p. 75). In my *Coping with Counsling Crises,* 1976, I wrote, ". . . the Lindemann grief work theory makes no room for essential distinctions between Christians and non-Christians" (p. 3). When the government begins sending preachers rather than psychologists, we will know its repentance is genuine!

15. Contrast this with view no. 2. Cf. *Coping,* pp. 100ff.

16. N.B., while Christian belief doesn't minimize or eliminate sorrow, it *lessens* it. Hope and faith make the difference.

help to meet needs. The bottom line to the article is found in these words: "Toccoa Falls College is in good psychological shape."[17]

The admission of the reality and depth of human pain and suffering, then, is balanced by faith in God's wise purposes in providence. The view that God cannot help was not what brought comfort to the Toccoa survivors; they found help in affirming the biblical view that God is sovereignly working out His purposes even through this. They saw life as meaningful, not absurd. By interpreting the disaster biblically, they came through this experience differently (and in a manner far superior to others).

The reason for the existence of misery is sin. But because of God's redemptive purposes in Christ, pain and suffering have been sanctified for the believer. While never losing the basic theme of penalty and punishment underlying *poena* (pain), Christians know that God has *lifted* pain and suffering up beyond this theme, and thereby has extracted much of the misery (that we engender by wrong attitudes toward suffering) from it. That was Toccoa's experience. More must be said about this later, as it relates to the title of this book. But for now I shall make one or two additional comments.

While the penalty (*poena*) theme is basic (and must never be lost in the discussion), it is clear from the book of Job that pain is not suffered in direct proportion to an individual's sin (cf. also John 9:1ff.). Job did not bring his suffering upon himself. What happened, happened to serve heavenly purposes about which we have only the barest glimpse and the slightest understanding. They were not fundamentally earthly concerns at all (though they had their beneficent effects upon Job as well). On the other side of the coin, surely (in this life) Hitler's misery did not equal what his crimes deserved.

Pain is *used* by God for numerous purposes. To mention a couple, God uses pain to *remind* us that all is not right here yet, and to fix our hope on the coming life, when it will be (cf. Rom. 8:18-25). Pain is used to purify and teach us (Heb. 5:8; 2:10).

The counselor's task is to help the counselee to put pain into a proper (biblical) perspective (cf. II Cor. 4:17, 18). This he does by setting it

---

17. Article by Greg MacArthur of the Associated Press, entitled, "Psychologists Baffled by Toccoa Survivors," *Macon* (Ga.) *Telegraph and News*, Nov. 5, 1978, p. 8c. Substitute the word *spiritual* for *psychological,* and this statement will be fully accurate.

over against eternal joy. By *comparison,* the severest pain is but light and temporary. He must help the counselee to see that others have faced it successfully (I Pet. 1:9; I Cor. 10:13), and that the answer is to go on trusting and obeying God (I Pet. 2:23; 4:19); there is, therefore, no excuse for letting the bars down. Pain does not excuse sinful attitudes or behavior. Of the fact that counselees often claim that it does, counselors must be aware. And, they must be ready to counter the thrust biblically (their familiarity with I Peter especially will stand them in good stead when handling such problems. In order to help counselors with this, I have published a practical commentary for counselors and preachers on I Peter, entitled *Trust and Obey*[18]).

The problem of the suffering Christian causes difficulty for some counselees. They seem to have difficulty understanding why Christians suffer. Why aren't they exempted from all misery when regenerated? Why must they suffer the consequences of pre-conversion sins (an arm lost in a drunken brawl isn't replaced when one becomes a Christian)? Why must they suffer for present sins (cf. I Cor. 11:32)? There are any number of short-term answers to these questions (and others like them): Learning and growth often take place under the discipline of suffering; the church must be purified; God wants to demonstrate the difference that salvation makes (e.g., the Toccoa experience). Ultimately, however, the answer to why God has done what He has done, as He has done it, falls in the category of those things covered by Deuteronomy 29:29. We may wish to speculate, but that would be wrong; it is stealing—such information does not belong to us; it belongs to God.

Thus, it is essential for counselors (1) to hold to the third view that pain is real and that for His own sovereign purposes God has decreed it; (2) to help Christians face misery as the Toccoa people, armed with this third view, did. Thus God will be honored in His church and before the world.

Not all Christians respond to God's providential working as the Toccoa Falls Institute people did. Not all Christians, as a result, honor God before men. Counselors are likely to encounter their share of those who don't. Their rebellion is one major reason why they are in need of

---

18. Published by Presbyterian and Reformed Publishing Co., Phillipsburg, N. J., 1978.

counsel.[19] It is the counselor's task to move them from doubt concerning or displeasure with God's sovereignty in such matters to a practical application of view number 3 that means meeting tragedy as the Toccoa Christians did.

How does one handle rebellion against the wisdom of God's decrees? The answer, of course, is in sympathetic (empathetic,[20] if you prefer) disagreement. While sympathy is important—the counselor must enter into the depths of the counselee's heartbreak and pain—the Christian counselor cannot, for a moment, excuse or countenance insubordination and rebellion toward God. Instead, at the proper time, and in the proper way, he must label it for what it is,[21] sin. And he will point out how misery is enlarged and pain increased by wrong attitudes toward it (physiological studies confirm this). In the final analysis, then, there is no other stance to take in such encounters than the one that God assumed when responding to Job:

> Who is this that darkens counsel with words without knowledge? . . .
> Will the one who contends with the Almighty correct him? Let him
> who accuses God answer him (Job 38:1; 40:2).

God stopped Job's mouth. He calls him to repent (rethink) of his attitude and words and to submit to His ways. Who is any man to object to what God does? (cf. Rom. 9:20). That is God's last word on the subject. And the only proper response toward which to lead the counselee is Job's final word:

> I am unworthy—how can I reply to you [God]? I put my hand over
> my mouth. . . . Therefore I despise myself and repent in dust and
> ashes (Job 40:4; 42:6).

There is no other easier way to deal with open rebellion. "But," you say, "think of my counselee's pain and misery." Well (I can only reply), think of Job's. Yet, that is how God handled him. In the end, remember, nothing will help more to relieve the pain than a proper biblical attitude toward it (that God will bless), while nothing will intensify it more than a wrong attitude (that the counselee cannot expect God to bless).

You must make it perfectly clear to the counselee that suffering can

---

19. Not to say that the Toccoa people didn't. Doubtless, much informal, mutual, strengthening counsel prevailed among them.

20. I make no great distinction between the two; in the N.T. the *sun* ("with") words describe the deepest sort of involvement with others.

21. Cf. *Coping with Counseling Crises* for details on this.

never be handled properly (or turned into the blessing God intends it to be for His children) until rebellion disappears. Hot-tempered rebellion so clouds one's perception of a situation that he sees nothing but the negative aspects of it. Pain and suffering for every Christian can *always* be turned to a blessing when *used* (rather than resisted or complained about) as God's Word directs.

Taking our cue from I Corinthians 10:13, we note that it helps to observe how others faced (and properly used) trouble and pain. Take Paul, for instance. Under the most severe pressures (cf. II Cor. 4; 11: 23-28), he never blamed God for wrongdoing or injustice, though he suffered more for Christ's sake than many of us lumped together. This he could do because of his attitude toward suffering (cf. II Cor. 4; Acts 16:22, 23, 25). In writing to the Philippian church, he made it crystal clear that he regarded his sufferings and misery as part of God's providential work in the spread of the gospel. Consequently, he could look for and participate in what God was doing (he witnessed to the soldiers of the Praetorian guard, rejoiced that other brothers were boldly preaching, that he could testify before the emperor, Nero, etc.). Surely that sort of perspective on pain makes a difference in one's ability to suffer well (the word *suffer* means, literally, "to bear up under"). When Paul suffered, he thought, "The Lord is up to something." Then he would search out some of the opportunities opened by the suffering, get excited about them and become involved in them.

Counselors, then, must be theologically aware of the problem of evil, ready to handle it as God does (and as He directs) and seek to help counselees to do so too. When the counselor's theology is weak, floating toward a denial of pain or doubt about God's control over and use of pain, he will flounder. He will communicate his own perplexities and confusion to the counselee, who (certainly) needs nothing more to further cloud the issue or encourage him in his sinful rebellion. It is vital, therefore, for a counselor to be thoroughly committed to a biblical understanding of sin.[22] The greatest help a counselor can bring to a counselee is to convince him of the fact that behind all suffering there is a good God Who—for His own righteous purposes—has brought all this about. Having done so, he may then show him ways to enter into the blessings of suffering as Paul did.

---

22. And for the counselee to be brought to this understanding too. It takes theological understanding (perceived as such or not) to handle suffering.

CHAPTER TEN

COUNSELING AND HABIT
(The Doctrine of Man, Continued)

For years, theologians and exegetes have puzzled and argued over the sixth to eighth chapters of Romans. Numerous questions have been raised, among which is the meaning of the word *flesh,* which has a specialized use in this place.[1] While I do not have space to exegete those chapters in detail (I do hope to do so in another book sometime, however), I wish to try to contribute something (at least) to the discussion.

Other passages—Romans 12, Galatians 5, Colossians 3, Ephesians 4 —pertain to the question of flesh and habit in the sinner; Romans 6–8 must not be studied apart from them. In all of these places, Paul considers the problem of sinful habits (or behavior patterns) acquired by the response of our sinful natures to life situations, and the difficulties that

---

1. Unfortunately, the translators of the NIV had a proclivity for settling exegetical questions in their translations, thereby becoming interpreters rather than translators. Among the most serious blunders resulting from this practice was the decision to translate the Greek word *sarx* ("flesh") by the theologically prejudicial phrase, "sinful nature." This is unfortunate, I say, because this obvious interpretive bias is *wrong.* The specialized use of the word flesh refers neither to man's sinful *nature* (i.e., the corrupt nature with which he was born) nor to the sinful *self* (or personality) that he developed (as some others think), but to the sinful *body* (as Paul calls it in Rom. 6:6). When Paul speaks of the body as sinful, he does not conceive of the body as originally created by God as sinful (as if he were a Gnostic), but rather of the body plunged into sinful practices and habits as the result of Adam's fall. There is no ultimate mind/body (flesh) dualism here, but only a tension in believers occasioned by the regeneration of the inner man and the indwelling of the Spirit in a body habituated to do evil. This leads to an inner/outer struggle. This warfare increasingly is won by the Spirit, Who renews and activates the inner man, who helps the body to put off sinful patterns and to put on new biblical responses. Bodily members are to be yielded less and less to sin and more and more to God (Rom. 6:13, 16, 19). This is possible because Christ has given life not only to the believer's soul (inner man), but also to his body (Rom. 7:24; 8:10, 11).

160

these raise for regenerate persons who seek to serve God. We are not now concerned with the task of overcoming these patterns (that falls under the heading of sanctification), but, rather, are anxious merely to recognize this problem as one of the significant consequences of original sin. Sinners, perverted from birth, will begin to develop sinful response patterns from the beginning of their lives (they cannot do otherwise before regeneration). Because of the great importance of habit in our daily lives, these patterns set up formidable barriers to growth in Christian living, with which counselees struggle, and with which counselors must deal. It is, therefore, of great importance for counselors to understand the biblical teaching concerning habit and what must be done about it. Unfortunately, systematic theology books rarely treat the subject.

That habit plays a large part in our every day living, and that the Scripture writers frequently speak about habit, are facts that careful investigation of their writings will confirm.[2] The effects of sin upon the human capacity for doing things by habit, therefore, is a significant issue for Christian counselors.

Habit—the capacity to learn to respond unconsciously, automatically and comfortably—is a great blessing of God that has been misused by sinners. Habit enables human beings to act without conscious decision in a variety of circumstances, so that they may put their minds to other matters instead of focusing upon hundreds of humdrum minutiae (tying shoe laces, buttoning shirts, etc., etc., etc.). But minute habitual acts tie together into patterns too (driving an automobile—foot, hand, eye, arm movements, etc., combine to form a behavior pattern called driving). These patterns are of larger scope. Yet, many Christians go through their lives never hearing a sermon on the problem of sinful habits and what to do about them.

Just how important is habit in our daily activities? Suppose that the capacity to act and react by habit were suddenly withdrawn for an entire day; think how that eventually would debilitate you. You awaken in the morning and lie there thinking, "Well, what do I do now?" After considerable thought, you decide, "I'll open my eyes." But then you are stuck with the question, "Which eye first—or shall I open both at

---

2. Cf. such additional passages as I Cor. 8:7; Heb. 5:13, 14; 10:25; Eph. 4:22; I Pet. 1:18; II Pet. 2:14; etc.

once?" Having hurdled that obstacle, you turn your attention to greater things: "What next?" You philosophize, and determine at length to get out of bed—"but how?" Finally, you conclude, "I'll throw over a leg." But *"which* leg?" and "over which side of the bed?" On and on it goes. Can you imagine the difficulties that lie ahead? You will have to think *consciously* (as though doing it for the very first time) about *how* to button a shirt, zip a zipper (without catching material in it), tie a shoelace, unscrew a toothpaste tube cap, squeeze the toothpaste out on a brush, use the brush effectually, and on . . . and on . . . and on—all just as you did the very first time! Awkwardly, deliberately, consciously (not comfortably, automatically and unconsciously, as habit now allows you to do) you must labor over each act. What a burden! Why, you'd be doing well to get to breakfast at midnight! No, there can be no question about it—habit is a vital part of everyday living!

Strange, it would seem, then, if the Bible (like so many preachers and theologians—not to mention counselors) ignored so large and important segment of our living. It doesn't; it is only Christian interpreters, bound by exegeticallly incorrect opinions who have done so. It is about time for the truth to be revealed, and the forceful impact of the Scriptures on this all-important matter disclosed. Understanding of biblical teaching about habit is essential for every Christian counselor.[3]

It is bad habit (the result of patterns stemming from the responses of one's sinful nature) that keeps some Christians from the fellowship of God's people (Heb. 10:25: "We must not abandon our practice of meeting together as some are in the habit of doing"). Sinners "train" —so as to habituate—their hearts in greed, according to II Peter 2:14. "Mature" Christians are "those whose faculties have been trained by practice to distinguish good from evil," says the writer of Hebrews (Heb. 5:14). Clearly, then, the Holy Spirit by His Word trains "in righteousness" (II Tim. 3:16) so that new practices are habituated in the place of the old ones. Habit capacity itself (like a computer) is

---

3. How to handle habit problems has been discussed thoroughly in two of my books: *Lectures on Counseling*, pp. 231ff., and *The Manual*, chaps. 17-19, pp. 161-216. Later, I shall quote from some of this material. But here I merely mention the fact that much of the data on this *crucial* issue will be omitted from the present volume *only because I have handled it in full elsewhere.* One aspect of of the question, "Radical Amputation," not dealt with elsewhere also will be discussed under the subject of "Sanctification."

neutral—you get out of it the results of what you feed into it.

Bad "behavior patterns" are "passed down" (by precept and example) from previous generations, according to I Peter 1:18 (". . . the useless behavior patterns that were passed down from your forefathers . . ."), and until Christ frees one from them, persons caught up in this process will continue to practice them and pass them on to their children.[4] When Christ saves someone, however, He makes it "possible to live the remainder" of his life "no longer following human desires, but following the will of God" (I Pet. 4:2). Many of these desires are the desires of the flesh—i.e., those things that the body "wants" to do because it has been programmed to do them automatically, unconsciously and with ease.

Sinful habits, formed in the old life, as unbelievers, are carried over into the new life, causing difficulty for everyone involved. Habits, the Bible says, are not easy to alter; Jeremiah asks, "Can the Ethiopian change his skin or the leopard his spots?" And then says, "Neither can you who are *accustomed* to do evil" (Jer. 13:23; cf. also 22:21).[5] Paul, commenting on the problem that habit posed for the Corinthians, wrote: "There are some who, out of habit formed in idolatry, still eat food as if it were offered to an idol, and because their conscience is weak, they are defiled" (I Cor. 8:7).[6] To mention one last fact (not that more could not be said), consider this sobering thought: even after good habits have been developed by Christians, if they are subjected to continued abuse by the practice of contrary behavior (especially as it is modeled by evil associates) these good habits can be lost. Paul warns, "Don't be misled, bad companions corrupt good habits" (I Cor. 15:33). Clearly, the place of habit in Christian thought and life is significant, and the Scriptures recognize this fact.

Nevertheless, as I have said, few (if any) recent theologians have discussed the relationship of habit to behavior. Their efforts have been expended on important questions having to do with Adam's sin, the

---

4. Counselors can look for similarities in behavior among persons from various generations.

5. See the *Manual*, p. 171, for more on the proper interpretation of this verse. Jeremiah's assertion is not intended to lead to despair. He is speaking to unrepentant (probably unregenerate) persons who (apart from God's grace) are unable to effect significant changes in habit.

6. The relationship of habit to conscience is an interesting study that I hope to consider in detail at some later point.

effects of sin upon the nature of his descendants and the process by which sin has been transmitted to his posterity. These are all vital questions, as I have noted in an earlier chapter. But so is the matter of habit—especially for counseling.

I shall leave the matter here (reluctantly), contenting myself with merely raising the problem, and referring the reader (once again) to my fuller treatments of the subject (as discussed in Rom. 6-8, Gal. 5, Eph. 4 and Col. 3) in *Lectures* and in the *Manual* (see footnote *supra*).

CHAPTER ELEVEN

HOW SIN AFFECTS THINKING

Total depravity (we have said) means not that a person is as bad as he might be (God's common grace restrains sinners from fully manifesting their sinful potential), but, rather, that in every aspect every person is affected by sin. That means (of course) that, among other things, his thought processes have been affected. At every point in the process of thought, breakdowns may—and do—occur. Because of Adam's sin—and their own—human beings do not think straight! That is an altogether important fact for the counselor to keep in view.

In speaking of the effects of sin, Paul put it this way:

> . . . because although people knew God, they didn't glorify Him as God or thank Him. Instead they became involved in futile speculations and their senseless hearts were darkened. Claiming that they were wise, they became fools . . . just as they disapproved of retaining God in their knowledge, so God handed them over to a disapproved mind. . . .[1]

These truths have great consequences for counseling. I shall mention one or two basic ways in which this is so.

The noetic effects of sin[2] upon daily living are quite varied. They creep into all areas of Christian living—the home, work, the church, prayer, etc. Constantly, in the Scriptures, we discover God correcting the results of sinful human thinking. The problem is so serious that He sets it forth in the sharpest terms of contrast[3] when He reminds us, "My thoughts are not your thoughts, neither are my ways your ways."[4]

---

1. Rom. 1:21, 22, 28 (note the way in which heart, knowledge and mind are used as synonyms).
2. *Noetic* means the effects of sin upon thought and thinking.
3. As does Paul in the above quotation: "Claiming that they were wise, they became fools."
4. Isa. 55:8. Note the parallelism between thinking and doing—"My thoughts . . . your thoughts" are chiastically paralleled with "Your ways . . . My ways." Later in this chapter I shall point up the biblical identification of learning with doing.

Again and again, in the Scriptures, we are confronted with the fact that sinful human thought reverses God's thought. And again and again, in counseling, Christian counselors struggle with this fact as it has destroyed the lives of counselees. Role *reversals* in marriage provide one clear instance of this (not to speak of the campaigning done by ERA proponents). To tell counselees, for example, that it is the *husband* who is responsible for love in the home, that it is *he* who is commanded to love, *normally* comes as a shock to all parties involved. If they have ever articulated their views at all—at least if you were to describe how they function in the marriage—in *most* cases, they (you) would have to say that they operate on thinking exactly opposite to that principle. To say that the (world's) idea that each partner ought to try to be fulfilled in marriage, and has a right to complain when he doesn't get what he wants in sex (to cite one area) and to demand those rights is totally wrong, similarly brings astonished responses. The biblical notion that one enters marriage in order to *give* the pleasures and joys of companionship to another (not to *get* what he can out of it), and that in sex his function is to fulfil his wife's needs, is totally foreign to most counselees. They must be *told* that it is "more blessed to give than to receive"; they neither believe this nor act upon it in many instances. And even when told so, often express grave reservations and doubts that are resolved (in many cases) only when, in obedience, they act upon the principle.

Human sinful thought has so perverted biblical values that an entire system of such value-reversal could be developed and seriously entertained as an option by many. Nietzsche, in fact, taught this explicitly.[5] But greed, self-assertiveness, looking out for "number one," etc., flourish even among counseling systems. Most of the appeal of counseling is hedonistic—"We can show you the way to happy, fulfilled, self-actualized living." It is grounded on selfishness, desire for power, wealth, etc., rather than on the desire to live in a way that pleases God.[6] This hedonism is directly opposed to the Christian emphasis to "seek first . . ." and to "lose your life." Indeed, these biblical statements seem epigrammatic only be-

---

5. Intellectuals (those who claim to be wise) still frequently cite him approvingly.

6. See many warnings to Christian counselors not to fall into the same trap in their appeals to counselees. Change must be desired as a way of pleasing God before it can be biblical change (cf. *Manual*, pp. 276f.; see my series of pamphlets— *What Do You Do When . . .*).

cause they are in such direct contrast to the usual thinking of society. Truly, then, the counselor, with Paul, must see himself engaged in an intellectual-moral battle. I say intellectual-*moral* because (as I shall explain later) it is not merely the "battle for the mind" (Sargent), but it is a battle in which the *whole* man is at stake. With Paul, he must ". . . tear down arguments and every high barrier that is raised against the knowledge of God [in order to] take every thought captive and bring it into *obedience* to Christ."[7]

Discovering the existence of the effects of sin on the understanding should give no counselor an occasion for surprise. No man thinks perfectly; Jesus Christ is the only One Who never made a mistake. This universality of error (not to speak of other sinful forms of thinking) has been captured well by the Peanuts cartoon in which Lucy says, "I've never made a mistake; I thought I did once, but I was wrong."

But the universality of error in thinking (everyone has used the eraser on his pencil—for some, the erasers wear out before the pencil!) is only a part of the effects of sin upon the inner man that Paul calls the "darkening" of the "heart" (elsewhere he speaks of "meaningless ways of thinking" in which men's "understanding is darkened,"[8] equating heart with understanding in these contexts). This "ignorance that is in them, resulting from the hardness of their hearts"[9] toward God and His Word, is not only error, but consists of rebellious plans and purposes, sinful scheming, lewd imaginations of the heart and the like. All this is said to stem from the heart (which is closely identified with the processes of thinking, planning, deciding, etc., as we have seen in an earlier chapter). It is "from the heart" that "evil thoughts" (not merely *erroneous* thoughts) proceed (Matt. 15:19).

Error in judgment (leading to error in action) at times may result from physical impairment. This dimension of the problems deepens our understanding of sin's effects, and must make us cautious in our approach to counseling and careful in our evaluations. Electro-chemical dysfunctions in the body—for instance—caused by organic failure (as a consequence of Adam's sin, but *not* the result of specific sins on the part of the individual in error) may lead to faulty perception. Such dysfunction may affect any one of, any combination of, or all of the perceptual gates—depth, sight, sound, taste, touch, smell. Error, in

---

7. II Cor. 10:5.   8. Eph. 4:17, 18.   9. Eph. 4:18.

such cases, is neither the result of wilful misreading or misleading; nor does it stem from sinful patterns of life.

On the other hand, one must deal with perceptual problems as well as any other physical impairments, righteously, not sinfully. And, to further complicate matters, error related to perception may (indeed) be the result of deliberate deception, or sinful practices, attitudes, beliefs that produce it. As a matter of fact the *very same* erroneous statements, "You have been frowning at me" (when you haven't), "I heard that voice telling me to do it" (when there was no voice), may be made because one wishes to deceive (e.g., statement one might be made to shift blame; statement two might be a lie designed to camouflage other sinful activtities) or because he has been deceived (by his own erroneous perceptions,

(1) as the result of sinful sleep loss, ingestion of drugs, etc., leading to faulty visual perception or hallucinations;

(2) as the result of bodily malfunctioning leading to faulty visual perception or hallucinations;

(3) as the result of erroneous doctrine, and failure to study the Scriptures adequately, leading to a strong desire for direct revelatory experiences, etc.

It is imperative, therefore, for the counselor (in each case) to discover precisely what is happening. The matter is complex; there may be multiple possible causes for the same effect; or multiple-combined causes for it! Error, then, is always the result of sin (Adam's sin), but not always, in addition, the consequence of actual sin by the one in error. The matter is not simple.

When a counselee *adopts* erroneous explanations of life or teachings, he is always responsible for doing so. At this point he may never be excused. And, furthermore, this error always plays some role (often the primary one) in his problems. False teaching and erroneous views of God's world (in whatever form) come ultimately from Satan—"the father [originator] of lies." Error (from the beginning) has always been a part of his counsel. As such, we are held responsible for rejecting it. But if, instead of rejecting error, the counselee accepts it, he is held guilty of, "two evils," not only of ignoring God's counsel, but also of "hewing out cisterns that can't hold water" (Jer. 2:13). The course that counselors must pursue, in such instances, is to call him to repentance (a change of *thinking*) for his arrogance against God and for believing and living lies. Positively, they must present God's truth and call him to believe and walk according to it.

Because it is obvious that all responsible behavior has a cognitive side, in my books I have not usually distinguished explicitly between changing one's thinking and altering his actions (the Bible doesn't draw sharp lines here either). For this reason some (wrongly) have concluded that nouthetic counseling is concerned with action alone (to the exclusion of concern about thought and belief). Such a reading of my writings is due either

    (1) to superficial study and thought, or
    (2) to such a strong bias by the reviewer that it blinds him to the obvious.

While I might (with some plausibility) be charged with lack of explicitness,[10] by no stretch of the imagination could one establish before an impartial judge the idea that I have not been concerned about teaching biblical truth to counselees.

Throughout my books, in any number of ways, I insist that the counselor must teach the counselee the ways God intends him to go. Indeed, others find my intense concern with teaching the Bible in counseling their chief complaint. From the beginning—in *Competent to Counsel*—I have said such things as one should use "authoritative instruction" in counseling (pp. 54, 55, etc.), he should teach through modeling (pp. 177ff., cf. also the *Manual*, pp. 335ff.), he must be aware of and freely utilize the "directive" teachings of the book of Proverbs and other Scriptures (pp. 97ff.), etc. I even suggest the use of turnover charts, etc., to use with such instruction. The *Manual* is filled with information about teaching, and volume II of *Shepherding God's Flock* has an entire chapter devoted to the subject, entitled "Instruction in Counseling."[11] In that chapter, I said such things as

> Because scriptural counseling is directive, and *counsel consists in large measure of giving information and advice,* by the very nature of the case, *teaching must be involved* [p. 121] . . . instruction in Christian living . . . must be conceived of as consisting of more than theoretical learning, acquired by attending courses. Much learning

---

10. But the same charge might be levelled against the biblical writers. Yet, it seems to me that the use of teaching is quite adequately taught.

11. I shall say nothing of the more than a dozen other volumes that also propagate such ideas.

comes only through discipleship,[12] which involves observation, participation, discussion and critique [p. 123]. . . . Often in an early session, repentance, forgiveness, reconciliation and such concepts will need to be explained [p. 127] . . . until the biblical instruction has been given in an applicatory manner, the [teaching] task is incomplete. Until he and the counselee have understood not only what the Bible means, but also what it means in terms of the counselee's situation . . . the counselor's instruction is inadequate [p. 127]. . . . frequently the instruction is stimulated by and grows out of the experience itself [p. 128]. . . . Give full instruction about what to do to avoid future failure [p. 129]. . . . Give full instruction about how to recoup in case of future failure [p. 129]. . . . The good news (gospel) is not a non-cognitive message, but contains factual historical elements. . . . To present the gospel is to give instruction [p. 130].

Patently, then, the charge that nouthetic counseling cares little about cognitive matters is absurd (indeed, it is seriously misleading). It is questionable whether any other system of counseling, purporting to be biblical, has (1) ever attempted to consider the various dimensions of such instruction as thoroughly, or (2) enjoined teaching so forcefully and insistently.

But why would such charges be made? One answer to this question leads into a very important issue. Because biblical counselors do not always begin with didactic instruction (but often let such instruction grow out of experience resulting from obedience to Christ's commands—as Christ did when instructing His disciples and various counselees), those who narrowly think of instruction purely in Greek academic (and abstract classroom) terms fail to recognize that in the Bible whole persons teach whole persons, acting as whole persons. They do not merely pack (or re-pack) heads. Biblical teaching and instruction is done fundamentally in life situational (cf. Deut. 6:4-9; 11:18-21) and discipleship milieus. In life situations, the teaching of truth grows out of the problems of living; in discipleship, truth is incarnated in life. The biblical construct—continually emphasized by numerous writers—is *walking* in the truth (i.e., relating and incorporating truth into life). Discipleship means "following" and "coming after" and being "with" Christ (Mark 8:34; 3:14). This involves *showing* as well as *telling*. At its core, biblical teaching is *learning through obedience* (cf. John 8:31; 13:13-17; 15:7, 8).

---

12. A subject to which I have devoted much space from *Competent to Counsel* on.

Because they have seen an emphasis upon obedience to Christ's Word in nouthetic counseling literature, they have caricatured this as non-cognitive, not recognizing that this often betrays their own scholastic, Greek approach to teaching, and failing to realize that the simple, elementary truth that in order to obey, one must be instructed in biblical truth, holds for counseling as well as other ordinary life circumstances. But the other, more subtle, yet crucial, point that they miss, is that in order to be fully instructed one must obey! Learning depends upon obedience.[13]

Some, with little biblical understanding about teaching, naively accept the pagan Greek *academic* model of teaching in counseling. They think that all that is needed is to tell people the truth, that they will accept and follow it. Biblical counselors know otherwise. Sometime ago I wrote,

> But before going further, let me warn the reader about one vital fact: the solution to the problems that counselees have is not *merely* educational. That means, for instance, that Fuller Torry's view that counseling should be *equated* with education is false. His substitution of the educational model for the medical model will not do. Because counseling involves teaching, the counselor must not conclude that all the counselee needs is the missing pieces to his puzzle, or that re-education and/or retraining will solve his problems. Nor must he see education (even in scriptural truth) alone as the sum of counseling. Counseling involves more—much more—than instruction; just as preaching involves more. Counselees are sinners who do not always automatically do whatever God wants them to do upon learning the truth. Often they don't (for various reasons) or won't. In addition, there must be reproof, correction, persuasion, encouragement, or whatever the situation requires. . . . And, of greatest importance, is the fact that the teaching must be done by the power of the Holy Spirit working through the various scriptural modes that the counselor employs.[14]

Education (of the purely cognitive sort[15]) is inadequate. God educates for *life*. True education, every counselor must understand, has to do with repentance, faith and obedience. Apart from these elements, education that is productive for problem solving does not take place.

---

13. Cf. John 7:17, "If anybody wants to do His will, he will know about the teaching." The *wanting*, here, means not merely desiring but willingness that leads to faith and obedience; it is genuine, life-affecting concern.

14. *Shepherding God's Flock*, vol. II, pp. 121-122.

15. In true biblical education the *whole* man—including his muscles—is educated.

That is why nouthetic counselors—in the spirit of the Scriptures—do not (like Albert Ellis, for instance) attempt to change people merely by attacking their beliefs and substituting new ones. They do not assume that new thinking will lead to new living. While they do attack falsehood, teach the facts about new biblical ways, and call counselees to faithful obedience to them (who has spent more time doing so?), nouthetic counselors at the same time also grapple with the problems that stand in the way of belief and/or action. Rather than separate teaching from obedience (because the Bible warns against doing so—cf. James 2:14ff.), as some counseling theorists seem to do, nouthetic counselors combine the two.

To put it another way—biblical counseling takes seriously the effects of sin on the thought and decision-making processes. Thinking and obedience are really inseparable. To know truth is not a neutral, "intellectual" matter (as many assume) but a moral fact demanding decisions and commitments about life. John 8:32 follows John 8:31: Knowing the freedom that truth brings is the result of knowing and obeying the Word of the One Who, Himself, is the Truth.

Biblical counselors, therefore, recognize that understanding is often (if not always) selective—based upon sinful bias. They know that far too frequently counselees *won't hear* what they are told, will *distort* what is said,[16] and they know that they won't always *do* God's will even when they *do* understand it. They take into consideration, therefore, the need to call counselees to obedience to Christ, not merely to instruct them in the ways and means of obedience.

There is much more that could be considered in this chapter (e.g., how sin has affected the human language with which we think and communicate in both its structure and uses—and, therefore, in its influence on life), but for now we must be content to point out the necessity for counselors to take into consideration, at all times, that the thinking of counselees has been affected by sin. Therefore, unlike the optimistic liberals of another day, who thought they could save the world through education,[17] the biblical counselor entertains no illusions. Yet, in the full face of the realities of human sin and error, he has hope for his counselees because they do not have to depend upon their own sinful

---

16. Cf. my article on this problem in *Update on Christian Counseling*, vol. 1.
17. It is about time for the pendulum to swing round to this error once more.

wits (or the counselor's) for change; the Word and the Spirit provide all that is necessary to renew the mind (Rom. 12:1, 2[18]) and enable them to understand, believe and obey. Thus, at once, the Christian's view of the matter is more realistic and more hopeful.

---

18. But notice that the renewal of the mind here, and in Eph. 4:23, is inseparably coupled to changed living.

CHAPTER TWELVE

MORE THAN REDEMPTION: THE DOCTRINE OF SALVATION

From eternity, God planned human salvation, choosing His people in Christ "from the foundation of the world" (Eph. 1:4). Jesus Christ, God's slain Lamb, died for "those whose names have been written" in His "scroll of life from the foundation of the world" (Rev. 13:8; 17:8). Peter says, "He was foreknown, indeed, before the foundation of a world" to be the Savior whose "valuable blood" would be "shed like the blood of a spotless and unblemished lamb" (I Pet. 1:19, 20). And it was for the benefit of the very same persons that God prepared eternal blessings through His Son "from the foundation of the world"[1] (Matt. 25:24). Clearly, then, salvation was no afterthought; it was not a last-ditch attempt by God to repair a world that had gone wrong. Instead, salvation is God's way of raising man higher than at creation (we shall look at this in some depth later in the chapter); He planned man's redemption from the beginning ("from the foundation of the [or a] world").

One must not picture God frustrated over sin, sitting in the heavens wringing His hands, wondering how He might make the best of a bad situation, suddenly striking upon the idea of sending His Son to die for guilty sinners. No, exactly not that—if it has any meaning at all, the phrase, "from the foundation of the world" has exactly the opposite import: salvation was in the picture from the beginning. All along, God intended to demonstrate His love through sending Christ. Whatever

---

1. The expression, "foundation of the world" (or of a world) presumably means from the creation or beginning of the world or universe (cf. Luke 11:50; Heb. 9:26, where no other meaning makes sense). The oft-repeated phrase probably may be equated with our "since the world began." It is plain from this that Christ's claim that the Father had loved Him *before* the foundation of the [a] world" (John 17:24) is a claim to deity. Jesus affirms existence prior to creation.

else he sees in salvation, it is important, therefore, for the counselor to recognize salvation as a part of the *eternal* purpose of God, Who determined that His Son should die. This determination was made not *after* sin came into the world, but before the world's foundation—before there was a man to sin or a world in which he would sin.

Many questions are generated over this realization, but there is one point I wish to make right off—through this salvation God planned to bring about *more* than through creation, which also means more than redemption. By this route He determined to elevate man *above* the state in which he was created. As we shall have occasion to observe later, this fact is all-important to the counselor's stance toward his counselee and his problems. And, speaking of problems, in passing let me suggest that the whole problem of evil (as it has been called by philosophers) takes on a different hue and perspective in the light of this eternal dimension—there is a plan behind history, and it involves God's glory through grace to man. History is not haphazard; in it God is doing something for the human race. The purpose of this grace is to lift man far beyond his original state.

What God the Father planned from eternity, Christ His incarnate Son accomplished in space and time—in human history. Redemption was not suprahistorical, but an event of this world's history (so much a part of it, indeed, that it set our calendars for us!). Jesus Christ, Who was God manifest in the flesh (note, *flesh* means body), accomplished God's purposes. He Himself said, "I came down from heaven not to do what I want, but to do what the One Who sent Me wants" (John 6:38). And what was it that the Father wanted Him to do? Listen to the next verse: ". . . here is what the One Who sent Me wants: that I lose none of all those He gave Me, but that I shall resurrect them on the last day" (John 6:39). God purposed, through redemption, to form a people who (like Jesus) were resurrected from the dead. That He accomplished His purpose, He Himself maintained in prayer: "I glorified You on the earth by completing the work that You gave Me to do" (John 17:4). Christ's death was no tragic, abortive termination to God's plans, but the very climax of them. So, when Jesus cried out, "It is finished" (John 19:30), those words were neither a sigh of relief nor a groan of despair—they were a shout of victory. He was saying, "I've done it! I have defeated the enemy; I have redeemed God's own!"

The Christian counselor, therefore, sees all of prophetic history from

Genesis 3:15 on—the whole sacrificial system in which thousands of animals were slain, all the types and figures of the O.T. period, etc.—not as some sort of human groping by Israel after the true God and the proper way to worship Him, but (rather) as an essential part of God's design in "leading many sons to glory" (Heb. 2:10). He Who was the "Leader of their salvation" did all that God's program required to assure their safe arrival.

That God's purpose included an eternal, divine program, and not merely the ultimate ends of salvation, is clear from the details of prophecy (*when* and *where* Christ would be born, minister and die, specifically *what* He would do and what would happen to Him, etc.) that were given in the O.T. Scriptures. Moreover, He continually spoke about that program: "My hour hasn't yet come" (John 2:4; cf. 7:30), "the hour has come" (John 12:23), "this hour" (John 12:27), "My time is not yet at hand" (John 7:6), etc. And it must never be forgotten that Christ came "in the fulness of time"—i.e., right on schedule (Gal. 4:4).[2] Salvation was no haphazard, makeshift, do-the-best-you-can-with-a-bad-situation affair, as some think. Instead, salvation was a carefully thought-through, well-planned and precisely executed program.

But the program for man's salvation was not merely planned and executed by God the Father and God the Son, it is also activated in each individual life by God the Holy Spirit. We must recognize that sinners, "dead in trespasses and sins" (Eph. 2:1), can never genuinely say, " 'Jesus is Lord,' except by the Holy Spirit" (I Cor. 12:3). In fact, they cannot even "welcome" or "know" (i.e., savingly believe or understand) the message of salvation apart from the new life that the Spirit gives. That is because the gospel "must be investigated spiritually" (I Cor. 2:14). That is to say, only those who have the Spirit of Christ at work in them can explore Christ's claims in such a way that they will repent and believe the gospel. Father, Son and Spirit, then, all participate in man's salvation. Salvation was designed by the Father, effectuated by the Son and applied by the Spirit. Salvation is a trinitarian work.

Now there are many other ways to view and discuss salvation. For instance, we might speak about the three tenses of salvation:

---

2. For more on scheduling, cf. *The Manual,* pp. 338ff., where I have also commented on the necessity for helping counselees to plan and schedule as God does.

PAST: We have been saved from the penalty of sin (justification).
PRESENT: We are being saved from the power of sin (sanctification).
FUTURE: We shall be saved from the presence of sin (glorification).

Or, it is possible to divide salvation into its divine side (what God does —atonement, regeneration, etc.) and its human side (what God's Spirit enables us to do—repent, believe, etc.). Or, we also might think of the objective elements in salvation (the atonement, justification, etc.) and the subjective ones (regeneration, faith, etc.).

I mention the three formulations above not because they exhaust the possibilities, but because I want to make it as clear as a storm-swept sky that since it is the central message and concern of the Scriptures, there is much to be said about God's redemption of man. Salvation is multidimensional; it may be approached from any one (or any combination) of its facets. (The three approaches noted are but illustrative of this fact.) So, then, all that might be said, won't be said here!

How, then, shall we approach the Bible's teaching about salvation in its relationships to counseling? To begin with, it is important to restate the fact that salvation is what makes Christian counseling possible; it is the foundation (or basis) for all counseling. This is the positive side of the coin mentioned earlier about the impossibility of counseling unbelievers.[3] When doing true counseling—i.e., working with saved persons to enable them to make changes, at a level of depth that pleases God—it is possible to solve any true counseling problem (i.e., any problem involving love for God and one's neighbor). Such assurance stems from the fact that all the resources necessary for change are available in the Word and by the Spirit.

No counseling system that is based on some other foundation can begin to offer what Christian counseling offers. How tragic, then, to see Christians giving out counsel based on other foundations composed of purely human ideas and resources. They offer little hope and have no good reason to believe that they will succeed; yet (sadly) many Christians lap up (and follow) such advice.

For several reasons, the hope that Christian counselors offer is unlike hope given by others. First, this hope is based on the unfailing promises

---

3. See also Appendix A.

of God that He has recorded in the Scriptures. That makes all the difference. How different from basing one's hope on—let us say—Freud!

Secondly, every command in the Scriptures implies hope: God never
tells His children to do anything that He fails to supply both the directions and the power to achieve. In II Peter 1:3 we read: "His divine
power has given us everything for life and godliness." We have all we
need to please God in the Bible and by the indwelling Spirit of holiness
(i.e, the Spirit Who through biblical direction and requisite strengthening
produces holiness). This fact of

Command + provision = potential for change

is hope-inspiring.[4]

Command	+ Provision	= Potential for change
Don't worry	1. Directions: Matt. 6; Phil. 4 2. Strength: Phil. 4	Work rather than worry

Thirdly, God Himself is the Counselor Who guides and directs
through His Word. The Christian counselor is not alone; for wisdom,
principles, etc., he depends not on his own strength, but on the written,
revealed will of God. Indeed, if a counselee doubts the truth of what
the Christian counselor advises, he may (1) ask him to show him
clearly the scriptural basis for the advice (at some point the counselor
should do this—unsolicited—anyway), or (2) check out the scriptural
teaching for himself (this is his obligation anyway, since it pleases
God—Acts 17:11). Since there is a divinely revealed source of information equally available to both counselor and counselee, (1) the counselee
ultimately isn't dependent upon the counselor, and (2) he can monitor
and evaluate the direction of counseling by following along in the Bible.
Counseling that doesn't carry conviction that it is biblical is deficient
(even when its thrust *is actually quite biblical*); the counselee must be
convinced that his decisions and actions are pleasing to God. It is not
proper for him to view them merely as expedient.

Genuine Christian counselors not only accept the counselee's interest
in checking out everything biblically, but (like Paul) *encourage* it.[5]

---

4. Counselors, at times, will find it helpful to write out this formula for their
counselees, together with particulars of the case:
5. Of course, some counselees misuse this privilege. One example is the "professional counselee" (cf. *Manual*, pp. 298ff.).

When a Christian counselee sees for himself that his counselor adheres closely to biblical principle, this too brings hope. This hope grows out of the fact that Jehovah is a covenant-keeping God Whose promises are dependable. He is also a God Who cares for the people whom He has saved and made His own (the covenant slogan appears in several forms but always includes the essential elements: "Your God . . . My people"). In other words, hope, in Christian counseling, is the direct result of one's salvation.[6]

Throughout earlier chapters, from time to time I have referred to the title of this volume—*More Than Redemption*—promising to explain it at length. It is here at last that I must fulfil my promise.

The facts to which that vital theme points provide the clearest view of the Christian counselor's stance in counseling. This is true especially in relationship to the hope that grows out of salvation, about which I have been speaking. And, the hope to which I refer is not pie-in-the-sky-by-and-by (salvation does promise that, it is true), but a hope that also says, "You can start slicing right now!"

So far, I have mentioned three important reasons for genuine hope in Christian counseling. But there is one more that—as important as these three may be—excels them. In fact, it provides the basis for them, and for all other hope in counseling. In it lies the explanation of the Christian counselor's hope; it is the truth signaled in the title, *More Than Redemption*.

First, let us be crisply clear about what the Bible means by the word *hope*. That word signifies far more than our pale approximation of that meaning in modern Western society. To us *hope* means "hope-so" (as in the fisherman's response to the question, "Do you think you'll catch any?"). But in the Scriptures hope never has such uncertainty connected to it. Indeed, certainty is inherent in the idea. Think of reading Titus 2:13 in the modern sense, "the blessed hope-so!" No, *hope* means something sure, something certain, that just hasn't happened yet. The *blessed hope*, accordingly, is "the happy expectation" or "the joyous anticipation." When we are told that we are "saved with hope" (Rom. 8:24), the hope —of the resurrection, to which the passage refers—is an assured certainty. God has promised it. We await a hope (biblically) because of

---

6. Hope for the non-Christian also stems solely from the preaching of the gospel (cf. Appendix A).

the sure promises of God. When counseling by scriptural principles, we have all the hope that those written promises of God afford.

But what is the nature of the promise found in the title of the book? To what ought one to look forward in counseling? What sort of hope does he have? Can he be assured that all true counseling problems[7] may be solved? If so, how? And—to what extent? The answers to these questions are of the greatest importance in formulating what I have called the Christian Counselor's Stance.[8]

The stance of the Christian counselor is fundamentally asymmetrical; what he promises (and seeks to get the counselee to anticipate) is *always more than he ever* had *before*—a *better situation than ever existed in the past*. In some ways, a recognition and utilization of this fact in counseling is the greatest contribution that this volume can make; that is why the title strikes this note.

The Christian counselor must never attempt to patch up what has fallen apart in his life, marriage, etc. Nor does he even offer a salvation like that of the Jehovah's Witnesses, who say that in Christ we have been returned to the state that Adam lost. The Christian counselor does not believe, *strictly* speaking, in mere renewal, or restoration or redemption (of what was lost); biblically, he believes in *more* than redemption. As a platform, upon which he develops his stance, he looks to a verse like Romans 8:20b:

But where sin abounded, grace far more abounded.

In that verse, Paul makes it plain that what Jesus Christ obtained for His people (by both His active and passive obedience[9]) was *more* than they lost in Adam's sin and the fall of the human race. Sin and its effects are great (misery, death, etc.)—and no biblical counselor *ever* minimizes the abounding nature of sin—instead of minimizing sin and its effects, he maximizes Christ and His redemptive work. Grace cannot be compared with sin—it (grace) "far more abounded."

Grace (and its effects) is greater than sin and its effects. Therefore, what Jesus Christ obtained for His people in salvation is not merely what Satan took away from Adam. Through His death and resurrection,

---

7. I.e., problems in loving God and neighbor.
8. And, subsequently, the counselee's stance as well as it is communicated by the counselor.
9. Both keeping the law for us and paying the penalty for our violation of it

Christ bought that—and *much more*. Thus to be true to the New Testament teaching, the counselor's stance must be based on the great truth that Christ offers counselees *more* than they ever had before.

Look at how this works. Adam was created "a little lower than the angels." By his sin, he plunged himself and all his posterity (Christ excepted) into the depths of further sin and its associated miseries far lower still. In the diagram (below) this is pictured clearly:

Angels

Man in Adam (at creation)

Man in Adam (after fall)

But in Christ, humanity has been raised (He had a human body and nature) far above principalities and powers (the very highest of the angels) into the heavenlies to sit at the right hand of God. A human being (Christ is that as well as divine) today sits in heaven! And, according to Colossians 3 and Revelation 2 and 3, this is what every believer can have fully some day in heaven and in part right now. This super-redemption is plainly indicated in the following diagram:

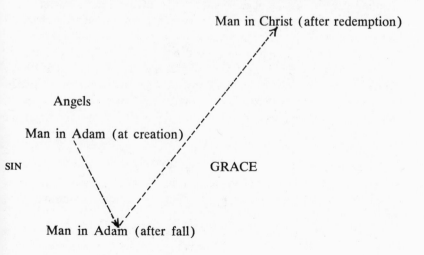

Man in Christ (after redemption)

Angels

Man in Adam (at creation)

SIN   GRACE

Man in Adam (after fall)

This diagram is not in the balanced, symmetrical shape of a V; rather, it is more like a check mark (✓)—all out of balance in favor of God's "far more" abounding grace. That is how Romans 5:20b describes the situation; what we now have in salvation far exceeds what we lost in sin.

Imagine you were a physician. A patient with a leg disability that has caused him to hobble from birth comes for treatment. He tells you that lately his problem has grown worse and that he can't walk at all, even with a hobble. Suppose all you could offer was to get him back on his feet, hobbling once more (as indeed it might be in medicine); is that all the Christian counselor has to offer? Is he in the business of getting counselees back to painful hobbling once more? No! Definitely no! What he has is comparable to offering a pain-free, hobble-free walk—something new, something better than the patient ever had before. Those who counsel in Christ's Name by grace have a stance superior to all others. We offer no one counseling that will merely help him to hobble; the hope of the Christian is that the counselee can run!

When counselees come with a marriage ripped to shreds, the Christian counselor doesn't merely offer to put the marriage back together again; he isn't interested in restoring the status quo that existed prior to the separation. No, as Christ had *more* in mind in His death than restoring the status quo, so does the biblical counselor. Such marriages—unlike the one in Eden—usually were begun wrong and never did go very well. That is why most counselees will tell you that they don't want to return to what they had before the marriage fell apart. To offer a return, therefore, is to offer no hope at all. And when they say, I don't want to go back to that," they are right. The Christian counselor alone has solid reason for believing that there can be a new (and *better*) future for that marriage in Christ; he has a theological reason—the doctrine of grace that I have referred to as more than redemption or as super-redemption. Christian counselors do not offer to do *repair* work. Because of grace, they always seek to turn crosses into crowns! So they say, "We aren't talking about going back to your former ways of living; what Christ can give you is a new marriage—a marriage that sings!" That is their stance; a stance of grace far more abounding!

Even though what Adam lost was perfect (although it wasn't yet complete), that wasn't enough for grace. Grace will settle for nothing less than the best. In Christ we shall obtain not only all that Adam had, but all that he might have had, but didn't. So too in Him, the counselees' hope is set on obtaining far more of what a Christian marriage should have been like than they have ever known before (it won't ever be perfect or complete in this life).

The counselor will explain his super-redemptive stance: "Even though it is sad that there has been so much unnecessary pain and misery and God's Name has been dishonored so greatly [notice, he doesn't minimize the effects of sin], let's thank God for bringing you to the place where that kind of marriage has come to an end. And let's thank Him that you are now ready for radical change, and that you aren't willing to go on as you did in the past any longer. He has put an end to your past way of life, not to send you back to it again, but to give you something brand new. And if you mean business with Jesus Christ, that's exactly what you can have—a marriage that sings!"

No matter what the problem is, no matter how greatly sin has abounded, the Christian counselor's stance is struck by the far-more-abounding nature of the grace of Jesus Christ in redemption. What a difference this makes in counseling! Thank God for this gracious implication of His many-faceted salvation!

CHAPTER THIRTEEN

FORGIVENESS IN COUNSELING
(The Doctrine of Salvation, Continued)

Man's greatest need is forgiveness. It is so easy for Christians to forget what it meant for them to come to Christ and be forgiven. But a lively sense of having been forgiven is essential to vital Christian devotion; without it, one easily leaves his "first love" (Rev. 2:4). And, without it, he will tend to lack the forgiving attitude toward others that is essential to proper Christian living and to dealing with many counseling difficulties. It is important, therefore, for counselors to learn all they can about forgiveness; and they must also spend time remembering their own forgiveness and reminding counselees about the pit from which they were dug.[1]

Christians are forgiven people—and should be thankful for it; that's what makes them unique. But this unique factor carries a responsibility with it: because they are forgiven, they must also become forgiving persons as Ephesians 4:32 says, "and be kind to one another, tenderhearted, forgiving each other just as God in Christ forgave you."

Within the Christian community, there should be much forgiveness going on all the time. The Christian home, the church and the counseling room are also prime areas for both seeking and granting Christian forgiveness. On all fronts, a Christian should be a forgiving person who never forgets how God forgave him. Counselors must realize the importance of this and work toward it in every counselee's life.

Matthew 18:23-35 is a graphic parable (to which we shall return later) that makes the Christian's *obligation* to forgive plain. We are indebted to God—not the debt that Christ paid for us but—to forgive others, sharing with them the joys of the same sort of forgiveness that we have experienced.

---

1. The Lord's Supper was designed for this very purpose. Clearly, the necessity for this memorial (reminder) demonstrates the propensity for sinners to forget.

Because it is so basic, there is a great emphasis on forgiveness in the Scriptures—not just Christ's forgiveness of us, but also our forgiveness of others (cf. Matt. 5—where forgiveness leading to reconciliation takes precedence over worship; Matt. 18—where church discipline is plugged into the willingness/unwillingness of brothers to forgive one another; Matthew 5—where our parental forgiveness is conditioned upon willingness to forgive, etc.).

Christian counselors need to learn the biblical teaching about forgiveness; they must know the subject thoroughly, traversing the entire field again and again until they are entirely familiar with it. They must be well acquainted with the exegetical, theological and practical sides of the issue. That is why I have decided to devote so much space to this subject at this point. I can think of no more important subject for counselors to understand fully.

The church is riddled with holes out of which power is leaking. Many of these holes are difficulties of all sorts in the realm of interpersonal relations. And most of those have never been plugged because of a failure to understand, teach and enforce the principles of Christian forgiveness. Counseling is a secondary activity designed to enable Christians to engage freely in primary activities. It helps people to begin to live as Christ wants them to live by freeing them from the obstacles that hinder them. Counseling is not an end in itself. It makes people fit for serving Christ in missions, evangelism, teaching, worship, etc. The subject, therefore, is quite pertinent for today. There is a great opportunity, during this time of world chaos, political and personal confusion, human unrest, to spread the gospel widely. There are personnel and funds available—we must not miss this opportunity, but enter into it fully, NOW. But the one thing that could most readily keep us from doing so is a church weakened by unresolved internal difficulties, looking inwardly, licking its own wounds. That is why an all-out effort in counseling is the strategy for the present hour. And, that is why forgiveness is so important a subject for counselors to study. A high majority of counseling cases, in one way or another, involve forgiveness.

Jack Winslow, head of a large British mental institution, declared, "I could dismiss half my patients tomorrow if they could be assured of forgiveness."[2] In my work in the mental institutions at Kankakee and

---

2. John Stott, *Confess Your Sins* (Philadelphia: Westminster, 1964), p. 73.

Galesburg, Illinois, during the summer of 1965, I found this statement corroborated by my own experience. When Karl Menninger wrote the book, *Whatever Became of Sin?*, he set forth an interesting thesis. He reported a significant change that had occurred over his long lifetime. Years ago, people talked about sin; they don't do so very much any more. It isn't that sin has lessened, of course. Rather, it has been re-labeled. What used to be understood as sin, now is called either crime or sickness. This change is significant because neither crime nor sickness can be forgiven. Crimes must be punished, sicknesses must be healed (or if that isn't possible, excused). As the result of this change, there are all sorts of people today who have sinned and need forgiveness, but (as he puts it) can't be forgiven. Menninger is right in this basic analysis, however wrong he may be in much else in the book (e.g., he thinks of sin only as wrongs against men; not against God!). There are many persons who know that something is wrong, something is missing, but they have been brainwashed into thinking it is something other than the need for forgiveness of sin. Until Christian counselors fearlessly tell them the truth—to call sin "sin" is the kindest approach possible—they will continue in their misery.

I propose, in what follows, first to investigate what the Bible says about forgiveness and then to show how God wants us to use biblical teaching in practical cases.

The Language of Forgiveness in the Scriptures

The Old Testament

There are two principal terms for forgiveness in the Old Testament with which every counselor must familiarize himself. The first is *salach*. This term is the basic one, and (therefore) the most important of the two. The fundamental idea in it is "to lighten by lifting." It becomes connected with forgiveness when it is used to describe God lightening a person's life by lifting the load of guilt from his shoulders. It is *always* used of God forgiving man (never man forgiving man) and is translated either "to forgive" or "to pardon." The word is translated in the LXX (Septuagint) by the Greek word, *aphiemi* (this word will be discussed below) but usually by *hileos eimi* or *hilaskomai,* "to be propitious to" (cf. Luke 18:13).

The term has connotations of restoration of an offender to divine favor. There is always some flavor of *atonement* that adheres to it. Frequently it is quite closely connected to atonement: cf. Leviticus 4:20, 26, 31, 35; 5:10, 14, 15, 18. Atonement, in these passages, leads to forgiveness. I shall return to that theme at a later point. Hebrews 9:22 provides the classic New Testament commentary: "without the shedding of blood, there is no forgiveness."

There are other sorts of references in which the word is used. To get the feel of *salach,* open your Bible to the following verses and follow the term through each reference. Some of these, you will discover, are very vital passages:

1. Numbers 14:19, 20 (interestingly, here even though sins are forgiven, consequences of sin follow; this question must be treated later).
2. Nehemiah 9:17
3. Psalm 103:3
4. Psalm 130:4. Here, notice, the opposite of forgiveness is keeping sin in mind. This is an important consideration, as we shall see presently.
5. Isaiah 55:7
6. Jeremiah 31:34. This critical passage is the one to which Christ refers when instituting the Lord's Supper. Forgiveness, here, as the synonymous parallelism indicates, means not remembering sins any more (cf. Ps. 130:4).

There are other passages to which we could turn, but these, doubtless, are sufficient to convey the richness and importance of this vital word.

The second term is *nasa.* It, too, is translated "to forgive" or "to pardon." The meaning is very close to *salach;* its special significance is "to take away by lifting up (or off)." While *salach* refers to the relief obtained from the lifting of the burden (of guilt), *nasa* focuses on *taking away* by lifting up. In other contexts, the word is used to speak of *lifting up* the eyes, head, face (Gen. 4:7), voice, heart or hand, of *carrying* a child, clothes, etc., of *bearing* fruit (as a tree), and of *suffering, enduring.* Of course, of importance to us is the idea of bearing *away* (or carrying *off*) sin.

Passages that give the flavor of the word include:

1. Genesis 50:17. Note that this word includes man to man as well as God to man forgiveness. In this it differs markedly from *salach.*

2. Exodus 34:6, 7. Here God is forgiving man of iniquity, transgression and sin (note that the words for forgiveness are not used exclusively with any one term for sin).
3. Psalm 32:1, 5. Forgiveness here is parallelled to covering. The original image in *nasa* (pardon by taking away) is eclipsed by the one in the context (pardon by covering). These are two ways of achieving the same end result: *removal* of sin. Comparing vss. 1 and 5, it is significant to note that sin is covered by God only when it is uncovered by man.
4. Hosea 1:6. The opposite of not forgiving = showing pity (cf. Ex. 34:6). There is a warmth about the word.

Perhaps even with these Old Testament studies alone it is beginning to become quite clear that the concept of forgiveness is rich. In the Scriptures the depth and breadth of the idea of forgiveness is vast; it is many faceted.

The New Testament

Again, in the New Testament, we shall study two words: *aphiemi* and *charizomai*. Of these, *aphiemi* is the principal term for forgiveness and in the LXX is related largely to *salach*. These Greek terms differ, yet have similarities. We shall consider *aphiemi* first.

Basically, *aphiemi* means "to let go, release or remit" (lit., to go off again). Similarity to the removal, lifting, etc., already discovered in the O.T. words is apparent. Yet, the figure varies slightly, as we shall see. The fundamental *usage* (as opposed to mere etymology) is for speaking of debts "forgiven" or cancelled (it can also be used for the *release* of a prisoner—where the idea of debt—he has a debt to pay for his crime—has not altogether vanished). The term is used in all sorts of legal-financial connections in the papyri, highlighting the concept of *debt paid* (or *cancelled*) in full. The Rosetta Stone (196 B.C.) has this phrase: *eis telos apheken* ("total remission" [of certain taxes]). The usage is quite typical.

The New Testament uses the word in this way, both literally and figuratively (cf. Matt. 18:27, 32; 6:12). The word *aphiemi* almost demands that the word "debt" follow it. When other words, like "trespasses" (Luke 7:41, 42) occur, they must be thought of in terms of the *liabilities* incurred. Trespasses place one in a place of debt; one is liable to God and likely to be called to account at any time; he is in a position where this obligation hangs over him at all times. In Acts 8:22, where we read of forgiving "the thoughts of hearts," the idea is *sinful* thoughts. Sin is plainly considered debt, obligation leading to liability incurred. The release, remission, relief of an obligation removed is paramount in the concept.

Aphesis is the noun form of *aphiemi*. It means dismissal, release, forgiveness. Eleven times it is followed by the word "sins" (*hamartia*), and once by "tresspass" (Col. 1:14). Cf. Mark 3:29; Ephesians 1:7; Acts 5:31; 13:38; 26:18; Luke 4:18. (Here, and in the LXX of Lev. 25:10, etc., it speaks of the release from obligations during the year of jubilee.)

The other New Testament term is *charizomai*. This word comes from *charis* (favor, grace), and means to bestow forgiveness *freely* or *unconditionally*. The forgiveness is always undeserved by the one who receives it (he deserves to pay the penalty or debt). The gift of forgiveness cost the giver, not the receiver (cf. Eph. 4:32; Col. 2:13; 3:13; Luke 7:42, 43—here the debt was *cancelled freely*).

Perhaps a note about the English word, *forgive,* also is in order. The prefix *for* (not fore) is a negative that in one way or another negates the word to which it is affixed (in this case, the word *give*). It means *"not to give,"* to refrain from giving (one what he deserves—a punishment or penalty of some sort). Of course, for other than illustrational purposes, the etymology of this term carries no real significance for this study.

The Meaning of Forgiveness

At this point, in a preliminary way, I wish to discuss the meaning of forgiveness. I say in a preliminary way, because what I shall do here will be rough and not precise. Much that I say will have to be qualified, amplified, systematized and developed as we go along. I am not yet ready to define forgiveness in one crisp sentence, or even in a precisely worded paragraph. What I want you to discover, above all at this point, is that forgiveness is a large, multi-dimentional concept in the Bible.

Let us begin by contrasting forgiveness with its opposites. Often the best way to understand an idea is to discover what it is set over against. (Cf. *heart*—in the Bible we have seen how illuminating it is to discover that heart is set over against lips, hands, words, outer appearance, not over against the head.) How does the Bible speak of unforgiving, non-forgiving, refusal to forgive? To begin our study, we shall turn to

1. Mark 3:28-30:

> Let Me assure you that all sorts of sins and blasphemies spoken by
> the sons of men will be forgiven them, but whoever blasphemes
> against the Holy Spirit will never be forgiven [lit., "never have for-
> giveness"], but rather will be held guilty for committing an eternal
> sin (this He said because some had claimed, "He has an unclean
> spirit").

This is the account of the famous unforgivable sin (for more details on
this, cf. chap. 37, *The Christian Counselor's Manual*). According to
Jesus, "all sorts of sins"[3] are forgivable. Only this one is unforgivable
vs. 29). The phrase "sons of men" is a simple variant for "persons"
or "human beings"; the word "blasphemy" means insulting speech. The
unforgivable sin is not adultery, masturbation, divorce, etc. (as some
counselees think), but, as the context makes clear, something quite
different. In verse 30 we are told that it has to do with blaspheming
(insulting) the Holy Spirit by calling Him an "unclean spirit." Nothing
could offend Him more. If there is one thing that characterizes the Holy
Spirit, it is His holiness. He is the Spirit of holiness (Rom. 1:4) Who
Himself is holy by nature and is the Source of all holiness among men
and angels. Holiness is separateness (from sin so as to make one
uniquely God's).

Persons concerned about committing the unforgivable sin have never
done so; persons who sin against the Holy Spirit oppose Him by turning God's values upside down—they call evil good and good evil (cf.
Isa. 5:20). They claim that the Holy Spirit is an unclean spirit (i.e., a
demon). But, enough for the background. Let us see what (by contrast) the passage has to say about the meaning of forgiveness.

According to verse 29, they will never have forgiveness (*aphesis*).
But what *will* they have? The second, contrasting portion of the verse
tells us: "but rather [they] will be held guilty of an eternal sin." An
eternal sin is a sin that for eternity will never be forgvien, and its effects
—eternal punishment—will be unending. That is the concrete result.
But notice the rest of the clause: "will be held guilty of." That is the
construct that stands over against forgiveness as its opposite. One who
is unforgiven is one *held guilty;* he is *liable*[4] for his sin. The word,

---

3. The word translated "sins" is *hamartema*, "acts" or "deeds of sin."
4. The English word *liable* comes from the Latin (through the French) word,
"to bind."

enochos, used here, means to be liable for or deserving of something (cf. 14:64, where the usage of the word is plainly seen: liable or deserving of death). A forgiven person, then, is one who is no longer held liable for his sin. He cannot be held accountable (cf. Rom. 3:19). Clearly, according to this usage, something is *held* against someone until he is forgiven. But when forgiveness occurs, he is *freed* from that condition; nothing is held against him any more. That liability to, or threat of punishment has been lifted, removed; it has been let go and has gone away.

2. Acts 7:60:

At the conclusion of Stephen's speech, as he is being stoned to death, he prays, "Lord, don't hold this sin against them." That is a prayer for forgiveness. Though the word forgiveness does not occur, there can be no mistaking the intent of the prayer; it is a sturdy echo of Christ's prayer on the cross ("Father, forgive them . . ."—Luke 23:34). Here, Stephen's exact words invite investigation. The prayer is negative; it is a request for God *not* to do the opposite of forgiveness, i.e., to hold their sin against them. Literally, the phrase, *me stese autois,* means "lay it not to them," "set it not down to them," or "let it not be made to stand against them." So, forgiveness (again) is seen as a condition in which one's sins are no longer charged against him.

In contrast, turn to II Chronicles 24:21, 22. Zechariah, like Stephen, is dying; he too is being stoned to death. But listen to his prayer: "Jehovah, look upon it and require it." The word *darash,* translated "require," means "to demand justice," "avenge" or "vindicate." It is to require a payment for what was done. The prayer is the opposite of Stephen's. Zechariah asks God to hold them liable for what they are doing, to call them to account for it and to pay them back for it. Stephen asks for the opposite. Because the circumstances are so similar—even to the uttering of a prayer for the enemy—the contrast in the content stands out all the more. What made the difference? The Lord's prayer from the cross had intervened; Stephen had a new model.

The result of forgiveness, then, is freedom from liability. A new outlook on life comes to the forgiven person. According to Jeremiah 50:20, even if one searches for sins, he won't find them when God pardons (cf. Ps. 103:12). All remembrances, traces of liability are gone. The forgiven person has a brand new record—freed completely from his past. Unforgiven persons carry the past as a part of their present; the liability of unforgiven sin hangs over their heads. The future belongs to forgiven people; others drag their contaminating past into the future, wherever they go, and destroy it for themselves. They are always in jeopardy. Forgiveness secures both the present and the future.

3. Hosea 8:13; 9:9:

Hosea declares that God will *remember* their guilt and *visit* their sins. Remembering and visiting are paralleled; they are used synonymously. And, in comparing the two passages, it is clear that visiting is used synonymously with punishing. To visit, in the Bible, is to come in blessing or in judgment (as here). The word never means making house calls. as some have thought (see my *Shepherding God's Flock,* vol. I, pp. 75-81, for a thorough study of the term). Here remembering, visiting, punishing all speak of God's judgment on sinners. Remembering is used as it is in III John 10. John is saying not merely that he will keep in mind what Diothrophes has done, but that he will *deal* with him on that basis; i.e., he will hold him liable for his evil deeds and punish him (perhaps by excommunication, perhaps in other ways) for them. The threat of such punishment is lifted for the forgiven person.

The Basis for Forgiveness
(Some Theological Considerations)

Having said that forgiveness is free to the receiver,[5] I immediately balanced that remark with the truth that forgiveness costs the one who grants it. Let's explore this fact and some of its ramifications.

First, it is crucial to recognize that God's forgiveness isn't an overlooking of sin, a by-passing of liability or a winking at guilt. It is not a pardon that is easy to give and costs nothing. Forgiveness was purchased at the cost of Christ's life. Forgiveness cost God His only Son. Hebrews 9:22 (cf. 10:18) declares that there is no forgiveness apart from the shedding of blood. This is bedrock; it may be neither doubted nor questioned by Christian counselors (remember how closely atonement is linked to forgiveness in Lev. 4, 5).

Of special importance is Matthew 26:28, where we are told that at the institution of the Lord's Supper Jesus spoke of "My blood of the

---

5. *Charizomai* stresses that element.

covenant that is poured out for many for the remission [*aphesis* = for-
giveness] of sins." The purpose, intention (or goal) of Christ's death
was to bring about the forgiveness of sins. Never, in theology, in counseling or anywhere else, may those two factors be separated.

Liberals ask questions like, "Why an atonement? Why the blood?
Why a sacrifice for sins? Why doesn't God simply cancel the debt and
remove the liability? Why do you say that He hinges forgiveness to
atonement?"

The question is important. Why did our forgiveness cost God His
Son? Because God is holy and righteous as well as merciful and com-
passionate. Both sides of God's person must be satisfied. In Romans
9:22, 23 we are told that God wanted to demonstrate *both* His wrath
and His mercy. Both can be seen in all of God's dealings with individuals and nations.[6]

As a God of order and righteousness Who rules His world with equity,
Jehovah ordained His laws and set forth the penalties for those who
violate them. He may not let man go scott free therefore; He must exact
the penalties that He has required. He may not upset His own order,
waive His former concerns and change His mind. His justice must be
satisfied. God's wrath over the personal and legal aspects of man's sin
must be appeased. Man not only broke God's laws; he also offended
God as a Person. Christ, by His active and passive obedience had to live
the life God's holiness required and die the death this justice exacted.
Because of these facts, the loving merciful, substitutionary death of
Christ has made it possible for God to be just and the Justifier of those
who trust Christ for forgiveness (Rom. 3:24-26). Mercy and wrath
kissed at the cross.

If I were to punch you in the nose, then ask someone sitting next to
you to forgive me, that wouldn't do. It is *you*—not he—that I have offended, and I must have *your* forgiveness. He can't forgive me; only the
one I have sinned against can do that. Forgiveness is a transaction that
always involves the two parties involved in the offense. Jesus Christ
wasn't a third party, sitting by; He was *God* manifest in the flesh. God
Himself—one of the interested parties—bore the cost by taking the
penalty upon Himself. In this way, all is satisfied that should be. In

---

6. A study of history, interpreted in the light of this thesis, would be enlightening.

contrast, the liberal view amounts to little more than a toleration or a condoning of sin.

Close to that liberal approach (in effect, if not in intention) is the view of the Christian psychologizers who equate *acceptance* with forgiveness. David Augsburger's book, *The Freedom of Forgiveness,* offers a fair sample of what is being said to the Christian public on a popular level:

> Christ's way was the way of giving forgiveness even before asked. ... To *live* forgiveness is to give wholehearted acceptance to others. There is no forgiveness without genuine acceptance of the other person as he is. ... Forgiveness is acceptance with no exception.[7]

The truth is that Christ's prayer on the cross for forgiveness (to which the first Augsburger quotation refers) was not forgiveness itself, as he claims ("that's forgiveness"[8]) but a *prayer* to God to forgive. Christ, of course had in view all that would happen to bring about that forgiveness; indeed, the death He was dying at the moment was the core of it all. To separate Christ's prayer on the cross from His crucifixion as Augsburger seems to do in this place is a tragic mistake.

We must not—as Christ certainly did not (otherwise, why did He die) —accept the other person "as he is." To do so, to forget all about sin atoned for and unconfessed (not properly dealt with) is not biblical. We forgive—and on that basis accept (I shall have much more to say about this and about *granting* forgiveness later on). Biblical forgiveness is conditional; it is not to be equated with Rogerian acceptance ("unconditional positive regard"). There is no basis whatever for that—except bad theology; the theology of Carl Rogers, who believes that at the core of his being man is essentially good.

Forgiveness never ignores sin, or tolerates it (accepting the other person *as he is*); rather, forgiveness is forgiveness of *sin* (seen to be, acknowledged and repented of *as sin*). Forgiveness focuses on the fact that there was an offense; it does not turn away from this fact but deals with it. Psychological doctrines of *acceptance* are cheap substitutes for forgiveness that deny the need for and efficacy of Christ's atonement— men can accept one another apart from that. Acceptance makes no

---

7. David Augsburger, *The Freedom of Forgiveness* (Chicago: Moody, 1970), pp. 36, 37, 39.
8. Ibid., p. 36.

demands; it is unrealistic, naive. Men are sinners and cannot be handled by acceptance.

Acceptance attempts (at best) a neutralism toward sin. I say attempts because it isn't really possible to be neutral about sin. Sin is against God, and it isn't possible to be neutral about God, Who has been offended by sin. Nonjudgmental attitudes actually condone and encourage sin. To accept a sinner *as he is,* means to say God was wrong in sending Christ to die for sinners *in order to change them.* God took sin so seriously that He punished His own Son with death for sin. If God punishes sin, we may not accept sinners as they are.

To say God forgives sin is true. But in saying it that way, we must never lose sight of the fact that it is *sinners* from whom the liability of guilt is lifted. God punishes *persons* and He forgives *persons.* Some try to distinguish between sin and the sinner: "God hates sin; loves the sin*ner.*" Such separation isn't possible. God sends sin*ners* to hell; they, not their sin, are punished eternally. Christ, not the sin He bore, suffered and died on the cross. We are concerned in counseling about the liability to unforgiven persons; sin*ners.* It does no good to obscure facts with trite sayings. Sinners need forgiveness.

It is important to use the word *sinner* in counseling when speaking of sin. It is not that we *want* to go around condemning people as sinners; that's not the point at all. What we want to do or don't want to do is beside the point. The only question is, What does God want us to do? The answer to that is plain: call sin *sin.* Only then can we point people to the forgiveness that is in Jesus Christ. Sin can be forgiven (mental illness, sickness cannot). Christianity is a religion based on forgiveness. The counseling that never speaks of sin and forgiveness, therefore, is not Christian—no matter what label it bears. Away, then, with the views of liberals and Christians who are psychologizers of Scripture! Let us return to the biblical basics.

"But didn't Jesus pray for His persecutors?" Yes. "Didn't He ask His Father to 'forgive them'?" Yes. "Did He?" Yes. "When? How?" Some were forgiven on the Day of Pentecost as the result of Peter's sermon; but *not* apart from conviction of sin (cf. Acts 2:37), and *not* apart from the message of salvation.[9] They had to repent and believe

---

9. Incidentally, the Apostle Paul's conversion was an answer to Stephen's prayer.

the gospel. Forgiveness came to them as the result of the atonement; *not* apart from it. These facts must be borne in mind by Christian counselors at all times when counseling. But the matter of guilt and the conviction of sin raises another matter with which (unfortunately) I must deal in some detail because of wrong views that have been insinuated into biblical circles by modern psychologizers of the Scriptures.

The Place and Purpose of Guilt in Christian Counseling

In order to pursue this matter as fully as possible, contrasting biblical teaching with modern distortions, with the hope of arriving at the place where God wants us to be, I shall focus for a time largely upon a book co-authored by Bruce Narramore and Bill Counts, called *Guilt and Freedom* (recently changed to *Freedom from Guilt*).[10] This book sets up most of the issues among Christian counselors concerning the place and purpose of guilt. I shall set forth some of its leading concepts, react to them and attempt to compose and contrast these with what the Scriptures teach. The book represents—and, perhaps, best sets forth—what has become a dominant strain of evangelical thought about guilt and forgiveness.

We must deal with guilt in depth because of its close relationship to forgiveness. The two can never be separated without peril. Forgiveness involves guilt; it presupposes guilt. Guilt is culpability for wrong done to God or God and man. All the words for forgiveness, as we have seen, have to do with lifting the burden of guilt, with canceling the debt charged to our account, with removing what was held against us. Narramore and Counts (from now on referred to as N/C) have chosen to discuss a very important subject; the only problem is that they try to lead us into a freedom from guilt by a way that, while purporting to be biblical, is not.

What is the purpose of guilt? N/C claim that guilt fails to achieve any good purposes. This is a strange claim to those who know their Bibles. The Bible, throughout, assumes what we have all experienced: that God made us so that we have a *sense of guilt*[11] whenever we are guilty of wrongdoing. That is to say, the awareness that one has done wrong leads to bad feelings. The conscience (the capacity for self-

---

10. *Guilt and Freedom* (Santa Ana: Vision House Publishers, 1974).

11. Throughout the book N/C speak of "psychological guilt" when thinking of what I prefer to call a *sense* of guilt. For them, this is the "feeling" of guilt.

awareness and self-judgment, leading to self-condemnation or exonera-
tion) in such situations triggers bad feelings in order to warn us that
something is wrong and must be dealt with. That is the standard, traditional viewpoint that most Christians have taken of the totality of biblical teaching: Guilt is an alarm and motivating factor to lead us to repentance.

Not so, say N/C. They want to change all that sort of thinking for
(what they say is) a more scriptural stance toward this question. They
speak of people who adopt the traditional position as playing (or being
in danger of playing) what they call "guilt games." Because of the sense
of guilt (which they see as altogether wrong), Christians do such supposedly improper things as trying "to obey the Bible to the hilt," "admitting" their wrong and "asking forgiveness."[12] But this is "too hard,"
they tell us, and (anyway) many confess sin only to get rid of bad feelings.[13] Then, N/C say, all of this leads to "a solid conclusion—guilt
doesn't work"[14] (the sense of guilt is what they are speaking about,
remember). This solid conclusion, however, constitutes a frontal attack
upon the structure of man as God made him, and much of what God is
up to in His relationships to men if the traditional understanding of the
Bible is correct. To say that guilt is a "total failure," as we are informed
on page 33, certainly goes pretty far, and assures us that what we are
reading is not a slight modification of previously held concepts, or a
warning about abuses of them, but a radical and absolute denial of
traditional interpretations and an attack leveled at them because they
see those interpretations as seriously wrong and dangerous. That, in
fact, is exactly what N/C are up to: they want to supplant the former
view with their own newer conception. What must we say about all this?

First, if N/C are correct, God must have wrongly made us. Forgiveness and confession of sin are but a farce on the N/C system. They are
merely words, drained of all their essential content, into which new and
strange meanings have been poured. Words are both misunderstood and
misconstrued; psychological content has been sewn up in them after
pulling out their biblical stuffings.

12. Ibid., pp. 27-37.
13. Interestingly, later on in the book, under a discussion of confession, N/C
claim that the purpose of confession is catharsis—the ventilation of bad feelings, and see this as a good thing. One of the difficulties a reader has with the
book is its inconsistencies.
14. Ibid., p. 33.

It is always important to ask (particularly in the field of Christian counseling) whether the writer derives the meanings he gives to words as well as his ideational constructs from the Bible through hard exegetical work designed to yield the correct biblical usage, or whether he obtains them from an outside source. Are the terms used as their biblical writers used them, or have they been shaped by the author of the book to fit a system of thought that he brings to the Bible? Narramore accepts a good bit of Freudianism; does his Freudianism influence his interpretation of the Bible? The answer is yes; many of the key scriptural terms have been reworked to fit a modified Freudianism. The pigeon-holes are set up; Bible verses and terms are then tucked into them.

Though at times (of course) guilt is ineffective—the Bible itself teaches that a sense of guilt doesn't always (or even most of the time) lead to repentance among men—that doesn't mean that it is wrong, or even ineffective. Because the majority head down the broad way to destruction, does that mean that salvation is ineffective? God's prophets plead, try to arouse a sense of guilt, etc., but often the people will not heed. That doesn't mean that guilt as a motivator is a failure; it means that people may harden their hearts—even to such strong feelings within. Moreover, to call the sense of guilt a "total failure" is far from the truth; the Scriptures are replete with evidence to the contrary. And such language is not only an attack upon a system, it amounts to a debunking of God's own approach; throughout history God has used this method (often very successfully!).

Again, to say that a sense of guilt was not built into man, but came only through parental training (N/C) denies the obvious fact that *Adam* fled, covered up, blameshifted, etc., out of a sense of guilt. Who was Adam's parent? He had none. Unless you want to say that God socialized a sense of guilt into him by His command, warning and penalty, you must say it was innate. Either way, the Source was God, not human parents. When God asks, "Who told you that you were naked?" He refers to the awakening of the sense of guilt that Adam's conscience brought upon him when he sinned. Conscience—the capacity for self-evaluation and self-judgment—had been there from the beginning, but until Adam sinned had always rendered a positive judgment about his actions and attitudes. Now, with the sin, his conscience began to accuse him and turned loose within him a feeling of misery that we call the sense of guilt. So, then, even if the majority of sinners

proclaim that their sense of guilt doesn't motivate them (this is questionable, however; it could be demonstrated that unsaved persons are
motivated by this sense of guilt to do all sorts of *wrong* things), that
misuse of the sense of guilt does not make it an improper motivating
force (cf. Rom. 3:4). Norms cannot be set by how many people do
or don't do something; we do not vote to determine what is and what
isn't righteous—God *tells* us. The sense of guilt as a motivator, in a
man who is basically oriented toward pleasing God, *does* work—quite
well!

What do the Scriptures themselves have to say about these matters?
Psalm 51 sets forth the traditional view:

> Vs. 1. Have mercy upon me, O God, according to Thy loving-
> kindness: according to the greatness of Thy compassion blot out
> my transgressions.[15]

This is a penitential psalm. After David sinned against Uriah and Bathsheba, and Nathan exposed his sin in the nouthetic encounter recorded
in II Samuel 12:10, he wrote this psalm. In it he describes the misery
of the period during which he impenitently refused to confess his sin.
The entire psalm exposes the inner misery of a man suffering from a
sense of guilt. This prepared him for the final confession to God when
Nathan came.

> Vs. 3. I am conscious of my transgressions and my sin is ever in
> mind.

He cannot get away from his guilt; it gnaws at him. The sense of sin
dogs him day and night. Now notice the next verse:

> 4. Against Thee, Thee only, have I sinned and done what is evil in
> Thy sight; so that Thou are justified in Thy sentence and pure in
> Thy judging.

Was God simply smiling at David with no barrier between except those
wrongly erected by David himself? Was God accepting and non-
judgmental? That is what N/C want us to believe, as they say later in
the book. But look at the text—God had judged and sentenced David.
It looks as if there was a charge against him; he was liable to punishment. God declared David guilty, and David said that He was justified
and pure in doing so. Who is right? David or N/C? Now look at verses
8 and 12:

---

15. I quote here from the Berkeley Version.

8. Cause me to hear joy and gladness, so that the bones which Thou hast broken may rejoice.
12. Restore to me the joy of Thy salvation. . . .

Clearly, David knew that it was God who brought the misery he was suffering into his life; it was not some residue of poor parental socialization. It was *God* Who broke his bones (a figurative expression denoting severe misery occasioned by excruciating pain. Few things cause such sharp pain as broken bones). That sounds like more than the "constructive sorrow" of which N/C will speak later on.

17. The sacrifices of God are a broken spirit; a broken and penitent heart, O God, Thou wilt not despise (cf. Ps. 34:18).

God desires broken hearts and spirits in His sinning children (cf. Joel 2:13).[16] He brings misery to break their rebellion, pride and self-centeredness. Brokenness, humility, is not wrong, but to be *sought*. Who breaks the spirit and heart? God Himself. But He breaks them not to leave them that way, as Isaiah said (58:15: He "revives" the spirit and the heart; cf. also Ps. 147:3).

God appreciates broken hearts in sinners; N/C tell us God doesn't want them to feel bad. They say that when you sin you ought not to feel guilty; instead, you ought to rejoice because of what God has done for you in Christ. There should be no pangs of guilt at all. Clearly, David and N/C are at odds.

But if Psalm 51 tells us that a sense of guilt is proper, Psalm 38 even more strongly says the same thing. I shall not quote the psalm or even verses from it. Surely, there is no indication that God smilingly accepted him in his sin, non-judgmentally looking upon him with favor, with no barriers between.[17] Rather we read of God's "indignation," "hot displeasure," etc. That's quite a difference. God Himself has been shooting arrows into David (not literally, of course, but in judgment); *His* hand has been resting heavily on David. Plainly, God was actively bringing misery into David's life because of his sin. There is no other way to read the psalm. The misery of the sense of guilt is vividly expressed in verses 2-10; nothing could be added to make the situation seem more miserable. It is all summed up in one succinct phrase: "I am

---

16. Note also vs. 12 for a picture of the attitude that accompanies a broken heart.
17. Ibid., pp. 83-85.

anxious because of my sin" (vs. 18b). What is going on here? God was at work bringing David to repentance. God was chastening him, and if there ever was a picture of the sense of guilt, it is in this psalm. And the misery of guilt could be removed only by confession (vs. 18a).[18]

N/C try to separate what they call "theological guilt" (culpability) from what they call "psychological guilt" (the sense of guilt). The first, they call "and objective fact"; the second, a subjective "feeling" (p. 34). This distinction is neat, easy and convenient; the sinner's standing is seen entirely apart from his state. Of course, there is a logical, paper disjunction that may (must) be made for the sake of analysis. But unless one's conscience has been "seared with a hot iron" and he is "past feeling," I would like someone to tell me how a Christian makes the distinction in actual life. David couldn't, Paul couldn't, Peter couldn't. How can a true believer, who basically seeks to please God, acknowledge his guilt as an objective fact and not in some way be inwardly moved by it? (cf. Ps. 38:18). A plainer invitation to antinomian Pharisaism hardly could be imagined. The doctrine is dangerous. In counseling, should it catch on, it could cause much damage. Fortunately, so far it does not seem to have been accepted widely.

N/C do allow for something that they call "constructive sorrow"[19] (taken from II Cor. 7:8-10), but they say that it doesn't "involve feelings of self-condemnation."[20] In discussing their obedience to his former letter regarding an offender, Paul does make a distinction between two kinds of pain: worldly pain and godly pain (vs. 10). The word *lupe,* sometimes translated "sorrow," is the standard word for *pain.* Paul's letter was so painful; he almost regretted sending it (that doesn't sound like taking a purely "objective" view of their sin!). But because of the results (*God* used it to produce pain leading to repentance) he was glad he did. This was a very painful sorrow that produced such results (among those for whom it was appropriate[21]) as "fear" and "mourning" (i.e., wailing, lamentation—vs. 7). And its results were effective. The description is not of a mild, objective response with some slight sorrow attached that led to constructive action. Rather, the reaction was *in-*

---

18. Unbelievably, N/C refer to Ps. 51 and write, "The miserable feelings of psychological guilt that David experienced weren't sent to him by God," ibid., p. 131. Read that sentence again, then read Ps. 51:8 and Ps. 38:2, 3.

19. Ibid., p. 34.

20. Ibid., p. 35.

21. There were other responses by those to whom it wasn't (cf. vs. 11).

tense! The entire section rings with strong emotion. The distinction is not between two kinds of sorrows—different in intensity;[22] rather it is between two kinds of sorrows—both painful experiences that differ in *source* and *result*. The sorrow that came from the world led to further sin, only to be the cause of further regret and sorrow; that which came from God led to good results, never to be regretted. The problem was not whether there was fear (there may be fear for different reasons) or not, but *why* the painful experience occurred. Godly sorrow led to self-condemnation among offenders all right, but that motivated them to repentance. In other words, godly sorrow over the guilt of one's offenses can be successful in leading to repentance. It is interesting that in the N/C book on guilt there is virtually nothing said about repentance. Of course, that is consistent with the basic viewpoint of the book. There is really no place for biblical repentance; that is why the concept is missing. Biblical repentance *always* requires self-condemnation; confession of wrongdoing toward God. But this godly sorrow, Paul says, led to repentance.

Triumphantly N/C say, "The Bible . . . never tells us to feel psychological guilt" (p. 36). Of course, this is true, technically speaking, because it doesn't use those terms. But the argument is specious. The whole Bible stresses the need for sinning Christians to become aware of, feel sorry about and repent of sin. There is no call for morbid introspection; the sorrow always should lead quickly to repentance. Perhaps James sums up the biblical position as simply as any writer:

> Be distressed and sorrow and cry; let your laughter be turned to sorrow and your gladness to dejection. Be humbled before the Lord and He will exalt you (James 4:9, 10).

So God never wants us to feel bad! So He never erects barriers to be removed by repentance! Nonsense!

N/C say that the "feeling" [regularly, they confuse judgments that lead to bad feelings with feelings themselves] that "I have failed; I should have done better" is wrong (p. 34). In other words, repentance for a believer is wrong (the essence of repentance is to acknowledge the fact that one has failed God and must do differently in the future). But I

---

22. Even Esau's "repentance" evoked strong emotion (cf. Heb. 12:17). The problem, however, was not that he had strong self-condemnation; rather, his regrets indicate the dominant concern was self-pity. Godly self-condemnation focuses on God, while self-pity focuses on one's self.

ask, was Jesus wrong when, again and again, in the letters to the seven churches, He calls Christians to repentance? Look at some of the detailed directions and comments that He gives along with that call.

In Revelation 2:4-5, Jesus tells the Ephesian believers, "I have this against you" (vs. 4—a phrase used throughout these letters). But to have (or hold) something against someone (we have seen in our discussion of forgiveness) is to hold him guilty. N/C have no place for this; there can be no barriers from God's side. Yet over and over in these letters Jesus erects this sort of barrier. Someone—Jesus or N/C— is wrong! The solution to the problem (i.e., what removes the barrier Christ erected) is not simply to smile and thank God that all is well in Christ, but to *repent* (vs. 5)!

When N/C claim that God doesn't want us to have a sense of guilt arising from our sinful failures and that He doesn't motivate us by this sense of guilt, by feelings of "lowered self-evaluation" or by "fear of punishment" (vs. 33), what do they do with the following passages?

1. Revelation 2:20-22. Is the "great affliction" of verse 22 to be feared? If so, why—if not to motivate to change? Why are there such warnings throughout these seven letters, and elsewhere in the Bible?

2. Revelation 3:2, 3. So, God doesn't want us to say, "I have failed"? Why tell the saints in Sardis, "I haven't found a thing that you have done complete before my God"? They are to "wake up" and "strengthen" the few bits and pieces that they have left—which are "about to die"—or else (warning) He will visit them in judgment ("as a thief"). If Jesus hasn't been painting a picture of *failure,* what has He been doing? Nothing was done completely—everything they started they didn't finish, they ruined along the way, etc. Very little worthwhile left—and that about to die: there is a picture of *almost total failure.* And for failing—unless they repent—Jesus warns them to watch out for a judgment upon their church (motivation by the sense of guilt and fear—just what N/C deny).

3. Revelation 3:16, 17. There must not be "lowered self-evaluation," say N/C. Here Jesus says, "You're lukewarm" and you make Me sick; "I'm going to vomit you out of my mouth" (vs. 16). Just the words themselves tend to lower self-esteem (Haim Ginott, *et al.,* would say talk about the act; not about the person; Jesus doesn't follow that advice at all)! But that isn't all; listen to what else He says, ". . . you say, 'I am rich . . . and have need of nothing' " (vs. 17). Then He con-

tinues, "and don't know that you are miserable and pitiable and poor and blind and naked" (vs. 17). If words ever were calculated to lower one's sense of self-worth, these words were.

4. Revelation 3:19. Here, in our last reference to the seven letters (there is plenty more; I simply don't want to waste space), Jesus sums up His purposes and methods; He lets us know what He is up to in writing such things: "I convict and discipline those about whom I care; so be zealous and repent." When N/C speak about conviction and discipline, it looks quite different from what we discover in these letters. In fact, we can say (without the slightest fear of contradiction by unbiased readers) that Jesus and N/C are on opposite sides of this issue.

But notice it is pastoral "care" that Jesus, the great Shepherd of the sheep, is exercising in such treatment of His flock. But that care is so deep that He will not countenance for one moment sins that destroy lives. Instead, by calling sin "sin," by crushing pride, by warning of potential punishment, by calling to repentance, Jesus wishes to bring conviction that motivates a sense of sorrow over guilt and leads to change. He didn't just smile and let it all pass by.

So, then, does God "make us feel guilty" as N/C put it (p. 36)? Is it possible to have what they call "guilt-free living" (p. 37)? No. Not when Jesus treats us that way. And, thank God we can't—we would be totally unconcerned about God if we lived that way. Now, when they speak of "guilt-free living," they aren't simply saying that if we didn't sin we could live guilt-free. No; exactly not that! We would all agree to that (theoretically possible) fact. What they are saying, N.B., is that *even while living a life in which we go on sinning* we can still live guilt-free (i.e., free from the sense or feeling of guilt)![23] Such thinking does not square with God's encouragement of a broken spirit and penitent (lit., "crushed") heart (Ps. 51:7).

We have been looking at some prime issues raised by N/C. What do they offer in addition on their non-judgmental system? With what would they replace the traditional view of Scripture? With what they admit is a view that "may seem incredibly far out" (p. 36). I can only

23. Unfortunately, A. A. Hoekema, in his little book, *The Christian Looks at Himself* (Grand Rapids: Wm. B. Eerdmans, 1975), leaves theology and psychologizes the Scriptures, adopting much the same view (p. 35). In his taped lectures on self-image, my colleague, John Bettler, deals in depth with Hoekema's book (tapes available from C.S.S. (250 Edge Hill Rd., Huntingdon Valley, PA 19006).

concur in this estimate; their view is far out—outside the Bible. They warn against preaching and counseling that (they claim) dumps guilt-loads on people. Instead, as the title of the book says, they claim to free Christians from a sense of guilt. How (we have already seen much of the system)?

1. By reminding us that what Christ has done for us should bring us a glorious self-image. This fact should carry us safely through sin-experiences, guilt-free (i.e., free from "psychological guilt" = the sense of guilt). John Bettler has pointed out (see note 23 for source) that what we need isn't a good or bad self-image, but an *accurate* one. Then, we can deal with our problems. Good self-images cannot be pumped up by telling yourself how great you are in Christ or by trying to ignore the consequences of your sin before God. True, in Christ we are perfect; and that is *important*. It is even very important for a Christian to *know* that this is true. But that doesn't alter the fact that *in ourselves* we are far from perfect. Justification (what we are in Christ) must not be confused with sanctification (what we are in ourselves). What we are in Christ gives us no warrant for ignoring the actual guilt in our own lives today, nor for feeling bad over it. Indeed, if anything, it should *increase* our sense of guilt. If we have already achieved something in Christ that we are failing to do in ourselves, we know that it isn't necessary for us to fail. In Ephesians 4 and Colossians 3 Paul's constant argument is that since you have something in Christ, you know you can have it in yourselves. He reasons: "Be (in yourselves[24]) what you are (already in Christ); your state must measure up to your standing." So this argument—confusing sanctification with justification—fails.

2. Next, N/C say, "We are so valuable . . . that Christ paid the ultimate price to restore us to fellowship with God" (p. 49). Is that why Christ died? Was it because we were so valuable He couldn't bear to lose us? Was the incarnation like Jesus crawling around on His knees in the mud trying to retrieve as many precious pearls as He can? No! Where is the vaunted N/C emphasis upon grace? There was nothing in us weak (no power), sinful (lawbreakers) enemies (who opposed Him) to commend us to Christ. Our salvation is wholly of grace. We deserve nothing but the opposite. What makes us valuable is Christ's death; N/C have the trailer before the car! What God told

---

24. By God's grace, of course.

Israel again and again when their self-image began to balloon was, "I didn't choose you because you were any better than anyone else." Unless N/C believe God thought *all* human beings were lost pearls, what they say leads again to pharisaical views (of course, if they do think *all* are pearls, they must think Christ failed, since most of the "pearls" go rolling down the broad road that leads to destruction). Salvation is by grace.

3. Again, N/C prove themselves bad theologians when they say that not all that is good comes from God (p. 52). Some (wrongly, they claim) teach that all good comes from God and none from us. Rather, N/C affirm, much comes from us. They ask, "At what point does God end and we begin" (p. 52)? No theologian would put the question that way (again, we see the importance of theology rather than psychology as the basis for counseling): God never "ends"! All the good that *we* do (and, against Charles Solomon, *we* do it; Christ doesn't do it *for* us, *instead* of or *in place of* us), we do by God's direction and strength provided for us in the Word and by the Spirit.

We may contrast several wrong views:

Charles Solomon	*N/C*[25]	*Self-Help*
God does all good through Christ in us. He does more as we cease trying and let Him do it for us.	God does some good; we do some good. Neither does all.	We do all good by our own strength (this view is the straw man that no evangelicals hold, but all fight against).

N/C stand in a mediating position between two faulty views. But it also is a false resolution of the problems presented by each. Rather, the biblical view looks like this:

Biblical View
All the good we do,
we do by God's wis-
dom and strength.

This view is based on the fact that God everywhere commands *us* (not Christ in us) to believe and to obey, but also says we can do so only by

---

25. Later in their book, N/C come to the biblical viewpoint. I am happy to acknowledge this; but the grave inconsistency of this statement is quite misleading.

His grace (wisdom and strength). See Philippians 2:13; 4:13; Colossians 1:11. I shall not take the space to discuss the question more fully.

4. We are to love ourselves, say N/C (p. 63). They write: "And we love ourselves because he [God] tells us to." I shall say nothing more on this point than to observe that there is not a single command in the Bible to love ourselves; the statement is completely false. For a discussion of the false psychologizing view that we should love ourselves, see thorough treatments in my books, *The Christian Counselor's Manual*, pp. 142-144, and *Matters of Concern*, pp. 91-98.

5. N/C assure us that God never punishes His children. This idea of punishment (the threat of punishment that forgiveness removes), we are informed, is only a hangover from childhood. Their essentially Freudian approach is plain throughout: Parents (and others) punished us in childhood, and now as "adults we continue to expect punishment" (p. 69). That's why we fear God will punish us. Are we "totally free from punishment" (p. 69) as N/C say? Is *"all* punishment" removed in Christ (p. 68) as they claim? Much must be said about this important issue before we have finished with it, but I shall respond only minimally at this point. N/C agree that God disciplines us, but see this as "entirely different" from punishment. Punishment, they say, is "payment for misdeeds" (p. 70), and Christ paid the penalty for these. God only *corrects* His children to remove faults, and that correction does not involve punishment. What N/C want to remove is all the elements of a sense of guilt and all fear that God would do something unpleasant to His children to motivate them (we have already responded to these views—cf. especially the discussion of Christ's dealings with the Christians in the seven churches of Asia Minor).[26]

All of us agree that God won't punish us as He did Christ. We all agree that anything that God does is for His honor and our welfare—not to make us *pay* for our misdeeds. Punishment, however, isn't to be restricted to payment (see note 26); it is fundamentally unpleasantness, pain, etc. But the goal of the unpleasantness may differ. Correction and

---

26. Punishment in the Bible isn't restricted to unbelievers and isn't limited to "payment for misdeeds." It is this faulty definition that confuses. Cf. II Cor. 2:6, for instance, on *punishment as church discipline.* Here *epitimia,* the word used for punishment, means "restriction of rights." And in vss. 7, 10, forgiveness of the wrong is extended following repentance. Punishment by pain, loss, restriction, etc., are all *punishments* intended to correct faults; as, indeed, was the case here.

discipline include some form of unpleasantness (cf. Heb. 12:5-11), despite what N/C want us to believe. Juggling terms does not change facts. Discipline is "painful" and it is unpleasant (12:11); the Scriptures themselves tell us so. He "whips every son" (12:6). The same punitive restrictions may be placed upon one person in order to make him *pay* that might be placed upon another to correct him. But to deny that (for their good) God does make it unpleasant—often *very* unpleasant—for His children, is to fly in the face of all of Scripture.

Punishment is a *part* of discipline (the "rod"), but not *all* of it. There are two sides to discipline (Eph. 6):

| (1) *nurture* | and | (2) *admonition* |

which are the same as the O.T.

| (1) *rod* | and | (2) *reproof.* |

These two concepts mean (as the usage of both O.T. and N.T. terms indicate):

| (1) structured discipline with teeth: reward and punishment. | (2) counsel: confrontation with the claims of Christ, motivating child out of love for Him. |

Both sides always must be present to be biblical. So far as I can see, N/C limit us to the first half of the first concept: reward. And, Paul tells us, we are to bring up our children in the discipline and nouthetic confrontation *of the Lord.* That means we are to follow God's example in disciplining us as we discipline our children. Clearly, then, this is how God disciplines us.

There is no eternal, *judicial* punishment in view, of course. But for the good of the children, for the welfare of the whole family, and for the sake of the family name, God uses *parental* punishment. This disciplinary punishment can be quite severe at times. Cf. I Corinthians 11:27-32: N.B., they "will be held guilty" (vs. 27)—a state needing forgiveness, as we have seen—"judged" (vss. 30-32, 34) and "disciplined." And according to verse 32 the Lord "disciplines" by "judging." Notice the judgment (vs. 30): some were weak, others sick, and a number had been put to death (the beautiful Christian figure is "slept"). Cf. also II Corinthians 10:6; Colossians 3:25; Matthew 18:21-25.[27]

---

27. Matt. 18:21-25. Here *forgiven* persons who are not forgiving are in view

Forgiveness in the Bible grows out of a genuine sense of guilt, contrary to all that N/C have to say. The forgiveness package contains all the elements that we have seen, and must not be depleted.

6. N/C discuss the question of what happens when a believer sins (pp. 82ff.). As expected, they say

a. If he feels a sense of guilt, that is wrong.

b. If he thinks that God requires repentance to be in fellowship with Him again, this is simply his "own mental gymnastics" (p. 83) and not true to the facts.

c. God has erected no barriers; only the counselee has done so in his own mind. He gets what he expects in this regard (p. 84).

d. God is only totally accepting. He doesn't condemn, judge, punish, etc. He isn't alienated (I John 1:7-9 is ignored along with I Sam. 59:12).

e. It is only that *sins* have *"built-in consequences"* (p. 87). These, not God, are what punish us. N/C write, ". . . every sin has some harmful effect on our physical or emotional lives." What we have here is a deistic approach: God Himself does not punish, but He has gone off and mechanically allowed His creation to do so for him.

f. There is also "false guilt" (pp. 119ff.): "Most of us feel guilty over a number of things God doesn't consider sins." I shall not comment on this since I have done so elsewhere.[28]

g. "Guilt feelings aren't the voice of God at all" (p. 122), but "always the products of our early family training." They are "the devil's tool. They do not come from God" (p. 123). We have already discussed this subject in some depth, but only as one additional factor consider Ezekiel 36:25-31, where believers "loathe" themselves *after* repentance and restoration (cf. also Ezek. 20:42, 43).

h. Conviction means being shown sins and urged to change (p. 124).

i. One confesses to avoid guilt; confession is catharsis (pp. 131,

---

(not fake professors, as some think). N.B., the terms "heavenly father," "you" (disciples), "brothers," etc. The torturers in the picture complete its exaggerated vividness (hundreds of thousands of dollars) and fit the other details in this contemporary scene. They are not to be made typical of punishment in hell.

28. Cf. *Competent to Counsel*, p. 14.

132). It is a matter of getting things out so that one feels better—it merely has to do with feelings, not with our relationship to God (p. 134). I shall not discuss this error further, since I have commented on it earlier. I shall say more about confession later.

So, we have seen the modern view of N/C (and a number of others who hold similar views) and have found that there is no biblical basis for it. I have taken the time and space to treat this viewpoint in detail because of the possibility that it may grow even more widely in Christian circles than it has in the past. If it does, you will be prepared to answer it.

Biblical Teaching

By way of contrast, I have already said much about what the Bible teaches on the subject of guilt as it relates to forgiveness as well as having done some basic biblical studies in a rough, preliminary way. It is now time to dig in more deeply, and tie together what has been learned systematically with what has been discovered thus far. That is what I propose to do at this point.

Let us begin, therefore, by grappling with the questions that N/C seek (but fail) to answer: What about forgiveness after forgiveness, punishment after punishment, repentance after repentance? Doesn't the traditional view, from which they depart, deny the once-for-all work and efficacy of Christ's death and resurrection? If we are forgiven in Christ, why repent, confess sin and seek forgiveness *again?* If He bore the penalty for our sin, taking the punishment on Himself, why should believers fear any future punishment at all? Those are the questions to which N/C unsuccessfully address themselves. We can commend them for raising these issues, because they are important to counselors.

I have been referring to the "traditional view"; perhaps it is time to state it clearly. I suppose that it is no more plainly set forth than in the Westminster Confession of Faith, Ch. XI, "Justification," sec. 5:

> God doth continue to forgive the sins of those that are justified; and, although they can never fall from the state of justification, yet they may, by their sins, fall under God's fatherly displeasure, and not have the light of His countenance restored unto them, until they humble themselves, confess their sins, beg pardon and renew their faith and repentance.

Without a doubt, the N/C book constitutes a direct attack upon that view—in general, and at every particular point.

We have seen that the N/C view is unscriptural, and that the Westminster view is thoroughly biblical. But we have not (as yet) dealt with the central problem of forgiveness after forgiveness—how can that be?

Let us turn to the teaching on forgiveness that accompanies the Lord's prayer in the Sermon on the Mount (Matt. 6:12b, 14, 15). Remember, throughout this sermon—of which this teaching is a part—Jesus is instructing His people about life in His community. He does not address unbelieving, unforgiven persons, but (rather) those who (by following His directions) can have righteous living that exceeds the righteousness of the scribes and the Pharisees.

Look at verse 4—"Your Father . . ."; verse 6—"your Father . . ."; verse 8—"your Father . . ."; and verse 9—"Our Father." The entire context has to do with God's children speaking to, and living in relationship with, their heavenly Father. They could not have missed that point; the language is far too explicit. Nor should we do so today. Similarly, in verses 14, 15, the forgiveness (or lack of it) about which Jesus speaks comes from a *father*. It is a matter of the heavenly Father forgiving (or withholding forgiveness from) His child. There is no question that, throughout, Jesus is speaking to forgiven (justified) persons about forgiving justified persons. In short, Jesus advocates forgiveness after forgiveness. And—don't miss this point—this prayer (including a prayer for forgiveness) and the discussion of it (vss. 14, 15) was designed to deal with the common, *everyday* events in the lives of forgiven persons. How can this be? How can truly justified persons need daily forgiveness?

Before answering that question, let me make one further observation. The point of giving the prayer was to provide a how-to pattern of brevity.[29] The Gentiles pray long, repetitious prayers (vs. 7). They think God wants to hear a lot of talking. That is wrong. Instead, one should pray like this, Jesus says—then, He gives the Lord's prayer, which (above all else) is a model of brevity. Yet, the one point in so brief a prayer, upon which He does elaborate, is forgiveness (vss. 14,

29. For more on the how-to nature of the entire Sermon on the Mount, see my *Update on Christian Counseling*, vol. 1 (Phillipsburg, N. J.: Presbyterian and Reformed Publishing Co., 1979).

15). Rather than downplay the idea, then, Jesus elevates this point to unmistakable prominence. Perhaps He emphasizes this feature because it is so difficult for some of us to seek forgiveness from the heavenly Father; perhaps because it is the factor that becomes the *sine qua non* in prayer (unless one is on talking terms with God, there is little use in praying for any other thing). At any rate, Jesus' concern to emphasize the point is evident from the enlightening commentary on verse 12 that appears in verses 14, 15.

Some take verses 14, 15 to mean that God will forgive His children on the basis of their own forgiveness; that isn't true. There is no forgiveness on the basis of human works. Others understand this to say that one evidence that one has been forgiven is his willingness to forgive others. That fact certainly is true, but that isn't what the passage says. He clearly states that God will withhold His forgiveness of us (based on Christ's merits, not on our works) until we are willing to forgive others. Well, then, are those who say that the passage is not for us today correct? Is this a legalistic way of salvation for a different time and place and people? No, not at all. There is but one way of salvation—in *all* times, for all people—by grace through faith in Jesus Christ.

What is the answer to the problem, then? It is very simple, yet profound—and satisfying. Christ here is not referring to *judicial* forgiveness, but to *parental* forgiveness. He had no intention of talking about the forgiveness that is a part of justification and that brings salvation. That was not in view. He was speaking to persons who were already *judicially* forgiven, once-for-all. We have seen that—He speaks to those who already call God their "Father" (indeed, in the Lord's prayer, He teaches them to do so). Those who get hung up on forgiveness after forgiveness, therefore, do so because they miss this *very obvious* point. That is the N/C difficulty; because they fail to distinguish the things that truly differ, they must distinguish the things that do not. Judicial forgiveness—forgiveness granted by God as Judge—is over and done with for those to whom Jesus speaks. He plainly calls God their heavenly Father (over and over again). The forgiveness under discussion in verses 12, 14, 15, therefore, is not *judicial* forgiveness, but *parental* forgiveness; to confound the two is to confuse people and leads to the misunderstanding of many profound truths for practical living. It is no minor error.

Is this idea new? No. Referring once more to a portion of the article that I quoted in the Westminster Confession of Faith, note these words: "God doth continue to forgive the sins of those that are justified. . . . because they fall under His *fatherly* displeasure" (emphasis mine). The writers of the Confession clearly understood the distinction between judicial forgiveness and that forgiveness that comes to God's children when they repent, confess and seek pardon for having displeased their heavenly Father.

In order to understand more fully the similarities and differences between judicial and parental forgiveness, consider the following chart.

God's Forgiveness of Us

JUDICIAL	Similarities and Differences	PARENTAL
GUILT—liability to eternal	S. D.	GUILT—liability to temporal
PUNISHMENT as just desert from	S. D.	PUNISHMENT as remedial and disciplinary from
GOD as Judge;	S. D.	GOD as Father;
REBUKE as condemnation;	S. D.	REBUKE as correction;
SENSE OF GUILT producing fear of judgment;	S. D.	SENSE OF GUILT producing remorse over offending the Father;
CONFESSION of an enemy surrendering;	S. D.	CONFESSION of a child submitting;
FORGIVENESS lifts threat of hell, establishes a new	S. D.	FORGIVENESS lifts threat of temporal punishment and improves previous
RELATIONSHIP with God	S.	RELATIONSHIP with God

An understanding of these differences and similarities will go a long way toward understanding how a counselor must deal with counselees as well as give him a handle for instructing counselees, many of whom are deeply confused over these very issues.

Clearly, a judge doesn't treat his own children in the ways that he treats criminals who stand before the bar. As a judge, one thing is required; as a parent, something else. Yet, in dealing with the wrongs of both criminals and children, there are (nevertheless) many similarities; because wrongdoing *per se,* is not altogether dissimilar, treatment will (in some ways) be similar. The chart distinguishes the things that differ and identifies those that are similar.

Let us review the items in the chart briefly once again.

(1) GUILT. Whenever one sins, he becomes liable. That, we have seen, is the meaning of culpability, and it is that which forgiveness "lifts" or "takes away." When, in parental forgiveness, one prays "forgive us our *debts,"* the idea of debts brings the notion of liability to the fore. The notion of liability to a Judge or to a Father may differ radically in many ways, but in respect to the question of liability itself— accountability, a debt to be handled, a burden unlifted—both in judicial and parental forgiveness, the fact is the same.

(2) PUNISHMENT. Surely, eternal versus temporal punishment makes a great difference, but with regard to the matter of the question of punishment itself, the two are the same. Fathers *do* punish their children for remedial and disciplinary purposes (not merely out of raw desert). We have seen evidence of this fact in earlier studies. Hebrews makes it clear that all children are punished—that is one evidence that they belong to the family (you don't go down the street giving the neighbors' children a licking!). But that is different from throwing them out of the family, disowning and disinheriting them, etc. All God's children will be punished, but all will live as joint heirs with Christ forever in the heavenly home.

(3) GOD is the same One Who punishes both His children and the children of Satan. Yet, how He does so is quite different. Like us, God wears different hats at times. He is both a Judge and a Parent. When wearing each hat, He always does that which is appropriate to each role.

(4) REBUKE. On the one hand there is condemnation; on the other, correction. The one rebuke is intended to *change* the child rebuked, while the other is not. Both lead to a

(5) SENSE OF GUILT. But in one, there is the fear, discussed in Hebrews 2 and I Corinthians 15; in the other a concern over the fact that we have dishonored and disobeyed the heavenly Father. A true sense

of guilt, in a child, therefore, focuses not so much on what is coming to one's self, but on the consequences to the Name of God and the welfare of His church. Actually, this sense of guilt rather than absent altogether (N/C) ought to increase, intensified by the fact that one has hurt his loving, saving heavenly *Father*.

(6) CONFESSION. The sense of guilt is designed to lead (in the judicially unforgiven person) to a surrender to God as an enemy. That is quite a different thing from the confession of a rebellious child now submitting to his father.

(7) FORGIVENESS. In both cases, guilt is lifted; but in the one case it is the liability to eternal punishment in hell, and in the other the threat of temporal punishment and fatherly "displeasure" and lack of fellowship that is in view.

(8) RELATIONSHIP. The new relationship of Father and child is established through judicial forgiveness whereas that same relationship is restored and deepened in parental forgiveness.

So, while there are obvious similarities, we must be careful also to observe the great difference between judicial and parental forgiveness. Only by doing so can we be true to the *whole* teaching of the Bible, preserving the truths of grace (on the one hand) and avoiding antinomian and undisciplined living (on the other). Few things, therefore, are more important for biblical counselors to grasp. Their views on this point are altogether crucial for proper counseling.

Repentance and Confession

Now let us examine two important biblical words that fit into the forgiveness package. The first of these is repentance. Repentance is a part of the Christian proclamation that is coupled with forgiveness:

> Christ must suffer and on the third day rise again from the dead, and . . . repentance and forgiveness of sins must be preached in His name to all nations . . . (Luke 24:46, 47).

The good news is that Christ died for our sins (a penal, substitutionary, sacrificial death) and that He rose (bodily) from the dead (cf. I Cor. 15:3). This good news must be announced to all the world. With that proclamation must go a call to a new way of thinking that leads to faith and forgiveness. This new way of thinking is repentance (*metanoia*). Repentance is (literally) a change of mind; a rethinking. It is wrong to hook all sorts of emotional connotations to that word. There is another term, *metamelomai,* that means "to be sorry about," and that focuses on the consequences of an act or attitude to one's self rather than on the rightness (or truth) of the act or attitude before God. One can be sorry about his own losses without changing his opinions, stance or attitudes. Repentance refers to a change of heart—a new orientation of the inner man brought about by the Holy Spirit. It involves a rethinking of one's relationships toward God, one's self, sin, Christ, others, etc. It leads to the conclusion that "I am a sinner who must trust Christ alone for forgiveness of sin." Repentance after repentance leads to a similar conclusion: "I have sinned against my heavenly Father; I must ask Him to forgive me through Christ." Repentance is known to be genuine when the inner changes of heart lead to outer changes of life. The two are connected, but must never be confused.

Confession is the second term. Confession also is a part of parental as well as judicial forgiveness (cf. Rom. 10:9, 10—judicial forgiveness; I John 1:8ff.—parental forgiveness). Judicial confession and forgiveness establishes fellowship; parental confession and forgiveness restores and improves it.

Confession is not catharsis (N/C). What is it? It is an essential part of the forgiveness package. Confession is, essentially, *agreement. Homologeo,* the Greek term, literally means "to say the same thing," as does the Latin word from which our English term *confess* is derived (the word *confess* means, exactly, "to say with"). To confess is to agree with someone else. In volume I, *Select Papyri,* of the Loeb Classical Library (Edgar and Hunt, eds.), the word *homologeo* is used constantly in those papyri that have to do with legal and business transactions. There, it regularly means "agreement." When two or more parties "agree" to do something or other, the contract drawn up is called an "agreement" or contains an "agreement." So too, a *confession* of faith is an agreement by those who subscribe to it that they hold to those truths articulated in it. Confession, then, is an acknowledgment on our part that we *agree* with God in what He has said about our sin in His Word. We stand on His side—the side of the One offended—and acknowledge that He is right in holding us guilty of an offense. Confession is a formal acknowledgment of the fact. It involves a personal, on-the-record admission of guilt. The confessee says, "I have sinned; I am liable."

We often excuse ourselves, rationalize away our guilt, blame others for our sin. Confession is the opposite of all such behavior. It begins with repentance—rethinking all such attitudes—and ends with owning up to one's sin before God (and any others whom we may have wronged). Confession is done to formally commit ourselves before God; He wants us to go on record before Him (not principally for His sake, but for ours). Examples of great prayers of confession are found in Ezra 9, Nehemiah 9, and Daniel 9 (the "9" chapters).

Proverbs 28:13 makes it clear that genuine confession never stands alone; it must always be followed by change. The writer links confession with forsaking sin. Note that in this Proverb, "concealing" = the opposite of "confessing." To "prosper" means "to be successful." To live successfully for Christ, then, one must confess sin and forsake it. Psalm 32:1, 5 interrelates various terms with confession. In verse 1 sin is covered by God; in verse 3 we read of the period when one is silent (i.e., when sin is still unconfessed, and covered by the sinner). Then, in verse 5, David says, "I acknowledged (note the parallelism here with "confess," "acknowledging" and "not hiding" sin). This leads to forgiveness. When he uncovered or opened up his sin to God (i.e., confessed it), then God covered it (vs. 1).

Confession is not morbid, unhealthy self-introspection. It is always done in the presence of another, to him. There is no self-focus. God (or God and another) is in focus. The concern is about the one who has been wronged. Confession always includes at least one other. That shows, of course, that it is not merely some kind of "catharsis." The goal of confession is reconciliation. The person to whom one confesses is the one whom he has wronged and who can (therefore) forgive him. All openness *groups,* or confession *groups* other than groups composed of wronged persons—and those who wronged them—are excluded.[30]

Confession, then, involves (1) personal recognition of guilt and liability, and (2) formal admission of this to God and any others wronged. It leads, quite naturally, to asking forgiveness from God and those others who may have been wronged, followed by the granting of forgiveness and the establishing of a new and better relationship to them.

There are other views of confession abroad in the church today. In a book, *How to Live with Your Feelings,* Philip Swihart takes a position on confession similar to some things that N/C have said, but then goes

---

30. For more on the use and misuse of groups in counseling, cf. *The Big Umbrella,* pp. 237ff.

far beyond. In the chapter on Confession[31] he describes confession as the confession of "emotions" and "feelings." Confession, according to Swihart, is "facing up to my own emotions, owning them as belonging to me and accepting the fact that they do exist in me no matter what they are." There is no confession of sin to God or others; merely confession of emotions to one's self. There is no biblical warrant for the Swihart teaching. What has happened is that a biblical term has been drained dry of its meaning and new psychological content has been poured into the word. Then, under the scriptural label, this psychological (not a biblical) concept has been palmed off as God's way. Using the biblical word to teach psychology is one way to gain authority for the latter among God's people. The Bible nowhere tells us that to get feelings out into the open and be honest about them is confession. The Bible is used to support psychological teaching; thus psychology is stamped with biblical authority while entirely by-passing what the Bible actually does say about confession. Such practices are altogether too frequently discovered in our day.

Now, I have mentioned the matter of confessing sin not only to God, but also to others (cf. Luke 15:18). That concern leads to several others.

First, note the importance of distinguishing between *heart sins* and *social sins*. These terms, without careful explanation, may be misleading. All sins (including social sins) are heart sins—i.e., at some point, the sin was in the heart before it was in the hand or on the lip. The sinner assents to the act, develops the desire, etc., in his heart. Even though he may never follow through in a social way, he has sinned. Perhaps out of fear, etc., the sinner fails to do what he desires to do; the sin never proceeds beyond the heart. So his sin has no direct[32] social effects. Such heart sins, nonetheless, are sins[33]—heinous and damning—and they must be confessed to God. Jesus called adultery of the heart "adultery" and not something else. The difference between heart sins

---

31. Philip Swihart, *How to Live with Your Feelings* (Downers Grove, Ill.: InterVarsity Press, 1977), pp. 43ff.

32. Inner attitudes and desires, persisted in, lead to *indirect effects* especially detected in deteriorating interpersonal relationships. The distinction between *heart* and *social* sins at points is rough, but important (as we shall see).

33. The inner temptation to sin must be distinguished from the sin. When temptation is inwardly resisted, there is no sin. Jesus had to entertain the possibility of sinning, when tempted by Satan, *in order to* reject it.

and social sins is the lack or presence of damaging social effects. Before God, desiring to violate any of His commandments is as rebellious as doing so. Of course (as His restraining common grace indicates), God hates the social effects of sin and is pleased to see His children not take the second step in which they put sinful thoughts into practice, but (rather) wishes them to repent and reject those thoughts before doing so.

But this discussion raises the question of how counselors should instruct counselees to confess heart sins. The matter is somewhat clearer with respect to sins with social effects. Counselees are instructed to confess them to God and to all others who have been wronged.[34] But what of heart sins, *directed* toward another brother or sister—let us say adultery of the heart, fornication of the heart, homosexuality of the heart.[35] All these desires go no further than the heart (the inner life), but they are sins. Does the sinner, in such cases, confess both to God *and* to the one at whom his inner sin was directed? Or does he confess to God alone?

The Bible indicates that a sin ought to be confessed as widely as the sin's direct effects extend (cf. Matt. 18:15ff.). First one goes *privately* to the *one* person who has been wronged (against whom a direct offense has been committed and from whom he is now estranged). He may not go to others (not even to office bearers). There is an endeavor to contain the problem. Only after every attempt at that level fails is he permitted to call in one or two others as arbiters or counselors (and ultimately as witnesses). Only if they will not be heard does the matter come before the church. Clearly, there is a reluctance to widen or spread matters any further than necessary. This is an important principle that applies to group counseling, etc., but that also has bearing on our question. It means that if no offense has estranged the counselee from another, he need not (must not) go.

That means that there are some sins that must be confessed to God alone. Lustful thoughts toward another is a good example. Counselees must be instructed to confess such sin to God (as a violation of His commandment) but not to the person who was the object of the lust.

---

34. There are problems associated with doing so, to which we shall come at length.

35. Bitterness, resentment, anger; self-pity, jealousy, envy, sinful doubt are other common problems.

No transgression against him/her was committed. There was no social issue involved; it was a heart sin only. If any social acts, words, etc., accompanied the lust (improper words or suggestive advances, for instance), these should be confessed to the one approached in this manner and forgiveness sought. The principle, then, is *a sin is confessed as narrowly as the offense;* in some cases, that involves God and the sinner alone. All sin requires confession to God, but only some requires confessions to other persons as well.

Next, let us ask, how does one confess sin to another? When confession of sin to human beings takes place, it must be done with great care. Counselors must explain how/how not to do so, warn of dangers, and (in general) safeguard confession against the many possible abuses that (so often) one finds associated with the practice.[36]

To begin with, *what* one says is important. In identifying his offense to another, the confessor must be careful about his content and his language. There are things that ought not to be said (Eph. 5:12). Today, under the guise of "openness," that passage is regularly ignored. Christians may *not* be free and open to say anything they please; they may say only those things that please God. In reporting sexual sins, for example, details are neither necessary nor proper. If a confessor seems caught up in titillating details of sexual exploits, the likelihood is that he has not actually repented of the sin, but is still vicariously trying to get kicks out of it. The attitude of heart in the confessor is important. While counselors cannot judge counselees' hearts, they can (must) warn them about the problem. One can confess sexual sin *cleanly*—as the Bible speaks of it. The Bible is neither prudish nor suggestive, but always strikes a frank, non-detailed, honest posture when reporting sexual sin. Clear direction, plain discussion of the point, etc., by counselors, is needed.

How does the counselor guard against such abuses? Let me suggest that he warn directly against several problems whenever it may be appropriate.

1. Tell counselees to avoid highly connotative language (language that tends to titillate, that tends to aggravate, etc.). They will do well to use simple, factual terms, and say what they have to

36. The suggestions that follow are but suggestive. Counselors should study the subject and be prepared for all of the many contingencies that may arise.

say as briefly as possible (Prov. 10:19).

2. Warn counselees against destroying good words by bad attitudes (Prov. 25:11). Urge them to be sure that they go for proper reasons in the right spirit.

3. Guard against someone ruining a confession by describing his own sin accusingly:[37] "Forgive me for saying what I did when you pulled that dirty trick on me." Look out for "but you too" attitudes.

4. Make sure that the counselee understands that he may not attach excuses to his confession. Here, watch out for "even though" qualifications: "Even though the pressures were great, I guess I shouldn't have done that."

Some habits of speech are so ingrained that counselees will find themselves saying such things without realizing it. Role play of the potential confession scene between the counselor/counselee often can be useful in detecting (and deflecting) such problems.

It is important to seek forgiveness when confessing rather than apologizing. To make this clear, let me quote from my book, *Update on Christian Counseling,* vol. 1:

DON'T APOLOGIZE

It is time to say it clearly—so that no one may misunderstand: the Bible nowhere advises or allows (and certainly doesn't command) apology.

Yet, in spite of this fact, Christians (and even Christian counselors) somehow seem to be addicted to apologizing and advising counselees to "go apologize" to others whom they have wronged. To all such, I have one piece of advice: Stop it!

"Well, what on earth is wrong with apologies?"

Fundamentally, two things.

I

An apology is an inadequate, humanistic substitute for the real thing. Nowhere do the Scriptures require, or even encourage, apologizing. To say "I'm sorry" is a human dodge for doing what God has commanded. And (as we shall see) since it is man's substitute for God's requirement (and has all but replaced that requirement),

---

37. He must first take the log out of his own eye. At a later time—after his own sin is cleared—he may raise other issues. The two must not be confused at the time of confession.

it has caused a great number of problems in the church. By replacing the biblical requirement for dealing with estrangement, it
has allowed estrangement in the church to continue unchecked.

"What is this biblical requirement that has been replaced?"

Forgiveness.

"Forgiveness?"

Yes. I shall not now develop this point by discussing the numerous
passages that speak of Christian forgiveness. Instead, I shall simply
refer you to other treatments of the subject.[38]

Thus, confession is always linked with seeking forgiveness. This is what
all the great prayers of confession do. Apologizing breaks that link.

As long as Christians continue to say to those they have wronged,
"I'm sorry" (or words to that effect), instead of "I sinned; will you
forgive me?," and as long as they receive the natural response, "Oh,
that's all right" (or something similar), the real solutions to the
many difficulties that could have been reached through forgiveness
will continue to be by-passed. The church will labor under the burden of resentments and bitterness on the part of its members.

"Why do you say that?" you may wonder. Let me explain; and that
explanation leads to a second point—apology is wrong, not only
because it is man's inadequate substitute for God's revealed method
of righting sour interpersonal relationships, but (as such),

II

apology elicits an inadequate response. When one asks, "Will you
forgive me?" he has punted; the ball has changed hands, and a response is now required of the one addressed. The onus of responsibility has shifted from the one who did the wrong to the one who
was wronged. Both parties, therefore, are required to put the matter
in the past. And, the proper response (Luke 17:3) is, "Yes, I will."
Like God's forgiveness ("Your sins and iniquities I will remember
against you no more"), human forgiveness is a *promise* that is *made*
and *kept*.

When one person says, "I forgive you," to another, he promises:

1. "I'll not bring this matter up to you again;
2. "I'll not bring it up to others;
3. "I'll not bring it up to myself (i.e., dwell on it in my mind)."

The response, "Yes, I'll forgive you," then, is a promise that en-

---

38. See *The Christian Counselor's Manual,* pp. 63-70, 88, 361; *Christian Living
in the Home,* chap. 3.

tails quite a commitment—one to which the forgiven brother (and God) may hold him, and one that (if kept) will lead to forgetting the wrong (not forgive and forget, but forgive to forget) and reestablishing a new, good relationship between the parties involved. So, an apology is an inadequate substitute because (a) it asks for no such commitment, and (b) gets none.

An apology keeps the ball in one's own possession. The other party is required to do nothing about it (and usually doesn't). To say "I'm sorry" is, you see, nothing more than an expression of one's own feelings. To say, "I have wronged you," and then to ask, "Will you forgive me?" is quite another thing.

Therefore, counselors (in advising counselees) must be quite clear about this matter. When they are, and when a proper understanding of this matter once again begins to permeate the Christian church, many of the current difficulties we are experiencing will disappear. Let's do our part in hastening that day.

In another place I wrote:

Now, let's take an example. Suppose you have told a counselee to ask God for forgiveness for a particular sin and then go to the person he has wronged by it and seeks his (or her) forgiveness as well. The counselee agrees. All looks well. When he returns for the next session, he reports that he has done so. (You fail to check out the exact particulars of what he said and did.) Pleased, you go on to other matters. Then, at the next session, the counselee announces that "this business of seeking a brother's forgiveness hasn't done any good." Things, he indicates, aren't any better; in fact, they seem worse. He says, "I'm sorry I took your advice."

There can, of course, be many other dimensions to such a problem (failure on the part of the offended party to forgive, or to live up to his forgiveness promise, etc. But, for the sake of simplicity in making the point, let's leave these possibilities aside for this discussion[39]). But let's say that this is what happened:

Your counselee heard your advice. However, he "translated" your words (even when written, this can happen), "ask forgiveness" into "make up with" or "tell him you're sorry" or "apologize." That isn't what you *said,* and it isn't what you *intended,* but it is what (in his sinful perversity) he *did.* What he did was *partial.* He went to the offended party as you directed, but it was also *perverted:* he did something qualitatively different. He did not follow directions. He said, "I'm sorry," instead of "I've sinned; will you forgive me?"

---

39. But not, however, in a genuine counseling context if the other party can be brought into the counseling session as well.

Now, there could be any number of reasons why he fulfilled the assignment in this way. Take two:

(1) It could be his pattern to "do things his own way."
(2) He could genuinely not have known the difference.

Let's consider (2) more closely. In this case, the counselor also bears some responsibility. Counselors ought to know about such perversions of biblical action; they should know that people substitute apologies for seeking forgiveness. And, therefore, they should know to spell out what asking for forgiveness entails. In fact, they should anticipate such a possible "translation" and guard against it by clearly distinguishing the two things when giving the assignment. Because so few persons recognize the difference, and because most people persist in confounding forgiveness and apology, of necessity good counseling involves spelling out *in detail* what is and (with equal clarity) what is *not* meant by the assignment. And it would be well to warn against substituting the one for the other. He might explain,

"Seeking forgiveness and saying 'I'm sorry' are two entirely different ways to handle the same situation. One is God's way; the other man's substitute. The former stems from repentance (leading to confession—an admission of sin—and to the granting of pardon); the other may stem from sorrow (often, as in Esau's case, mentioned in Hebrews 12:15-17, sorrow arises over the *consequences* of sin, rather than the fact of sin as an offense against God and others, and his inability to reverse them). The two differ radically. An apology is no more than a statement about one's feelings: 'I'm sorry.' It is non-specific—is he sorry about what happened to himself or to others? Does he recognize the fact that he has sinned, first and foremost against God? What do the words mean?

"Because they are non-specific, the words of apology elicit some non-committal response (if any is forthcoming at all). Why shouldn't they? They are vague, and (indeed) ask for no commitment from him. Having made an apology, one may *assume* that the matter is closed. The truth is that it is not. Neither party has committed himself to closing the question; nothing has been done about the past act or about their future relationship. This leaves all options open.

"In contrast, asking for forgiveness is quite specific, when done biblically. Say to the one you wronged, 'I have sinned against God and against you [Luke 15:18]. I have confessed my sin to God [if you have], and I know He has forgiven me; now I ask you to do the same. Will you?' Such a statement is specific. By it you recognize the serious nature of what you have done—it is sin, against both God and him. Secondly, it asks for a concrete response on the part of the one that you have wronged (don't settle for a non-committal reply like 'Forget it.' Say, 'No, this was sin. That requires forgiveness. I want to set the matter to rest; will you forgive me?'

"Sometimes the person wronged is willing to settle for less so that he can go on holding the offense against you. If he dodges an answer, or refuses to forgive, remind him of Luke 17:3-10. If he still refuses, Matthew 18:15ff. comes into play (with another believer).[40] He must say either 'yes' or 'no.' You must know the answer.

"When you go to another, the object isn't merely to express your feelings—even of regret. You must go (as the Scriptures make clear) to be reconciled to him. The substitute, 'I'm sorry,' does nothing about the *relationship;* the biblical way opens the door on a new beginning.

"And, one more thing—if either you or the person to whom you go doesn't understand what forgiveness is and, therefore, what the granting of forgiveness entails, let me tell you plainly. Then you can explain to him what you have in mind. Forgiveness is a *promise.* When God forgave you in Christ, He promised not to 'remember your sins and iniquities against you any more.' The one who asks for forgiveness also asks for *that;* the one granting forgiveness promises *that*—and nothing less. This promise is threefold in his case.

(1) 'I won't bring the matter up to you again;
(2) 'I won't bring it up to others;
(3) 'I won't bring it up to myself (i.e., allow myself to sit and brood over it in self-pity).'

"Asking and granting forgiveness implies future effort to work for a new, biblical relationship. When God reconciled us to Himself, He didn't leave the matter with forgiveness. Once the sin was forgiven, He insisted on building a new, proper relationship with us (cf. Eph. 4:17).[41] Now, what do you think of this? Is it clear? Do you have any questions?"

Some such presentation of the assignment must be given (whatever the subject may be). By going into it in some detail (you may even want to *read* this to a counselee at times) you will forestall all sorts of problems. By giving an opportunity for feedback at the close, often you can discover whether the counselee understands, believes, intends to follow directions, etc. His response usually will lead to further clarification of the issues.

What about restitution? Often, restitution is necessary. God required

---

40. In seeking forgiveness from an unbeliever, follow Rom. 12:18 (for a thorough discussion of this, see my book, *How to Overcome Evil*).

41. On this see my *Matters of Concern*, pp. 36ff., where I discuss how reconciliation must lead to a new relationship.

restitution in addition to sacrifice (cf. Num. 5:5-7). Luke 19:1-10 shows how one man spontaneously far surpassed that requirement. A chief difference between the sin offering and the trespass offering is the fact that the latter was for *social* sins and usually was accompanied by restitution (cf. Lev. 6:4f.). The O.T. worshiper was to restore the value of the loss plus one-fifth more. Zacchaeus far exceeded this requirement. He said, "I'll give four times the original." For every dollar of value, the law required $1.20 in restitution. Zacchaeus said, "I'll pay four dollars for one." Paul agreed to pay Philemon whatever Onesimus may have owed; his conversion did not free Onesimus from obligations entered into prior to his conversion.

At this point, I am tempted to reproduce my sermon on Luke 17:3ff. on the subject of forgiveness, in which Jesus tells us that the person wronged is (1) required to take the initiative and go to the one by whom he was wronged, (2) required to rebuke him in love, and (3) required to forgive him

    a. if he repents,
    b. as often as he repents (7 times a day if necessary),
    c. on the basis of his word alone, "saying, 'I repent,'"
    d. whether he feels like it or not,
    e. because God commands it.

But I shall not.[42] The principles in the passage are, however, of great importance.

In the discussion of Luke 17:3ff. the idea of *rebuke,* leading to forgiveness, appears. In the chart presented earlier the word *rebuke* appears. It is useful, therefore, to understand something of the biblical meaning of rebuke.

The basic O.T. term for rebuke is *yakach.* This word occurs frequently and is often translated "reprove." Inherent in it is the idea of reproaching or rebuking through reason. It presents not the idea of strong emotion but rather of measured, logical argument. The notion has to do with making something clear by presenting the facts. The concept of conviction attaches itself to the word. The issue is to be *discussed.* Obviously this says much about *how* rebuke is to be done. Some typical passages in which *yakach* occurs are: Genesis 31:42; Leviticus 19:17;

42. The sermon is available on tape from Christian Study Services, 2540 Edge Hill Rd., Huntingdon Valley, Pa., 19006. In its fullest form, it is found in the taped series of studies on Christian Forgiveness.

Psalm 6:1; 38:1; Proverbs 9:7, 8; 24:25; 28:23.

Another term is *tokachath* = reproof, correction by words, arguing down, showing what is right. This is a great word in Proverbs (1:23, 25, 30; 15:12; 6:23; 10:17; 12:1; 13:18; 15:5, 10, 31, 32; 29:1, 15).

A third O.T. word is *gaar* = to rebuke, scold, threaten[43] (used of a father rebuking a son; but also used more widely), instruct, punish, warn, reprove. This is a somewhat stronger term. Sample passages are Proverbs 13:1; 15:31, 32; 19:25; 27:5; 28:23.

There are also two N.T. words for rebuke. The first is *elengcho* (found in I Tim. 5:20; Tit. 1:13; 2:15; Heb. 12:5; Rev. 3:19). The word means to convict. It is a legal term, taken from the courtroom, meaning to so pursue a case against another that he is *convicted* of the crime of which he was accused. It is not merely rebuke or reproof, but *effective* rebuke or reproof.

The other N.T. word is *epitimao,* meaning "to set a weight on, to chide." It frequently appears in the Gospels, but is also found elsewhere (e.g., II Tim. 4:2; Jude 9). It appears in Luke 17:3 (the passage mentioned earlier). The word is much more *tentative* than its N.T. counterpart.[44] It is *rebuke that may be undeserved* (cf. Matt. 16:22) *or ineffectual* (cf. Luke 23:40). When one goes to rebuke his brother (Luke 17:3), he often must do so with certain reservations. He may not know for sure that the rebuke is deserved until he hears his brother's response. In this rebuke, one raises the issue, and brings the evidence that he has so far. It is most important, therefore, in counseling others to go and present their cases to offending brothers and sisters, to explain that the attitude in which they go must possess this quality of tentativeness. That should be so, even when the case *seems* open and shut. The one going to rebuke another must go in love; but among the qualities of love are these: to "believe all things" and to "hope all things" (I Cor. 13:7). The one raising the issue must be prepared (have a mind set) to hear new evidence, and must show a willingness to give his brother the benefit of any doubt. In effect, he says, "Here are the data that I have; now let me hear your side of the story."[45]

---

43. This element must not be applied to such passages as Luke 17:3ff.

44. Trench, R. C., *Synonyms of the New Testament,* has an excellent comparison of the two terms.

45. For more on love as "believing all things," see my *What About Nouthetic Counseling?,* pp. 51ff.

Now, turning from the notion of rebuke (which, as you can see, is multidimensional), let us ask the question, "What is forgiveness?" We are almost ready to say a final word on this subject. But first, let us be clear about one thing: forgiveness is not a feeling. The Luke 17:3ff. passage is plain about that. Against all his feelings to the contrary, the slave had to refrain from tasting his master's meal as he was preparing it. Out of obedience, he restrained his own hunger, just as the one who forgives another often must restrain his feelings (to pay back, to withhold forgiveness, etc.) and grant forgiveness to the one who seeks it the seventh time. No, forgiveness isn't a feeling.

Well, then, what is forgiveness? Forgiveness is a *promise*. When God forgives a sinner, He does not simply become emotional over his repentance. No, instead, He goes on record that He has forgiven by making (and keeping) a promise to that effect: "Your sins and iniquities will I remember against you no more" (Jer. 31:34). When Bushnell once disparagingly wrote, "Forgiveness is only a kind of formality," he missed the whole point. Of course forgiveness is a formality—but what a glorious one! "Only a kind of formality," indeed! Thank God for a formal promise not to bring up our sin any more; if it were not for that "formality," we'd always be unsure of our salvation. Forgiveness is a *wonderful* formality, the basis for all our comfort, peace, security, certainty. Our forgiveness is modeled after God's forgiveness (Eph. 4:32). That means that for us forgiveness is also a promise that offers assurance for the future.[46]

So, when a counselee says, "I forgive you," to another, then he also makes a promise. This promissory aspect is an essential element of forgiveness. Forgiveness is a formal declaration to lift the burden of one's guilt and a promise to remember another's wrong against him no more. It is a promise (as we have seen) that involves three elements: I won't bring it up to you, to others or to myself.[47] The one to whom such a promise is made may hold him to it. And a promise can be made whether or not one *feels* like it (e.g., a husband, out of conviction—against his feelings—may say, "Honey, I'll take you out to dinner Fri-

---

46. Of course we may, and often do, fail to keep our promises. In such cases, we too must seek forgiveness for having done so.

47. The third element of the promise is often the hardest; self-pity can destroy the good effects of forgiveness. Counselors can find help on how to keep the promise in *Lectures on Counseling*, pp. 138ff., and *Matters of Concern*, p. 11.

day"), and his promise can be kept (in the foregoing example it had better be), whether or not one feels like it (even on Friday).

So, we are ready to put it all together now:

> Forgiveness is a lifting of the charge of guilt from another, a formal declaration of that fact and a promise (made and kept) never to remember the wrong against him in the future.

"Wait!" you ask. "Does the Bible teach that we must 'forgive and forget,' as the saying goes?" No, it does not. It teaches that we must forgive *in order to forget*. Whoever makes and keeps those three promises will forget; that is the only way to do so.

Looking once more at Luke 17:3, 4, I should like to note that forgiveness is conditioned on repentance. Forgiveness may not be granted to another person until he says, "I repent, please forgive me" (or words to that effect). This should be obvious to anyone who thinks through the facts about forgiveness. After all, if one must rebuke an unrepentant brother or sister (as Luke 17:3 requires), and *pursue* the matter to repentance and reconciliation, he may have to bring it up again and again in the process (Matt. 18:15ff.). On this matter, see the discussion of "Church Discipline" in *Matters of Concern* (pp. 69-74, esp. pp. 72ff.).

"Well, then, if a person refuses to seek forgiveness, and you hold something against him inside you, won't that lead to the self-pity you were warning us against in the last footnote?" Again, the answer is *no*. "Why not?" First, because Christians are not allowed to become bitter and resentful, and there are ways to avoid doing so (cf. *Competent to Counsel,* pp. 220ff., and similar discussions in any number of my books). But, even more to the point, there is a very important passage in Mark 11:25 that we must consider:

> And when you stand praying, if you have something against anyone, forgive him, so that your Father in the heavens also may forgive you your trespasses.

How can we square this verse with the idea that forgiveness may be granted only to those who seek it in repentance?

Let us look more carefully at Mark 11:25. Note, you may not sit around and wallow in self-pity or become bitter; that much is clear. But what do you do? Do you forgive or don't you? Does God forgive us when we don't repent? No. Forgiveness and repentance are always snapped together in the Bible. John the Baptist came preaching forgiveness through repentance; Jesus did the same. And He taught us to preach the same (Luke 24:47). Well, then, what does Mark 11:25 mean?

First, it doesn't mean that you stop bringing up the matter to the offending, unrepentant brother; Matthew 18 requires you to bring up the issue until repentance occurs.

Secondly, it doesn't mean that you stop bringing it up to others— Matthew 18 may require you to bring it up to one or two others, or eventually to the elders of the church as well.

Does his failure to repent give you the right to become resentful? No, that is no license for self-pity. The words in Mark 11 apply to the third element in forgiveness—precisely this matter of self-pity. You must empty the matter from your heart in prayer; you may not dwell on it— you have given it to God. Note, especially, you do this *before God,* not before the *offender.* You must tell God of your *willingness* to grant him forgiveness, that you *want* to be reconciled and that you won't sit and brood about how you were wronged. In that sense—and that sense alone—you forgive him: *before God.* But Mark 11 *doesn't* require you to *grant* forgiveness to the offender; the passage speaks only about one's own personal attitude. You are not making a formal promise to the offender when you tell God you won't be bitter toward him. This passage speaks of forgiveness of the *heart.* Forgiveness of the heart is essential in *all* cases. The heart and the promise on the lips must conform.[48] The only commitment in Mark 11 is a commitment to God; none is made to the offender. It is forgiveness before God. At every point, a matter is set to rest as quickly as possible, where it *can* be. According to Mark 11:25, *one* person can resolve at least one part of the problem right away. Counselors must call them to do so.

There is one other issue to consider. Even though a person may be forgiven, that does not cut off *all* consequences which may flow from his sin. If a person puts his arm through a plate glass window in a drunken brawl, and lacerates it so badly that it must be amputated, he doesn't sprout a new one when he is forgiven. He must learn to overcome these consequences and by God's grace use them for God's honor in days to come. Forgiveness lifts the weight of guilt and removes liability to punishment. It does not lift *other* consequences.

---

48. To do something "from the heart," remember, is to do it sincerely.

Some may think that all such consequences *are* punishment, failing to recognize the possibility of other factors. Probably the most striking example of this situation is the case of David and the death of his child born out of that adulterous union with Bathsheba (II Sam. 11, 12). Nathan comes, tells the story and mentions some consequences (the sword will continue with you; there will be trouble in your own family— these were consequences that God [for His own reasons] said would be set in motion by his sin and that would continue until fulfilled). David repents and is assured of forgiveness (and the removal of his punishment: "You will not die"). But then he is told, "Nevertheless," because your sin provided such an occasion for the Lord's enemies to ridicule, your son will die. And he did. *This was not punishment;* it was a consequence that involved the Lord's Name and His witness to His enemies (to show them that God doesn't countenance sin). Sure, it was tough on David; certainly it had sanctifying effects on his life—but those questions were secondary. The fundamental reason is given—the witness to God's enemies.

This fact of further consequences (following forgiveness) must not be forgotten (or by-passed) in counseling. Too often, counselors look on forgiveness unrealistically, neglecting to mention this possibility,[49] thereby failing to prepare counselees for it and setting them up for some nasty jolts in the future.

How does one help the counselee to handle the after shocks of sin's earthquakes? Again, he teaches them from the super-redemption stance discussed in detail earlier. Even such liabilities can be turned to assets, by God's grace. He must help them to see how. Every consequence of sin can become a blessing. God is greater than any problem and loves to turn liabilities to His own advantage; He is the One Who makes even the wrath of man to praise Him.

Because forgiveness (and its many ramifications) is such an important issue in counseling, I have taken a great amount of time to deal with the question. I cannot overestimate the need for every counselor to thoroughly familiarize himself with the biblical data on the subject. But

49. Note how Paul did not fail to mention such matters in his letter to Philemon. Paul knew that Onesimus was fully forgiven, yet he recognized that there were still obligations (1) to return to Philemon, and (2) repay anything that he may have owed Philemon. He hoped (and hinted), of course, that Philemon would forgive him not only the wrongs done, but the obligations (consequences) remaining. Cf. also Num. 14:19-23.

before leaving the subject of forgiveness, let me append one footnote.

Frequently, these days, one hears words like, "I know that God has forgiven me, and Bill has forgiven me, but I just can't seem to forgive myself." How does a Christian counselor handle that problem?[50] First, he points out that the words represent a psychologizing rather than a biblical construct of the situation. Yes, there is something more to be done, but it is not a matter of more forgiveness. Nowhere does the Bible command us to forgive ourselves. That simply isn't the real difficulty.

The actual problem lies elsewhere; there is a dynamic at work that must be understood and properly dealt with, and not masked by such unscriptural notions.

When a counselee has been forgiven by God and others, but recognizes that this is "not enough," he is right. Forgiveness isn't only an end; it is also a new beginning. Forgiveness closes off certain relationships, but it also opens up the possibility (and need) for new ones. Forgiveness is a *watershed*. There is truly a need for something new—but it is not more forgiveness (remember, the forgiveness chart closes with a new relationship).

The dynamic behind the counselee's uneasiness is twofold. He senses, but often cannot articulate clearly the fact that:

1. Though forgiven, he is still the same person, unchanged, who did the wrong. Something more is needed, then, to keep him from doing it again; he must change.

2. Though forgiven, he has done nothing more to establish a new and better relationship with God and his neighbor. Unless he does, the future relationship will drift, and is likely to be bad rather than good.

These are vital issues and must be handled well by Christian counselors. I have dealt with the second one in *Matters of Concern* (pp. 36, 37), where I have shown that *barriers* removed do not constitute *bonds* cemented; those are two separate things. Indeed, barriers removed leave *breaks* existing if bonds are not cemented. Forgiveness is but a part of the larger concern of reconciliation, which involves making and cultivating new relationships as well (see also the *last* element listed on the similarities and differences in forgiveness chart).

The first item—becoming a new and different person—is a vital one and must be considered in full in the next chapter.

---

50. For more on this, see *Matters of Concern*, pp. 7-9.

CHAPTER FOURTEEN

COUNSELING AND THE NEWNESS OF LIFE: THE DOCTRINE OF SANCTIFICATION

In *Competent to Counsel*[1] I observed that counseling has to do with the process of sanctification. That is why counseling has to be done with believers (with unbelievers only precounseling—i.e., evangelism—is appropriate[2]). True counseling is done at a level of depth; it is a work of the Spirit that involves change from within. This takes place in the heart of a regenerate human being as he responds favorably to the ministry of the Word because of his new life tendencies.

Perhaps, for those who may be unfamiliar with theological terms,[3] (and, sadly, so many who wish to do counseling are), the following chart and explanations will help to put some (not all) key concepts in place.

Doctrine	Act	Process	God alone does it	God enables man to do it
Regeneration[4]	✓		✓	
Conversion: Repentance and Faith	✓			✓
Justification	✓		✓	
Sanctification		✓		✓
Glorification	✓		✓	

1. Pp. 73-77.
2. See Appendix A.
3. See also my list of theological definitions in *Update on Christian Counseling*, vol. 1.
4. There is both a broader and narrower use of this term. The Bible also sometimes refers to the whole new life as regeneration; theologically, regeneration = quickening.

The chart clearly indicates that, of all the key doctrines listed, sanctification alone involves a *process*.[5] This is significant. Moreover, along
with conversion, this is the one other doctrine that describes a work not
performed directly by God alone, but indirectly by God, using human
agency.[6] In conversion, by the Spirit's wisdom and power, man repents
and believes (God enables him to do so, but then *he* does it); in sanctification man trusts and obeys (again, God enables him to do so, but
then *he* does so).

Sanctification, then, is like conversion in that the human being himself
plays more than the passive role he does in regeneration, for instance.
Since this is true, it is possible (indeed, often necessary) for others to
assist him. As in conversion, so also in sanctification, the ministry of the
Word is paramount. The Spirit uses the preaching of His Word to bring
about conversion (cf. Rom. 10:14, 15). Sanctification takes place in
a similar way (the close ties between the process of conversion and
sanctification are noted in Gal. 3:2, 3). It is the Word, ministered to
counselees that brings about spiritual change (II Tim. 3:15-17) and
growth (I Pet. 2:2). This takes place through preaching and teaching,
through mutual fellowship and encouragement and (because sanctification is a process, not an act) through one or more (often several)
counseling sessions.

Now, at this place, it is appropriate to develop an understanding of
the process of sanctification in relationship to counseling. To avoid
doing so in this book would be a tragic mistake. But there is a problem.
In the *Christian Counselor's Manual* I have already considered at great
length the fundamental matter of putting off the old ways of the pre-
Christian life and the putting on of new ones. My problem, then, was
to decide how to proceed here. Should I omit that material entirely and
simply refer the reader to the appropriate passages in the *Manual*,
should I quote all of it, or what? After considering the alternatives, I
decided to quote extensively (but not entirely) from the Manual.

Effecting Biblical Change

Change: The Goal

Biblical change is the goal of counseling. But change is hard. Joel

---

5. In Hebrews (and perhaps elsewhere) sanctification is considered an act.
6. Cf. earlier discussions of this. For more on the subject of the "Human/
Divine in Counseling," see *Matters of Concern*, pp. 65-67.

Nederhood pointedly refers to the title of an article by Amitai Etzioni entitled, "Human Beings Are Not So Easy to Change After All." In this article Etzioni cites the failures "to bring children of disadvantaged backgrounds up to standard . . . indicates that driver's training has reduced accident rates somewhat, but [only at the cost of] $88,000 for every life saved," and other similar information. Jeremiah pointed out the difficulty of breaking into an established life pattern when he quipped:

> Can the Ethiopian change his skin
> Or the leopard his spots?
> Then you also can do good
> Who are *accustomed to* do evil
>   (Jer. 13:23, emphasis mine).

Calvin, in his commentary, observes that this passage has been interpreted wrongly as referring to the sinful nature with which men are born. The interpretation still is common. Instead, he insists, it should be understood as a description of "the habit that is contracted by long practice." Careful attention to the exegesis of the passage shows that Calvin is right. Jeremiah, elsewhere, makes the same point in another way:

> I spoke to you in your prosperity;
> But you said, "I will not listen!"
> This has been your practice from your youth,
> That you have not obeyed my voice (Jer. 22:21).

Change Is Hard

Counselors must be realistic about the work to which they have been called. While in Christ there is a genuine basis for hope of change, as we have seen, this change is hard. Children, who have "learned" to slam doors have a hard time relearning the process of closing them; young marrieds must make many adjustments of their former habits to construct a third way of life that will be different from their two backgrounds; older persons upon losing a life partner discover change inevitable but not easy.

Change, then, is necessary, but change is hard. One of the major reasons Christians founder is because they are either unwilling to make changes or do not know how to make the changes that God requires of them in order to meet the vicissitudes of life.

Counselors should not be surprised, then, when counselees protest, "I'll never change," or "I guess that's just the way I am," or words to that effect. Counselees *continually* confuse learned behavior patterns with inherited nature (*phusis*.) Counselors may take it as a rule that any quality of life, attitude of mind, or activity that God requires of man may be acquired through the Lord Jesus Christ. Thus, whenever a counselee protests, "But I just don't have patience," and means by those words, "That's the way that I was born and nothing can be done about it," the counselor must protest and insist that patience can be acquired, since the Scriptures list it as the fruit of the Spirit.

While it is true, for instance, that not all of the *gifts* of the Spirit may be acquired by all Christians, for He distributes them to whomever He wills and in the quantities that He sees fit (I Cor. 12:4-11; Eph. 4:7), all of the items in Galatians 5 that are said to be His *fruit* are available to every Christian.

Failure to Effect Changes That Stick

The repetitive pattern of sin-confession-forgiveness, sin-confession-forgiveness, that is so well known to counselors as well as to counselees, probably accounts for as much discouragement and failure in counseling as any other factor. Why do counseling resolutions, following the style of the traditional New Year's resolution, so often fall so flat? Why is change so frequently temporary? And . . . what (if anything) can be done about the problem?

Well, let us answer by asking another question (actually, the first line in a child's joke):

"When is a door not a door?"

You know the answer, of course: "When it is ajar!"

Now I did not tell this joke for its humor value (which is doubtful), but because it can become a useful paradigm for the discussion that follows. Let's ask and answer the question again, with a slight change:

Q. "When is a door not a door?"

A. "When it is something else."

In thinking about change, the biblical data indicate just *that*— change takes place not merely when certain *changes* occur, but only when there has been a *change*. The change of an activity is not the same as the change of a person. The former may involve actions sporadically or temporarily sustained by certain conditions; the latter involves a pattern developed as part of the fabric of the person's life that brings about those actions in spite of conditions.

Let us take an example or two and clarify this concept. Ask the question once more with blanks:

"When is a . . . . . . not a . . . . . .?"

The blanks may be filled in with the counselee's problem. For instance, they may read:

Q. "When is a liar not a liar?" or
Q. "When is a thief not a thief?"

What are the answers? Should they read as follows:

A. "When he stops lying";
A. "When he stops stealing"?

No, precisely not. There is no assurance whatever that a thief who is not stealing has ceased being a thief. All that the cessation of stealing indicates is that *for the moment* or *at present* he is not stealing. Perhaps all that this means is that it is strategically not wise for him to steal at this time. Or it may mean that he has made a good resolution to stop, yet what he will do when he finds himself under economic pressure is another matter. In other words, since thieves do not steal at all times, liars do not always lie, and drunks are not always drunk, cessation of these activities is (in itself) no indication that there has been a permanent change. Indeed, if that is *all* that has taken place, the Christian counselor must conclude that changes, not change, have occurred, and with confidence he may predict the future failure to which I have alluded in the opening paragraph of this section.

What, then, is wrong with the answers given above? Simply this: they do not conform to the paradigm that the revised answer in the joke sets forth:

A. "When it (he) is *something else.*"

Dehabituation and Rehabituation

Let us consider the biblical base for this framework and the scriptural principles that underlie these assertions. In Ephesians 4, Paul deals directly with the problem of change. As we have noted elsewhere, he is discussing the need for walking in new working relationships among Christians; unity is essential. But that requires a change in lives. But unlike some present-day conservative ministers, Paul not only exhorts, he explains *how* change can be effected.

We shall skip over the early part of the chapter and begin with verse 17, in which he stresses the necessity for such a change:

> This I say therefore, and affirm together with the Lord, that you walk no longer as the Gentiles walk. . . .

That is as strong an imperative as he could have laid upon his reader. The words "and affirm together with the Lord" underline the need, strengthen the emphasis, and show that there is no question about the matter. The exhortation is to change: "walk *no longer* as the Gentiles walk." "You *once* did, when you were a Gentile (i.e., heathen, unbeliever), but now that you have become a Christian, your walk (manner of daily activities; life style) must change."

Do not fail to note how plainly Paul speaks of more than the cessation of some objectionable actions; he calls for a change in the "manner of life" (cf. vs. 22). Paul calls for genuine change; change in the person. Not merely in his actions. There is hope in that—God expects His children to change. If so, such change must be *possible;* if so, He Who commands also must have provided the *ways and means.*

Again, we shall pass over verses 17b-21 with only a comment or two. What Paul describes in those verses as the Gentile style of life amounts to the description of a life that is focused upon self; what we have called the desire-oriented and motivated life. This comes to the surface especially in 19b: (they "have given themselves over to sensuality, for the practice of every kind of impurity with greediness, and in verse 22, in accordance with "deceitful lusts." Notice that the change contemplated is directed toward *a way of life,* not merely toward some of the activities involved in such living. Paul speaks of it as a "walk" (vs. 17), as a "practiced" way to which they have "given themselves over" (vs. 19), as a "former manner of life" (or as the Berkeley Version has it, "previous habits") and as "the old man" (vs. 22). In describing the change, it is as if one must become a "new man" (vs. 24), one that has been renewed in "mind" (vs. 23), in "righteousness," and in "holiness" (vs. 24)—a man like Jesus Christ. These changes issue, he says, "from the truth" (vs. 24b). The change is a change in the man; he is renewed by changing his entire life style. The new style must conform to the image of Christ so that in his new manner of life the Christian truly reflects God. Nothing less will do.

This is the setting for the "how to" which is described in verses 22-24 that is vital for every counselor to understand. The key fact here is that Paul does not only say "put off" the old man (i.e., the old life style), but also says "put on" the new man (i.e., the Christian life style).

Change is a two-factored process. These two factors always must be present in order to effect genuine change. Putting off will not be permanent without putting on. Putting on is hypocritical as well as temporary, unless it is accompanied by putting off

Let us return, then, to the liar and to the thief. Ask again,

Q. "When is a liar not a liar?"

A. "When he is something else."

Very good, but *what* else? When he *stops* lying what must he *start* doing? By what does the Bible say that lying must be replaced? (That is the kind of question that counselors continually should be asking and answering.) Well, what does Paul say? Look at verse 25:

> Therefore [he is now applying the principles of change] laying aside falsehood [putting off], speak truth, each one of you with his neighbor, for we are members of one another [putting on].

There you have it.

Q. "When is a liar not a liar?"

A. "When he has become a truth teller."

Unless he has been "reprogrammed" or rehabituated, when the chips are down—when he is tired, sick, or under great pressure—a counselee's good resolves and temporary cessation of lying will not last. He will revert to his former manner of life because he is still programmed to do so. The old sinful habit patterns have not been replaced by new ones. Until that occurs, he will remain vulnerable to sinful reversion. Dehabituation is possible only by achieving rehabituation. The counselee must be repackaged. New patterns of response must become dominant. It is to these instead that he must learn to turn habitually under life stresses.

Let's do it once again:

Q. "When is a thief not a thief?"

When he stops stealing? No. Look at verse 28:

> Let him who steals steal no longer [putting off] but rather let him labor, performing with his own hands what is good, in order that he may have something to share with him who has need [putting on].

A thief is still a thief if he has only stopped stealing. He is simply a thief who *at the moment* is not stealing. Under pressure, he is likely to revert. But if after repentance he gets a job, works hard at earning his money honestly, and learns the blessings of giving, he is no longer a thief. A thief is not a thief when he has become a hard-working man who gives. He becomes dehabituated to stealing only when he becomes rehabituated to hard working and sharing.

All through the Scriptures, the two-factored process appears. In this chapter, for instance, notice what Paul says about anger (vss. 26, 27):

put off: resentment (holding anger in);

put on: dealing with problems daily (letting anger motivate to biblical solutions).

Consider his words about speech (vs. 29):

put off: unwholesome words that cut up others;

put on: words that build up another.

He advocates in place of the nasty verbal or physical expression of "bitterness, wrath, anger, clamor, slander and malice," tender-hearted forgiveness (vss. 31, 32).

The two factors occur in Peter:

Not returning evil for evil or insult for insult / but giving a blessing instead (I Pet. 3:9);

and in John:

Beloved do not imitate that which is evil / but that which is good (III John 11);

in Hebrews:

Not forsaking our own assembling together as is the habit of some / but encouraging one another (Heb. 10:25);

and scores of other places. The works of the flesh must be replaced by the fruit of the Spirit (Gal. 5). The way of the ungodly must give way to the way of the righteous (Ps. 1).

The discipling method of Christ, in which the disciple must become *like his master* (Luke 6:40), involves the two-factored process:

If anyone wishes to come after Me, let him deny himself, and take up his cross [put off] and follow Me [put on] (Matt. 16:24).

The new life style of Christ's disciple is acquired by dying to self (putting self to death on the cross) and / living to God (following Christ). It was begun by turning *from* idols / *to* the living and true God (I Thess. 1:9). Sanctification continues as the believer turns *from* sin / *to* righteousness.

Breaking and Establishing Habits

A way or manner of life is a *habitual* way of living. God gave man a marvelous capacity that we call *habit*. Whenever one does something long enough, it becomes a part of him. Counselors must remember that their counselees (as well as themselves) are fully endowed with this capacity. Sometimes, however, counselors must point out the dynamic of habit to their counselees. When they do so they may need to stress the fact that habits are *hard* to change because we have become comfortable with them, and because they have become unconscious responses. One counselor puts it this way: "Fred, let's take an example: did you put your left or right shoe on first when you got up today? Ah, it took you a minute to answer that, didn't it? Maybe you don't even know yet. You don't think about where you begin any more; you just *do* it. You don't consciously say to yourself, 'Now, I'm going to put my shoes on this morning; I shall begin with the right foot.' You don't think about that at all. You just do it without thinking about it. You just get up and unconsciously do what you have done hundreds of other mornings. You probably don't know which arm you put into a shirt first, or hundreds of other details. We no longer find it necessary to think about details. That is the capacity that God gave us. Take another example: think of the first time that you sat behind an automobile wheel. What a frightening experience that was. There you sat, thinking, 'Here is a wheel (it looked about ten times bigger than it was), and here is a gear shift, here is a complex instrument panel and foot pedals down below. I have to learn how to use and coordinate all of these! And at the same time I must look out for stripes painted down the middle of the road, and signs along the roadway, and pedestrians and automobiles, and . . . How will I ever do it?' Can you remember back to that time? But now —*now* what do you do? At midnight, on a moonless night, you slide into the car seat as someone else slips into the seat beside you. Deftly you insert the key into the slot without scarring the dashboard, turn on the motor, shift the gears, depress the gas pedal, back out of the driveway into the street and start down the road, all the while arguing some abstruse point of Calvinism! What an amazing feat that is when you think about it! Well, just think about it. You have learned to perform highly complex behavior unconsciously. Think of what Brooks Robinson and Willie Mays have learned to do *in the same way*. How did you learn? How did they? By practice, *disciplined* practice. You drove the car long enough that driving has become a part of you. It has become second nature to you. That is what Paul was talking to Timothy about when he wrote, 'discipline yourself for godliness' (I Tim. 4:7). That is how one establishes a life style and lives according to it—by habit."

The writer of Hebrews (Heb. 5:13ff.) speaks clearly about this matter. There he is upbraiding the Hebrew Christians because, although they had received so much teaching of God's Word, yet they had not profited from it. The reason was that they had not *used* it. Consequently, when they ought to have become teachers they still needed to be taught. He says that everyone "who partakes only of milk is *not accustomed* to the word of righteousness, for he is a baby" (vs. 13). He continues: "But solid food [meat and potatoes] is for the mature who *because of practice* [because they have done it so often] have their senses *trained* to discern between good and evil." There it is. The practice of godliness leads to the life of godliness. It makes godliness "natural." If you *practice* what God tells you to do, the obedient life will become a part of you. There is no simple, quick, easy way to instant godliness.

"But," you protest, "I don't seem to be able to do it." The protest is invalid. You already have. You have practiced and learned *something;* you have developed some unconscious patterns. As a sinful human being bent toward sin, you have practiced sinful practices so that they have become a part of you, just as they have become a part of all of us. There is no question that the habit capacity is there. The problem is that it has been used for the wrong purposes. The capacity of habit works both ways. It operates in either direction. You can't avoid habitual living, because this is the way that God made you. He gave you the ability to live a life that does not demand conscious thought about every action or response. It is a great blessing that God made you this way. It would be unbearable if every time you did anything you found it necessary to think consciously about it. Imagine yourself each morning saying, "Now, let's see, how do I brush my teeth? First, I have to get the toothpaste tube and roll it from the bottom, etc., etc." It is a great benefit that you don't have to consciously think about everything that you do, or you probably would not get to breakfast by midnight.

But practice itself is indifferent; it can work either for you or against you, as a blessing or as a curse, depending upon *what* you have practiced. It is what you feed into your life that matters—just like the data fed into a computer. A computer is no better than the data with which it operates. The end product is good or bad according to the raw material provided for it. That is just like habit capability. In II Peter 2:14, Peter speaks about people whose hearts are *"trained* in greed." Trained is the same word that Paul used (*gymnazo*), the word from which *gymnastics* comes. A heart that has been *exercised* in greed is one that has faithfully practiced greed so that greediness has become natural. Without consciously thinking about it, such a person "automatically" behaves greedily in various situations where the temptation is present.

Since God has made counselees with the capacity for living according to habit, counselors must reckon with habit when seeking to help counselees change. They must help them consciously to take a hard look at their life styles. They must help them to become conscious of life patterns by carefully examining their unconscious responses. The unconscious must again become conscious. As they become aware of life patterns, they must evaluate them by the Word of God. What the counselee learned to do as a child he may be continuing to do as an adult. Pattern by pattern the counselor must help him to analyze and determine whether it has developed from practice in doing God's will or whether it has developed as a sinful response. There is only one way to become a godly person, to orient one's life toward godliness, and that means pattern by pattern. The old sinful ways, as they are discovered, must be replaced by new patterns from God's Word. That is the meaning of disciplined living. Discipline first requires self-examination, then it means crucifixion of the old sinful ways (saying "no" daily), and lastly, it entails practice in following Jesus Christ in new ways by the guidance and strength that the Holy Spirit provides through His Word. The biblical way to godliness is not easy or simple, but it is the solid way.

When the counselor undertakes this task, he knows that he and the counselee do not have to do it alone. He may assure the counselee, "It is God Who works in you" (Phil. 2:13). All holiness, all righteousness, all godliness is the "fruit of the Spirit" (Gal. 5:22, 23). It takes nothing less than the power of the Spirit to replace sinful habits with righteous ones, for a ten-year-old or a fifty-year-old. God never said that once a person reaches forty or fifty or eighty that he is incapable of change.

Look what Abraham did as an old man. Look at the tremendous changes that God demanded of him in old age. If anything, age and the *experience in change* that it brings should help, as we have observed already under the discussion of *hope*. The Holy Spirit can change any Christian, and does.

Christians never should fear change. They must believe in change so long as the change is oriented toward godliness. The Christian life is a life of continual change. In the Scriptures it is called a "walk," not a rest. They never may say (in this life), "I have finally made it." They must not think, "There is nothing more to learn from God's Word, nothing more to put into practice tomorrow, no more skills to develop, no more sins to be dealt with." When Christ said, "take up your cross daily and follow me" (Luke 9:23), He put an end to all such thinking. He represented the Christian life as a daily struggle to change. The counselee can change if the Spirit of God dwells within him. Of course, if He does not, there is no such hope.

Week after week, counselors encounter one outstanding failure among Christians: a lack of what the Bible calls "endurance." Perhaps endurance is the key to godliness through discipline. No one learns to ice skate, to use a yo-yo, to button shirts, or to drive an automobile unless he persists long enough to do so. He learns by enduring in spite of failures, through the embarrassments, until the desired behavior becomes a part of him. He trains himself by practice to do what he wants to learn to do. God says the same is true about godliness.

All of the stress that the Bible puts upon human effort must not be misunderstood; we are talking about grace-motivated effort, not the work of the flesh. It is not effort apart from the Holy Spirit that produces godliness. Rather, it is through the power of the Holy Spirit alone that one can endure. Of his own effort, a man may persist in learning to skate, but he will not persist in the pursuit of godliness. A Christian does *good works* because the Spirit first works in him.

Now the work of the Spirit is not mystical. The Holy Spirit's activity often has been viewed in a confused and confusing manner. There is no reason for such confusion. The Holy Spirit Himself has plainly told us how He works. He says *in* the Scriptures that He ordinarily works *through* the Scriptures. The Bible is the Holy Spirit's book. He inspired it. He moved its authors to write every wonderful word that one reads there. This is His book, the sharp tool by which He accomplishes His work. He did not produce the book only to say that it could be laid aside and forgotten in the process. Godliness does not come by osmosis. Human ideas and efforts will never produce it. There is no easier path to godliness. It always requires the prayerful study and obedient practice of the Word of God.

The Spirit took pains to raise up men and mold those men to fitly write His book. Under His good providence they developed the vocabularies and styles in the kinds of life situations that He required. Thus they could write a book of exactly the sort that He wanted to meet our needs. He was careful to assure that not one false word was penned; in His book there are no errors. It is wholly true and inerrant; it is the dependable Word of God. After going to all of that trouble, one must not think he will zap instant holiness apart from the Bible. He doesn't work that way. The Spirit works through His Word; that is how He works. So to help a counselee to discipline himself toward godliness, a counselor must insist upon the regular study of God's Word as an essential factor.

It is by willing, prayerful, and persistent obedience to the requirements of the Scriptures that godly patterns are developed and come to be a part of us. When we read about them we must then ask God by His grace to help us live accordingly. He has given the Holy Spirit to us for this purpose. The word *grace* has several meanings in the Bible, one of which is *help*. The Holy Spirit gives help when His people read His Word and then step out by faith to do as He says. He does not promise to strengthen unless they do so; the power often comes *in the doing*.

In II Timothy 3:17, Paul mentions four things that the Scriptures do for the believer. First, they *teach* what God requires. Secondly, they *convict* of sin by revealing how one has fallen short of those requirements. Thirdly, they *"set us up straight again."* Lastly, they *train* or *discipline* in righteousness. This fourth benefit of the Bible means a structured training in doing righteousness. Using the Bible every day disciplines. Disciplined, biblically structured living is what is needed.

Structure alone brings freedom. Discipline brings liberty. People have been brainwashed into thinking the opposite. They think freedom and liberty come only by throwing over structure and discipline.

Liberty comes through law, not apart from it. When is a train most free? Is it when it goes bouncing across the field off the track? No. It is free only when it is confined (if you will) to the track. Then it runs smoothly and efficiently, because that was the way its maker intended it to run. It needs to be on the track, structured by the track, to run properly. Counselees need to be on the track. God's track is found in God's Word. In God's round world the counselee cannot lead a square life happily; he always will get the corners knocked off. There is a structure necessary for the commandment-oriented and motivated life; that structure is found in the Bible. Conforming to that structure by the grace of God enables Christians to change, to put off sin, put on righteousness, and thus to become godly men.

This, then, is the counselor's biblical answer: regularly read the Scriptures, prayerfully do as they say, according to schedule, regardless of how you feel.

That last factor points to what is perhaps the biggest problem of all. Counselees give up because they don't *feel* like doing something again. Counselors must tell their counselees: "You probably didn't *feel* like getting up this morning. But you had to do so in spite of how you felt. After you were up and around awhile you began to feel different, and you were glad you *acted against your feelings*. From that first decision on, the rest of the day is filled with similar decisions that must be made on the basis of obedience to God rather than capitulation to contrary feelings."

There is much that people do not feel like doing. But there are only two ways to live. These two ways of life reflect two kinds of religion and two kinds of morality. One religion and life and morality says, "I will live according to feelings." The other says, "I will live as God says." When man sinned he was abandoning the commandment-oriented life of love for the feeling-oriented life of lust. There are only two kinds of life, the feeling-motivated life of sin oriented toward self, and the commandment-motivated life of holiness oriented toward godliness. Living according to feeling is the greatest hindrance to godliness that we face. Godly, commandment-oriented living comes only from biblical structure and discipline.

We have seen, therefore, that breaking a habit is a two-sided enterprise that requires regular, structured endurance in putting off and putting on. Dehabituation is *more* than that; it also involves rehabituation. When a counselee turns his back upon his old ways, at the same time he must turn to face God's new ones. If he does not, what he turns to face instead may be equally as bad or worse. If the new way is vague and indefinite, he may vacillate from one thing to another, becoming confused and exasperated rather than developing new biblical ways of living. The process, then, should be clear to both the counselor and, through him, to the counselee.

The following form may be used to establish plainly the twofold nature of biblical change for the counselee.

Change . . .

is a two-factored process

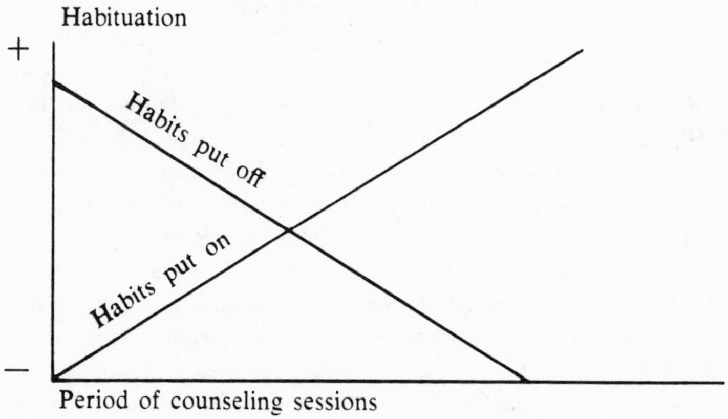

Dehabituation
(List habits to put off:)

Rehabituation
(List habits to put on:)

Figure 2

Counselees, in conjunction with their counselors, early should identify and list sinful habit patterns in the left-hand column that God in the Scriptures says must be put off. The corresponding biblical patterns to be put on should be listed in the right-hand column. Early identification of these can clarify the work that needs to be done and keeps everyone on the track.

We have seen that a counselee is no longer a thief when he "puts on" the righteous way of life that accords with honesty in getting gain. That is to say that he does not cease to be a thief when he stops stealing. If his whole life is still programmed toward stealing, he is still—*in character*—a thief even though (at the moment) he may not be stealing. He has not become dehabituated because he has not been rehabituated. If he does not become reprogrammed by the Word and the Spirit, when the pressures of life grow heavy he will react to them according to the only habit patterns that he knows. That is why Paul insists not only that he must steal no more, but also that he must learn a new way of life that consists of (1) toiling with his hands to earn money and (2) giving to the poor. Until he has developed a life characterized by toil and giving, he is still *characterologically* a thief.

The reversion to character will be more than a mere temporary reversion in some instances. In cases that counselors see, it may involve discouragement, heartache, and many times other negative factors that make it even more difficult for the counselee to change. The situation, at times, may seem to entail conditions similar to those that existed when the unclean spirit returned to the cleaned-up house along with seven others (Matt. 12:45). So the key to change is to recognize the double-faced nature of the process. We must now consider *how* this change may be brought about.

This material sets forth a viewpoint and approach to change that counselors should find helpful. Because so little has been said by the theologians about habit—even though it is an altogether vital subject—it was necessary to focus on it here. Counselors, in particular, will find that they cannot avoid the subject.

CHAPTER FIFTEEN

COUNSELING AND THE SPIRIT'S FRUIT
(The Doctrine of Sanctification, Continued)

Elsewhere, I have made the point that not all of the Spirit's gifts are for all believers,[1] but all of the Spirit's fruit is. The goal of sanctification is not only to put off the works[2] of the flesh, but in its place to put on the fruit of the Spirit.

First, let us consider the important, carefully chosen word *fruit*. The Spirit's fruit presupposes a living tree (vine or bush); it is never produced in the lives of those who are spiritually dead. Fruit grows in those who have been given new life through regeneration (again, the Spirit's work). A sign of life is growth, producing fruit.

It is the Spirit's fruit, not in the sense that He is the tree that bears it, but (rather) that He is the One Who has both planted (regeneration) and cultivated it (sanctification). Moreover, we who have come to Christ belong to the Spirit—we are His orchard! The fruit that He gathers brings honor not only to Him, but to the Father and Son as well.

The qualities of life described by the list of items in Galatians 5:22, 23, called "fruit," are appropriately named. The figure of speech (fruit) denotes something that *grows*. Growth is gradual; man can assist producing it, but cannot initiate it or assure its production. Fruit cannot be manufactured, but growth may be promoted by providing such important elements as light, water, nutrients, etc. The growth of fruit depends upon care and cultivation. Counselors, ministering the Word, work under the Spirit in His orchard, to provide such care. So, then, both the progressive nature of sanctification and the necessity for care and cultivation are aptly depicted by the term *fruit*.

In the chart that appears at the beginning of the previous chapter, I noted that sanctification is a doctrine that involves both God and man;

---

1. The *Manual*, pp. 344-347.
2. Sinful attitudes and actions appropriately are called "works"; they are purely the product of the sinful "flesh" (see earlier discussion of this), for which we alone are responsible.

God *enables* man to produce fruit in his own life. But Paul's term, "the Spirit's fruit" (Gal. 5:22), at first glance, seems to preclude human effort. Is man passive, as in regeneration? No. To understand how "love, joy, peace, patience, kindness, goodness, faithfulness, meekness [and] self-control" are produced, we must compare other passages of Scripture as well. To fail to do so is to err seriously and to read into the passage a kind of quietism that is entirely foreign to the New Testament.

Let us, then, compare the following two passages (not the only ones that might be considered:

> But you, man of God, flee these things; pursue righteousness, godliness, faith, love, endurance, meekness (I Tim. 6:11).
> . . . pursue righteousness, faith, love, peace . . . (II Tim. 2:22).

Clearly, the qualities (and even some of the actual terms) overlap those listed in Galatians 5. But here, note, Timothy is commanded to *pursue* these things. The production of the Spirit's fruit, then, involves human agency; it is not procured passively, but by "pursuing" it. The pursuit of fruit is a large factor in the task of Christian counseling. We must discover how this pursuit of fruit takes place in counseling and how the Spirit produces fruit in the life of its pursuers. A discussion of these factors must precede a consideration of the individual items that are designated "fruit."

The Pursuit of Fruit in Counseling

The pursuit of fruit in counseling is a top priority. The characteristics listed—"love, joy, peace," etc.—are all qualities that both counselees and most counselors[3] would deem desirable. They, then, become goals for Christian counselors to pursue in all their counseling. Because they are—and because goals are so vital—it is essential for every Christian counselor to understand the basic meaning of each term and how it may be pursued. Counselors must become adept at locating such lacks in their counselees, identifying strengths and weaknesses, and in describing each quality in depth. In short, they must understand the Spirit's fruit thoroughly.[4]

---

3. All Christian counselors, of course. But even most non-Christians might approve of the items listed in the abstract (i.e., undefined by Scripture and unapplied according to scriptural principles) with the possible exception of meekness.

4. The list in Gal. 5, though incomplete, is a good base from which to work. For purposes of our present discussion, we shall use the qualities listed in Gal. 5 plus those found in I Tim. 6:11 and II Tim. 2:22.

Much has been written about personality; but even Christian counselors have failed to take seriously the vast amount of material on the subject in the Bible. While I cannot engage in a long (or definitive) study of personality in the Scriptures, I do want to make at least several vital points regarding the way that God speaks about human personality in the Bible, especially in terms of the personality possibilities of the Christian (I have already spoken about fallen man in some depth). It is a tragedy that no one to date has even begun to make a serious attempt to systematize biblical data on personality. To do so would require a study of personality at birth, its growth and development apart from Christ, its transformation in regeneration, and its growth and development in Christ.

Now, let us make two important statements:

1. The Bible everywhere looks on personality as fluid. No one is "stuck" at any point in his life with a certain personality. Personality consists of the basic nature (*phusis*) with which one was born, how he has used and developed it in responding to life, plus how God has changed and molded it up until the point of consideration.

2. The foregoing fact of changeability leads naturally to the second factor: counselors very definitely can help counselees to effect personality change (for good or for ill—depending, of course, on whether or not they minister the Word faithfully and whether or not the counselee submits to God's Word). The Spirit's fruit, from one perspective, may be said to consist of a fairly comprehensive list of desirable personality traits, the acquisition and development of which ought to be a goal of counseling. It is safe to say that a person who has learned to produce such luscious fruit in profusion is a person who has overcome his difficulties and (except for occasional instructive guidance, perhaps) needs no further counseling. So, the pursuit of fruit in counseling represents the positive (or, to use the language of Paul elsewhere, the "put on" side of sanctification.[5]

Now, we must ask, how does the Spirit produce His fruit, and how do counselors help counselees to pursue it? These two questions may be

---

5. I could discuss the "put off" side of eliminating the works of the flesh, but it would take too much space to develop the negative terms as well as the positive ones. Strategically, to know the positive goals is most vital.

answered jointly; they are but two aspects of the same question. The basic answer to these questions is that the Spirit's fruit is cultivated and produced by the prayerful, regular study and obedient application of the Scriptures. The word *pursue* used in I Timothy 6:11 and II Timothy 2:22 (*dioko*) is a strong word meaning "strive after, pursue, hound, track down," even "persecute." The word is used of being pursued by a lion. That is how zealously (from the human point of view) one must pursue it if he wishes to "bear much fruit." The word clearly speaks of dedication, persistence, concern and serious effort.

To take one example, let us look at *peace* (mentioned earlier; worked out here). How does a Christian obtain peace? Philippians 4:6-9 tells us. There are three fundamental steps in acquiring peace in the place of worry that distresses the heart and mind. These steps involve putting off as well as putting on. Here they are (notice how peace comes by pursuing it; it does not appear magically at 3:00 A.M. on Thursday morning as the Spirit zaps one with it):

1. *Pray about problems* (vss. 6, 7). The heart must be unburdened, casting cares (specifically; the various terms indicate specific prayer) upon God, together with thanksgiving both for the trial itself and in advance for what God will do about the problem.

Many Christians (erroneously) stop with verse 8, failing to recognize that verses 9 and 10 also speak of how to obtain this peace. When it doesn't come, they give up on themselves, on God, on prayer (or on all of the above). Prayer is but the *first* step. It is a formal recognition that (at bottom) the fruit that comes will be the work of the Spirit. But He wants us to pray, *and to do two more things,* as He works in us.

2. *Repackage* the heart and mind with proper thoughts and concerns (vs. 8). It is not enough to empty one's heart and mind of worries; if it is left empty, more worries will rush in to fill the void. Instead, there must be a subsequent refilling of the mind with proper and productive thoughts that fit the categories mentioned in verse 8.

3. *Do what God commands* through precept and practice (vs. 9). Prayer must be followed by action. Whatever the apostles (and other scriptural writers) command (or show by example) that ought to be done about a particular problem should be done by the counselee. But to do it once, again, is not sufficient; he must learn to do it regularly, habitually, by "practice" (vs. 9). That comes,

of course, only by *pursuing* it. "Then" (when it has become a vital, regular part of his life) "the God Who gives peace" will be with him. Peace comes in no lesser way.

Clearly, this pursuit of fruit called *peace* is not magical or mystical. It lies in the path of understanding (of the Bible) and obedience. So, too, does the other fruit appear, develop and grow as one pursues it in such a biblical fashion.

The counselor's task is to guide the counselee along the proper biblical course leading to each quality, pointing out the inadequacy of the other routes so frequently taken by failing counselees and encouraging him to persevere in his pursuit of godliness. Counselees so often will want peace (or love or joy, etc.) "right away." They will want to use gimmicks and shortcuts to get it. Counselors must warn against these tendencies and fully develop (in clear-cut, practical ways) the biblical passages that point to the proper method of pursuit, at the end of which lies the desired quality.

The Fruit That Is Our Pursuit

Now, let us turn to the list of qualities found in Galatians 5, I Timothy 6:11 and II Timothy 2:22 (a fairly comprehensive and workable, though not complete, list[6]). Here is the entire picture:

Galatians 5	I Timothy 6:11	II Timothy 2:22
1. Love	Love	Love
2. Joy		
3. Peace		Peace
4. Patience		
5. Kindness		
6. Goodness		
7. Faithfulness (or faith)	Faithfulness (or faith)	Faithfulness (or faith)
8. Meekness	Meekness	
9. Self-control		
10.	Righteousness	Righteousness
11.	Godliness	
12.	Endurance	

6. Presumably, Paul thought such representative (though incomplete) lists were of great practical value.

This even dozen terms presents quite a picture of Christian life and personality! The pursuit of these qualities can be dramatically life-changing, as even a casual perusal of the list should indicate.

Love

The first word, love, is found in all three places (as is faith, or faithfulness), showing its importance in Paul's thinking. Since love (*agape*) has been discussed so fully by so many writers, since Paul so beautifully and fully describes it in I Corinthians 13,[7] and since the concept is deeper than any human being can fathom, I shall say little about it.[8] To sum up, we may safely say that the love in view must be produced by the Holy Spirit; no man (unaided by His presence) can attain to it (cf. Rom. 5:5). In essence, it is desire to obey God in order to please Him and to do whatever He says is best for others. It is not a feeling first, and depends upon nothing in the one to be loved, but is generated in the lover and moves out toward the loved one, even when he/she is unloving, unlovely or unlovable (love conquers all). Such love is the sort God had for sinful men. It always involves giving of one's self to others; but nothing is expected in return.

Joy

Christianity is joyful; the noun joy (*chara*) appears 60 times in the N.T., and its corresponding verb 72 times. The word refers to a deep-seated attitude and confidence toward life that only a Christian, who knows that God is sovereign, can have. Such joy isn't dependent upon favorable happenings in life, as "happiness" is (cf. James 1:2; Phil. 4:4; Col. 1:24). To view the Christian life as a sombre, serious, miserable existence—as some have in the past and some do at present—is to seriously misrepresent it. Because Jesus came that "our joy might be full" (John 15:11, 16:24), two facts are clear:

1. This joy is not attainable apart from Christ;
2. This joy is attainable through Christ; it is not an illusion. He actually came to effect it in our lives.

---

7. Early in their ministries, all Christian counselors should do a thorough exegesis of I Cor. 13.
8. Eph. 3:18 indicates that to understand love, one must pursue its meaning together with other believers; no one person can do so alone.

This leads to a third:

3. Such joy is possible for every true (Christian) counselee.

But, as the passages quoted indicate, joy isn't the automatic possession of every Christian; rather, it belongs to those who understand, trust and obediently follow God's will. Joy seems to be associated most closely with fellowship with God and other believers (cf. II John 12; Phil. 4:1) and with Christian service (Acts 15:3; III John 4). But, fundamentally, joy is a basic, bedrock confidence lying beneath the shifting sands of daily happenings. In order to face and conquer trials, counselees need this quality; yet so few know much about it.

Joy is closely aligned to faith, issuing (as it does) from a certainty that God knows all about those trials and is working all things together for their good. It starts with a trust in God's sovereignty that leads to this confidence about life under God. Without this base—this basic joy that God has it all in His pocket—there can be no place to stand and evaluate life. All is flux; all is meaningless—indeed, life is absurd. Counselors, therefore, will be careful (somewhere along the way— usually, early in the counseling process) to discuss these facts with their counselees, perhaps referring to James 1:2 or I Peter 1:6-9[9] as he does.

Peace

Closely related to and, indeed, a part of this joy about which I have just written, is *eirene,* peace (cf. Phil. 4:4-9 for something of this interrelationship). I shall not say much more about this *shalom* from God than what I have written several paragraphs earlier when considering Philippians 4:6-9. It might be well, however, to note that peace is not merely a negative thing; it is not to be thought of simply as the absence of hostilities and cares. Positively, peace may be considered a joyous sense of well-being that views all things as good. In it is a sense of satisfaction that comes from knowing one is right with God in Christ. Since, however, it "passes all comprehension," no one will ever be able to describe it adequately; so why try?

Patience and Endurance

The word *makrothumia,* patience, means "long-tempered." It is the opposite of that which is referred to in our expression, "short-fused."

---

9. Cf. especially my commentary on I Peter, *Trust and Obey,* pp. 17-20.

Patience is the ability to contain one's self (in one passage a writer speaks of wrath "restrained by long suffering as it were by a rein"— M & M, p. 386). Negatively, patience is not losing one's temper; positively, it is putting up with others. So patience is not a bad translation.

Makrothumia indicates *self*-restraint, whereas *hupomone* often describes successful endurance of *outside* pressures; Christians are urged to exercise patience among themselves and endurance in the face of hostility from unbelievers (I Cor. 6:7). *Makrothumia* refers to patience with persons, while the focus of *hupomone* is on a bearing up under impersonal forces. The former may be ascribed to God, but the latter to men only (God never need bear up under outside forces!).

How many Christian counselees need to learn to become patient with one another! Counselors must teach the virtue constantly, and help counselees to cultivate it. But how does one learn such patience toward others?

To begin with, patience is bound up with love (I Cor. 13:4). The two (like joy and peace) go together. The loving act (attitude) often is to restrain one's words or actions. If one cares for another—i.e., sets his love on him—he will work at restraining his words and actions. The commands and insights Paul gives us in Romans 12:14-21 (see my exposition of this passage in *How to Overcome Evil*), properly applied, also lead to self-restraint. Not only does he discover what is not his prerogative in reprimanding another, what he must give place to God to do, but he is supplied with another, better way of responding.

Probably the most definitive passage regarding the source of *makrothumia* is Colossians 1:9-11. It comes from God in answer to prayer, but not directly. It is the outgrowth of other factors. Paul prayed that the Colossians would be "filled" with "knowledge" of God's "will," together with "spiritual wisdom and understanding" (to know how to put God's ways to work in life) that would lead to "walking" in ways that are "pleasing" to God and that would produce "fruit." Through these ways he expected God to empower them to "learn" the "joy" of "enduring" and becoming "completely patient." Again, in a very pointed manner, the interrelatedness of joy, endurance and patience (three of the fruitful qualities we are studying) is most apparent. It is beginning to appear that the several aspects of this fruit cannot be separated and sought singly; they interpenetrate (and interdepend upon) one another. According to Colossians 1:9-11, prayer, leading to truth wisely applied in daily conduct, enables one to learn to endure what he cannot change (*hupomene*) and to put up with what he doesn't have to, but will, for Christ's sake and for the welfare of another (*makrothumia*).

Kindness, Goodness

Chrestotes ought not to be translated "gentleness" (though there is something of the flavor of gentleness in it), but "kindness." Kindness is the broader term. Of course, at times, kindness may require gentleness. In the N.T. the word is frequently used to speak of God's attitude toward men. Since there is no definitive passage either describing this kindness or telling us how to obtain it, we must do our best to understand the word from its usage. First, it is instructive to note that in Romans 11:22 *chrestotes* is opposed to the word *apotomia* ("severity"). This latter term can mean such things as untempered exactness, harshness or even cruelty (of course, not in Rom. 11:22). *Chrestotes* is the opposite of that. Trench says that this *kindness* is a spirit "pervading and penetrating the whole nature, mellowing [one form of the word is used of mellowing wine] there all which would have been harsh and austere."

Chrestotes is used together with *agathosune,* the term next appearing in Galatians 5, and ought to be compared and contrasted with it. The difference between the two is that there is more activity in *agathosune* (Lightfoot), which is translated "goodness." *Goodness* is the outgoing action of a *kind* spirit; its expression is in concrete deeds. Thus "goodness" speaks not so much of the person exercising it (though his own goodness must be presupposed) as it does of that which characterizes his words and deeds toward another.

Plainly, both kindness and goodness are terms that accompany one another; where one exists, usually so does the other. Both are needed by counselees; yet they are rarely exhibited by them. Of essence to both terms is the existence of others toward whom such an attitude and such actions would be appropriate. The problem of many counselees is a self-centeredness that (so long as it continues) precludes any such outgoing relationships. On the other hand, repentance over self-centeredness can best show fruit that is appropriate to it by developing a kindly spirit. Other counselees, in their attempts to build relationships, fail either because of austerity and harshness, or because of lack of effort growing from a concern to do good for them that leads to concrete deeds.

How may these qualities of attitude and action be cultivated and developed? First by recognizing their importance—God desires them. Secondly, one must actively temper his demands of others. Can he ask his child to turn off the TV *when the program he is watching is over* (assuming it is one of the few good ones) instead of insisting that he leave the TV immediately to do something for him? Can he work out *other* legitimate ways of achieving goals that might better fit the lives of his employees, instead of demanding that what is most convenient for him be done? To become mellow, one must work at devising ways to be kind toward others. That begins by *thinking* of others. A counselee might be given the task of reviewing the activities of the week to come, thinking of others in relationship to each job and developing (on paper) ways of making it easier (more convenient, nicer) for others to participate. Thus kindness and goodness combine.

Basically, counselors ought to study the *chrestotes* of God toward man as Paul describes it (only Paul uses the word) in Titus 3:4, Romans 11:22ff., Ephesians 2:7. By understanding God's kindness toward men in providence and in redemption, one can begin to understand what He requires of us.

Agathosune occurs three times in the N.T. outside Galatians 5 (again, all in Paul's letters: II Thess. 2:17; Eph. 5:9; Rom. 15:14; this last use speaks of goodness as a trait essential to good counseling). Remember, *goodness* is the activity by which one *does good* toward others because he cares for them. The word has been contrasted with the term *justice*. Justice says, "Give a man what he deserves"; goodness responds, "No, I shall give him what he needs." There is generosity in goodness.

Faithfulness

This term, *pistis,* which can be translated "faith" or "faithfulness," appears also in I and II Timothy. In all three places it ought to be translated "faithfulness" (note especially this usage throughout II Timothy). It means reliability, trustworthiness, loyalty, dependability. The concept is straighforward and need no elaboration.

Constantly counselors struggle with the problem of unfaithfulness in counselees. They are unreliable in many ways. They cannot be depended upon to keep their word, to do their homework assignments, and even (at times) to show up for counseling sessions. There are any number of causes for this common failing; each must be treated appropriately. It may flow from lack of genuine faith or lack of concern. It may stem from bad habits or misunderstanding. But one very common cause (especially likely to be the cause when the counselee basically doesn't *want* to be that way, and shows genuine disgust with himself over it) is lack of discipline. Since I have written extensively on discipline (cf. my book, *God Has the Answer to Your Problems,*[10] pp. 24ff.), I shall do no more than mention the fact here.

Counselees must be taught the importance of faithfulness, not only to a spouse, a parent, an employer, etc., but first and foremost, to Christ. They are His stewards—stewards of His money, His time, His gifts. One thing (above all else) is required of stewards—faithfulness (I Cor. 4:2). Much is said about the faithfulness of stewards in the gospels (cf. Matt. 24:45; 25:21, 23; Luke 12:42; 16:10-12; 19:17).

Meekness

We come now to *prautes,* perhaps the most misunderstood word of the lot. Many people equate meekness with weakness. The notion is false. Moses was meek, but he certainly wasn't weak. Sometimes the word is translated "gentleness," but that somewhat misses the mark. There is no English equivalent. The word had in it the notion of soothing (as an ointment soothes or as the words of a peacemaker soothe the parties to an argument). A meek person knows how to pour oil on troubled waters while not ignoring problems.

The term *meekness* also carries with it the idea of humility; a meek person is never proud or boastful, and he is humble toward God and others. In this very humility lies his strength; it gives him the entree into the lives of others whom he may influence for good.

Meekness is a quality, then, that enables a Christian to know when to speak or act, how to speak or act and what to say or do for another. It is the one element in the Spirit's fruit that is demonstrated in the context (there should be no new chapter division in Galatians at this point, because chapter 5 flows naturally into the discussion that opens chapter 6). Paul goes on (in Gal. 6:1ff.) to show how meekness can lead to help in counseling others.[11] The person who has the Spirit is the one who can assist his brother or sister who has fallen into sin. His

---

10. Evangelical Press (Welwyn, 1979).
11. For a full exposition of the passage, see my book, *The Big Umbrella,* "You Are Your Brother's Counselor."

attitude of meekness is essential for such work; without it he will do more harm than good. But in a truly humble and soothing way he says something to this effect: "I'm not here because I think I'm better than you; I am a sinner too. Indeed, for all I know, I may need similar help from you next month. No, I am here because Christ sent me, because you have a need and because I care. May I help?" That is meekness—strength—in a concrete context.

How counselees need to be taught to exercise meekness in every "touchy" relationship to other Christians! But there is no better way to teach it than for counselors to demonstrate it in their own lives as they offer guidance and help.

Self-Control

The last term in Galatians 5 is *egkrateia,* a word that embraces a very important concept in counseling. Barclay (*Flesh and Spirit,* p. 121) calls it "Victory over Desire." The exercise of self-control, doubtless, is a fundamental problem for many counselees, as (indeed) it was for Felix (Acts 24:25)—and for many of us! It has to do with curbing or restraining one's desire (the use of the verb in I Corinthians 7:9 makes this perfectly clear), and the notions of disciplined restraint and control are always present.

Because of the feeling orientation of our society, discipline and self-control are poorly taught and learned. Anger, sorrow, frustration, sexual desire—all sorts of emotions—must be restrained or directed. Counselors must help counselees to learn to do so. There can be no self-control apart from prayerful disciplined effort to learn it. The main original root word in *egkrateia* has to do with "holding" or "gripping" something. The self-controlled man is the one who has a hold or grip on himself. Discipline in practicing the proper biblical outlets for emotion is what is needed (see, e.g., material on anger in the *Manual*).

Righteousness

In both the I and II Timothy passages, Paul directs Timothy to "pursue righteousness." The word is *dikaiosune,* a frequently occurring word (66 times in Paul's writings), must be understood. Here it refers not so much to the declaration of righteousness (though such imputation of Christ's righteousness is a prerequisite) by which believers are justified as it does to their becoming righteous by the power of the Spirit transforming their lives. One who is righteous is one who is full of the quality of being right and just. He has a disposition characterized by the desire to do what is right. He does not rationalize his sinful behavior, try to find ways around God's commands or make excuses. He, like his Lord, loves to do right (cf. Heb. 1:9). He knows that what is right is what God says is right in His Word. Therefore, he pursues righteousness by studying the Scriptures diligently and endeavoring in every way to conform to their precepts.

Counselors cannot help others to become righteous apart from teaching them the Scriptures. According to Hebrews 1:9, lawlessness (ignorance and violation of biblical principles and precepts) is the opposite of righteousness. Therefore, all counseling must focus upon God's revealed ways as the standard for attitude and action and every counselee ought to be encouraged to begin his own regular study of the Bible.[12] Righteousness, remember, is essentially rightness according to what God, in Scripture, says is right. It is rightness of thought, belief, attitude, word and deed.

Godliness

Lastly (I dealt with endurance under the discussion of "patience") we come to "godliness" (*eusebeia*), the word found in I Timothy 6:11. The term occurs frequently in the pastorals, indicating that the life of the pastor (counselor) must be godly so that he may model and inculcate godliness in those to whom he ministers. The term means piety toward God and toward God in relationship to others (e.g., Christian reverence for parents). It has to do with a sense of reverence and awe that is to pervade one's entire life and his life style. It is the life approved by God because it acknowledges God in all things. It is not the godliness of worship or any other activities specifically labeled "religious." Rather, it is a manner of life in which reverence for God conditions and influences all of one's thoughts, words and activities. *Eusebeia* must be the driving spirit (power) behind any Christian world view: respect for God must characterize the work of a Christian in business, science, politics, study, homemaking, etc. All of life—not just "church life" (in which God is formally acknowledged)—must be lived in reverent re-

---

12. Cf. the book, *Four Weeks with God and Your Neighbor*, which was designed to help counselees begin fruitful Bible study.

lationship to God. All human relationships must be sustained in the light of that greater relationship.

There is an outward form (or appearance) of piety that is not truly *eusebeia* (II Tim. 3:5); because it has no inner reality, it lacks power with God or men. It is a sham, hypocrisy at its worst. Counselees must be warned against mere outer conformity, and steered from models that promote it (3:5b). *Eusebeia* comes about as one orients and disciplines his thinking and living *toward* it (I Tim. 4:7). That is to say, he must consciously try to relate God to every aspect of each sphere of life. Disciplined living in accordance with biblical teaching[13] will promote *eusebeia*, just as thinking about ways to relate God to each area of life will promote disciplined living; it works both ways. When this fruit begins to grow, it may influence some to trust Christ, but others will respond quite negatively (cf. II Tim. 3:12; perhaps even other believers who like to live a compartmentalized one-day-a-week Christianity will join in such persecution).

Thus we have considered the fruit of the spirit. It might do well for some counselors who are unfamiliar with the meaning of these terms to write them out in a chart on the blank pages in the back of their *Christian Counselor's New Testament,* together with (1) the meaning of each, (2) some applications of each to counseling, (3) ways of promoting each in the lives of others and (4) key passages in which each occurs.[14] This would make this important issue more practically useful in actual counseling sessions. Because I consider it of importance in counseling to have a good grasp of this material, I have taken the time and space to discuss this issue. One way for pastoral counselors to indelibly impress the words in their minds is to preach a series of nine or twelve messages on them.

---

13. Cf. Titus 1:1c: Paul speaks here about "truth" that "brings about godliness" (*eusebeia*).

14. Next to the passage in Gal. 5, he would write a note to refer to the chart.

CHAPTER SIXTEEN

COUNSELING AND RADICAL AMPUTATION
(The Doctrine of Sanctification, Continued)

We have seen that sanctification is a matter of growing out of old ways while growing into new ones. These ways of thinking and doing were brought into the new life from before conversion. One who is truly regenerated is changing without (in putting off old patterns and putting on new ones) because he is changing within. The word *sanctified* means "set apart" or "separate." Negatively one is set apart *from* sin, positively, *for* God. He is separated from others, unique; special to God.

We are already separated, completely sanctified, *in Christ.* His whole righteous life is attributed to us—we are circumcised with Christ, crucified with Christ, buried with Christ, risen with Christ, seated in the heavenlies with Christ. But we do not have all this in daily living in this life. That is why sanctification is taking place—to enable us, day by day, to become in actuality more of what we are reckoned to be in Christ. We must become in ourselves (but not by ourselves) what we already are in Christ. This is quite distinct from self-actualization (becoming what you may be in and by yourself); sanctification is becoming in yourself (by the Spirit's work) what you already are counted to be in Christ. This "third force," Maslow self-actualization doctrine is a dangerous, subtle substitute for the real thing. When it is integrated into Christian circles, it fosters a fundamentally Pelagian attitude (teaching human self-sufficiency by self-help methods). Maslow's self-actualization sees no need for either the Word or the Spirit; it is purely humanistic.

How, then, does sanctification take place? Patterns of thinking and living change as one is "renewed by the Spirit" (Who is working) in his "mind" (Eph. 4:23). While I have considered in part the human side of this renewal (vss. 22, 24), I must here say a word about the Spirit's work in renewing God's image by renewing the mind (cf. Col. 3:9, 10; Rom. 12:1, 2).

In Ephesians 4:23, there are two key words ("mind"[1] and "renewed") and one key concept to understand (the Spirit changes us by changing our minds). The word *renewed* (here, in Rom. 12:2, Col. 3:10) is *anakainoo* (the noun form is *anakainosis*), which means "to make new again in quality" (not new in time). The old, worn out, sinful ways of thinking (vs. 17) must be replaced by fresh, biblical ones. The transformation of the patterns of living into which the members of the body have been habituated (Rom. 12:1, 2—these words pick up the discussion of chapter 6–8), which must be "put off" and replaced by new ones (Eph. 4, Col. 3), takes place as the direct result of the Spirit's work in changing and influencing the counselee's mind.

Because the Spirit works in the inner person, to change one's thinking and attitudes, counselors will focus on inculcating the biblical data that (1) set the standards for Christian behavior, and that (2) point to specific principles and practices of Christian living. Moreover, they will take the time to show how (practically) these can be integrated into the particular situation that each counselee faces. Since the Holy Spirit uses the Scriptures, they can count on Him (in His own way and time) to bless their faithful ministry of the Word. But He does so, especially, when we adopt His practices set forth there.

In this chapter I wish, therefore, to take up one important biblical dynamic (that I have not discussed elsewhere) for "putting off" sinful practices. Counselors must become aware of it and use it, if they wish to experience lasting change in their counselees. I have called it "Radical Amputation."

The words of Jesus on this subject are found in Matthew 5:27-30:

> "You have heard that it was said, 'You shall not commit adultery.' But I tell you that whoever looks at a woman with the intention of desiring her already has committed adultery with her in his heart. So if your right eye causes you to stumble, tear it out and throw it away from you; it is to your advantage to have one of your members perish than for your whole body to be thrown into Gehenna.

---

1. *Nous,* mind, is discussed in depth at an earlier point in this book. This word *mind* refers specifically to the logical, intellectual and reasoning functions in a human being, as well as to the opinions, viewpoints, beliefs and attitudes that are formed by exercising these capacities. Here, and in Rom. 12, the latter idea (what is the result of thought) seems to be the dominant idea; not the process itself. The Spirit is at work challenging and changing our thinking, making our minds (attitudes, beliefs) conform to the mind of Christ.

And if your right hand causes you to stumble, cut it off and throw it away from you; it is to your advantage to have one of your members perish than for your whole body to go away into Gehenna."

A vital part of sanctification is putting off old ways. Speaking figuratively (there is no call to actually maim the body), Jesus calls on us to incapacitate ourselves so that we find it extremely difficult to sin again as we did in the past. That is the gist of the passage. But there are four prominent factors in achieving this.

First, *we must recognize the fact that we will be tempted to repeat our sin.* Forgiveness does not automatically preclude repetition. If we are not aware of these facts, we will not be concerned about them. If we are not concerned, we will do nothing to prevent a repetition of the past. So, first, counselees must be realistically alerted to the possibility of future failure.

Secondly, *we must prepare ourselves to meet and defeat temptation* in the future. We get into trouble largely because we do nothing to prevent it. Jesus is concerned not only about forgiveness; He is even more concerned to help us take every precaution against future failure. That is why He spoke about the necessity for radical amputation. A counselor's work is never complete until he has done preventive as well as remedial work. This work of radical amputation is fundamental to the dehabituation process.

Thirdly, if the problem of past patterns surfacing in the future cannot be avoided (by hoping it will go away, for instance), then something definitive must be done to prevent the counselee from falling into old sinful ways. The passage in Matthew 5 directs him to *take definitive, concrete, radical action.* The offending member—eye, hand, foot; it doesn't matter—must be removed so that it no longer can be used to commit the sin in question: that is radical amputation. The concept seems to grow out of the problem of sinning in the heart by lusting after a woman with the eye. In such a case the eye must be torn out and dispensed with. But mention of the hand—and in another place, the foot—extends the principle to all of life.

Fourthly, *nothing must be spared* in this process: it is radical. Even the *right* eye, the *right* foot, the *right* hand, must be forfeited if necessary. That is to say that it is so important to take this preventive action that even the most valuable organs must be eliminated when necessary. Improper conduct must be curtailed even at the greatest cost. And the means used is radical (but effective)—amputate; after all, an amputated limb cannot be used again.

Now, what does all this mean? Obviously it is not to be taken literally. A man who lusts after a woman can continue to do so in his "mind's eye," even if *both* of his physical eyes are removed.

There are several elements to note. Clearly, the counselee (somehow or other) must *make it very difficult* (if not impossible) *for him* to sin the same sin again. To do so, he may have to put impediments in his own way. He may have to excise certain things, people or practices from the orbit of his daily life. Whatever it takes, he must develop a preventive situation where

1. He automatically becomes aware of the temptation and possibility for sin. To have to hobble over to a place of sin on his one remaining foot (so to speak) alerts him to what is going on—there will be no unconscious *drifting* into sin.

2. Stumbling blocks (occasions for falling into sin) will all be removed from his daily pathway so far as he is able to rearrange the circumstances to do so.

The believer is warned against ignoring this procedure by suggesting, as the alternative, that the *whole* man (not just a foot, or eye) might be thrown into hell. This is not a salvation by works, or a suggestion that saved persons might ultimately be lost. Rather, it is a strong warning that if there is no concern about sin, no desire to keep from offending Christ, no struggle or effort made to prevent future failure and no progress in doing so, then there is no evidence of salvation to begin with. Counselors might keep this in mind when dealing with counselees who seem totally uninterested in the preventive dynamic of radical amputation.

Such radical, definitive, preventive action may take any number of forms—breaking off bad influential relationships (I Cor. 15:33—note the first clause: "Don't be deceived . . ."; counselees constantly fool themselves into thinking that they don't have to do this), getting rid of pornographic materials, changing one's job, etc., etc. But, whatever it takes, radical, effective action must be taken; and it is essential to sanctification. Christ commanded it—and attached a warning. Dare we neglect it?

CHAPTER SEVENTEEN

COUNSELING AND PERSEVERANCE
(The Doctrine of Sanctification, Continued)

Perseverance of the saints is the name of the doctrine; not "eternal security," or "once saved always saved." And for good reason. The latter two alternatives are true enough, but, dangerously, they put the emphasis on only one side of the truth. The phrase, "perseverance of the saints," plainly emphasizes that it is through efforts involved in sanctification (a saint is one who is set apart) that one remains secure—not apart from them. All truly saved persons will persevere, however.

The comments about "abiding" in John 17 are to the point. The word *abide* simply means "to remain, to continue, or to stay" somewhere.[1] Hence, verse 5b should read:

"The one who stays [remains, continues] in Me and I in him is the one who bears much fruit . . ."

and verse 6:

"Unless a person continues with [remains in] Me, he is thrown outside like a branch and withers. . . ."

To be a fruitful branch, one must continue his relationship with Christ. That is, he must persevere in the faith. If he doesn't, his faith is not genuine and he will end up "in the fire" (vs. 6).

I shall not pile up passages that teach the perseverance of the saints but would simply comment on the fact that it is through faith that they persevere (cf. I Pet. 1:3-5). Those who do not have lasting faith never had genuine, saving faith from the beginning. But, of course, that faith is, itself, the gift of God. Nevertheless, human agency is involved—the believer believes; the Holy Spirit doesn't do the believing for him.

---

1. There are strange, unbiblical views of abiding afloat that see it as a sort of super state that some believers enter. All saints abide (remain) in Christ.

Both sides of this doctrine are significant in counseling:

1. The saints do persevere.
2. Saints are secure because they persevere.

It is important for sanctification to know that all true saints do persevere. Rather than focus one's attention continually upon himself—and whether he will/will not make it (the problem of uncertainty for one who disavows the teaching—he can't turn his attention to loving and serving God and his neighbor. Curiously, it isn't by focusing on one's self that he grows; it is when he turns his attention from himself to others that sanctification occurs. But there is no way to do this when utter uncertainty about salvation (leading to continual self-evaluation) is the only "hope" one has. Such bad doctrine leads to serious consequences.

When God brings children into His family, He does not turn them out of the house, disinherit them, kill them spiritually, hand them over to Satan and place them once again on the road to hell when they backslide. Rather, the Father disciplines them for their own good and for the sake of the family name (Heb. 12:5-11). What kind of a Father would God be if He could not handle His own children any better than some suggest?

There are only two places where anything could go wrong with our salvation—something might happen to the inheritance itself or to the heir. But God has promised to protect both (I Pet. 1:3-5). And this protection extends throughout life to the point of his ultimate salvation.

Perhaps the firmest ground of all for the believer's assurance is the love of God. Nothing—absolutely nothing—can separate him from the love of God (Rom. 8:35-39). That love, manifested in the cross, was a love that *saves;* not merely one that makes salvation available. Christ died for my sins; I cannot suffer eternally for what He has already suffered. God exacts no punishment twice.

Closely related to the false doctrine of the non-perseverance of some saints is the erroneous concept of sinless perfection. It may seem strange that those who put so little stock in the power of *God* to preserve Christians at the same time heavily lean on the ability of *man* to live a perfect life. Yet, on reflection, it is not so strange after all. Both concepts exalt man; both demean God.

There are only two ways to keep people saved on the basis of the non-perseverance doctrines:

1. To hold that there are two kinds of sin; sin that is bad enough

to send people to hell, and sin that isn't so bad. Is there, then, some sin (the not-so-bad kind) that God allows in heaven? The Bible makes no such distinctions about sin.

Because this doctrine is totally untenable, a second—sinless perfectionism —was conceived.

2. The not-so-bad kind of sin was changed to the category of non-sin. Only the wilful (bad-enough-to-send-a-man-to-hell) type of sin is now called *sin*. The rest is called mistakes, etc., but not sin.

So long as one does not transgress a greatly diminished number of injunctions, he has not sinned (according to this construction). In other words, the only way for one to have confidence about his salvation is through some kind of "second work of grace" or "second blessing") that enables him to avoid committing the "bad" kinds of sins. Then, if he is sinless, he can have peace at last.

There is little that needs to be said to refute this lie (as John doesn't hesitate to call it, I John 1:8, 10). Mostly, I wish to point out that the doctrine has dire consequences. Counselors, in pointing out various sins, will find difficulty in doing so with those who do not view sin as sin. This truncated view of sin, for example, makes it impossible to convince counselees to repent and seek forgiveness. In addition, they may discover counselees doing sinful things with impunity while refusing to call them sins. And that means that, first, before they can help them in any other ways, they must help the counselees to develop a *true* view of sin. Apart from that, counselees will not be able to handle many problems in their lives in a biblical fashion. Here is one of those instances in which false doctrine either causes the problem or complicates it.

Two facts also become apparent:

1. Counselors cannot avoid dealing with doctrine because
2. Doctrine influences life.[2]

Those are reasons why every counselor not only must be a good exegete, but also must know doctrine (the systematic understanding of what the Bible teaches on various subjects). Sometimes (as in the foregoing example) the counselor will get nowhere unless he first removes the doctrinal barrier.

---

2. Titus 1:1 makes this fact evident. Paul calls himself God's slave and Christ's apostle "to promote the faith of God's chosen people and the full knowledge of the *truth that brings about godliness*" (emphasis mine).

Getting back to perseverance, it is interesting to note that God continually admonishes believers to persevere (Matt. 10:22; 24:13; Rom. 2: 7-8). This note is one that constantly should be on the lips of counselors too. After all, many counselees come as defeated persons, crushed under problems. Their "who cares" or "what's the use" attitude is in strong contrast to the biblical emphasis. Counselors must say in no uncertain terms that if they are truly saints (God's own), it *does* matter; *He* cares. And saints *will* persevere; sooner or later they will come to realize this, so they might as well face it now and get out of their doldrums, self-pity (or whatever) and begin to act like saints. Eventually—why not *now?* If they begin to face and solve problems God's way, they will save themselves a lot of heartache and suffering. So get with it!

CHAPTER EIGHTEEN

COUNSELING AND SUFFERING
(The Doctrine of Sanctification, Continued)

In the last chapter I ended on the note of suffering, self-imposed. There is, however, another kind of suffering, for which one is not responsible. It is suffering which, as in the case of Job (or Christ, for that matter), one did not bring upon himself by his own sin. I should like to discuss both sorts in relationship to counseling.

Counselors must have a biblical view of suffering[1] from which to instruct and help counselees. The problem is widespread; everyone (at one time or another) suffers. Counselees in particular complain of the suffering they undergo. Indeed, in one form or another, it is some sort of suffering that brings counselees to the place where they seek counseling. Suffering can be the primary problem in counseling—how do I handle it; it can be a complicating problem, or it can be a symptom.

Suffering is universal because the fall and its effects are universal. All suffering may be traced back to Adam's sin. Had Adam, our representative, not sinned, there would be no suffering; it was the result of God's curse upon Adam and his posterity. But that does not mean that an individual's suffering is the result of each individual's own personal sin.

The choice is not between pain and no pain in this life; we have no such choice. Rather, choices lie in these areas:

1. How are pain and suffering viewed by the counselee?
2. How are pain and suffering used by the counselee?

The cross dignified suffering by giving it meaning and demonstrated that it can have far-reaching effects for good. Christian counselors must recognize these facts and bring them to bear upon the lives of coun-

---

1. For much more on this, see my commentary on I Peter, a handbook on suffering, entitled *Trust and Obey*.

selees. Because of the cross, no Christian should face suffering as an unbeliever does.

How do unbelievers (and, alas, all too many Christians) respond to suffering and pain? By whining and self-pity (seen in every sort of situation from handicapped and shut-ins to disappointed lovers), denial (actually this futile attempt so focuses one's efforts on the pain that it actually can intensify it), seeking relief at all costs (the TV commercial and medical mentality seeks "pain-killers," tranquilizers, etc., but never meaning in suffering; pain is always an enemy, never a friend to such persons).

Rightly viewed and used, pain must be interpreted biblically and applied biblically. Otherwise pain may be wasted, misused, dreaded bitterly, fought, hated.

What is this pain from which we all suffer? I am not interested in a physiological explanation at this point (though that can be both an interesting and instructive study). We may loosely define the pain of which we are speaking as sharp bodily discomfort. "But what of mental anguish?" When it becomes serious enough, such difficulty brings about bodily discomfort (a headache, aching muscular pain in the neck, or something worse).

Pain is a warning that something is wrong and that something must be done about it. There are physiological (or organic) causes of suffering and non-organic ones. Physical sickness, disease, injury all may produce pain. These pains are indicators that something is wrong in the body. And if the problem cannot be remedied by the person himself, he ought prayerfully to seek a physician's help (cf. James 5, and commentary on oil and prayer in *Competent to Counsel,* pp. 105-110). Then, too, there are non-organic causes of suffering and pain. They may be connected with loss, sorrow, the sense of guilt, fear, etc. They indicate that there is something wrong in the attitudes or the behavior of the one who suffers. It may be his way of responding to outside pressures or to the inner pressures that he himself generates that leads to the pain. Either way, something is wrong.

Of course, there are some losses and sorrows to which pain and suffering are the proper response (grief over the death of a loved one, over the sin of a child, etc.); not all pain and suffering are wrong. Christ suffered pain (on the cross) from physical causes (nails, thorns, beatings) but also from nonphysical ones (cf. Ps. 22). We must rid ourselves of the TV commercial mentality that all pain is bad. Indeed, as its inclusion in this section suggests, suffering, intense suffering—even suffering of *every* sort mentioned above—can (in the end) be turned into a means of grace to help one grow spiritually. Even Christ *learned* through suffering (Heb. 5:8).

What I have said thus far points to helping counselees to grow through suffering by helping them to interpret and use pain biblically.

How does one interpret pain?

First, he must recognize that pain usually isn't easy to handle. This will be of special import in the case where a counselee has *never* handled pain well. Simple solutions either are not available or are not proper. Because of his own experiences in suffering, a counselor ought to be able to show compassion on counselees (cf. Heb. 10:32-34; II Cor. 1:4ff.).

Next, the counselor must help the counselee to gain a proper perspective on pain and suffering. This perspective is chalked out by the Apostle Paul, who suffered more pain than any of your counselees will ever have to endure:

> This temporary light affliction is producing for us an eternal weight of glory that is beyond all comparison (II Cor. 4:17).

He calls it *temporary*.

"Temporary? Why Mary has been on a bed of pain for 12 years!" you object.

"Yes, temporary," Paul would retort. In comparison to an eternal pain-free existence in glory with Christ (Rev. 21:4), what is 12 (or, for that matter, 50) years? It all depends on one's viewpoint. If he takes a purely earth-bound attitude toward life, 12 years can seem a long time. In comparison with eternity (and, note, Paul contrasts *temporary* with *eternal, light* with *weight, affliction* with *glory*) 12 years is very short. What one believes and where he focuses his eyes in suffering can be the all-important factor in determining how he handles it.

But the suffering is temporary in that it *will* end. Paul makes this point in I Corinthians 10:13c. And the story of Job shows not only that suffering has an end, but that it is, in itself, limited by the purpose and wisdom of God (as, indeed, I Cor. 10:13b also teaches). Suffering is limited in time and extent. Even the body itself has been equipped with a chemical, endorphin, that acts as an agent to keep pain from becoming too intense.

Again, the counselor will point out that in contrast to the heavy weight of glory Christ has prepared for those who love Him, *any* pain one can experience can only be considered light. This is not a matter of not treating pain seriously; it is a simple (but profoundly important) fact. Paul wasn't a person who knew nothing of pain; read II Corinthians 4:16; 6:4-10; 11:23-29. He knew pain. He called suffering, suffering—there is no denial in his words. But Paul could endure such pain *because* of his viewpoint (or perspective) on it. Often we hear people say, "Oh, what a burden this pain is!" But, in contrast, says Paul, "Oh, what a burden—of peace and joy in glory—you will have to carry in eternity. You will be *so* loaded down then, with *so* much, that this present load (and it is a load) will seem light. Therefore, let that thought lighten your load today!" That is the reason he could say (in the previous verse—vs. 16): "We don't give up" (cf. also 4:1, 8).

Other points could be made. Suffering is not unique (I Cor. 10:13 makes the point that others—including Christ—have borne up under similar suffering successfully). I Peter 1:9 and Hebrews 2:18 are supporting verses.

But what of the purposes of pain?

A. Suffering sometimes comes to further God's Word and the progress of the gospel. That's what Paul discovered in jail (Phil. 1). But he could rejoice at and enter into that purpose only because instead of complaining (why me? why this? why now?), he looked in the trial for the hand of God at work. Suffering is in God's control. Therefore, counselors must get counselees to ask, "What's God up to?"

B. Suffering sometimes is chastening. Often it is a warning; it may be intended to purify (cf. I Cor. 11:30-32). The Latin word *poena* = punishment, is the word from which our *pain* comes. The frequent connection between the two was early noticed (cf. Gen. 3:16). Those who are alert to discipline from God (or who by a faithful counselor are alerted to it) can say with the psalmist, "Before I was afflicted I went astray, but now I observe your Word" (Ps. 119:67).

C. Suffering sometimes is instructive. But if we do not help counselees to look for God's teaching, they will lose the benefit of it. Cf. Psalm

119:71: "It is good for me that I have been afflicted that I may learn your statutes." If suffering doesn't encourage a Christian to search the Scriptures, then he is missing God's blessings in it (cf. also Heb. 5:8; 2:10).

D. Suffering sometimes comes simply to honor God (Job; John 9:1ff.).

All these meanings (and more) from time to time properly describe the purpose for a counselee's sufferings. Perhaps *one* is dominant; perhaps all are present. But every counselor ought to be prepared to have such reasons at hand when a counselee (in earnest—not in complaint) asks, "Why?" A large part of the solution to the problem of bearing up under suffering is in *knowing* that it is not meaningless.

Now the other great fact about suffering is that it may be used. Pain is no excuse for letting down the bars (cf. *Trust and Obey* on I Pet. 2:22, 23). To "suffer," etymologically means "to bear under (*sub* = under; *ferre* = bear, carry). Consider the following: God provides strength to endure (II Thess. 1:4; I Pet. 2:19) even unjust suffering brought simply because one names the name of Christ. Yet such endurance witnesses to His Name. That is one *great* use of suffering. In the hospital room, the Christian's demeanor, itself, ought to be an initial testimony to nurses, roommates, visitors, doctors.

A great purpose (and use) of suffering is *growth through testing* (I Pet. 4:1). Those who can handle this, who pass the test and thereby grow in knowledge and strength, are those who *expect* such things: "Dear friends, don't be surprised at the fiery ordeal that is coming upon you to test you, as though something strange were happening to you." To warn counselees of further tests through trials is important. Good counseling looks ahead and prepares others for what they may encounter in the future. One can bear to look ahead to the immediate future if he has first looked far ahead to the ultimate future.

CHAPTER NINETEEN

COUNSELING AND THE CHURCH: THE DOCTRINE OF THE CHURCH

Counseling in the Church

When I spoke at the Rosemead Graduate School of Psychology a few years ago, the thrust of my brief opening remarks was, "This program has no reason for existence. Not only can you not integrate pagan thought and biblical teaching, but what you are trying to do is to train people to attempt the work of the church without ordination, outside the church. That is distorting God's order of things. Counseling may not be set up as a life calling on a free-lance basis; all such counseling ought to be done as a function of the church, utilizing its authority and resources."[1]

To my amazement, I discovered that to many students this was virtually new material. They had not seriously considered such a question; it seemed as if they were encountering the thought for the first time. Indeed, they continued to raise questions about this point for the entire discussion period. The question of the church and counseling is a live issue today!

In many quarters, there is very little knowledge about and concern for the visible church on the part of Christians. Some of this is understandable (though not excusable) from an historical point of view. This appalling lack largely has grown out of a reaction to denominational liberalism combined with the lingering effects of an anti-church Darbyism that pervaded Bible-believing churches during the past generation. Both led to a basic distrust in the organized church, and provided the impetus for extra-church agencies. This bevy of para-church agencies which was spawned in turn did much to develop a do-it-yourself-outside-

---

1. Cf. *Shepherding*, vol. II; the *Manual*, pp. 11ff.

the-church mentality. This independent mentality neatly fitted the growing professionalism of the modern counseling movement which, during the same period, developed alongside of it. A number of other factors collaborated[2] to produce the present situation, in which young people can grow up in a Bible-believing congregation, graduate from a Christian college, enter a graduate doctoral program, and never be confronted with the biblical truth that counseling is the work of the church.

Only in most recent times has there been a healthy change of direction. Conservative churches have been growing strong, liberalism has waned and there is a new emphasis on the organized church (as opposed to the "remnant theology" that previously tended to stress the invisible (or unorganized) church alone. The bankruptcy of modern counseling theories (in addition) has tended to encourage pastors to rethink the entire question of referral. These—and other factors that I cannot discuss now—have combined to create a new mentality that (at last) is beginning to turn the tide. More and more, the idea of counseling as the work of the organized church (in general) and the pastor and elders (in particular) has begun to emerge.[3]

Because of this happy change—and concomitant with it—has grown a necessity to think again about the place of the church in counseling and the place of counseling in the church. This subject (again) demands, at the very least, a definitive book or two.

When the church really develops a biblical form of counseling within its purview, not only will many of the present problems encountered in counseling sessions be diminished, but a new day of preventive counseling will dawn. The emphasis in free-lance counseling is basically remedial—that's all it could be. It has neither the platform from which nor the resources by which it may do preventive work. Nor do most self-styled "professionals" make any effort to rectify this situation.

Just to take one area (about which I am currently writing a book) as an example, consider the problems and complexities connected with divorce and remarriage counseling. I would estimate from extended experience that more than 75 percent of the complications in such marriage counseling could have been eliminated at the outset (if not avoided al-

---

2. I have discussed these in detail in *Lectures*, pp. 40-45.
3. There are sad retrogressions. E.g., Dallas Theological Seminary's Practical Theology Department in recent years has turned to psychiatrists for training in (supposedly) "pastoral" counseling.

together) if the church had known what to do, when and how (and had done it). Because the church failed, because most "professionals" know as little or even less about what the Bible requires, most counselees who sought help about divorce got poor advice. Consequently, when those who do know how to help biblically come into the picture, it is often too late, or requires hours simply to untangle many unnecessary complications.

To mention just one other area, consider also the realm of interpersonal relations. More often than not, the church has failed to instruct its members biblically about principles involving interpersonal relations, and (on top of that) either doesn't deal with violations of those principles adequately or adds to the problem by violating them itself (e.g., receiving gossip, talking negatively about persons behind their backs, failing to insist that the steps in Matthew 18:15ff. be followed, etc.).

But—as I said—all this is now changing, rapidly. There is new concern to be biblical. And even where there may not yet be much knowledge, there is study; where there may not be much practice there are attempts. All this is encouraging.

The Church in Counseling

God has given (1) the ordained teaching and ruling officers (2) the task of changing people's lives (3) through the authoritative ministry of the Word (II Tim. 3:15-17). When that authority is exercised properly (biblically), Christ promises to be "in the midst" giving encouragement, furnishing wisdom and providing strength (cf. Matt. 18:15-20). Both *exousia* (externally conferred authority) and *dunamis* (internal power and capability) are granted these officers by virtue of their calling to the work of ministering the Word. The *exousia* authorizes them to command respect and obedience (I Thess. 5:13; Heb. 13:17); the second empowers them to carry on their work (II Tim. 1:7).

All too few officers—pastor included—recognize and exercise their authority and power (and too often some who do abuse it and, as a result, put it in the wrong light for others). No wonder, then, that counseling limps. Ordination is important because it is the orderly appointment of a man to his office and work; in Christ's name it grants him the right to authoritatively use the gifts that the Holy Spirit has already given (the recognition of the gifts is one of the bases for ordination). The authority for counseling is granted through Christ's Church.[4] Ordination brings one's counseling under the scrutiny and regulation of other elders. He acts under—not apart from—the counsel and admonition of Christ's divinely instituted order, the church.[5]

When a pastor of a congregation may claim that his ministry keeps him too busy to counsel (as some do), his claim is *always* false. Surely he could not be busier at the Lord's work than the Lord Jesus (Who found so much time to counsel individuals) or even the Apostle Paul (who followed his Lord's example in this—cf. Col. 1:28; Acts 20:31). If the pastor really is too busy (and that claim is not merely an excuse), then something is radically wrong. He must examine his activities to discover what it is that is keeping him so busy, because (surely) it will not be the ministry of the Word. Perhaps he has been wasting time; perhaps he is busy doing much that is not really the work of an elder, has failed to delegate work (especially to deacons—cf. Acts 6:2-4[6]), has not yet taught his elders to join with him in his ministry, etc. He must check his priorities. Perhaps he is running all over the map to committee meetings. Whatever the reason, he cannot be too busy to counsel. Because it is a ministry of the Word—his ministry (II Tim. 3:15-17; Col. 1:28)—he must never be so busy with the ninety-nine sheep that he neglects the hundredth.

Counseling, like preaching, is a ministry of the Word (when psychology replaced the Bible in counseling, no wonder pastors began to ask whether they had time for it); it is, therefore, an integral part of the pastor's ministry. He is a pastor-teacher (Eph. 4:11), not merely a teacher only. Pastoral work involves ministry of the Word to individual Christians (note Paul's frequent reference to "every man"). Public and private ministry of the Word are of a piece and supplement (and contribute to) one another. When a pastor (who has been counseling)

---

4. Others, doing counseling in a free-lance manner outside the church may have the gifts, but they (1) neglect the resources of the whole body and (2) act in a wholly unauthorized way. They should seek ordination and bring their work under the supervision or review of the church.

5. One problem is that many disgruntled pastors, who could not make it in the church, have gone into free-lance counseling. Some of them have been anxious to be relieved of the mutual counsel of their brethren. This may be understandable for those who have left liberal denominations (though not excusable), but certainly only is a form of rebellion by others.

6. His task is prayer and the ministry of the Word—publicly (in preaching) and privately (in counseling); cf. Acts 20:20.

preaches, he does so differently from the one who preaches only. When a preacher counsels only, he does so differently than if he also preaches. The former is more down-to-earth in his preaching; it sounds less bookish. People begin to say, "He knows! He understands my problem," and they come for counsel. A preacher who preaches as well as counsels, on the other hand, counsels more biblically—because in order to preach, he must continually expound the Scriptures. From this exposition, greater confidence develops, and he has more help to offer his counselees. The two go together. In fact, whenever one is separated from the other, both suffer.[7]

Let the church, then, assume her counseling duty, and let Christians of all sorts encourage her to do so. Let no one stand in her way, lest he be found opposing her Head and King Himself!

---

7. Pastors may *emphasize* one side of the ministry of the Word over the other, but never to the exclusion of it. Ironclad divisions between preaching pastors and counseling pastors are unscriptural. All such elders are pastor-teachers (Eph. 4:11).

CHAPTER TWENTY

COUNSELING NEW CONVERTS
(The Doctrine of the Church, Continued)

What I am about to say in this chapter is—so far as I know—an entirely new emphasis in the modern church (but not in the biblical one). Yet, it is an all-important preventive measure that could do much good.

There always have been problems with how to assimilate new converts into the church and how to help them to grow. Too many converts in a year or two stop growing (perceptively, at least), develop lethargy and (generally) become like so many of the older members— unexcited about their faith. Why? Many things may contribute to these symptoms. But surely one is a failure to counsel them adequately immediately after conversion. If the suggestions that follow are taken seriously and implemented, they could bring about a quiet revolution for good.

For a long time, a conviction that comes from biblical data has been growing. These data have been thrusting themselves upon me as I have been studying the Scriptures in order to find answers to various problems that trouble the church. And, all these problems surface in the counseling room. Let me share the conclusion I have reached from this study.

My basic suggestion is simple: you should set up counseling for every new convert who comes into your congregation. How did I reach this conviction?

First, every new convert should be encouraged to obey Jesus Christ *immediately*. We should not wait until someone gets into trouble months (or years) later in order to instruct him. We now teach new converts basic doctrine (and that's good), but not what to do with it—i.e., how to transform it into daily living (and that's bad). We teach a few (usually four) personal activities: Bible study, prayer, church attendance and witnessing (and that's good), but there are a host of other things we neglect (and that's very bad).

The greatest need for a new convert is to recognize that his life *as a whole* must change. Christ wants him to be different across the board. We must tell him so, demonstrate examples of such change in every area of his life, and be prepared to help him do so. That means that every congregation must have a purposeful plan and practical program to accomplish this.

Let us consider a powerful verse that forcefully compels me to make such a proposal. The more I looked at it, the more it troubled me—it got under my skin. I began to ask, "how?"—"how can it be implemented?" The verse is Ephesians 4:17:

> So then, I say and testify this together with the Lord, that you must no longer walk like the Gentiles do. . . .

The fourth chapter of Ephesians contains the practical consequences of the doctrines taught in chapters 1–3. Paul's words in verse 17, at first, may seem strange. Didn't he write all his biblical letters "with the Lord"? Of course. Well, then, why make a point of it here? For emphasis. What he says here is of great significance. This was one way of saying, "If you get anything, be sure you get this," or "Now hear *this.*"

What, then, should we hear at all costs? That new converts must no longer walk like Gentiles (pagans, unbelievers) do. That is what every new convert needs to hear.

In Paul's letters (of course, in Peter's and elsewhere too) you can discover that this is precisely what the apostles did. Take time to study the N.T. data on the subject, and you will be amazed to find out how much new converts were told right away. Not only were they taught basic doctrine, but all sorts of implications of these truths for life (often in surprising detail). And, you can't miss the fact that the apostles seemed to cover the waterfront!

Take Paul's letters to the infant church at Thessalonica (where Paul stayed so briefly) and note what sorts of things Paul incidentally *says* he told them in that brief span of time (probably he taught much more, that he had no reason to mention).

The basic truth is set forth in I Thessalonians 1:9, 10:

> . . . you turned from idols to serve the living and true God and to wait for His Son from the heavens.

That statement presupposes a radical change that is in keeping with the admonition of Ephesians 4:17. It involves (as the rest of the letter shows) teaching about the second coming, and how that geared into their daily living. In I Thessalonians 2:11, 12, the matter of the Christian's walk (cf. the commentary on this in Eph. 4–6) was *thoroughly* discussed. And note (vs. 11) that this counseling was not just general; it was done with "each one"—i.e., each new convert. As much individual concern was shown as a father would show each of his children.

But about what sorts of things did Paul counsel them? According to I Thessalonians 4:1-8, he even got down to discussing sexual questions, how to acquire a wife properly (vss. 4, 5), etc. According to 4:11, 12, he gave this sort of instruction in all areas (business, interpersonal relations, etc.). More could be mentioned.

But to show that this happened *right away* elsewhere (and not only at Thessalonica), consider Paul's teaching at Crete, where the church had not even been formally organized. Consider Titus 2:14; 3:14—all sorts of good deeds in every area were to be taught from the outset.

The new convert must not be ignored once he is converted. At this early point, when he is willing and ready to learn, when he is ready to change, when he *expects* it—we must not disappoint him with our usual too little, too late approach. While he is still basking in the warmth of his "first love," we must begin to counsel him seriously about *every* front in his life. He needs to know (it is for us to show) that he can be different in *every* aspect of life. We must confront him with Ephesians 4:17 (or its equivalent) and go to work helping him according to a thorough, comprehensive plan and program for doing so.

Instead, we wait till problems come. When the wheel begins to squeak, we get out the grease gun. But it is usually so rusty by then that it is very difficult to solve the problem. Paul wanted to prevent rust.

At John's baptism all sorts of people repented and were baptized. Was that all? No. They, themselves, sensed the need for more—for change in all of life appropriate to their repentance—so they asked, "What should we do?" John told them—in specific how-to detail that related to each person's circumstances, whether they were soldiers, tax collectors, etc. (cf. Luke 3:10-14). From the beginning, they knew that their whole lives would be different because of Christ. And he told them right away; he didn't wait until two months (or two years) later, when they were in a pack of trouble! To turn from idols to serve the living God means lots of changes in lots of particulars—whether the idols be images of wood and metal or wooden homes and metal automobiles! A lot of new ways must be learned.

The terms of the Great Commission make the point too (Matt. 28: 18-20). This is an educational commission. Consider the educational milieu: ". . . make disciples" (i.e., students) . . . "teaching them. . . ." That is not conversion alone; it is discipleship.

If Christ says anything in this passage, it is that the church is an educational institution. The church is a school. Students matriculate by baptism (that word means, literally, "uniting" or "joining"[1]), learn from Him (Matt. 11:29) from that day on, and are expected to translate His truth into life ("teaching them *to observe"*). Converts come into Christ's school (the church) precisely for this reason: *to learn to do "all" that He commanded.* That has to do with all of life: the curriculum is explicit.[2] This is a vital education for life—not merely for academic excellence!

Of course, everything can't be taught all at once. But from the outset the new convert should know about the purpose of the school he joins and should be keenly aware of the curriculum. He must also see that total change should *begin* right away.

Instead of holding the new members' course *before* a person enters into the fellowship of the church, it ought to be held after admission. Then, he gets the idea that education begins (rather than *ends*) with admission into Christ's school. The class should survey all areas of life, suggesting aspects in each where change must occur. Growing out of this, special counseling sessions may be held to help those who are having difficulties in any of these areas.

How many new converts have ever had anyone talk to them about their physical lives, for instance, telling them about the body as the temple of the Holy Spirit and urging them to develop regular sleep habits? Usually (tragically), we wait till sleep loss leads to serious irritability (or even hallucinations) before we say a word! Families often

---

1. *Bapto* = "dipping, immersing." *Baptizo* (from which the word baptism comes) means "mersing" (or as the English, "merging"; that is, uniting, joining). For details, see my book, *The Meaning and Mode of Baptism.*
2. Yet what church or Sunday school has developed a curriculum based on a study of the commands of Christ? How we have missed the basics!

have to be talking divorce before anyone suggests counseling. Why not talk about such matters right off?

Surely a business man can't be conducting his business affairs according to the principles of Colossians 3 *before* he comes to know Christ. Well, then, why not tell him about the need to be working for Christ rather than for an ungrateful employer? A new convert's family relationships can't be Christian before he is, so why not ask about the family right away?

There is no printed program available for this; you will have to develop your own program. Once you do, establish it in the church, so that when you leave, the program doesn't. Have two or three capable elders sit in on early sessions, then turn it over to them. You dare not ignore this important matter; the whole future of your new converts (not to mention your own counseling program) may depend upon it.

CHAPTER TWENTY-ONE

COUNSELING AND CHURCH DISCIPLINE
(The Doctrine of the Church, Continued)

Because it is so important to counseling, I must once more bring up an old subject that (nevertheless) is new (or possibly unknown) to so many churches: church discipline. Unfortunately, the failure to discipline church members amounts to withholding from them the privilege of being confronted by others, and by the church, when they err in doctrine or life. Christ granted them this right; we have no right to withhold it from them.

Many Christians who think that they have done all that they can to solve their problems have not yet begun to do what Jesus Christ requires. So counselors must do all they can to instruct them about this fact.

When you tell them so, it sounds surprising. They may not even believe it. They may protest, "Now wait a minute. My husband and I have been having problems all these years, and I've tried everything . . . *everything*. There isn't *anything* more to do. I even went to a good Christian friend (or to my pastor) and asked if there was anything more, and he said he didn't know of anything. He thought that I was doing everything that I could do."

In response I say, "If you're a Christian, if your husband's a Christian, there is *always* a way to solve that problem between the two of you. You are never out of resources."

The answer to the problem does not lie in mysticism. It isn't a matter of saying, "Well, I'll leave it all in God's hands and hope that it works out for the best. After all, all things work together for good for those who love God, who are the called according to His purpose." Now that verse is a wonderful comfort. And there are times when we can say, "Well there's nothing more that can be done about this situation." But it's not the time to say that when two Christians are involved in a relationship that has gone sour. The only time to say that is when there is

286

an *unbeliever* and a Christian involved in an impasse (Rom. 12:18).

Matthew 18:15, 16, 17 gives us a very important clue about how to solve problems that don't seem to be getting solved any other way. This is a neglected area, and yet it is an extremely valuable portion of the Word of God to understand. It deals with church discipline. "Church discipline?!" Yes, church discipline. "Aw, c'mon. Church discipline is just the way that you get rid of troublemakers in church." That's the response so many give. If that's what church discipline has meant to you, or if that's what it's meant to your congregation, then that is church discipline abused.

Church discipline is not intended to get rid of anybody. At every point in the disciplinary process, the whole concern is to bring about reconciliation.

Now let's look at that passage a little more closely. There are three steps in church discipline.

First: Verse 15 says, "If your brother sins, go and reprove him in private. If he listens to you, you have won your brother."

Sometimes Christians go this far, but very rarely. Most of the problems that we have with others, that go on for weeks or even years, could be solved if we just simply did what this first step says. The counselee who has been sinned against is to go with the facts and the data, and to face his brother with the problem, simply, plainly and straightforwardly. Now it doesn't say go in the spirit of nastiness. It doesn't say go in order to tell the other guy off. It says to tell him about the problem. Counselors must warn about going in the wrong way.

Many times problems aren't resolved simply because we don't tell the other person about them. He doesn't even know that we've taken offense. He doesn't know that he's stepped on our toes. And so, he doesn't come to us. No reconciliation takes place. We stand there folding our arms, saying, "Well, let him come," but he doesn't even know that there is a problem.

It's the obligation of the offended party to go, as well as the obligation of the offender if he knows that he's offended another. That's the first thing to see in verse 15. "Go and reprove him," but notice—"in private." You don't advise him to tell the church, or all his friends and neighbors. You don't let him talk about another behind his back. You say, "Go and talk to *him*." Keep the facts as private as the offense itself was in the first place.

And the purpose for which he goes is mentioned in the last part of the verse. He wants the other to acknowledge his sin, or to straighten out any misunderstandings. He wants him to *hear* what he has to say, so that the two may become reconciled once again. It says, "if he *listens* to you, you have won your brother."

That's what he wants; not to get rid of somebody. The first step of church discipline, then, is an informal step that any individual in the church may take. It has one main goal and purpose to it: to win one's brother.

The counselee may respond, "But did you say that I could do this with my husband (or wife), or with my parents, or children?" The counselor answers: "Yes, I did. If there is any Christian brother or sister with whom you are unable to work out affairs in any other way, you may go and you may talk to that person about what is wrong. If problems continue to separate the two of you, you need to straighten out those matters by first going to that other person."

"But I'm supposed to be subject to my husband." Or, "I'm supposed to be subject to my parents. I can't go and *reprove* them, can I?" Of course you can. Subjection and reproof are two entirely separate and different matters. Reproof is in no way inconsistent with subjection. Subjection has to do not only with *what* you do, but *how* you do it. If you go in a submissive manner, in that proper recognition of your relationship to that parent or to your husband, you may reprove him. Remember, Nathan reproved David. He was able to reprove the *king,* in spite of the authority that had been given to him as king. Authority is not limitless. Authority in the Bible is limited by the Bible itself.

And so, your counselee must go in a submissive spirit, one that recognizes his proper relationship to the other. He must be certain that he really is seeking to win the brother back. He must be seeking reconciliation. If he goes in that manner, he can speak about anything that's wrong between them.

We have been talking about the values, privileges and right of church discipline. Every believer in Jesus Christ has the right to be disciplined. Counselees may say, "That's the kind of right I can do without." No, they can't. Church discipline is extremely important.

Discipline is not some process that God has given to get rid of troublemakers in the church, as a lot of people think, though it might do that, at times. But that's not its main purpose. The purpose of church discipline is to win others back to the Lord and to bring about reconciled conditions between brothers.

Jesus says that if two brothers are having problems with one another, they are to go to one another. That's the first step that we talked about— it does not say wait for the offender to come. Of course, the offender is obligated to come if he recognizes his sin. But the offended party is always to go to his brother. He is the one who is always aware of the problem because he's the one whose toes hurt. One who is offended is thereby obligated.

He may say, "Well, that doesn't seem right. The offender should come." Of course he should, but suppose he doesn't realize that he has offended you. Then nothing happens. And week after week, year after year, people go on with the same old bitternesses and grievances against one another, simply because the one who is offended sinned also. He sinned by not following verse 15. It says, "If your brother sins, you go; you who have been offended, go and reprove him in private. And if he listens to you, you have won your brother." Not to go is sin.

That, of course, is the purpose of church discipline, to bring about peace—peaceful relations, peaceful communication, peaceful friendship between the two. Brothers ought to be at peace with one another.

But suppose the offender doesn't listen when the offended party goes to him. Suppose he gets all the more angry. Suppose he says, "Look, I've had enough of this. You've come here five or six times. I don't want to do anything about it. I've had it. I don't want to see you again." Then what do you tell him to do?

First, make sure he has exhausted that first resource. When the offender says, "Don't come again," turn to verse 16: "If he does not listen to you, take one or two more with you, so that by the mouth of two or three witnesses, every fact may be confirmed."

All right. So he then takes a couple of arbitrators along with him. They stand between the two. They become counselors. They do everything within their power as neutral observers and concerned, interested parties, who are part of the Body of Christ, to bring about reconciliation.

In other words, Jesus says, "Don't stop if you yourself fail. Go get an elder, a pastor. Take them along with you. And the three or four of you, sit down and talk this matter through and pray about it. This is the second step.

It is rare that the second step has to be taken if the first is followed. But there are times when it must be taken, and in that case he must take it. He has no option. He can't say, "Oh, he won't pay any attention to them." Or, "He'll just get all the more angry." He has no right to talk that way. He has no idea how God is going to work. Not everything depends on the brother. When he says, "Well, that's why I haven't tried," he is prejudging the situation, but he has no right to do so.

Jesus works in the way in which He Himself told us He would. Indeed, at the very end of this section He says, "Where two or three are gathered together in My name, there am I in the midst." That's no warrant for small prayer meetings. He's not even talking about prayer meetings. He's talking about church discipline. Jesus promises to be there in a very special way, working through church discipline. The counselor may say, "If you let this go on and on between the two of you, bitterness and resentment building up, differences growing, the matter of the two of you and your relationship getting sourer every day (in a marriage, in a home, in personal relationship at church, whatever it may be), don't tell me that you've done everything that you can do! You tell me that the other person isn't going to respond properly, and will make things worse? You don't know that. Christ can change him. And even if things do get worse, you are to follow what Jesus Christ says anyway. You must do what you have to do; you have to go."

Well, what happens if he doesn't listen to them? Suppose they go back four or five times, and he finally says, "Look. I've had enough of this. Get out of here and don't come back!" Verse 17 spells out Christ's third step in church discipline: "And if he refuses to listen to them [that is, the arbitrators, the counselors you bring with you], tell it to the church, and if he refuses to listen even to the church, let him be to you as a Gentile and a tax collector." Now what does that mean?

Well, if he won't listen to you personally, as you go privately, if he won't listen to the counselors you take with you, then you are to bring the matter officially before the elders of the church. And they are to order him in the Name of Jesus Christ to be reconciled. This Christ-given power and this authority is to be wielded with love, but also with firmness.

Finally, if he refuses to hear even the church, then they are to excommunicate him, not for the particular sin that he committed, but for his arrogance, his refusal to heed the authority of Jesus Christ, exercised by His church. And so they excommunicate him. They put him on the outside, where the Gentile (the heathen) and the tax collector who had been excommunicated were. But even then the idea is not to get rid of him. Even then (like that man in Corinth) his excommunication is to lead to repentance.

In II Corinthians 2:6-8, after the man did repent, Paul says, "Quickly, lest there be too much sorrow on his part, receive him back, reaffirm[1] your love for him and forgive him."[2] Not only should the church be quick to excommunicate when someone refuses to hear the authority of Christ (after all attempts at reconciliation), but it ought to be even more quick to receive him back, once he has repented of his sin.

And so we have a wonderful process given to us by Jesus Christ. If you've never used it, start today. Start right now. Use the principles in the Word of God that have been given to you. Otherwise you do not counsel properly.

Discipline, when exercised, must be recognized and supported by other pastors and churches. Typically, in the rare cases in which a church *does* exercise discipline, it is undermined by other congregations (in such cases, the pastor and elders of the disciplining church ought to request a meeting with the pastor and ruling board of the undermining congregation and confront them about the matter.[3]). The disciplined person simply runs down the street to the next evangelical church, where he is received—no questions asked—with open arms. That practice is wrong, self-defeating, a disgrace to Christ, and must be remedied.

Instead, the pastor of the second church should try to bring the disciplined person to repentance and send him back to the original church (he may want to *take* him back). He should announce his policy toward straying or disciplined sheep: "We try to help sheep having difficulties (other than doctrinal difficulties) in their own fold to work these

---

1. The word here is a legal term. This speaks of a formal reconfirmation into the body. A written record ought to be made declaring the matter closed.

2. If members refuse to forgive, whisper about him or ostracize him, they too are subject to discipline.

3. It is possible that the disciplined person misled them. More likely, they, too, need confronting because of poor policies. Among churches of the same denomination, there should be means of recourse. If no results come in talking to the officers of a church of a different denomination, every attempt should be made until they shut off discussion. In such cases they should be treated as (a functional judgment) a non-church.

out with their shepherds or other sheep. How may I help you?"[4]

How vital it is for as many Bible-believing pastors in a community as possible to work out (as some have) a set of agreed-upon policies and procedures for handling straying (the most frequent problem) and disciplined sheep. In that way *only* can church discipline become effective. The church that receives a disciplined sheep into its own fold gets no bargain; it takes a Jonah on board and has but to wait for the storm to break.

If you do not know how to go about achieving some agreement on policies and procedures, you might do one of two things: (1) bring the matter up at the local evangelical ministerial meeting; (2) visit individually other pastors who might wish to participate in such a cooperative effort. One way to get it under way is to read this section of this chapter and ask for discussion. Here is one place where true biblical ecumenicity can be shown; one place (despite other differences) where brothers can work together to help each other's ministries.

If you are not sure of the soundness of the ministry in another church, you (or you and your elders) can go with the straying sheep to see if the problem *can* be worked out (you'll learn what you didn't know by doing so. And, you'll have an opportunity to influence the other pastor and his board) with the other congregation. They cannot object to you bringing a straying or repentant disciplined sheep back, surely. If they do, you have learned too. Such circumstances may lead to helping other weaker congregations or (what is equally important) to discovering that a congregation is basically not willing to carry on a biblical ministry (in such cases, if you can't influence, you shake the dust off your feet, and take the straying sheep back with you to his new church home).

"But you have been judging people; I thought you shouldn't," someone objects when he hears about church discipline being exercised. The objection is almost inevitable. Your response is, "Yes and no. I am judging as Christ taught us to, but not in the way that He forbids." It is not the wrong sort of judging (after proper disciplinary process) to excommunicate another and treat him as a heathen. You do not call him a heathen; you simply say, "He has been acting like one—refusing to heed Christ's authority; so we must treat him *as* one." That is what

---

4. There is no problem about taking sheep away from a wolf in shepherd's clothing.

Christ taught us to do in Matthew 18. We make no judgment about his heart condition; man can look only on the outward appearance—God alone looks on the heart. We simply make a *functional judgment*. The congregation must relate to him in some fashion; Christ said, treat him *as* a heathen when he rejects the church and acts like one.

One precaution. It is very important for pastors and others to exercise extreme care in handling accusations and evidence when confronting others. Qualifications are important; exact wording can be crucial. Hearsay, gossip, indirect evidence, jumping to conclusions—all these are wrong. Testimony (if the person is willing to back up his charge) is admissible, but to make a charge stick, there must be at least two witnesses. In love (I Cor. 13 says, "believe all things, hope all things"), the best construction ought to be put on acts or words until hard evidence demands otherwise. Care in church discipline is essential.

CHAPTER TWENTY-TWO

COUNSELING AND WORKS OF MERCY
(The Doctrine of the Church, Continued)

The work of mercy in Christ's church continues His work of "going about doing good." But, sadly, it has been all but forgotten by many Bible-practicing churches and barely acknowledged by others. In a day of insurance, social security, Medicaid, etc., there has been a tendency to say, "Let the government take over the work." But the government, or pagan business, cannot do what God told the church to do. To think that any other agencies could truly replace the church in doing such work is a great mistake. A cup of cold water in Christ's Name (which means that it is accompanied by a ministry from the Word) can never be matched by water in the name of the U.S. Government! Widows and orphans must be cared for ("visited" means cared for).[1] We must "do good to all men [unbelievers included], but especially to those who are of the household of faith [believers]," says Paul in Galatians 6:10. It is that diaconal ministry to those who belong to the household of faith (cf. Acts 6) that I wish to mention very briefly in this totally inadequate chapter (an entire book must be written on this subject in relation to counseling). There should never be a need for a member of Christ's church to turn to a social worker.

The pastoral counselor constantly will turn up hardship cases of one sort or another (they don't all have to be matters of financial need) as he speaks with people who are in trouble. Sometimes these problems will be brought upon themselves by counselees; often not. A mother needs some sort of help with her children, a new convert needs assistance in kicking the heroin habit, a family is facing financial ruin; in another there is the need for a change of jobs. In the course of an ordinary day's counseling, at least one or two such problems are likely to arise. What does the pastoral counselor do? Is he restricted to his own resources plus

---

1. On this, see *Shepherding God's Flock*, vol. I, chap. 11. pp. 75-84.

referral to pagan social services? Not at all. He has (1) the resources of the entire church, in general (cf. vol. II, *Shepherding God's Flock*, "Mutual Ministry") and (2) the diaconate (board of deacons), in particular, to draw upon. There is, potentially, a wealth of resources in the church body (largely untapped in most congregations, unfortunately) to which he may turn.

But, note, he does not call in church aid carelessly. Where finances are needed, for example, if the family or the individual ought to (and can) do something to offset the need, he will not ask the church to do it instead. To do so would be bad counseling—it would encourage parasitism. God says if a person (who can) won't work, he shouldn't eat (II Thess. 3:10). This sort of policy was followed even with widows (cf. I Tim. 5:3-16). If a widow's family could help, they should be told to do so and expected to meet the need. The church should not be burdened unnecessarily. If the widow herself could get a job or remarry, she should. And, note (vs. 10), only those who have helped others should be helped. (Would this rule be relaxed in the case of repentance?) Clearly, there were qualifications that one had to pass to receive help—and they were strict. Money was not to be given away indiscriminately. But there were cases of genuine need for prisoners, widows, orphans, the sick and others who could not help themselves or find help elsewhere, and the church was to meet their needs in full.

I have spoken of financial need. The counselor must not ignore financial needs, but he must think more broadly (in terms of Gal. 6:10). He encounters all sorts of problems in the counseling room; not just financial ones. And there are all sorts of things that various members of the congregation can be asked to do to help, as well as the body of deacons, whose specific task is to lend aid. (Indeed, the two ought to be coordinated: pastors ought to get their diaconate to organize the members for such work. Then, the pastor may simply call upon the diaconate, who, in turn, will draw upon the list of persons gifted, recruited and trained by them to lend aid in various ways.)

But how does the pastor know when to call in help from others? Whenever something arises in counseling that (if he pursues it) requires him to leave the direct work of the prayerful ministry of the Word to minister in some other way, it is time for him to do so (cf. Acts 6:2, 4). The diaconate is a catchall board dealing with ways and means of accomplishing all the temporal tasks that the elders turn over to them.

It meets temporal needs by organizing and implementing the programs and policies of the elders. In general, anything that otherwise would take the elders away from their tasks ought to be handed over to the deacons.

If, in a counseling session, it becomes clear that John needs someone to show him how to find and hold a job, the pastor ought to ask the deacons to help John in this matter. It is wrong for the pastor (beyond teaching the biblical principles and showing him how they apply to his life) to spend time showing him how to make out a dossier, how to present himself to an employer, where to go, etc., if he has deacons (or they know of others in the congregation) who could do this as well as the pastor—or better. It is not a matter of such work being "beneath" him; it is a matter of focusing upon the tasks assigned by Christ and learning how to delegate (as the apostles did in Acts 6) so that all the members might share in the blessings of helping others by using their gifts. If a new convert is uncertain about many of the particular ways in which she ought to relate her new faith to her family, at length, the pastor may turn her over to a mature Christian woman (solicited by the deacons, perhaps—but not necessarily so) to help her (cf. Tit. 2:3-5).

Finally, let me note that Luke indicates (in Acts 6) that special persons (wisely, Hellenists to serve Hellenists), spiritually qualified, were chosen with great care to carry out the work of mercy. Not just anyone will do; and not just anyone of those qualified in every case. Care and wisdom in the selection of helping personnel are essential. Moreover, clearcut policies were established and formally carried out by the church—note: (1) lists were kept of those qualified to receive funds, (2) judgments were made among various persons seeking aid to qualify only those who (3) met specified, published criteria (cf. I Tim. 5:3-16). Everything was done in an orderly fashion.

Counselors, who have the privilege of utilizing this great program as an adjunct to pastoral counseling, must do so freely. But they may neither abuse it themselves nor allow others to do so. They must use it with caution and care. By encouraging and maintaining a businesslike (in the *good* sense of that term) approach, they will enhance the work of the diaconate (from the lowly status that it so often has) in bringing great blessings to many, while—at the same time—reaping many benfits for counseling.

CHAPTER TWENTY-THREE

COUNSELING, DEATH AND DYING: THE DOCTRINE OF THE FUTURE

"It is appointed for people to die only once. . . ." All human beings, except those believers who are alive at Christ's second coming, will die. People, therefore, have a vested interest in death. It is no wonder, then, that the pseudo-scientific death-and-dying (or thanatology) movement associated with Elizabeth Kubler-Ross, Raymond Moody and Robert Monroe has been attracting much attention. The Christian counselor must put the claims of this movement into perspective (1) to answer inquiries of counselees, (2) to warn persons dabbling in it and (3) to develop their own biblical approach to such matters.

All three—Kubler-Ross, Moody and Monroe—are closely related. Kubler-Ross's original work was done in the area of dying; Moody investigated reported experiences of persons declared clinically dead (who revived) and those who had gone through near-death experiences. Monroe has been involved in O.B.E. (out-of-body-experiences) work and in spiritism, into which Kubler-Ross and Moody also have been drawn in more recent days. (Kubler-Ross claims to have her own "spirit-guide," whose name is "Salem"; she claims also to have taken at least two out-of-body trips herself. Moody claims some sort of direct revelation, and Monroe is supposed to have learned his tape technique for inducing O.B.E. trips from the spirits.[1]) Each of the three has written:

Kubler-Ross, *Death and Dying* and *Death: The Final Stage of Growth.*

Moody, *Life after Life.*

Monroe, *Journeys Out of the Body.*

I shall not duplicate my basic work on death, counseling the dying and

---

1. Cf. the article, "Thanatology: Death and Dying," in *The Journal of Pastoral Practice* II, 2 (1978), pp. 139ff.

ministering to the grief-stricken found in *The Big Umbrella* ("Grief as a Counseling Opportunity") and *Shepherding God's Flock,* vol. I ("Visiting the Dying"), pp. 128-134. In those places, I have discussed the basic hope of the Christian found in I Corinthians 15 and Philippians 1, the distinction between the way that Christians and non-Christians face death (I Thess. 4)—an altogether crucial distinction ignored by Lindemann, Kaplan and others in the "grief-work" movement[2] (see my *Coping with Counseling Crises*). The fallacy and utter paganism of the grief-work hypothesis is shown as well as an alternative pattern for counseling that grows out of biblical presuppositions (and that doesn't minimize or ignore the all-important problems of sin, repentance and forgiveness). The importance of the counselor's own beliefs about and attitudes toward death is discussed. All these questions—and many more —are taken up in the three references mentioned above. While I consider that material to be vital for successful counseling, I do not think it would be profitable to repeat it here. I shall (therefore) presuppose that the reader has read these books as a background for the present chapter.

Kubler-Ross and Moody (Monroe is less well known) have aroused interest in death and dying, but their conclusions must not be accepted by Christians, for a number of reasons (some of which I shall now list).

1. They make claims about reported experiences and personal involvements from which one is led to infer that all persons (irrespective of whether they are Christians or not) find death and dying an enjoyable experience. Presumably, all go to heaven. Sin is made light of (sinful deeds are even viewed humorously)—all are warm and comfortable, greeted by the "being of light" whose love and acceptance permeates everything.[3] The teachings of the Scriptures about hell, heaven, judgment, etc., are undermined by this movement.[4]

2. Their evidence is suspect. Kubler-Ross develops a model of dying that fails to discriminate between how genuine Christians face death (in the light of Heb. 2:14, 15; I Cor. 15:54-57; Phil. 1:21-24) and

---

2. The distinction is also ignored by Kubler-Ross, who finds the same "stages" (*denial,* leading eventually to *acceptance*) present for *all* terminally ill patients.

3. Cf. Raymond Moody, *Life After Life* (New York: Bantam Books, 1975), pp. 59-63, 97, 98.

4. Moody writes, "So, in most cases, the reward-punishment model of the afterlife is abandoned and disavowed, even by many who have been accustomed to thinking in those terms" (ibid., p. 97).

how others who are not Christians do so. Since she gives absolutely no evidence of Christian faith (but, to the contrary, seems to be mixed up in spiritism), she cannot be expected to take such a distinction seriously (cf. I Cor. 2; in light of vs. 15, she wouldn't even know how to identify a Christian). But neither can Christians, who have a direct revelation from God in the Bible, accept a viewpoint that rejects and contradicts that revelation. We know that all do not enter bliss at death, as Moody's book implies. So we must conclude that if the recorded experiences are true (not trumped up, manipulated or exaggerated —and since no sources are documented by Moody, we cannot know), they do not really speak of death. Clearly, the people who spoke to Moody were alive—they were not dead and never were. Because scientists do not have a universally accepted definition of death, it is impossible to say that any of these persons died. From a Christian perspective, we must say that they did not. Moody was talking with persons who had been in a state of unconsciousness who (probably) were hallucinating. Hallucinating periods can lead to O.B.E.-like experiences. Much of the good feeling associated with such experiences may have been due to the body's own adaptive mechanisms that help handle extreme pain (e.g., recently a new bodily manufactured anesthetic, endorphin, has been isolated. Who knows what other bodily factors—yet unknown—may come into play at such times?).

3. Because Kubler-Ross, Moody and Monroe all have been involved in spiritism, against expressed biblical prohibitions (Deut. 18: 9-14), we must be extremely wary of their writings and viewpoints, and we must warn others of the dangers inherent in what they have been doing.

4. While protesting against denials and avoidance of the facts and realities of death, Kubler-Ross and Co. are leading their followers into another type of avoidance—the acceptance of a kind of universalism that makes no distinction between Christians and non-Christians during or after dying, and that finds in the reports that they publish great hope and comfort for all apart from Jesus Christ.

5. This kind of talk of a glorious, warm, painless experience after death—without a judgment—where all (and all alike) find acceptance and love, could very well lay the groundwork for justification of euthanasia (why let old people suffer here when they can be freed from that and enjoy such blessing with the "being of light"?).

In summary, it may be said that the thanatology movement has been trying to take the sting out of death apart from the cross of Christ, where (alone) is found the death of death. With no other data required, we know (*a priori*) from the Scriptures that this cannot be done and ought not be attempted. I do not have space here to suggest further implications of such teaching, but must simply urge Christian counselors to avoid and oppose it wherever it may appear.[5]

Christian teaching about death does not stop with the words, "It is appointed for people to die only once . . . ," quoted at the beginning of this chapter. That verse continues, "and after that, they face judgment" (Heb. 9:27). In the same book we read of ". . . a fearful anticipation of judgment and the fury of fire" that belongs to "God's adversaries" (Heb. 10:27). Moody's book is wrongly titled *Life after Life*. To many there will be only death—the second death—after life. Existence in eternal separation from God and punishment is not even called *life* in the Bible. Life—eternal life—is a qualitative term, signifying the blessings and joys of living with and serving God for eternity. But life is only for the sheep on Christ's right hand.

The subject of judgment—including the discussion of rewards and punishment—is so important for counseling that I shall devote the entire next chapter to it.

---

5. Some unthinking Christians have hailed the thanatology movement as a return to biblical thinking, because they see in it a confirmation of the truth of life after death. It is not. The two are antithetical. The Bible needs no confirmation from spiritists; it is to be accepted by faith on its own word.

CHAPTER TWENTY-FOUR

COUNSELING AND JUDGMENT
(The Doctrine of the Future Continued)

As we have seen in the last chapter, the Bible teaches there will be a judgment for all after death. The word *krino,* "to judge," has (as its fundamental idea) the concept of separating (or sorting out) one thing from another; i.e., discrimination (cf. the Hebrew *taam*—taste, discrimination). The most important O.T. word for judgment is *shaphat* ("to judge"), which has as its root meaning the notion of setting something up straight or erecting it. Thus it comes to mean upright evaluation. This seems to be the import of the question, "Won't the Judge of all the earth do right?" (i.e., deal uprightly—Gen. 18:25). Putting it all together, we may safely say that inherent in the concept of biblical judgment is the idea of just evaluation leading to the sorting out of things that differ.

Sometimes negative results are assumed in the use of the word *krino* (John 3:17, 18; 16:11), but this same thought is communicated most frequently (and more clearly) by the compound *katakrino* (judgment against, condemnation). Some Christians (wrongly) use the word *judgment* in the negative sense only and thereby misunderstand and misuse the term (cf. Girdlestone, *Synonyms of the O.T.,* on this point[1]). When they think of all persons (including Christians) being brought into judgment, they become confused. We are freed from condemnation (Rom. 8:1); that is a truth that must not be lost sight of. But it is also true that (as Paul says when speaking to Christians), "We shall all stand before God's judgment seat" (Rom. 14:10). He declares also that "each of us will give an account of himself to God" (vs. 12). Indeed, Vos tells us: "by far the majority of instances where the last-judgment-idea occurs speak of believers."[2]

---

1. R. B. Girdlestone, *Synonyms of the O.T.* (Grand Rapids: Eerdmans, 1948), p. 251.
2. Geerhardus Vos, *Pauline Eschatology* (Grand Rapids: Eerdmans, 1952), p. 270.

The import of judgment, then, is to sort things out justly. That is what we see. The sheep are separated from the goats. Varying degrees of reward or punishment are allocated to each, respectively. Wrongs are righted, tables turned, God's Name, His Son and His people vindicated, God's righteousness proclaimed. Some aspects of this judgment are negative, it is true; but others are positive. It is the harvest time, when the wheat is separated from the tares, when the hypocrites are separated from the sincere believers, when good works are separated from dead works. That is judgment. And the punishments and rewards are meted out in justice by the omniscient One Who judges all things according to His publicly declared standard, the Bible.

The preliminary sorting process will discriminate between the sheep and the goats (Matt. 25)—the saved and the lost. Here, the final determination will be made on the basis of the presence or absence of the fruit of salvation (cf. Matt. 25:34-46). That does not mean that salvation is by works, but (rather) that on the day of final discrimination between those who have already been saved and those who have not, the basis for that judgment (who has been saved and who hasn't) will be their works (cf. Rev. 20:12). Since believers are "His handiwork, created in Christ Jesus *for good* works" (Eph. 2:10), it is altogether fitting that judgment (sorting out the sheep and the goats) should be made on this basis. Both Paul and James have made it perfectly clear that genuine saving faith always will produce character and conduct that are discernibly appropriate to salvation (as the fruit of the Spirit), and that "faith without works is dead." Jesus taught us that it is right to discriminate among various sorts of trees by looking at the fruit that they bear. He said, "Every good tree produces fine fruit, but every rotten tree produces bad fruit . . . it is by their fruits that you will know them" (Matt. 7:16-20). Here, Jesus taught us that the principle of discrimination was fruit—works—whether good or bad. The tree (the man) is known by its fruit (Matt. 12:33; Luke 6:44).

Notice, again, it is not what one does that saves him—when it is judged, the tree is already a good tree—that's *why* it bears good fruit (its fruit-bearing doesn't make it a good tree). One's works *identify* him as a good tree, wheat, a sheep, a Christian. Conversely, the bad tree, goat, tare and the unsaved man (like a child) is also "known by his doings" (Prov. 20:11). See Romans 2:6-8 in the light of this principle.

The preliminary sorting out process, in which goats and sheep are discriminated is followed by a secondary one. This second judgment is designed to discriminate among those who in the first have been shown to be Christians, and among those who have been shown not to be. To each of the latter will be assigned various gradations of punishment that have to do with the nature of their sin, the degree of their enlightenment, etc. All will be punished eternally, some (however) more than others (Matt. 11:21-24; Luke 12:47, 48; 20:47; Rom. 2:12-16). Believers will join in administering this judgment (I Cor. 6:2). On the basis of that fact (and the additional fact revealed in vs. 3), they are called upon to exercise church discipline, adjudicating matters of dispute or wrongdoing among the saints within the church rather than spreading their dirty linen before unbelievers in the courts. In drawing this all-important implication, Paul shows us how vital the doctrine of the future can be for everyday affairs right now. (Incidentally, this point itself is of great significance for counselors to stress in divorce cases. Believers have no right to go to court against one another—even for divorces.)

But it is important, too, to see that believers will be judged for allotment of rewards (at this judgment, sins will not be mentioned—Christ dealt with those sins on the cross, once for all; God has promised to "remember them no more"). There are a large number of passages that teach us about rewards. These are intended to motivate.[3] Vos lists the following: I Corinthians 1:4-8; 3:8; 15:32, 58; II Corinthians 4:16; 5:10; 9:6-8; Galatians 6:5-10; Philippians 1:10, 26; 2:16; Colossians 1:5; 3:24; I Thessalonians 3:13; 5:23; II Thessalonians 1:7; I Timothy 2:18; 4:8; 5:25; 6:18, 19; II Timothy 2:11; 4:4, 8, 14, 16; and Vos comments, "What strikes one most is . . . the matter-of-fact manner of its expression."[4] There is no issue made of the fact that God will reward us; it is presupposed everywhere.

Now, lest anyone misunderstand, let it be said right away—these rewards are given in grace, not because of merit. When we have done all that God requires of us (and no one does), that is still not more than we ought to have done. We have done only what was expected of us; no more. Therefore, we are "unprofitable servants" (Luke 17:10). By "unprofitable servants" Christ means servants who have done nothing

3. Cf. the section on reward/punishment as motivation in the *Manual*, pp. 164-167.
4. Vos, op. cit., pp. 75, 276.

above or beyond the call of duty—they have accumulated no merit. Thus a reward (*misthos*), though according to the usual meaning of the Greek term is "a payment for work done" (Arndt and Gingrich), in this case is the fruit of the Spirit, which is nonmeritorious. It is a wholly *gracious* payment; God owes us nothing. That is the peculiarity of biblical reward.

These rewards are given not *because* of our works (as though we earned them), but *according to* our works. God determined to reward believers for works He enabled them to do, purely out of His grace. There was no necessity upon God to grant any rewards at all. In His decision to grant rewards, He also determined to relate the degree of reward to character and conduct.

The judgment is inextricably bound up with the coming of Christ (cf. II Thess. 1; II Tim. 4:7, 8). That is one reason why His coming can be associated with exhortations to watchfulness, work and purity (Col. 3:4, 5; James 5:7, 8; I Cor. 1:7, 8; I John 3:2, 3; cf. also Luke 12:35, 37, and parallel passages). We are urged to look forward to His coming with joy and anticipation. If we serve Him faithfully, we can do so. It isn't wrong, then, for counselors to warn counselees of the possibility of being ashamed at His coming (I John 2:28) and urging them to be on the alert (I Thess. 5:4-8). These emphases can have a powerful impact upon true believers. Moreover, the hope of reward is firmly established as a vital motivational factor by the Bible itself.

At this point it is important to distinguish between the reward/punishment (aversive control) system found today in behaviorism and the system of rewards and punishment found in the Scriptures. People are continually confusing the two, and accusing anyone who speaks about reward/punishment (or about behavior) of being a behaviorist. To do so is to be guilty of superficial examination of the facts—or worse. The two differ all along the line.

Let me, however, sketch one *essential* contrast. It is of the essence of Skinnerian behaviorism to reward *immediately* the behavior to be reinforced. Therein lies a significant point of difference; and it has to do with rewards as motivation—the question that we have just been considering. We shall now see that as the result of two radically differing focuses there are two radically different outcomes. Skinnerian behaviorism employs animal training techniques that it attempts to apply to human beings. This is consistent with its presupposition that people are only animals. This technique, as I said, is to reinforce desired behaviors by *immediate* rewards (after all, cats and dogs are not motivated by long-range goals—especially those that occur after death!). The Bible, on the other hand, presupposes that man is more than an animal. While he shares certain characteristics with some animals (breathing, eating plants and meat, walking on the crust of the earth), man is more than an animal *because* he was created in God's image. In the garden, before sin, the warning and hopes that God gave him had long-range consequences in view. Even today, as a sinner, he continues to live toward long-range goals which strongly motivate him.

Because this is true, the attempt to train a human being as one would train an animal (if it were possible to do so[5]) would lead to animal (in man, criminal) behavior: "I want to avoid all immediate pain and get all the immediate pleasure I can grab; and I want it *now*." Long-range goals would be sacrificed for immediate gratification; that is the attitude that behavioristic training would inculcate. Morality, especially Christian morality, which is linked to eternity, would be impossible.

In speaking of the biblical reward/punishment dynamic (in contrast), Hebrews 11 comes to mind, especially verses 13, 24-26. The kind of faith described in that chapter looks on immediate gratification as unsatisfying. There is no strong motivation in the present—people with faith like that have something better in sight. They are not about to sell the day to buy the hour. They are virtually travelers (pilgrims and strangers), rootless sorts who are on their way somewhere; they have not yet found their home. Their taproot is sunk deep in the future. The present world, with all its pains and pleasures, no longer exerts the dominant influence on their lives.

This world has a certain recognizable entropy, a deteriorating force that makes everything run down as the result of the curse. That is why it can give no lasting satisfaction. The Christian knows this and (by the eye of faith) sees the promises from afar and presses on (11:13). How then can Christian counselors encourage motivation on a lesser level?[6] When one knows that his citizenship is in heaven (and lives like it), his whole attitude toward life is different. He can say, "So, I lost that big business deal! It was only money that I lost. What is money, anyway?

---

5. It seems that it is possible to do so only in part.
6. All temporal goals of Christians must be conditioned by eternal ones.

It has value for this world only. Surely, I should be a good steward, and I have been. After doing all I could, I lost it. So what? I'm on my way to the place where money grows on trees!" How does one trained in Skinnerian values handle this?

Or, take another case. Compare the difference that the two perspectives make on the lives of parents who have just lost their only child in an accident. With a stress on the long-range and the eternal, a Christian counselor can point beyond the range of immediate vision to the bright light at the end of the tunnel. Then, there is reason to keep on *moving*.

So, you can see that a clear conception of (and focus upon) the future is absolutely essential to all good counseling. Without it, much of life would seem unfair, chaotic, absurd. There would be no hope of finding answers to all those questions to which there are no answers now. But to know that judgment is coming—in which all will be righted forever—that changes everything. The counselor must help the counselee to develop an eternal perspective on temporal issues. When he does—and only then—he sees them correctly for the first time. When studying pain, we saw how Paul handled pain from the eternal perspective (II Cor. 4:16, 17; cf. also Rom. 8:18). Out there in the future, beyond the curse, is God, and the blessing! That is the attitude that counselees need.

And, contrary to the accusation sometimes made, this long-range outlook does not lead to irresponsibility now. In fact, it leads to morality and industry; the doctrine of eternal rewards sees to that! Which is more likely to motivate—an eternal reward or an M and M? Look at Paul himself. He fought the fight (against incredible odds), kept the faith through unparalleled hardships), and finished the race (a winner!), he tells us in II Timothy 4:7, at the end of his life. And, he lets us know in the next breath (vs. 8) one fact that urged him on: ". . . the winner's wreath . . . lying *at a distance,* that the Lord (Who is the righteous Judge) will award to me on that Day." Then, as if to commend the same effort to Timothy (and to us), he added, "and not to me alone but also to all those who have loved His appearing" (II Tim. 4:8).

CHAPTER TWENTY-FIVE

CONCLUSION

We have come a long way, traveling through all the basic loci of systematic theology. Yet we have by-passed so much. How I would like to have lingered longer and explored each area more fully, developing (for instance) some of the implications of the sacraments for counseling, looking into many other aspects of sanctification and so on. But that is not for now. The book already has grown too long.

All along the way I have tried to point to doctrines that ought to be explored much more fully in relationship to counseling. It is my hope that many of these challenges will be taken up by biblical counselors in the near future; the need is so great.

One desire—above all others—has been to convince the reader that truth and godliness are interrelated in such a way that it isn't possible to have one without the other, and that, therefore, counselors must become biblical theologians if they would see their counselees grow by God's grace.

How well (or poorly) I have accomplished my ends only time will tell. The task has been a formidable one; but I must say that what it did for me personally was worth it. I hope that something of the power and necessity of using the Word in counseling has been conveyed to you. After spending this time working closely with scriptural truth, and in discovering my own inadequacies, I can only marvel at those counselors who seem to think that a thin veneer of Sunday School study of the Scriptures is all that is required for counseling, and who, therefore, spend their time immersing themselves in the writings and vagaries of pagan psychiatrists and psychologists. The study behind this book has taught me several things afresh:

1. No one has even begun to scratch the surface of the Bible truth that relates to counseling (including myself). I have a lot more work to do—for the rest of my life.

2. The biblical data are totally relevant and pertinent to today's problems and needs.

3. Systematic theology need not (dare not) be dry and dusty; the lives of God's elect are dependent upon it.

4. God blesses us in His Word, by His truth—not apart from it. What a joy it has been to engage in this study!

5. All we need—or ever will—for life and godliness may be found here. If we don't know what to do, we have only ourselves to blame.

Now, let me commend the study of theology to you once again. Do not stop here! If you have been informed and helped, let me assure you that there is much more knowledge and aid where this came from—the Word of God! Search it daily, systematically, for both truth and life. Such is the background and daily sustenance needed for a truly Christian counselor.

APPENDIX A

WHAT TO DO WHEN YOU COUNSEL AN UNBELIEVER[1]

The topic tonight is "How Do You Counsel an Unbeliever?" What do you do when an unbeliever comes for counseling? I have held hundreds of conferences with pastors, and I don't believe that I can remember a single conference where there was a question and answer period in which someone did not ask the question, "How do you counsel an unbeliever?" So, instead of waiting for that question to be raised in this conference, I shall address it right now.

I

First, there are significant differences between counseling an unbeliever and counseling a believer. If you counsel Christians and unbelievers the same way, there's something wrong with your counseling. You're not doing *biblical* counseling. Indeed, you've missed the most significant point of all: Does the man know Jesus Christ as his Savior or not? There is no more significant first question to ask. It may be provisional, to be sure, but at least some kind of answer to this question is necessary. If you don't think that it makes any difference, that tells me your counseling is deficient. I think that this deficiency will appear as we develop this theme.

Counseling—Christian and non-Christian—has one goal in view: to change people. Everybody who counsels believes that people need to be changed. The hope is to change people's lives. But the first and most significant difference between Christian and non-Christian counseling lies in the kind of change that other systems have in view.

---

1. Originally delivered to the Annual Meeting of the National Association of Nouthetic Counselors, October, 1977, and published in Howard Eyrich, ed., *What to Do When* (Phillipsburg, N. J.: Presbyterian and Reformed Publishing Co., 1978), pp. 39-53 (revised for this Appendix).

All non-Christian systems, regardless of what they say, are really changing people on a superficial level. *All* unbiblical systems, even when they speak of doing "depth" counseling, change people at a surface level. No unbiblical method of counseling can really get down into the heart of a human being and change him at that level. But that's exactly what a Christian system must do, to be truly Christian.

In Matthew 15, Jesus talked about man. He said, "From the heart come evil thoughts, murder, adultery, sexual sins, thefts, false testimonies, blasphemies; these are what defile a person, but to eat with unwashed hands doesn't defile a person" (vs. 19). "Out of the heart," says Jesus, "these things come." And this list was not exhaustive, but merely suggestive of the kinds of things people do that get them into trouble. Then they come for counseling. Note, the source of the problems is the heart: "Out of the *heart* these things come."

Freud and others who have followed his psychoanalytical approach talk about depth counseling. They speak about getting down into the deepest recesses of a human being, where his motivation really stems from. The fact is, they don't have the faintest idea of what is involved in doing that. Yet, pastors have often been told (and their parishioners have often thought), "This person's problem is *much too deep*" (the key word that is used all the time is "deep") "for a pastor to handle. He will need professional help. I'll have to send him to a psychiatrist."

My friends, it ought to be the other way around! The only person who can really operate at a level of *depth* is the person who knows how to go to the *heart* of a man's problem. That's because the heart *is* the man's problem. The only way to go to the heart of a man's problem is through the gospel of Jesus Christ ministered in the power of the Holy Spirit, Who transforms the heart of man and *thus* transforms his life patterns. The murders, the adulteries, the evil thoughts, the sexual sins, the thefts, the false testimonies, the blasphemies (and all the rest) can be changed only in some superficial way, unless the heart out of which they come and by which they are generated is transformed by the Spirit of God using His Word. And—never forget this—in such work the *pastor* is the professional—*God's* professional.

Now we ought to believe that if we believe the Bible. I don't need to turn to twenty-five other passages and do a lot of Bible flipping with you; I don't believe in doing that kind of study (it's not the kind of study to do in the pulpit). You can go home and do that on your own. We need only one verse to tell us something; then we should believe it. But there are at least 125 passages that clearly tell us in one way or another that man's problem stems from sin down deep in the heart. Human beings inherited hearts corrupted by Adam's sin. And unless something can get at that corrupt heart, people won't be changed at the level of depth that is necessary to alter the source of their problems. Anything else that is done is equivalent to putting a plug in the bottle, putting a lid on the problem, screwing a cap over it. You can't really solve a person's problem at the level of depth necessary unless you use the Word of God, empowered by the Spirit of God, and bring it home to the heart.

The Bible uses a number of terms to talk about the make-up of human beings. It speaks, for instance, of loving the Lord your God with "all your *heart,* all your *mind,* all your *soul* and all your *strength."* These words—heart, mind, soul, strength—all these words describe aspects of human nature. It's not quite as easy to cut and categorize people as some think. They make easy divisions like "man is spirit, soul and body" that don't quite fit the fulness of the scriptural description of man. "Heart" is a word that encompasses all other terms for the inner life. The biblical term, however, doesn't mean what we mean when we say "heart" today. When somebody says, "I love you with all my heart," he's thinking about one thing—feelings and emotions. The Valentine's Day heart typifies the modern usage. There you see lace doilies, cupids and cherry-cheeked cherubs with bows and arrows shooting arrows into hearts. Today "heart" means emotion, feeling. But that isn't what heart is in the Bible. When you read passages in the Bible that use the word heart, you must never interpret the meaning in terms of the feelings, or you will misunderstand every one of those passages. Perhaps some of you have been doing so for years. If so, it's high time for you to realize it.

When the Bible talks about feelings, it talks not about the *heart* but the *bowels*—the guts. Did you know that? It does. It speaks about "bowels [feelings] of compassion." The Bible is much closer to the facts than we are in our modern culture. The Bible calls the bowels the seat of the emotions. Where is it that people get ulcers—on the heart? No—in the gut, where so much emotion is centered.

Well, then, what does the Bible mean by "heart" if it is not talking about feelings? What the Scriptures are talking about is *the inner life* of a human being. This is the inner man—his *whole* inner life, *including* the inner aspects of the feelings, thinking, decision-making, etc. "Why

do you *reason* thus in your heart?" asks Jesus. *Plans* are said to origi-
nate in the heart. When a person talks to himself ("the fool has *said* in
his *heart* . . ."), he does so in the heart. That is where one thinks with
himself, reasons with himself, accuses and excuses himself, etc. According to the Bible, that whole inner life that you live is your heart.

You do know that you live two lives (or, better still—one life on two
fronts), don't you? You live a life in reference to other people, and you
live a life in reference to yourself. And of course you live both of them
in reference to God. God is over both. What is it that makes you do
what you do? What is it that makes you think what you think? What is
it that motivates you the way you are motivated? What is it inside of you
that produces the kinds of words that pour out of your mouth and the
kinds of actions that your hands perform? It is the inner life, the heart;
and that is what needs to be changed, says Jesus. This planning and
motivational center of your being must be transformed so that you can
begin to do things that please God and that benefit your neighbor. Until
that takes place, you haven't begun to change at a level of depth.

And of course nobody can learn to love God and learn to love his
neighbor as he should until he has first come to know the love of Jesus
Christ for him. It simply can't be done. *"We* love," says John in his
first letter, "because He *first* loved us." And it is only when we come
to a recognition of our sin and when we come to a relationship with
Jesus Christ through faith in Him that transforms us and changes us
to be different people *within,* that we can become different people *without.* This is the work of the Spirit of God. Look at Romans 5:5. "God's
love has been poured into our hearts through the Holy Spirit Who was
given to us." You can't love others, you can't love God, until the Holy
Spirit has been poured into—what? Your feelings? No. Until He is
poured into your heart—i.e., your innermost being—to change and transform and mold and remake the inner structure of your thought life. It
was corrupted and twisted and warped through Adam's sin. So that's
where you must begin. Without that viewpoint about counseling, you
might as well not even start to think about changing people, because all
you're going to do is to exchange one set of bad behavior patterns for
another. You're not going to do anything at the level where it needs to
be done—at the inner core of the human personality.

When the Spirit of God changes hearts, His inner alterations lead to
change of outward actions and life relationships. There isn't time to go

into that in detail; I'm still in the introduction! But you can read about it in Romans 8:10, 11; Romans 6:2; Galatians 5—how the Spirit of God enables believers to transform the habit patterns of the "members" of the "body" by changing their hearts (for more on this, see *The Use of the Scriptures in Counseling*).

If you stress outward change, as so many people do, what happens? You will develop a legalistic liberalism: "Do this, don't do that." The notion will get abroad that you can change persons by changing from the outside their environment or their behavior patterns, or something of that sort. This legalistic liberal approach really says, "The cross is not necessary; all you have to do is obey the rules." We are not liberals; we believe the Bible, and that the cross is the essential message that every Christian must proclaim. We are not legalistic; we believe that a man must operate out of love, not out of rules imposed upon him, to which he has no commitment whatever. A person obeys His rules, even when he doesn't feel like it, because he wants to please a God who had sent His Son to die for him. That makes all the difference in the world.

On the other hand, if you stress the inner change alone and forget that that the inner change leads to outward changes in behavior patterns as Romans 6, 7 and 8 tell us, then you get a cold orthodoxy that is great on doctrine, but doesn't do much to change people's lives. They get all this information tightly packed into their skulls, but it never gets into the fabric of everyday living. They do not walk in the truth, as the Scriptures beautifully put it when with perfect balance they combine the inner/outer sides of changed living. So it is absolutely essential to see that inner change is essential, but also that it leads to outer change. These two sides are part and parcel of one another. If there is really no outer change—none whatsoever—there has been no inner change. If there are no works, there is no faith. But if there is minimal change (as there so often is), it may indicate that there hasn't been much good counseling; there has been only evangelism.

Now that's the first presupposition that I want to get across: counseling must be done on a level of depth, a level deep enough to transform the human heart. That fact makes a tremendous difference when you're counseling an unbeliever.

II

The second fact grows out of the first: you must recognize the limitations that exist when counseling an unbeliever. First of all, unbelievers do not know Jesus Christ, and they do not care about knowing Him in any significant way. So anything you say to them about obeying, loving, or serving Jesus Christ falls on deaf ears. The difference is explained in John 3:19-21:

> And this is the judgment: . . . the Light has come into the world, but men loved darkness rather than the Light because their works were evil. Everyone who practices evil hates the Light and doesn't come to the Light so that his works won't be exposed. But whoever does the truth comes to the Light so that it may be clearly seen that his works have been carried out for God.

In I Corinthians 12:3, Paul puts it this way: "I want you to understand [and we had better understand] that nobody who is speaking by God's Spirit ever says, 'Jesus be cursed.' And nobody can say 'Jesus is Lord,' except by the Holy Spirit." Now Paul doesn't mean that a person can't utter the words with his lips hypocritically. Of course many thousands of people have done so, and there could be people right here who have fooled others around them because they have done just that. But they've repeated words that they don't really mean. They are not subject to Christ as Lord. Pushed on this question, Paul would say, "Nobody can say this *from his heart.*"

When the Bible speaks about believing something "with all your heart" or saying something "from the heart," what it means is that you're not just saying it with your lips. It is the *lips* and the heart that are contrasted in Scripture, not the *mind* and the heart. We talk about head-knowledge/heart-knowledge, but that's not a biblical contrast. It's lips and heart that are contrasted; what we speak and what we believe (the contrast is between the inner and the outer man). To speak of doing something from the heart is to talk about sincerity, not about feelings over against intellectual thought. The contrast is between sincerity and hypocrisy. There may be someone here who has said, "Jesus is Lord," with his lips and never said it with his heart. The man who believes in his *heart* that God has raised Christ from the dead, will be saved. It must be genuine; it's got to come from the core of the being, from the inner person. This says that no man can say "Jesus Christ is Lord" (that way) *until the Spirit of God has enabled him to do so.*

If that is true, how are we ever going to get people to change in counseling, if they can't say, "Jesus is Lord"? If they can't say, "Jesus is

Lord," they can't obey; if they can't obey, they can't follow Him, they can't be His disciples.

You say, "What are you doing? It sounds as though you're proving that it's impossible to counsel unbelievers." Well, just hold on for a little bit. Please be patient.

Let me go one step further. Unbelievers can't understand the Scriptures either. Remember, we're trying to face the limitations honestly. In the second chapter of I Corinthians—among other startling things in that chapter—Paul says in the fourteenth and fifteenth verses:

> But a natural person does not welcome the teachings of God's Spirit; they are foolishness to him and he is not able to know about them because they must be investigated spiritually. But the spiritual person is able to investigate everything while (on the other hand) no one has the ability to investigate him.

What is a natural person? Just a plain old natural person, nothing has happened to him; he's just the way he was born by nature and that's it. He has never been transformed at any level of depth; he's just a natural person who has been born once with a sinful nature that can do only those things that displease God. A natural person is one who does not have the Spirit of love poured into his heart, so he cannot love God and his neighbor, and he does not welcome the teachings of God's Spirit.

Suppose you try to do biblical counseling with an unbeliever. You say, "There's a solution to your problem," and you turn to the Bible and tell him, "Here's what God says in His Word." What's his response? He says, "Huh!" He says (in effect), "So what?" And if he doesn't say "Huh!" out loud, he goes out and lives "Huh!" He doesn't *welcome* the teachings of God's Spirit. Why? The passage goes on to say, "They are foolishness to him and he is unable to know about them because they must be investigated spiritually." He does not have the ability to investigate the Bible on his own. He has only *natural* equipment with which to investigate it. He has his own nature, his own abilities, his own insights, his own strength to do it. But this equipment won't do. To investigate Scripture properly takes something more, and he doesn't have what it takes to really understand that Book.

What is it that he needs? He can't investigate these things because they must be investigated spiritually. When the Spirit of God comes into a person's life through regeneration, he enables that person to read the Bible with new eyes, and to understand it with a new mind. He transforms the person so that he comes to the Book with a new heart, and he begins to see things that he never saw there before. Have you ever talked to an unbeliever who says, "Aw, the Bible—that's a dead book"? I've heard that dozens of times from unbelievers. And I say to them, "No, you're a dead person, the Book is alive." You get the same effect, whether the book is dead or the person is dead. Because he doesn't have spiritual life, the life that the Spirit of God gives to enable one to understand this book, it is dead to him.

Think of a corpse lying in a casket. We could cook the most delicious meal you ever tasted—mountains of potatoes, lakes of gravy, fields of green peas, and forests of roast beef reaching towards the sky. The aroma could fill this whole huge auditorium. And then—a dessert that looks like Niagaras of whipped cream cascading over cliffs of apricots! And we bring this huge, magnificent meal to the corpse, and say, "Here it is! Look at it! Ah, doesn't it get to you?" Not a shiver. Not even a sniff. Why? Because that body is dead. It is insensitive to the aromas, the beauty, the magnificence, the taste and everything else. Here—in this Book—is a far more wonderful meal. God said that we can't live by bread alone, so He gave us His Word. But everywhere there are spiritual corpses walking around who don't know Jesus Christ, who have no spiritual life, and who can't appreciate it. Are you as a counselor going to change them by using the Word of God? Are you going to tell them what they should do to get their three squares for that day so that they can live by God's Word? No! They won't have any part of it; that is what it says here. They don't welcome it; they aren't able to know about it, because they can't investigate the Bible spiritually.

Now I Corinthians 2 goes on to say, "The spiritual person" that is, the person who has the Spirit of God in his life, "is able to investigate everything while [on the other hand] no one has the ability to investigate him." The unbeliever can't understand the believer. He sees him as a strange character. He looks at him and says, "I don't understand him." He talks about varieties of religious experience, the psychology of conversion and all these things, but it's all off base. When you read such things, you laugh and cry, because you know that they come nowhere near the truth. Unbelievers can't understand why you do what you do, and why you don't do what you don't do; why you take an interest in a prayer meeting and sing in a choir. They don't understand any of these things. They can't. It takes the Spirit of God living in a man to enable him to understand.

So the unbeliever isn't going to understand and appreciate the Christian counselor either.

Right here in this room tonight are all kinds of things that you don't see or hear, but they are here. There are all sorts of pictures—beer advertisements, commercials, etc., and all kinds of music—rock and roll, popular, classical—right here, right now. You didn't know that, did you? "Right here in the First Baptist Church in Atlanta?" Yes, they are here. I could bring in a television set and turn it on and let you see and hear it all. It would all take place right here because those sounds and those pictures are all around us in this room. We don't hear them. Why? Because we don't have a receiving set, and we're probably just as well off that we don't! But that's the way the unbeliever is when it comes to the Word of God and the things of God. Listen to what Paul says, in verse 9, "What *eye* hasn't seen and *ear* hasn't heard"—that's just like the absence of the television set; without it you can't see and can't hear. Let's go on, ". . . and hasn't been conceived by the human heart, is what God has prepared for those who love Him. And to us God has revealed it by His Spirit." That's what we must realize: that poor unsaved fellow who sits in front of you in the counselee's seat seeking help, can't see or hear. How are you going to help him? If you (as a good biblical counselor) turn to the Scriptures and advise him, he can't even get it. Your words and the Bible's words are sounds coming through the air, but he doesn't have the receiving equipment to pick them up. That's what it is like when you use the Word of God to counsel an unbeliever. You have to get that clear. There are serious limitations in counseling an unbeliever. It is essential to recognize that.

"Well," you say, "Things are going from bad to worse. It looks as though it is utterly hopeless to try to counsel an unbeliever. Would you please get to what I *can* do? I thought you were going to talk about how to counsel." Now please be patient. I have just a bit more to say first.

Now we have seen that unbelievers don't have the power to understand the Scriptures, but that isn't all—there is still another limitation. Even if they *were* able to understand the Scriptures, even if they wanted to obey the Scriptures and obey Christ, they couldn't because *they don't have the power of the Holy Spirit to enable them to obey.* I don't have time to get into it, but look at the third chapter of Paul's letter to the Galatians, where he reminds them that you must begin the Christian life by grace through faith, by God's doing everything for you in Christ—

you cannot save yourself. Then Paul asks them, "What is wrong with you; beginning by grace, do you think you are going to grow by your own strength?" The implied response is "absolutely not." The only way a Christian can grow is if the Spirit of God continues to change him and make him different in the days to come. So what are we going to do for unbelieving counselees?

There is no holiness apart from the power of the Spirit's giving us strength to obey God's Word. Now there is a very important point to get clear about this. People today are teaching false doctrine that sounds good. I am saying just as clearly as I know how that we cannot depend on our own strength to make changes that please God. That's what I've been saying all along. The Spirit of God must enable us to understand the Word, must give us the power to obey the Word, must give us the ability to declare Jesus Christ as our Lord and to really live as His servants. So, since this is true some say, "That means that I must do nothing, absolutely nothing. All I do is give up. All I do is recede into the background, and the less there is of me and the less there is even of my obedience or efforts or anything else, the more there will be of the Holy Spirit." And that sounds good, doesn't it? And it is, if you interpret that rightly, but it isn't if you interpret it wrongly. And they are interpreting it wrongly; they are interpreting it as passivity.

A Christian must obey God. A Christian must believe that the Holy Spirit does not do the believing for us, and the Holy Spirit does not do the obeying for us. We are responsible beings who are going to be held responsible for believing and doing what God says; but we dare not do the obeying or believing *in our own strength*. We must rely upon the strength of the Holy Spirit. That's the point. It is the Spirit Who enables us to believe, and it is the Spirit Who enables us to obey. We must not try to do these things in our own strength, or we shall do them wrongly. But this is crucial—*we* must do them. He doesn't do them for us, as some are teaching. So, then, you've got to recognize these limitations when trying to help an unbeliever.

III

"Well, then, if we can't counsel him at a level of depth, and make those kinds of changes, what can we do for him? I guess we'll have to settle for something less." *No! Never!* No, you can settle for nothing less than changing him at a level of depth. "But we can't change him at a level of depth. You yourself said so. He won't listen to us; he won't listen to the Word; he has no power; he does not have the Spirit; he's a natural man; he does not have the receiving set; all of these things are impossible! How are we going to do what we can't do?" That's the dilemma.

But before we try to solve that dilemma, let me make it very clear that you may not settle for something less; you *must* not settle for something less. You cannot do band-aid work when your counselee needs radical surgery. You dare not. That's the most cruel and heartless thing a person could possibly do. When someone goes to a surgeon and says, "I think I have cancer," the surgeon puts him through all the tests. If the surgeon knows in his heart that this man has cancer, and that unless he operates on him, the man is going to die within a year, what does he do— settle for something less? Does that surgeon say, "I just can't bring myself to tell this man such terrible news. I want to make him happy, and I don't want to be unhappy myself. I don't want him to be upset with me. I don't want to see him cry; I don't want his wife to cry, I want him to leave here happy. 'Here, sir, is a salve that you can put on that sore.' " If he says that, the surgeon makes the man happy, and the surgeon feels better too, because he didn't have to go through the cancer scene. But when the man realizes six months later that there is no hope now, because the surgeon didn't do the hard thing that he should have done, then that man hates the surgeon and the surgeon feels worse. The man may even sue the surgeon for malpractice. The same is true for you—you must not give band-aids to people with cancer. You must not say to an unbeliever, "Look, let's change a few superficial things and settle for that." God hasn't called us to reform people. That's always the beginning of liberalism—when people settle for something less than a change at a level of depth; a change in the heart of a man.

And if we did settle for something less, if we did settle for changing a few outward things, shifting certain patterns of life here and substituting patterns of life there; if we did settle for something on that level, what would we settle for? We would settle for misrepresenting God's whole message and mission in sending Christ. We would say (in effect) that the cross is a cruel mockery; a farce, a ridiculous waste. And we would say to people by that, "God has a way to change your life without Christ. You don't need to trust Him as Savior." And that would misrepresent God.

Moreover, we would foster thereby a false assurance in unbelievers. We would lead them to think that they were all right with God when they were not. Pretty soon they would be let down hard, when the new patterns turned out to be no better than the former. Then they would think that God let them down. No, we dare not settle for something less.

"What then can you do for an unbeliever? It looks as though you can't counsel him." You're right. That's what I've been telling you. You can't counsel an unbeliever; no, you can't. You've been concluding that all along, and I agree with you; you can't counsel an unbeliever. There's no way to counsel an unbeliever. Now I'm not going to walk off the platform at that point and leave you there. You can't counsel an unbeliever if you mean by counseling what the Bible means by counseling—changing his heart; changing him at a level of depth. The man won't listen, because his heart is not oriented toward the Book, so he can't hear what it has to say, and he doesn't have the power to obey the Book, even if he wanted to. You can't counsel an unbeliever in the full biblical sense of that word counsel. What then can you do for an unbeliever?

There are some things that you can do for an unbeliever so long as you make it clear all along that you haven't started counseling yet. Continually as you work with an unbeliever, you've got to make it evident to him that anything and everything that you're doing before he comes to know Jesus Christ as his Savior is not counseling; it's not what God is offering to people as the remedy for their problems. It is something introductory to what will bring about this greater thing (if indeed he comes to know Christ).

What you do then is preliminary; it is *pre*counseling.. And that is all that you can do for an unbeliever; you precounsel him; you can't really counsel him. And all that precounseling means is that you are going to do some problem-oriented evangelism. That's what precounseling is—problem-oriented evangelism. That's what you can do for an unbeliever. Now, how do you do problem-oriented evangelism?

IV

There are many things I could say about that, but I shall mention only a few. Jesus helped many people, sometimes with superficial problems on a superficial basis first, but always in connection with evangelism. When healing bodies, for example, He always connected the greater healing of the eyes of the *heart* or the paralysis of the *heart* or the leprosy of the *heart* with the physical healing. That's just what you must do in counseling. You must approach unbelievers with both hands. You have something in both hands to offer: in one hand something very minimal, and in the other the entrance into real counseling, change at a level of depth that begins with the gospel of the Lord Jesus Christ.

This involves four things that I will quickly mention. First, it means removing obstacles to a presentation of the gospel. The phone rings. The pastor picks it up. What does he hear at the other end? *All right, Pastor, this fine Christian wife of mine has her bags packed. What are you going to do about it?"* Is that the time to evangelize Joe? Hardly. What you say is, "Joe, put Mary on the phone." He gets Mary to the phone and you say, "Mary, we've talked about I Corinthians 7 many times before. It says that if your husband wants to stay with you, even if he is an unbeliever, you are to make your marriage as good as you possibly can. You are to do everything you can do as a believer. You are to really hang in there, you're to try to win him and your children to the Lord Jesus Christ. Now packing you bags and threatening to leave him is sin. This is wrong, and you *know* it's wrong. So get those bags unpacked and you and Joe get over here as fast as you can. I'm going to a funeral in twenty minutes." (You know, a funeral comes before anything else.) So, Mary grudgingly says, "All right."

Ten minutes later she gets there with Joe. You have ten minutes left. Joe comes in feeling a little better, but he is still upset. He doesn't know what is going to happen. And you get him in there. Is that the time to evangelize? Absolutely not. You have ten minutes. You're under pressure to go to a funeral. What do you do? You say, "Look, Joe, Mary; I just want two fur-lined, ironclad promises from you. First of all, Mary, I want you to promise that you won't threaten Joe with this sin again. We've got to get this out of the picture. And secondly, I want a promise from both of you that you'll be here at 7:00 tonight. We're going to start counseling to find out what is going wrong in this marriage and what God says can be done about it."

If the pastor can get them to make those commitments, he's done some pretty good precounseling. He's done a few things minimally to help them, but he hasn't really done any counseling yet (except possibly with Mary). When Joe and Mary come back at 7:00 and he begins to talk to them, it is possible that he can begin to evangelize Joe. So you see, sometimes there are obstacles to the presentation of the gospel. When a man is all upset about his wife with her bags packed, and she's heading for the airport, that's no time to talk to him about the Lord. You had better stop her first; then he might listen. Often you have to do pre-counseling of that sort.

Secondly, sometimes you have to give precounseling hope to those who have lost it, by making certain minimal efforts. In the case of the man born blind recorded in John 9, Jesus put clay on his eyes. It wasn't Jesus' saliva that healed him; there was nothing mystical or medicinal about it. It wasn't the clay on his eyes that healed him, either; neither of those things themselves had anything to do with the healing. Christ's action was designed to give him hope. Here was a man who was *born* blind; he had no hope of ever seeing. Nobody ever heard of a blind man seeing. But when Jesus put the clay on his eyes, He gave him hope. The man began to think: "If only I could wash my blindness away as I can wash off that clay, I could see." Hope began to well up within him, for the first time, perhaps, since he long ago laid aside any hope of such a miracle taking place. And Jesus at that moment said, "Go wash in the pool of Siloam," and the man went and washed, and came back seeing. He wouldn't have gone if Jesus hadn't given him hope. He would have said, "This is foolishness." Sometimes you have to give hope by something you do for somebody first.

Thirdly, you have to approach each person differently. Jesus approached Nicodemus quite differently from the way he approached the woman at the well. Nicodemus comes and says, "We know that you are a teacher from God because no man is able to do these miracles unless God is with him." And Jesus said, picking up on his very phrase, "No man *is able* to enter the kingdom of God unless he is born again." Nicodemus comes and says, "I want to talk about theology." Jesus says, "I want to talk about your life." *Pow!* Right smack in the teeth. That was a "Brother are you saved?" evangelism approach (without the "brother") if there ever was one. There were teeth lying all around the upper room when He was done with Nicodemus.

But look at His approach to the woman at the well. It was supremely gradual; He led her through buckets, ropes, husbands and hills. She says, "Oh, you're a teacher," then she says, "You're a prophet" and at last, "You're the Messiah!" He leads her there very gradually. With the blind man, He didn't even talk to him about salvation at first; He just healed him and disappeared. People came to him and said, "You're in cahoots with that man Jesus." But he answered, "This one thing I know. A man named Jesus made clay, put it on my eyes, sent me to the pool and I came back seeing." His parents came to him and he told them, "This one thing I know. . . ." The Pharisees came to him and he said, "This one thing I know. . . ." He told them all the same story all over again. They threw him out of the synagogue, but he still protested all the way to the doorstep," "This one thing I know. . . ." Why? Because that's all he knew. Jesus hadn't told him another thing. It was only on the next encounter that Jesus talked to him about the blindness of the heart, the inner life.

All three situations differed, but there is one thing that is true of every one of them—the same message of Jesus Christ's death on the cross in the place of guilty sinners, and His bodily resurrection from the dead. That's the good news. Paul puts it very plainly in I Corinthians 15: "This is the good news that I preached to you, by which you are saved." There is only one good news, one message: Christ died for our sins according to the Scriptures; He was buried and He rose the third day according to the Scriptures. These two facts were predicted in the Old Testament Scriptures: the death of Christ for sinners, and His bodily resurrection from the dead. Go through the whole book of Acts some rainy Sunday when you don't have anything else to do and look up every time somebody in the book of Acts preached the gospel or talked to somebody about the Lord, and always the death and resurrection will appear. The death and resurrection, the penal, substitutionary death and bodily resurrection of Christ—that's the good news. That's what Jesus and all the apostles and everybody else proclaimed. In evangelism, that is what you must call all men to believe.

In closing, let me suggest three approaches that you might use in dealing with people who need precounseling. When you have given certain precounseling help, you might point out where the precounseling came from, why you were motivated to help Joe get his wife back from the airport. And you can stress what it was that motivated her to come back. This woman agreed to stay home and unpack her bags only because there was an authority over her life; an authority that brought order, change into her life, even at that point.

I had a couple in counseling one time where the wife sat down, and the husband wouldn't. He was storming all over the place and stomping around. Between his expletives, I patched this story together. He said,

"My wife is a Christian and I'm not, and she knew I didn't want to come to a Christian counselor. She deceived me. She said, 'We're going for counseling,' but she didn't tell me it was *Christian* counseling and I'm mad." (He didn't have to mention the last fact.)

When I heard his story, I began to talk to her; I just let him go stomping around. I turned to her and said, "Is this true, are you really a Christian?" She gave some evidence of really believing. Then I said, "Now what he says about you, is this true—that you deceived him and so on?" She said, "Yeah, he wouldn't have come any other way." So I ignored him and began to give her a little mini-sermon, to show her from the Scriptures that this was sin. I began to show her from I Peter 3 that she had dishonored God, she had lied to her husband, she had not been submissive to him, etc. About half way through that mini-sermon he began to calm down and listen, looking at her and looking at me. Next thing you know, he was standing still and edging over, listening. Then he sat down on the chair and put his elbow down on the desk, listening. Before long he said, "Give it to her." Now there was a fellow who was getting hope. You must understand that he had a long way to go; this was still precounseling. But he got enough hope from it to stay throughout all the counseling sessions to come. Why? Because, as he said, for the first time, somebody somewhere could control his wife! And I made it clear to him that it was the Holy Spirit who controlled her through this Book. It wasn't I. She wasn't listening to me. She wouldn't have cared any more for what I said than she did for what he said. But she had a basic commitment to Jesus Christ and He was controling her life, in spite of her feelings.

So, one thing is to point out where the precounseling help comes from. Secondly, there is a point at which you have to say in precounseling, "Whoa!" (One of the greatest words in counseling is "Whoa!" or your own personal equivalent.) There is a place where you have to bring precounseling to a screeching halt and say, "This is as far as it can go." There comes a time when you've given all the precounseling help you can give. Then you have to say to the unbeliever that if he doesn't trust Christ, after you've been talking to him about the gospel, "We're up against a brick wall. I want to give you real counseling. I want you to experience all the changes that the Holy Spirit can make in a person's life." And you can even describe them. Then you can say, "I'd like to do all these things for you, but we're up against a brick wall because all those things are on the other side of the wall and you're on this side. There is only one way to get through it—through the Door, through the One Who said, 'I am the Door.' " You can describe what you'd really like to see happen, and how you would like to counsel at a level of depth, but you can take him only to that point in precounseling. Then you tell him, "I can do no more for you until you go through that Door."

I've often said to people at that point, "Look, if you came to my house and you didn't bother to ring the doorbell or knock on the door or anything, but you just opened the door and walked in, and then you walked into my kitchen and opened my refrigerator door, and you made yourself whatever you liked (a big ham sandwich or whatever) and you munched away at that and drank a nice big glass of Coke or Pepsi and then you said, 'Well, I'm feeling better, but I'm a bit sleepy,' so you marched upstairs and slept in my bed just like in the Three Bears story, would you expect me to protest, or do you think I'd be happy to let this go on?"

"Not on your life."

"Why not? Because you're not a member of the family. If my children walk through the door without knocking, they have a perfect right to; I don't expect them to knock every time they come to my front door. I even give them keys. My wife can come in too; I never expect her to knock on the door. She can sleep in my bed, etc. (Now I do draw the line at my toothbrush.) Why can they do all these things and you can't? Because they are part of the family. God has provided biblical counseling for His children, that is at a level of depth. But not for others. All the wonderful promises of the Scriptures you can have if you become a member of the family, but now you're not a member of the family." I turn to John 1:12 and read, 'As many as received Him, to *them* gave He the right to become children of God.' You must receive Him first by faith. That comes first. All of this is on the other side of the brick wall and Christ is the Door."

Now, let me say one more thing in closing about what to do if he doesn't believe, if he won't pay attention to your precounseling. You can do a lot of things, of course, but there is one thing I've done that God has blessed in a number of situations, although not uniformly. Not everybody believed when Jesus Christ spoke to them, and it's not always your fault if people will not believe you when you talk to them. It may be your fault, of course; it was never Christ's fault. You have only two problems, and I have two problems; He had only one: people, not Himself. Our problem is that we have to check out whether we did the right thing as well as whether or not the person did the right thing. With Christ, the play was a success, but the audience was a failure. So, you have to keep that in mind too.

But what if a person won't believe? What if you've checked yourself and you believe under God that you've done the best you can, and it really is his rebellious attitude toward the gospel? Well, you conclude that you can lead a horse to water, but you can't make him drink. And you repeat all through that last session (as it becomes apparent that this will be the last)—I try to weave it in twenty times and even write it down on a piece of paper, if possible—a verse that he can carry with him. I try to indelibly impress it upon him so that he'll never forget it. All through that last session I quote Proverbs 13:15. It's short, it's to the point, and it's memorable. I say, "Well, if you're not going to believe this message, I want you to remember that God says, 'the way of the transgressor is hard.' And when you get out there and start facing this problem or that and such and such a thing happens, you're going to find out that 'the way of the transgressor is hard.' Remember that if such and such a thing happens, that's when I'd like you to think about the fact that 'the way of the transgressor is hard.' " I keep saying it and saying it, and saying it. And I've had people come back in six months and I've asked them, "What has brought you back here?" "I've found out that the way of the transgressor is hard." I think you have to put a burr under his saddle. The best burr I know is the Scriptures.

Let me say it once more: you can't *counsel* unbelievers in the biblical sense of the word (changing them, sanctifying them through the work of the Holy Spirit, as His Word is ministered to their hearts) so long as they remain unbelievers. The change they need is the regenerating work of the Holy Spirit. So do precounseling: present the gospel, and pray that the Holy Spirit will open their hearts to receive it in faith. Evangelism is essential. That must come first.

INDEX OF PERSONS

INDEX OF SCRIPTURE REFERENCES

OLD TESTAMENT

NEW TESTAMENT

John
1:1 — 1
2:4 — 176
3:32, 34 — 91
4:9 — 22
4:24 — 116
5:18, 20, 30 — 91
6:38, 39 — 175
7:17 — 171
7:30 — 176
8:26-38 — 91
8:31 — 170
8:34-44 — 5
9:1 — 140, 156, 275
12:23, 27 — 176
13:13-17 — 170
14:9 — 91
14:13, 14 — 12, 85
15:7 — 84, 170
15:11 — 254
15:15 — 128
15:21 — 12
16:23-27 — 12, 85, 254
17:4 — 175
17:24 — 174

Acts
2 — 132
2:37 — 114
3:21 — 17
4:13 — 89
4:28 — 124
5:4 — 114
5:31 — 189
6 — 279, 294, 296
7:54 — 114
7:60 — 191ff.
8:10 — 34
8:29, 30 — 124
12:1-16 — 80
15:3 — 255
16:13,16 — 71
16:22 — 159
16:64 — 143
17:11 — 20, 178
17:18, 30 — xii
17:28 — 1, 49
20:31 — 279
24:25 — 260
26:18 — 189

Romans
1:16 — 35
1:21, 22, 28 — 165
1:26, 27 — 99
2:6-8 — 302

Romans
2:7, 8 — 270
2:15 — 45
3:4 — 199
3:23 — 101, 150
4:15 — 150
5:12 — 143
5:20 — 40, 133
6:6 — 160
6:16-19 — 142, 160
7:24 — 160
8:6 — 110
8:14 — 26
8:8 — 121
8:18-25 — 40, 140, 156, 306
8:20 — 180ff.
8:28, 29 — 44, 73, 120
10:8-10 — 115, 216
11:22 — 257
11:36 — 47, 86
12 — 160
12:1, 2 — 110, 173
12:14ff. — 53, 127, 256
14:14, 15, 20 — 32
14:23 — 31, 146f.
15:14 — 258

I Corinthians
1, 2 — 46
1:4-8 — 303
2 — 110
2:4, 5 — 176
2:7 — 124
2:9, 10 — 42
2:14 — 176
2:20 — 115
3:8 — 303
5:9-11 — 127
6:2, 3 — 303
6:14 — 107
6:15, 16 — 132
7 — 26, 126
7:4 — 131
7:9 — 260
7:34 — 111
7:39 — 26
8:7 — 161ff.
9:4 — 137
10:13 — 157, 159, 273ff.
11:30ff. — 208, 274
11:32 — 157, 274
12:4-11 — 236
12:13 — 176
13:7 — 227, 254
13:9-12 — 47
14 — 110
15:33 — 163

INDEX OF SCRIPTURE REFERENCES

INDEX OF SCRIPTURE REFERENCES

II Timothy
1:7 — 278
2:11 — 303
2:22 — 250ff.
3:5 — 262
3:15, 17 — x, xiii, 16, 25, 34, 36, 234, 278
3:16 — 162
4:2 — 227
4:4 — 203
4:7 — 242, 304, 306
4:8 — 203, 304, 306
4:14 — 203
4:16 — 203

Titus
1:1 — 262, 269
1:13 — 227
2:3-5 — 296
2:4, 5 — 92
2:13 — 179
2:14 — 151, 283
2:15 — 227
3:14 — 283

Philemon
Book of — 231
7, 12, 20 — 114

Hebrews
1:9 — 261
2:2-4 — 25
2:10 — 86, 156, 176, 275
2:15 — 153
3:7, 8 — 17, 66
4:7 — 17
4:12 — 111ff., 114, 115
4:13 — 66
4:14-16 — 54
4:16 — 72, 86
5:7 — 73
5:8 — 156, 275
5:13ff. — 161, 242
5:14 — 161f.
9:7 — 151
9:26 — 174
9:27 — 40, 300
10:15ff. — 26
10:16 — 17
10:18 — 192
10:22 — 115
10:25 — 161ff., 240
10:31 — 40
12:5-11 — 208, 227, 268
12:6 — 208
12:11 — 208
12:15-17 — 202

Hebrews
12:23 — 3
13:17 — 278

James
1:2 — 255
1:5 — 55, 81
2:14 — 172
2:26 — 109
3:9 — 119, 120
4:2, 3 — 82
4:9, 10 — 202
4:14-16 — 12
5:15 — 71
5:16-18 — 12

I Peter
1:8 — 163, 255
1:9 — 157, 255, 274
1:18 — 161
1:19, 20 — 174
2:2 — 234
2:23 — 140, 157, 274
2:24 — 143
3:9 — 240
3:20 — 116
4:1 — 117
4:2 — 163
4:14 — 84
4:19 — 140, 157
5:10 — 84

II Peter
1:3 — 25, 178
2:14 — 161, 162, 243
3:1ff. — 36
3:9, 10 — 52
3:13 — 106, 127
3:18 — 121
4:1 — 275

I John
1:1 — 106
1:3 — 40
1:6 — 40
1:7 — 40
1:8, 10 — 269
1:9 — 40
3:4 — 147
3:19, 21 — 115
3:17 — 114
4:2 — 106
5:15 — 73
5:6-8 — 106
5:19 — 41

II John
Book of — 130

INDEX OF SUBJECTS

N

Names, ch. 5, 85ff., 183, 229
Nature, 2, 98ff., 118, 141, 150, 160, 236
Need, 72
Neutrality, 8, 39, 43, 44, 172
Noetic effects, ch. 11
Non-judgmental, 194, 195ff.
Norms, 98ff., 100ff.
Notes, 62
Nouthesia, ix

O

O.B.E., 297
Obedience, 170, 171ff.
Observation, 90
Omnipotence, vii, 11, 71
Omnipresence, vii, 11, 71
Omniscience, vii, 11, 71, 302
Opinion, 21
Order, 135, 193, 296
Ought, 45ff.

P

Paganism, ix, xi, 43, 44, 61, 91, 276
Pain—*See* Suffering
Patience—*See* Endurance
Planning, 174ff., 176
Peace, 31, 77f., 82, 252ff., 255
Penalty, 154ff., 156
Perception, 126, 167ff.
Perfection, 2, 102, 152
Perseverance, 253, ch. 17, 267ff.
P.D.I., 73ff.
Personality, 48ff., 60, 89, 96, 117, 124ff., 251
Petition, 69, 72, 73
Pharisees, 13, 82f.
Postponement, 67
Power, 34ff., 48
Practical living, 46
Prayer, vii, 12ff., ch. 6, 211ff.
Preaching, 12, 13, 279ff.
Precounseling—*See* Evangelism
Predestination, 124ff.
Preference, 29
Pressure, 64ff.
Prevention, 122, 277f., ch. 20
Professionalism, 13, 277ff.
Prostitution, 132
Psychiatry, psychiatrists, x, xii, 13f., 16, 35, 39, 50, 144, 277
Psychology, psychologists, x, xii, 13f., 16, 20, 35, 39, 50, 144, 154ff., 218

Punishment, 154ff., 191, 207ff., 214, ch. 24, 302ff.
Purpose, 2, 41, 44, 75, 156, 157
Pursuit of fruit, 250ff.

Q

Questions, 5
Quietism, 250ff.

R

Radical amputation, ch. 16
R.E.T., 45
Reality, 41
Rebellion, 1, 4, 148, 158, 159, 279
Rebuke, 139, 213, 214, 226ff.
Reconciliation, 120ff.
Record, 291
Redemption, 101, ch. 12
Reformation, 120
Regeneration, 36, 120, 177
Regularity, 135
Rehabituation, 237ff.
Relationship, x, 1, 14, 41, 102, 215
Relativism, 2, 50ff.
Remedial, 139, 277
Renewal, 110, 111, 119, 120, 121, 173, 263f.
Repentance, xii, 201ff., 215ff., 233, 291ff.
Resentment, 49, 53, 81f.
Responsibility, 5, 120ff., 125, 166, 168
Resurrection, 36, 133, 175
Retirement, 136f.
Restitution, 225ff.
Revelation, 1ff., 6, 7, 8, ch. 3, 25, 49, 60, 168ff.
Reward, 118ff., ch. 24, 302ff.
Righteousness, 119ff., 168, 193, 253ff., 260
Role reversal, 166ff.
Roman view, 114
Rosemead, 276
Ruin, 148, 203

S

Sacred, 43f.
Salt, 128
Salvation, 34, 36, 55, 115, 120, 132, ch. 12, 233
Sanctification, 36, 37, 55, 120, 205, ch. 14, 233, 262ff., ch. 16
Satan, 4ff., 22, 35, 107, 153

62081